Peace Journalism

Jake Lynch

and

Annabel McGoldrick

Hawthorn Press

Peace Journalism copyright © 2005 Jake Lynch and Annabel McGoldrick

Jake Lynch and Annabel McGoldrick are hereby identified as the authors of this work in accordance with Section 77 of the Copyright, Designs and Patent Act, 1988. They assert and give notice of their moral right under this Act.

Published by Hawthorn Press, Hawthorn House, 1 Lansdown Lane, Stroud, Gloucestershire, GL5 1BJ, UK
Tel: (01453) 757040 Fax: (01453) 751138
info@hawthornpress.com
www.hawthornpress.com

The ideas expressed in this book are not necessarily those of the publisher.

Publication of this book was funded by the Joseph Rowntree Charitable Trust.

Photographs were taken by the authors and are their copyright, unless otherwise credited.

Cover illustration *Guernica* by Pablo Picasso copyright © Succession Picasso/DACS 2005
Cover design by Hawthorn Press
Design and typesetting by Lynda Smith at Hawthorn Press, Stroud, Gloucestershire
Printed in the UK by The Cromwell Press, Trowbridge, Wiltshire
Printed on paper sourced from sustained managed forests and elemental chlorine-free

Every effort has been made to trace the ownership of all copyrighted material. If any omission has been made, please bring this to the publisher's attention so that proper acknowledgment may be given in future editions.

British Library Cataloguing in Publication Data applied for

ISBN 1 903 458 50 1

Guernica, by Pablo Picasso, is known as perhaps the most powerful modern image of the cost and horror of war. An Indonesian official once welcomed Peace Journalism because, he said, it would make reporters less inclined to cover the violence visited on people in Aceh by troops his government sent into the province. No misconception could be more damaging – Peace Journalism entails disclosure, not suppression. Both Guernica and *Guernica* have been on the frontline of that battle. The infamous massacre in the little Spanish town, by German Air Force bombers in 1937, was falsified by the double agent, Kim Philby, in his guise as a *Times* reporter, to imply that landmines planted by the Republicans might have been responsible. Decades later, the tapestry depicting Picasso's masterpiece, at UN Headquarters in New York, was covered by a curtain as US Secretary of State Colin Powell faced the world's media to make the case for invading Iraq. We are on the side of *Guernica*, the painting, if it is a side; in favour of full and honest reporting of both conflict and violence, including images and perspectives of non-violent responses and solutions. That is what Peace Journalism is all about.

Phillip Knightley, author, *The First Casualty*

The aim of this ambitious book is to spark off a revolution in journalism – to change the way the media reports wars. It is important and long overdue. Behind it is the fact that the relationship between media and military has undergone a major change. The way a war is fought has now become a media event, presented as a struggle between good and evil with only two outcomes possible – victory or defeat. This has left war correspondents disorientated and confused, faced with the choice of being regurgitators of government and military propaganda or cynical onlookers struggling to explain events that shape the lives of people and nations.

Lynch and McGoldrick insist that there has to be a better way. Journalists should go back to first principles. They should give a voice to all parties. They should show empathy and understanding, focus on suffering, expose untruths on all sides, explain the background, highlight peace initiatives and stop demonising one side while glorifying the other.

Of course, all this is easier said than done. But this is not just a book of theory. It is packed with sensible, easily understood, practical exercises in understanding peace journalism. It is suitable for both old hands and newcomers alike. You cannot put it down without being convinced that the authors are right and that the world will be a better and safer place if their recipe for a reporters' revolution wins the support it deserves.

Stuart Rees, Professor Emeritus and Director, Centre for Peace & Conflict Studies, University of Sydney

In powerful and empirically rich analyses, – with examples from Iraq to Northern Ireland, from Indonesian provinces to Rwanda, from Morocco to Afghanistan, from Israel to the White House – Jake Lynch and Annabel McGoldrick show how reporting which reinforces official versions of reality has a huge and dangerous influence on public understanding...

In *Peace Journalism*, two skilful and astute journalists show how society at large can think about and value non-violent responses to conflict. This elegantly written, often humorous and always encyclopaedic book could have a major influence on the way events are reported and how the public perceives them. Whether this potential is realised will depend on the willingness of media owners and journalists to replace pre-conceived views of reality with a consideration of how violence may be explained and how ways of reporting could help to resolve conflicts instead of inflaming them.

If this significant work is studied and promoted, journalists could become more discerning and more analytical, less prone to be co-opted – or embedded – by official accounts of 'the way it is.' In the task of using non-violent perspectives to report conflicts, journalists and political scientists, educators, politicians and the general public now have available the most refreshing and constructive analysis of media practice which has appeared for years.

Majid Tehranian, Professor and Director, Toda Institute for Global Peace and Policy Research

Peace Journalism is a daring and sober guidebook for journalists to practise what journalism should be all about: to inform without fear or favour. The authors, two distinguished journalists, call it 'peace journalism' in order to contrast it with what is the prevalent practice today, namely 'war journalism'. Through lucid presentation and practical exercises, the authors demonstrate how a journalist can be a humane observer-participant in un-humane circumstances. They apply the insights of social theory to global journalism and show how to avoid the prevailing prejudices and stereotypes. This book should be required reading for all students and practitioners of journalism in a world that desperately calls for understanding instead of obfuscation, compassion instead of loathing, and sustainable peace instead of cycles of violence.

Kim Sengupta, special correspondent, the London *Independent*

This is an important study of how conflicts are influenced by the way they are reported in the media, how journalists are so often not just observers but play an active part in shaping events on the ground. The analysis and conclusions in the book will not be to everyone's liking. But the authors have provided a valuable service in focusing on an issue which is of special relevance now amid the continuing and bitter recriminations over the Iraq war.

Associate Professor Chris Nash, Director, Australian Centre for Independent Journalism

This book is worthy of the goal it has set itself: how journalists could and should insert the missing question 'Why?' back into their coverage of war and conflict. It comes from two seasoned international correspondents at a time when our news seems drenched in mindless bloodshed, to make a compelling argument: to stop the violence, we have to change the way we report it. This book deserves a place on the desk of every reporter, and every thinking person.

Contents

Acknowledgements viii

Introduction by Roy Greenslade
Guardian media commentator and Professor of Journalism at City University, London . . ix

Preface by John Kampfner
Editor, *New Statesman* and author of *Blair's Wars* xii

Foreword by Philip Hammond
Senior Lecturer in Media, London South Bank University xiii

Prologue xv

- A critical self-awareness
- Conflict Analysis tools for journalists
- Responsibility and the Feedback Loop
- A paradigm shift, a journalistic revolution?
- Using this book
- The name – a problem?

Chapter 1 The Peace Journalism Model 1

- Why do we need the Peace Journalism model?
- Definitions of Peace Journalism
- Invading Iraq – a case study
- Two versions of a suicide bombing – as War Journalism and Peace Journalism
- Seventeen tips for practical Peace Journalism

Chapter 2 Conflict Analysis – Anchorage for Journalists 33

- Why study conflict?
- What is conflict?
- Conflict theories and terminology
- The Conflict Orange
- Mapping a conflict
- What do we mean by Peace?

- Two versions of Casablanca bombings – using Conflict Analysis in reporting
- An alternative '5 Ws'
- A code of practice from India

Chapter 3 Reporting and Understanding Violence 57

- Two versions of a violent incident in Macedonia
- A typology of violence – Direct, Structural and Cultural
- The Rwandan genocide
- A note on 'evil'
- The struggle for context
- Understanding and condemning – two child murders by children
- Explaining or excusing? The suicide bomber's brother
- Hard cases – al-Qaeda and the Bali bomb
- Literacy in non-violence
- Heroes of non-violence
- The legacy of violence – Kosovo, Afghanistan, Iraq
- Consequences for reporting
- Realism versus the Cycle of Violence
- A framework of understanding

Chapter 4 War Propaganda 95

- How to recognise it and why it works
- NATO's war on Yugoslavia – a case study
- Developing strategies to resist propaganda
- Truth and lies
- The psychology of propaganda

Chapter 5 Scenarios and Dilemmas 125

- 'Tension is rising'
- Beginnings of violence
- Early warning – Rwanda before the genocide, a case study
- Parties to a conflict not communicating
- What if you can only report on one party?
- Reporting on massacres
- Reporting on refugees
- Stalemate – how do you get it on the news?
- Reporting on peace proposals, talks and 'deals'
- A facility with the men of violence

Chapter 6 Doing Peace Journalism 161

Re-conceptualising, re-sourcing, re-framing and re-writing:
- The story of a single violent incident – a bombing in Indonesia
- Follow-ups in the Israel/Palestine conflict
- A major international story – Iraq's 'dossier' on what happened to its banned weapons
- The Sliding Scale of Peace Journalism – two stories from the Philippines

Chapter 7 Why is News the Way it is? 195

- Gatekeeper theory
- The Propaganda Model
- The liberal theory of press freedom
- Journalistic Objectivity – the big 'O'
- Objectivity and War Journalism
- Structuralism and the Linguistic Turn
- The Feedback Loop of cause and effect
- Deconstruction
- Conclusion

Epilogue – Struggles and Opportunities 227

- Journalism education
- Journalist training
- Public service and media campaigning
- Media monitoring for Peace Journalism

List of Exercises 233

List of Discussion Points 237

Appendix A – Dialogue with the Devil's Advocate 240

Appendix B – Physical and Psychological Security for Journalists Covering Violent Conflict 245

Appendix C – Resources 255

Select Bibliography 260

Index 261

Over the years we have had cause to be grateful for the help, encouragement, guidance, enthusiasm and constructive criticism of many colleagues and friends, including Johan Galtung, Indra Adnan, Rune Ottosen, Danny Schechter, Phil Hammond, Mark Brayne, John Owen, Majid Tehranian, Stella Cornelius, Stuart Rees, Carol Sansour, Judith Large, David Loyn, Nick Mawdsley, Sirikit Syah, Kai Frithjof Brand-Jacobsen, Hannes Siebert, Firoze Manji, Umit Ozturk, Pat Kane, the SGI and Taplow Court and the Newsroom, the *Guardian/Observer* Archive and Visitor Centre in London.

The list is in no particular order, and doubtless omits some whose names should be there – to them, our apologies. Finally we are thankful to our parents, for their patience and support, and to Finn, our son, who arrived to bless our lives with his joy and innocence just in time to sustain us through the birth pangs of this book.

Introduction

There is no more important a task for journalists than reporting on war. It is journalism's litmus test because it forces reporters and editors to confront a host of ethical dilemmas and to question the nature of their occupation. How do they report fairly, accurately and compassionately? How do they place isolated events in an historical context? What efforts do they make to try to tell the truth? What is the truth anyway? These difficulties are compounded by the fact that most modern wars are fought as much through the media as they are on the ground. It is obvious that the theatre of war now includes newspaper offices as well as military headquarters, television stations as well as the trenches. In this situation words and images have become as lethal as missiles. Therefore journalists who inform the public about war bear a heavy responsibility for what they write and broadcast. Given that journalism's central mission – to tell the best possible approximation of the truth at the earliest opportunity – is tricky enough when dealing with relatively mundane events in times of peace, it is clear that in times of war it is infinitely tougher. All governments fighting wars do their best to put the best possible gloss on their activities and in pursuit of that goal are prepared, at best, to be economical with the truth and, at worst, to lie (and even murder). Official secrecy is always hard to penetrate and, during wars, it becomes harder still. So the journalist's job in war is certainly daunting. But, as off-putting as that sounds, if reporters and editors are to act properly on behalf of the public they represent then they must rise to the challenge.

Reporting on war is bedevilled by several overlapping problems: where do the boundaries lie between truth-telling and patriotism; between factual information and propaganda; between describing events and interpreting them; between the narrow focus and the broad canvas; between professional detachment and human emotion; between glorification and denigration? Nor is this an exhaustive list of the dichotomies journalists face during the heat of battle. It is one of the strengths of this book that a whole range of problems are raised, from the nitty-gritty matter of the choice of value-laden words and phrases to broader issues about the underlying ideology of the news agenda, the mind-set of journalists working to that agenda and the insidious nature of propaganda. Most importantly, it offers journalists a coherent, practical set of guidelines for facing up to these problems and, whether one agrees with their solutions or not, the undeniable merit of the authors' approach is that it makes journalists think more deeply about their overall responsibilities to society. They are not being merely counter-intuitive by asking journalists who cover war to think consciously of peace as they go about their daily tasks; they are advancing a coherent strategy which strikes at the very notion of conflict as a method of settling disputes. Their approach recognises that if the media are the central locus of war-mongering then, logically, they have the capability to be the catalyst for peace-mongering. No wonder the authors speak of the application of Peace Journalism as 'bring[ing] us to the point of a journalistic revolution'.

A brief retrospective view of the history of war coverage by the British media is instructive. It is generally agreed that it all began in 1854, during the Crimean war, with William Howard Russell of *The Times*. His reports of battles illustrated the futility of the war but one emotive despatch, about the charge of the Light Brigade, also managed not only to glorify war but also to take pride in defeat (inspiring Tennyson's poem, which did even more to romanticise the notion of blood sacrifice). More significant however were Russell's revelations about the inadequacy of the British army administration, which had provided soldiers with inappropriate kit, and his descriptions of the horrific deprivations of the army during the winter months, especially the lack of proper medical facilities. This led directly to the raising of a fund, inaugurated by *The Times*, to send out nurses who, most famously, included Florence Nightingale. Meanwhile, Russell and his paper were castigated by the government, which did its best to discredit him and his supposedly exaggerated reports. Many of these establishment attacks, not least from Queen Victoria, suggested that Russell and *The Times*'s editor, John Delane, were lacking in patriotism.

So, from its inception, many of the elements familiar to war-reporting down the ages were to be found. A single, dedicated reporter did his best to tell the truth, though with the benefit of hindsight we can see that he was occasionally factually inaccurate, often guilty of sensationalism and, while questioning the conduct of war, he did not trouble to question the war's motive. The government and the military authorities lied, tried to cover up and did their best both to censor the press and to discredit it. As one senior politician remarked: 'If England is ever to be England again, this vile tyranny of *The Times* must be cut off'. Yet the key aspect, the 'vile tyranny' of war itself as the solution to political differences, was not confronted.

In three subsequent conflicts – the Boer war, the 1914-18 first world war and the 1939-45 second world war – the press gave largely unquestioning support to the British government and journalists tacitly accepted that they were part of the war machine itself. Anything less would have been deemed unpatriotic. The very concept of Peace Journalism would have been anathema to the khaki-clad journalists who followed the troops into battle. But in the Korean war of the early 1950s there was an interesting incident involving James Cameron, a pacifist who believed war could never be justified and whose reports therefore tended to reveal the horrors and inhumanities of war. In one despatch to his London-based magazine, *Picture Post*, he told of the brutal treatment of political prisoners by the South Korean authorities on whose side the United Nations – led by the United States and Britain – was fighting. Cameron argued that if there was a just reason to make war in Korea then it was of overriding importance to ensure that the cause was not corrupted by siding with totalitarian oppression and cruelty. The magazine's owner refused to let the editor publish the article, arguing that it would give 'aid and comfort to the enemy'. Cameron resigned and his editor, Tom Hopkinson, was dismissed. The pair were stoutly defended by several journalists, one of whom referred to the editor having been 'interrupted in a public duty' by being fired. This is a wonderful phrase – public duty – because it evokes the image of journalism's real place in society, not as part of a commercial enterprise, not as part of the entertainment industry, not as an extension of a government propaganda machine, but as a serious activity that justifies its existence by informing the people about what is being done in their name. Is that not patriotic too? Indeed, if there could ever be a scale of patriotism, surely Cameron's journalism deserves to rank in the higher reaches.

In some senses, the Cameron affair is a precursor to the concept of Peace Journalism advocated by Jake Lynch and Annabel McGoldrick because it relied on a reporter's belief that there was more than a single narrative during war. He was willing to place in a wider context the nature of the conflict on the Korean peninsula. He could see beyond the war to ask whether peace might conceivably have come quicker – or that war might never have started at all – if there had been a greater understanding of the dispute. Though he may not have been aware of it at the time, his reporting also raised a much more fundamental matter. Patriotism is routinely defined as the zealous defence of one's own country. But if one steps outside the nationalistic straitjacket then it is perfectly feasible to be zealous in the defence of people across borders, to defend the rights of all human beings, especially those so often referred to as the innocents of war. Wars prosecuted by Britain since Korea – such as Suez, the north of Ireland, the Falklands, in Kosovo and Iraq – have never attracted the whole-hearted support of journalists in the manner of previous conflicts. But opposition to a certain war is only ever a first step. Even journalists who oppose wars usually employ a war-like lexicon when writing and broadcasting about conflicts. It is this problem that Lynch and McGoldrick deal with when they challenge journalists to think more deeply about their craft.

Some of the practical suggestions offered by the authors may not strike everyone as realistic. That, however, is less important than their wholly refreshing attempt to make journalists think more carefully about what they are doing and, most particularly, to think beyond the narrow confines of their own government's political position. Many of the tips in this book – about how to avoid viewing complex disputes in simplistic terms, for instance, or about the need to be scrupulously fair – should be second nature to journalists. The fact is that, all too often, they are not. The coverage of the conflict in Iraq was, and continues to be, both too superficial and lacking in contextual analysis. Journalists may not believe that their work can contribute to peace, and they may certainly bridle at the suggestion that they seem to favour war over peace. The record, however, shows that they have done so for far too long.

Roy Greenslade, Guardian media commentator and Professor of Journalism at City University, London

Preface

Journalists are curious beasts. Many of them, or should I say us, live off adrenalin. No matter how much we might deny it, nothing beats a fast-moving story. Nothing, sadly, beats a war. The story of the Iraq War of 2003 is a sorry one for the media, and not for the reasons of government versus BBC (although that was bad enough). No, the problem has deeper roots than the unseemly but cyclical battle between politicians and broadcasters. As Jake Lynch and Annabel McGoldrick point out in their compelling book, the industry tends to lose its head when it comes to war – any war. The natural scepticism that is an adjunct of the contemporary British trade is suspended by the prospect of gunfire. The language changes. The tone changes. Much of the rationalism disappears.

In the case of the Blair-Bush joint venture of 2003, this was a calamitous abrogation of responsibility. For all the complaints afterwards about government deception, where was the restraint by editors and reporters when presented with the false assertion that Britain was 45 minutes away from an attack by Saddam Hussein? Where was the probing about weapons of mass destruction *before* the invasion? Who was asking the right questions about the legal advice? Hindsight is a cheap weapon that the gullible deploy to conceal their failings.

These failings were even more in evidence once the 'shock and awe' had actually begun. The boys took to their toys with alacrity.

Access was all, and as the White House's chief spin doctor at Central Command in Qatar told me at the time, the 'real heroes' of the war were the embedded correspondents. Those with access fought to get on air or on the front page. With a number of honourable exceptions, reports were replete with hyperbole and lacking in context. What would I have done in their shoes? I'm not sure very much different. That is why, come the next conflagration, the same tactics will be used.

Peace Journalism provides some useful pointers, even if I find the title itself cloying. Journalists' job is to do what little they can to provide reliable fact and analysis. The authors demonstrate just how hard this has become, pointing out that the majority of television viewers believe that it is the Palestinians who are the 'settlers' in the West Bank and Gaza. Where do you begin to explain? Other examples extend to the Balkans, to Rwanda, to Indonesia.

The merit in this book lies as much in the prescription as the critique. The authors have provided an important set of guidelines for the rest of us to follow. It is not definitive. It is not universal. But it is as good as anything published so far. Will it be heeded? I would like to think yes, but I fear that once the crackle of gunfire is heard in the distance, lessons will be too readily forgotten.

John Kampfner,
editor, New Statesman *and author of* Blair's Wars

Foreword

Contemporary war is fought as a media event. In the 2003 invasion of Iraq, from the 'shock and awe' bombing, through the 'rescue' of Private Jessica Lynch, to the toppling of Saddam Hussein's statue outside the media hotel in Baghdad, the military campaign was conducted throughout with one eye on how it would look on television. Similarly, after the Kosovo war British Prime Minister Tony Blair's then press secretary, Alastair Campbell, argued that 'the modern media has changed the demands of modern conflict.'[1]

Whereas in the past propaganda was generally understood to be a secondary factor, designed to support the military effort, the implication of Campbell's remark is that media presentation is now a key consideration in shaping how wars are conducted. As Jake Lynch and Annabel McGoldrick argue, media coverage of conflict is not simply a question of reporting the facts: journalists are part of a 'feedback loop', whereby sources deliberately create 'facts' in order to be reported...

In the media-friendly 'War on Terrorism', some military operations have apparently been undertaken primarily so as to create good propaganda, rather than to fulfil any strategic military objective. The US special forces who went into Kandahar in October 2001, for example, were ostensibly engaged in a 'covert operation', yet they videotaped themselves and the footage was broadcast around the world. The operation was of dubious military value since, as Seymour Hersh revealed in the *New Yorker*,[2] army pathfinders had already gone in beforehand to make sure the area was secure.

At least outside the United States, however, much media reporting has been less than enthusiastic. Particularly in coverage of the Iraq war, there was sometimes an acute self-consciousness about reporting the contrived photo-opportunities and sound-bites, as when a reporter on the BBC's *Newsnight* programme noted that a ship delivering aid had been met by a 'reception party of journalists' who had been 'bussed in... by the military's press handlers', and observed that 'like many of the events of recent days laid on by they coalition, there was a very clear message they wanted to get across'.[3]

Similarly, many in the media responded with knowing irony to Bush's 1 May 2003 speech announcing 'the end of major combat operations' in Iraq. BBC reporters described the performance, during which Bush co-piloted a fighter jet and strode around the deck of an aircraft carrier wearing a military flight suit, as 'carefully choreographed', 'stage-managed', 'made for American TV' and 'pure Hollywood',[4] one correspondent even suggesting that the war itself had merely provided a 'useful prop'[5] for Bush's re-election campaign. While this sort of self-conscious cynicism may do little to encourage support for war, it also side-steps the journalist's responsibility to offer analysis and explanation.

In *Peace Journalism* Lynch and McGoldrick engage with the testing ethical dilemmas of reporting contemporary conflicts, drawing on their own extensive journalistic experience. Readers may not agree with the authors' analysis of all the different conflicts mentioned in this book, but its spirit of critical enquiry will surely be welcomed by everyone with an interest in understanding contemporary conflicts and military interventions. Above all, *Peace Journalism* is a call for an analytical approach to conflict, as an alternative to both the traditional 'bang-bang' school of military correspondents and to the moralistic victimology of more recent advocacy journalism.

One of the most refreshing aspects of the book is the authors' willingness to question orthodoxies and to look beyond the conventional view of the conflicts they discuss. As well as examining contemporary debates and controversies about journalism and propaganda, the book also has a highly practical orientation. The ideas presented here by Lynch and McGoldrick have been sharpened in discussions with fellow professionals, and refined in their work in training reporters and teaching university journalism courses.

At a time when so much media coverage of conflict seems to be trapped between the uncritical reproduction of propaganda and a distanced and disengaged cynicism, *Peace Journalism* is a valuable resource for all of us concerned to improve journalistic practice.

Philip Hammond,
Senior Lecturer in Media,
London South Bank University

Endnotes for Foreword

1. Alastair Campbell, 'Kosovo: Communication Lessons for NATO, the Military and the Media', speech at the Royal United Services Institute, London, 9 July 1999.
2. Seymour M Hersh, 'Escape and Evasion', *New Yorker*, 12 November 2001.
3. 28 March 2003.
4. BBC Radio 4, 3 May 2003.
5. BBC1, 2 May 2003.

Prologue

To journalism, and to journalists, the world has much to be thankful for. In the West, we helped to make democracy work, by weaving together public opinion and keeping watch over the exercise of power. We breathed life into the public sphere, in which authority must account for itself, if it is to be seen as legitimate.

Thomas Jefferson, a founding father of the modern world's first democracy, even went so far as to say: 'Were it left to me to decide whether we should have a government without newspapers or newspapers without a government, I should not hesitate a moment to prefer the latter.'[1]

In the global South, we helped awaken and connect the stirrings of awareness that ultimately overthrew colonialism. Kwame Nkrumah founded the Accra *Evening News* to provide 'practical guidance on how best to promote the independence struggle'; Gandhi made sure the press were on hand as he went to the sea to make salt, in defiance of the British Raj.

Above all, journalism brings the reassuring sense that someone, somewhere, is monitoring developments – summed up by the legendary war correspondent Martha Gellhorn: '... any form of keeping the record is better than just letting things drift away'.

Even on that qualified basis, however, such views have become unfashionable, and can seem a little starry-eyed. Two of journalism's most august institutions, the *New York Times* and the *Washington Post*, felt obliged to issue unprecedented apologies for their misleading coverage of Iraq. They coincided with tenth anniversary commemorations of the Rwandan genocide, one of the worst atrocities of a violent century, in which the media played a sinister role.

'Mass media technologies, institutions, professionals, norms and practices constitute one of the fundamental forces now shaping the lives of peoples and nations.'[2] So says Professor Robert Karl Manoff of New York University's Center for War, Peace and the News Media. Could the force be somehow directed or harnessed – and if it could, should it? 'The media constitute a major human resource,' he continues, 'whose potential to help prevent and moderate social violence begs to be discussed, evaluated, and, where appropriate, mobilised.'

How could this be done? When and where would it be appropriate? How far is it compatible with the job of keeping the record? Peace Journalism pulls these threads together. It represents a rethinking – or perhaps a *thinking* from first principles for the first time – of news about conflict; one of the journalist's most important jobs.

The concepts and methods we explore in this book are put forward as ways to make conflict reporting more accurate and more useful. But why should new concepts and methods be needed, here and now, to achieve these aims?

That notion of journalism as a record – a reliable account of what is really going on – is built into many of our assumptions about the world and the way it works. 'Reliable' because it promises *scrutiny*, sifting what is true and important from the mass of verbiage around us – 'making sense of it all', to quote a marketing slogan used by *BBC World*.

To tackle this formidable task, many of its practitioners still go equipped with nothing more, in the way of conceptual tools, than Gellhorn's own advice to budding reporters: 'Limit yourself to what you see and hear. Do not suppress and do not invent.' Compare that with what Ron Suskind – a highly experienced reporter – heard from a senior adviser to President Bush shortly before his election triumph in 2004:

> 'The aide said that guys like me were in what we call "the reality-based community", which he defined as "people who believe that solutions emerge from your judicious study of discernible reality". I nodded and murmured something about enlightenment principles and empiricism. He cut me off. "That's not the way the world really works any more", he continued. "We're an empire now, and when we act, we create our own reality. And while you're studying that reality, judiciously, as you will, we'll act again, creating other new realities".'[3]

'Empires', it could be argued, have always done this; all that changes is the way they do it. The important thing for journalism is that today's new realities are characteristically *discursive*. After the September 11th attacks on New York and Washington, British Prime Minister Tony Blair confided:

> 'I kind of think that the decisions taken in the next few weeks will determine the rest of the world for years to come. As primary players, we have the chance *to shape the issues that are discussed* [emphasis added].'[4]

The 'War on Terrorism' and the 'Axis of Evil' that followed were media strategies as well as military ones. Shadowy international menaces, familiar only to specialists and the intelligence community, lie, by definition, outside most people's direct personal or social experience. So media representations of conflict grow in relative importance. They now form a key site for the exercise of power, seen as such by 'primary players' and many others besides.

It means that journalism needs some workable form of *reflexivity*, analysing and addressing its own role in shaping discussions and creating realities. Without this, it is fated to collude and conceal. In the words of John Lloyd, a senior editor at London's *Financial Times*:

> 'Power has to be interpreted, power has to be interrogated. One could say that's our mission, our mission statement as journalists. But we *are* now the power to some extent... because the media corporations control access, to communications, to fantasy, and information, they control real power.
>
> We need to take our power, media power, seriously. And we need to unpick what we are doing to the world because we are *constructing* the world, through advertising, through the new media, the e-media, through media corporations themselves, through television, radio, through to newspapers and magazines.'[5]

A critical self-awareness

If journalism is to be reliable, accurate and useful, therefore, it has to join the long list of endeavours to develop a critical self-awareness. How is it we end up being in a position to see and hear some things, and not others? How come it's always the same things, or at least the same sorts of things? On what basis do we sift, select, scrutinise?

How come Iraq's non-existent 'weapons of mass destruction' dominated the news agenda for so long? Why is 'terrorism' treated, in UK and other media, as a bigger security issue than global warming, when experts including the UK's chief scientific adviser know the emphasis should be far, far in the opposite direction? Why was south-east Europe the centre of world attention in the years around the turn of the century while millions perished in the Congo?

To 'report the facts', in the time-honoured phrase, *is* to suppress – inescapably, since there are so many more facts than reports. How do we decide what to put in and what to leave out?

It's those decisions, above all, that control access to information and communications and, in the process, construct the world around us. But journalism is stuck on the other side of the fence, in the reality-based community of empiricism, still trying to convince us that it is 'up to' nothing more than sending reporters out with a blank page, to reflect what they see and hear.

To pull off this sleight-of-hand, decisions about what to report, and how to report it, are commonly disguised as natural and obvious – 'indexed' to an apparently authoritative external register, usually the public pronouncements, comings and goings of political leaders in particular, and 'officialdom' in general.

This means that subjects officialdom does not care to discuss, facts and perspectives omitted or suppressed from official discourses and representations, tend to go missing from the news, even where they are vital to understanding what is going on, and why. 'We are being set up for a war against Saddam,' veteran Middle East correspondent Robert Fisk observed months before the invasion, but 'we will not – repeat this one hundred times – we will not mention oil'.[6]

For the same reasons, news prefers events – things that have, indisputably, happened – to process, which is inherently disputable. Hence the exaggerated importance of 'terrorism' compared with climate change.

The instinct to camouflage key decisions also means there is a ready market for anything appearing to offer 'balance' – even to the point where form triumphs over content. Think of the Swiftboat controversy, in the election that put Bush back into the White House. John Kerry's status as a Vietnam war hero came under attack from Swiftboat Veterans for Truth, a group financed by Texan backers of the Bush campaign.

Their claims proved groundless, but Kerry's military record, as a factor in the election, was successfully occluded – not despite but, in a sense, *because of* journalists' best intentions. They felt honour-bound to put the allegations to Kerry and his handlers, then test the answers by going back to the other side, effectively keeping the story in the news. To ignore or downplay them would have been to invite complaints that they had set out on the story with 'an agenda', especially given well-worn claims of a liberal media bias.

Peace Journalism: Conflict Analysis tools for journalists

Today, we are less likely to think of media scrutiny than media *glare*. Scrutiny is critical, active and selective; the media's glare is unblinking, instantaneous, too close and constant to maintain perspective – think of 24-hour news with its pressure to 'update regardless'.

It was in the rapids of 'real time' media that the Swiftboat campaign could float. The episode points up the other urgent need for journalism – to find its own anchorage in the constant stream of information, a firm basis on which to distinguish it from the misinformation and disinformation mingled in.

We add, into this potent mix, the deliberately provocative concept of Peace Journalism. Provocative because it proposes that most journalism, thinking itself neutral and 'objective', is actually War Journalism, biased in favour of war; also because it requires us to see that the practical methods journalists use to do the job should also be understood as a set of conventions, or theoretical constructs.

Peace Journalism provides reflexivity, or a critical self-awareness; but it also provides anchorage. It proposes that, when covering conflicts, we can tread down to find solid ground beneath our feet, by studying and applying what is known and has been observed about conflict, drawing on the overlapping fields of Conflict Analysis and Peace Research.* We can use this knowledge to help us decide for ourselves what is important, and to identify what is missing from what we are told by interested parties. Key findings include:

- **Violence never wholly its own cause**
  Conflict is made up of structure, culture and process – the context, without which no account of a violent event is complete or, indeed, correct.
- **Non-violent responses always possible**
  There is always more than one way of responding to conflict. Many people, in many places, are devising, advocating and applying non-violent responses.
- **More than two sides**
  There are always more than two parties to any conflict – some, whose involvement or interest is hidden, need to be put on the map. Others, presented as having a solid aggregate view, may contain important internal divisions, and need dis-aggregation.
- **Every party has a stake**
  Parties to conflict should be seen as stakeholders, pursuing their own goals, needs and interests – some openly acknowledged, but almost invariably some hidden as well.

Summary of contents

- Chapter 1 explains how the reporting of conflict generally omits or occludes the key factors just listed, thereby producing the distorted form we call War Journalism.
- Chapters 2 and 3 harness the insights of Conflict Analysis and Peace Research to look in more detail at key concepts –

examining what conflict is, how it works, and the nature of, and explanations for, social violence, together with their implications for journalists.
- Chapter 4 offers a theory of propaganda and its effect in a conflict, explaining how to recognise it and discussing how to counter its distorting influence.
- Chapters 5 and 6 consider real-life scenarios and stories that put our propositions to the test, working through possible journalistic responses, including both individual reports and entire editorial and reporting strategies.
- Chapter 7 is for those who wish to take critical reflection a step further. It shifts the focus to the question of why news is the way it is – why War Journalism is dominant. We argue that it rests on unexamined nostrums, about both news and conflict, now in urgent need of critical analysis. It also outlines Feedback Loop theory as a way of understanding the influence of journalistic responses on the actions and motivations of parties to conflict.
- Appendix A deals with objections to Peace Journalism. What about Fox News? What about 'blogging'? Do they alter the fundamentals of the case we examine here, about the news and its role in conflict and political process? These and other points are dealt with in the form of a 'Dialogue with the Devil's Advocate'.
- While the rest of the book is concerned mainly with the effect the journalist has on the story, Appendix B examines the effect the story has on the journalist, offering a brief introduction to issues of trauma and safety.
- Appendix C lists organisations working in and around the field of media-and-conflict, with brief notes and web addresses.

---

*These fields are, of course, as nuanced as any, with their own controversies. However, they have useful things to say to journalism below and before the point where these 'kick in'. In this book, we quote a range of sources, and we do not intend to suggest that they all think the same things; but neither, for this reason, do we dwell on differences of emphasis between them. The four propositions listed here, for instance, command widespread agreement.

Responsibility and the Feedback Loop

How does journalism shape the lives of peoples and nations? What are journalists responsible for? Is the meaning of a news story generated chiefly at the moment of production, or the moment of reception? Does the reporter load, as it were, a hypodermic syringe, which is then injected into the consciousness of anyone reading, watching or listening? Or do the messages communicated by newspapers and programmes depend on broader cultural conditioning, and its influence on the way they are interpreted?

We do not set out to explore this controversy in any depth, but the book is unavoidably based on the proposition that public understanding of key issues depends, at least to some extent, on how they are reported. There is some wisdom in the familiar observation that news cannot necessarily tell people what to think, but it may be more effective in telling them what to think *about*.

Then, of course, news itself has a part to play in the process of 'cultural conditioning', or perhaps more than one part. Peace Journalism may cut across familiar narratives by raising unexpected questions, whereas War Journalism, we suggest, 'reiterates what we already think of as the answers'.

There is, moreover, another mechanism by which the effects of journalistic response are transmitted, which arises, not from its effect on public opinion as such, but from people's assumptions about its effect, actual or potential.

These assumptions, we suggest, feed into the media strategies of parties to conflict – strategies which in turn influence their behaviour, their words and deeds, which may then be reported as 'the facts'. Sources, journalists, readers and audiences are connected by a Feedback Loop of cause and effect – another index of responsibility which merits consideration here, irrespective of which side is, ultimately, 'right' in the production/reception debate.

A paradigm shift

The phrase 'paradigm shift' has become a cliché of everyday conversation. But we may be at one of those rare moments when its use is justified on the terms in which it was first coined, by Thomas Kuhn in *The Structure of Scientific Revolutions*.[7]

Journalism from 'the reality community', based on claims of empiricism and objectivity, is the equivalent of 'normal science', 'predicated on the assumption that the scientific community knows what the world is like'.[8] But it 'often suppresses fundamental novelties because they are necessarily subversive of its basic commitments'.[9]

The non-appearance of Iraq's weapons, and the concocted Swiftboat controversy, are examples of what Kuhn called 'anomalies' which 'subvert the existing tradition of scientific practice... the tradition-shattering complements to the tradition-bound activity of normal science'.[10]

To draw on the insights of Conflict Analysis to establish a frame of reference – to decide, in advance, that we intend to use it, to assign meanings and draw distinctions – is to risk the ire of the journalistic community and beyond: 'Journalists who try to tell these stories, connect these dots, and examine these links are demeaned, disparaged and dismissed.'[11]

But journalism has now spread its wings to become a fully-fledged subject in universities, part of its long transition from trade to profession. University subjects generally are distinguished by their preoccupation with deriving and applying frames of reference, and with developing a critical self-awareness, or reflexivity. To apply this approach to journalism, as we do in this book, is perhaps to bring us to the point of a journalistic revolution.

Steady on

If there's to be a journalistic revolution, does it entail taking over the commanding heights of the media economy? Not necessarily. In one sense, both government and commercial media have their own interests in creating images of 'self' and 'other' – to command allegiance, and to sell products and services, respectively. 'The two systems thus tend to exacerbate international tensions by dichotomizing, dramatizing, and demonizing "them" against "us".'[12]

So War Journalism has powerful political and economic imperatives at its back – an important argument for diversity in patterns of media structure and regulation to extend and strengthen the concept of public service. But that doesn't mean there is no scope for Peace Journalism, whether consciously pursued or not.

Indonesia's leading newspaper, *Kompas*, deliberately adopted Peace Journalism, *Jurnalisme Damai*, as a strategy for covering conflicts, large and small, in the years following the fall of Suharto's New Order regime in 1998.

Latterly, *The Independent* bucked a trend in the London newspaper market by increasing sales as it downsized to a tabloid or 'compact', and picked up multiple accolades and awards for its coverage of Iraq and the 'War on Terrorism' – much of it recognisable as Peace Journalism. Still more is visible in the work of countless editors and reporters around the world, in many media, covering many conflicts.

The 'embedding' of television crews with forward units in the invasion of Iraq has fixed, in our mind's eye, an image of conflict coverage as something carried out by a breathless reporter in helmet and flak jacket, crouching to avoid bullets flying overhead. But this is only one aspect among many.

In this book, conflict is considered as a system of relations influencing many apparently diverse discourses and social interactions. The journalism of conflict is discernible in the way many stories are covered. The news agenda is saturated with it. The Peace Journalism approach is, therefore, relevant to a broad sweep of journalistic activity.

Using this book

Bringing about Peace Journalism is a gradual, multi-layered and multi-dimensional process. This book is designed to help. It has been written to be accessible to the general reader, or perhaps the active citizen for whom these issues could now be construed as an urgent concern.

The book can also be worked through, using the large number of exercises, examples and discussion points. It can be used in training workshops for mid-career journalists, as well as courses for students of various disciplines, including:

- Journalism and Journalism Studies
- Media and Communications Studies
- Conflict and Peace Studies
- International Relations and Politics

In each case, some of the ideas discussed here will be more familiar than others.

There are **Discussion** points, denoted by grey shading, which can be used as stopping-off points in seminars or workshops, as stimuli for whole-group working. The **Exercises** can be set for private study or to break-out groups or working in pairs. Or you can simply use them to gather your thoughts.

Throughout the book, we extend the approach advocated in this Prologue, to consider practical methods as conventions, or theoretical constructs, and to test theoretical perspectives at the 'newsface' of practical experience. There is a gap here for Peace Journalism to fill. Evangelia Papoutsaki, an NGO media expert, was invited to devise and teach a conflict reporting course at the journalism department of Tbilisi State University:

'I decided to use this approach after extensive searching for course material led me to the conclusion that most approaches to media and conflict situations were either too academic and thus out of practical application, or personal and thus partisan accounts of journalists who have worked as war correspondents.

The Peace Journalism approach

offered a more holistic view of conflict and media and it was very appealing to students who were able not only to relate media and conflict but incorporate in their learning conflict resolution techniques, essential for journalists in the region.'[13]

The name – a problem?

The phrase 'Peace Journalism' will not appeal to everyone. In the first place, 'peace', until you start to analyse it – as we do later in the book – seems too vague and open to interpretation to make a promising starting-point.

Peace Journalism is often misunderstood as 'advocating peace'. Not so – 'giving peace a chance' in national and international debate, by ensuring that non-violent responses to conflict get a fair hearing, would be a better way to think of it.

Then, if you are a professional member of the journalistic community, you might recognise the nervousness about anomalies and fundamental novelties that prevails in the scientific community. To fly a banner may be to invite unwelcome exposure – one reason, Kuhn said, why scientific revolutions tend to be 'invisible' until viewed in retrospect.

The Independent, for instance, does not label its journalism – why should it, when the coverage speaks so eloquently for itself? Our project for London-based journalists, introducing Peace Journalism concepts in discussions about issues of representation and responsibility in international news, was called, simply, 'Reporting the World'. Many of the ideas set out here were tested and honed in that stimulating series of exchanges.

So why is this book called *Peace Journalism*? Firstly, because it's time Peace Journalism *had* a book. 'Google' the phrase in double inverted commas and it brings up, at the time of writing, over 14,000 hits, testimony to the number of journalists and others round the world who have worked to develop it.

Its value, hopefully, is to galvanise, shake up, send a seismic energy through sedimented layers of tradition, assumption and definition.

It's also intended to be distinctive – you may have bought this book because it looked and sounded different from many others on the same shelf. And a book is, after all, something you may consume in private. However, we hope you will find some way to put the ideas presented here into practical application, whether by introducing them as Peace Journalism, or not.

Some may even share the experience of Declan Hill, an award-winning reporter and anchor-man from Canada's CBC Television and Radio:

> 'It was in Ankara, Turkey on a cold, grey March day... I got a letter from a friend – in it was an essay written by a British journalist about what he described as "peace journalism"... It was an epiphany for me. In a few brief words the journalist had articulated all my vague desires and ideas into a concrete plan.'[14]

Endnotes for Prologue

1. To Edward Carrington, 1787.
2. Robert Karl Manoff, quoted in Jake Lynch, *The Peace Journalism Option*, Conflict and Peace Forums, Taplow, UK, 1998, p 15.
3. Ron Suskind, 'Without a Doubt', *New York Times* 'Magazine', 17 October 2004.
4. Interviewed by Bob Woodward for *Plan of Attack*, quoted by Chris Patten in 'Out from the shadows', review of *Free World: Why a Crisis of the West Reveals the Opportunity of Our Time* by Timothy Garton Ash, London *Guardian* 'Review', 3 July 2004.
5. Quoted in Jake Lynch, *Reporting the World – A Practical Checklist for the Ethical Reporting of Conflicts in the 21st Century*, Conflict and Peace Forums, Taplow, UK, 2002, p 109.
6. Robert Fisk, 'We are being set up for a war against Saddam', London *Independent*, 4 December 2002.

7. Thomas S Kuhn, *The Structure of Scientific Revolutions*, University of Chicago Press, Chicago, 1996.
8. Ibid, p 5.
9. Ibid, p 5.
10. Ibid, p 6.
11. Bill Moyers, 'Journalism under Fire', remarks to Society of Professional Journalists conference, 11 September 2004.
12. Majid Tehranian, 'Peace Journalism: Negotiating Global Media Ethics', *Harvard Journal of Press/Politics*, Vol 7, No 2, April 2002.
13. Evangelia Papoutsaki, 'Peace Journalism Approach: A Teaching Experiment from the Caucasus', *Georgian Times*, 29 September 2003.
14. Declan Hill, review of *News from the Holy Land* by Jake Lynch and Annabel McGoldrick, in *The Canadian Friend*, December 2004.

Chapter 1

The Peace Journalism Model

This chapter will introduce and explain the basic Peace Journalism model for identifying and predicting patterns of omission and distortion in conflict coverage.

'Distortion' because the way conflicts are generally represented does not match what is known and has been observed about conflict *per se*; because certain prevalent reporting conventions hamper journalism in doing the job expected of it – to provide a reliable account of what is really going on.

Like Darwin's theory of evolution by natural selection, the Peace Journalism model, we argue, is the only one left standing after the application of two tests: not only does it fit the individual pieces of observable evidence, it also offers an overarching account of how they are connected. It explains how particular biases and shortcomings in coverage reinforce and articulate with each other.

Above all, it comes with a built-in case for change, delineating the options for journalists committed to offering readers and audiences a fuller and fairer account of the issues at stake in conflicts, from local to global.

The chapter:

- Summarises the case for Peace Journalism as an analytical model
- Offers definitions of Peace Journalism
- Tests the Peace Journalism model, in the context of coverage of the US-led invasion and occupation of Iraq, from 2003
- Provides War Journalism and Peace Journalism versions of a story about a violent incident

- Suggests a list of Peace Journalism 'dos' and War Journalism 'don'ts'

By the end of this chapter, the reader will be able to:

- Diagnose War Journalism
- Identify Peace Journalism
- Understand the consequences of each for our understanding of conflict
- Report conflicts with basic techniques for avoiding War Journalism and doing Peace Journalism instead

Why do we need the Peace Journalism model?

We have been fortunate indeed to gain our experience as journalists in the British media. The journalism of professional editors, reporters and producers here – our colleagues – has a strong claim to be considered the best in the world.

The BBC runs the top global newsgathering operation, and regularly sweeps the board at international awards ceremonies – especially for the reporting of conflict. The *Economist* and *Financial Times* are the leading brands in their respective fields. Reuters, the most prestigious global news agency, is headquartered here; and latterly, websites such as *Guardian Unlimited* have registered as many hits from the US and further afield, as from the UK.

London's daily press is praised and criticised in equal measure, but the world's most competitive newspaper market is a uniquely fertile and stimulating environment for a highly variegated crop of news and views.

So, when it comes to the crunch, how do we perform? Take, for instance, the invasion of Iraq. Rewind to the middle of 2002. As he toured the US campaigning for the mid-term Congressional elections, George W Bush was beginning to make the case for 'regime change' to overthrow Saddam Hussein. Karl Rove – 'the president's brain'[1] – advised him to concentrate on 'security' to 'maintain a positive issue environment'[2] for the Republicans, as a distraction from state budget crises, rising unemployment and the waves of corporate malfeasance washing around the very pillars of the White House.

The polling evidence was clear – Americans would back a war on Iraq, but only if Sheriff Bush was at the head of a posse of allies. London's position was crucial. If the closest ally declined to join in, the mission was doomed – especially as other capitals would see it as a signal that they, too, could afford to give this one a swerve. Support in the US for *unilateral* military action hovered around the 20 per cent mark, and no president could afford to embark on a risky foreign adventure on that basis.

Britain did join in, of course, and papers leaked from the Foreign Office, 18 months after the event, revealed that Tony Blair, the man Bush called 'the Primester',[3] had secretly committed himself to 'regime change' as early as March 2002. One particularly well-sourced account of Britain's political and diplomatic path to war had already identified this meeting as the one where Bush told his guest, 'we don't want to do this alone'.[4]

Now the London *Sunday Telegraph* showed its readers that people around Blair were well aware of the difficulties in the job they had taken on. Officials begged understanding for his task of having 'to manage a press, a parliament and a public opinion that was very different from anything in the States'.[5]

Just six weeks before the invasion, Blair had plenty of managing still to do. London's biggest ever demonstration saw between one and two million people rally against the war, and polls revealed public disapproval – by 53 to 29 per cent, according to one pollster, ICM, which tracked the issue over many months.[6]

Peace demonstration, Hyde Park, London,
February 2003

By the time of the first night of 'shock and awe' over Baghdad, however, this had turned around. ICM's survey of 11-13 April showed the British *in favour* of the war, by 63 to 23 per cent. MPs on the governing Labour benches, feeling sentiment in their constituencies see-sawing beneath their feet, blessed the policy in two separate parliamentary votes, albeit by fairly narrow margins.

Bush only got his war because Blair was at his side. Blair only got there because he had public opinion on his side. But the British were convinced, at least at the initial level, only for a short period – the six weeks leading up to the war, plus the month or so it took to overthrow Saddam and a shortlived interlude of 'euphoria' thereafter.

'Swing voters' quickly swung back again as key claims were shown to be unfounded –

chiefly about the weapons, of course, but also perhaps about the possibility of avoiding significant casualties and about the likely impact of an invasion on the political and security situation, both in Iraq itself and around the world. By September 2003, ICM's respondents felt the war had been unjustified, by 53 to 38 per cent – proportions subsequently sustained as minds were, apparently, made up.

Journalists reflected ruefully on the yawning gap between the way the case was reported in advance, and the actual out-turn of events, especially the failure to find 'weapons of mass destruction'. According to Ed Pilkington (foreign editor at the time) of the London *Guardian*:

> 'The weird thing about this war, and uniquely in my experience, is that the war itself is becoming increasingly a sideshow. The talk about embedding and talk about Basra, talk about Umm Qasr and all that – it is becoming increasingly marginal to the main question of how did we allow Tony Blair to get away with telling us that he had his own special intelligence and we must trust him? And he knew the truth? And we now know that he didn't have his own special intelligence and in fact virtually the entire lot of it was at least four years old and pre-1998, and we let him get away with that.'[7]

Michael Wolff of *Vanity Fair* spent part of the war at Centcom, the military briefing centre in Qatar, where he asked the (in)famous emperor's-new-clothes question: 'Why are we here?' Now he, too, looked back on gaps in media coverage at the time and saw connections with the course of the conflict itself:

> 'Clearly, the war will be more of a story. It gets bigger every day. Not least of all because the media is now having to rewrite itself. The questions we failed to ask, the stories we declined to pursue, have surely helped to get us into the present mess.'[8]

A closer look

So, *wha'ppen* in those six weeks? A continuation, broadly speaking, of well-established patterns of reporting. One study, by the journalism department at the University of Maryland,[9] examined coverage of Iraq at regular intervals over a six-year period – right up to the invasion – giving both US and UK media 'a failing grade': 'Too many journalists acted as virtual stenographers' for the authorities. They presented 'weapons of mass destruction' as a 'monolithic menace', lumping nuclear, chemical and biological weapons into a single category, thereby obscuring differences in potential harm, availability and ease of use – 'a pattern of imprecision'. There was, moreover:

- too little critical examination of the way officials framed the events, issues, threats and policy options
- too little coverage of policy options beyond 'pre-emptive war' and 'regime change', with alternative views hidden away in back pages or late-night discussion slots

One of the newspapers studied, the *New York Times*, implicitly accepted the findings, with a fulsome apology to its readers:

> 'Editors at several levels who should have been challenging reporters and pressing for more scepticism were perhaps too intent on rushing scoops into the paper. Accounts of Iraqi defectors were not always weighed against their strong desire to have Saddam Hussein ousted. Articles based on dire claims about Iraq tended to get prominent display, while follow-up articles that called the original ones into question were sometimes buried. In some cases, there was no follow-up at all.'[10]

A separate academic study of UK television news supported the criticism that official 'frames' too often went unchallenged. For instance:

'The government's case for war was based partly on the idea that most Iraqi people wanted liberation and hence supported the invasion. So to what extent did TV news portray the Iraqi people as welcoming US and British troops? This turned out to be a dominant theme of the coverage: across the news as a whole, the Iraqi people were around three times more likely to be portrayed as pro-invasion than anti-invasion.'[11]

As for the claim that the BBC was biased against the war, *fuhgeddaboudit* – it crumples under anything more than the most cursory examination:

'Far from revealing an anti-war BBC, our findings tend to give credence to those who criticised the BBC for being too sympathetic to the government in its war coverage. Either way, it is clear that the accusation of BBC anti-war bias fails to stand up to any serious or sustained analysis.'[12]

Interestingly, the Maryland study hints at a systemic failure – that particular shortcomings over this story may be woven into the very warp and weft of general reporting conventions:

'The inverted pyramid style of news writing – which places the most "important" information first – produced much greater attention to the Bush Administration's point of view on WMD issues, at the expense of alternative perspectives.'

An intelligent account?

Researchers stated, at the outset, the normative criteria against which journalism about the war was to be assessed: 'The public relies on the media to separate facts and tangible realities from assumptions and spin',

so as to provide, in the terms we have used, a reliable account of what is really going on.

There are clear and widely understood ideas about what journalists are supposed to be doing. These have a rich heritage (for further discussion, see Chapter 7) and they are written down in, for example, broadcasters' public service agreements. Each agreement contains some variant on a key concept: 'Audiences should receive an intelligent account that enables them to form their own views'.[13] But as the studies quoted above and others found, the media largely failed to deliver on this promise:

- propaganda was too seldom challenged
- alternative views and perspectives received too little attention
- as a result, readers and audiences were bamboozled into supporting the war, on a series of premises that turned out to be either false, or misleading, or both

In this book, we explore, in detail, a number of examples to show:

- this pattern is a familiar one, from the conduct and coverage of many other conflicts, in many media around the world
- war propaganda, in its character and content, is imbricated* with the way conflict is habitually framed by news reports
- the framing grows, in turn, out of reporting conventions held by many journalists to be so self-evident as not to require ongoing examination or justification

Iraq is far from being the only story where the public has been led, even by UK media, in the opposite direction from some of the most important facts.

Despite almost nightly dispatches on the

---

*Imbricated – an unusual word and one you will meet several times in this book. Literally, it means 'interleaved' as with, say, the slates on a house roof. In this case the sense it is intended to convey is that War Journalism on the one hand and war propaganda on the other are shaped in such a way as to fit snugly together, like a mortice and tenon joint in carpentry; or perhaps to articulate with one another, as the hipbone does with the femur. We say 'imbricated' to avoid seeming to make any claim that one is logically prior to the other: they are better seen as being 'coterminous', ie taking place at the same time and in the same conceptual space.

Israel-Palestine conflict, Glasgow University researchers who spoke to British television viewers found that more of them believe 'the settlers' are Palestinian than know they are Israeli, and substantial numbers think it's the Palestinians who are occupying the Occupied Territories.[14] 'They just thought "occupied" meant someone was there, a bit like a bathroom is occupied.'[15] Many have only the vaguest idea of where 'the refugees' come from. 'Afghanistan' is not an infrequent guess. On another intensively reported story, the Refugee Council commissioned pollsters to set British people a multiple choice question, asking them to say how many of the world's asylum seekers they believed were ending up on their shores. The most popular answer? Between 25 and 30 per cent. The true figure? 1.98 per cent.

We argue that it is not sufficient, as the *New York Times* pledged itself to do, simply to carry on as before, only try harder. Shortcomings in the way news is reported, in each of these stories, are *systemic*. They result from the application of well-established reporting conventions, familiar from many media, the world over – built into the values and practices of journalism.

These values and practices are linked, in turn, with underlying concepts of both news and conflict – concepts which often pass unexamined or even unacknowledged. The Peace Journalism model offers a basis for identifying and rethinking concepts, values and practices alike.

As a theory, it has the cardinal merit – like Darwin's theory of evolution by natural selection – of not only fitting the separate pieces of observable evidence, but also explaining how they are connected.

The examples we consider here, along with countless others, reveal characteristic patterns of omission and distortion in the reporting of conflicts. These patterns not only leave the public misinformed. They also usually lead us, or leave us, to overvalue reactive, violent responses – and to undervalue developmental, non-violent ones.

This is why we refer to the dominant

discourse of reporting as War Journalism. Peace Journalism, therefore, can be defined against it.

Definition of Peace Journalism

Peace Journalism is when editors and reporters make choices – of what stories to report and about how to report them – that create opportunities for society at large to consider and value non-violent responses to conflict.

Peace Journalism:

- uses the insights of conflict analysis and transformation to update the concepts of balance, fairness and accuracy in reporting
- provides a new route map tracing the connections between journalists, their sources, the stories they cover and the consequences of their journalism – the ethics of journalistic intervention
- builds an awareness of non-violence and creativity into the practical job of everyday editing and reporting

---

Peace Journalism can be seen as a set of tools, both conceptual and practical, intended to equip journalists to offer a better public service. As we shall suggest in later chapters, it intersects with struggles being waged, within and around media in many parts of the world, over issues of representation and context.

The picture of reporting on Iraq painted by academic researchers is not all gloomy. 'Some reports are exemplary,' the Maryland study says. Our own verdict on the performance of UK media was that it was 'of a noticeably higher standard'[16] than in previous recent conflicts, and our necessarily astringent comments here should be seen in that context.

There are many journalists, in British media and elsewhere, who engage in these struggles with determination and skill. One of the intentions behind this book is to fortify them in their work, by opening debates on a number of different levels about what we are doing when we report conflicts, about how and why we are doing it.

What is Peace Journalism?

The original Peace Journalism model was set out, in table form, by Professor Johan Galtung, a founder of the academic subject of Peace Studies and the set of analytical and fieldwork methods known as Peace Research:[17]

PEACE/CONFLICT JOURNALISM	WAR/VIOLENCE JOURNALISM
I. PEACE/CONFLICT-ORIENTATED	*I. WAR/VIOLENCE-ORIENTATED*
explore conflict <u>formation</u>, x parties, y goals, z issues general 'win, win' orientation	focus on conflict <u>arena</u>, 2 parties, 1 goal (win), war general zero-sum orientation
open space, open time; causes and outcomes anywhere, also in history/culture	closed space, closed time; causes and exits in arena, who threw the first stone
making conflicts transparent	making wars opaque/secret
giving voice to all parties; empathy, understanding	'us-them' journalism, propaganda, voice, for 'us'
see conflict/war as problem, focus on conflict creativity	see 'them' as the problem, focus on who prevails in war
humanisation of all sides; more so the worse the weapon	dehumanization of 'them'; more so the worse the weapon
<u>proactive</u>: prevention before any violence/war occurs	<u>reactive</u>: waiting for violence before reporting
focus on invisible effects of violence (trauma and glory, damage to structure/culture)	focus only on visible effect of violence (killed, wounded and material damage)
II. TRUTH-ORIENTATED	*II. PROPAGANDA-ORIENTATED*
expose untruths on all sides / uncover all cover-ups	expose 'their' untruths / help 'our' cover-ups/lies
III. PEOPLE-ORIENTATED	*III. ELITE-ORIENTATED*
focus on suffering all over; on women, aged, children, giving voice to voiceless	focus on 'our' suffering; on able-bodied elite males, being their mouth-piece
give name to all evil-doers	give name of their evil-doers
focus on people peace-makers	focus on elite peace-makers
IV. SOLUTION-ORIENTATED	*IV. VICTORY-ORIENTATED*
peace = non-violence + creativity	peace = victory + ceasefire
highlight peace initiatives, also to prevent more war	conceal peace initiatives, before victory is at hand
focus on structure, culture, the peaceful society	focus on treaty, institution, the controlled society
aftermath: resolution, reconstruction, reconciliation	leaving for another war, return if the old flares up again

War Journalism, Peace Journalism and the invasion of Iraq

This section makes the case for Peace Journalism as an analytical model to predict, identify and connect shortcomings in reporting of the then proposed invasion of Iraq: it concentrates on the crucial period in the battle for public opinion, mainly in UK media.

We consider the following key questions:

- Were parts of the story omitted or marginalised at the time?
- How strong was the evidence for them?
- How important were they to the 'reliable account of what is really going on' that journalism is expected to provide?
- How strong, therefore, were their claims for inclusion – or for playing a more central role – in the coverage?
- What was the effect of their omission or marginalisation?
- Was it, indeed, to lead us or leave us to overvalue violent, reactive responses to conflict, and undervalue non-violent, developmental ones?
- In other words, to what extent can this pattern of coverage be said to merit the description 'War Journalism'?
- Does the Peace Journalism analytical model explain this pattern, and how the individual elements of it fit together? Did the model predict this pattern?
- Would Peace Journalism therefore represent a remedy, for systemic shortcomings or distortions in coverage, arising out of this pattern of omission and marginalisation?

We divide our consideration of these questions into the sections of Professor Galtung's table, explaining, in the process, some of its key concepts – interlocking and overlapping, to a certain extent, as they are.

War/Violence-orientated vs Peace/Conflict-orientated

What does it mean, that claim in the table, that War Journalism presents us with two parties, one goal – a general zero-sum orientation?

This *Newsweek* cover,[18] from six months before the invasion of Iraq, is literally a frame, formed by the masthead at the top, price bar at the bottom and (if you look closely) the piping down the sides.

Front cover of Newsweek, *30 September 2002 (international edition) reproduced with permission Photograph of Saddam Hussein Agency Pool image Photograph of George W Bush copyright © Chris Usher*

But it is also a *story frame*. The magazine decided to represent the conflict of the moment as consisting of only two parties, Iraq and the US, personified in the two presidents, George W Bush and Saddam Hussein.

> DISCUSSION: What connects a decision to frame a conflict as a battle between two parties with the question in the middle – who will win?

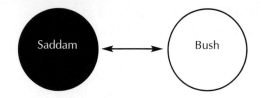

The component parts of War Journalism are mutually reinforcing. The question is implicitly posed in the initial framing decision.

Here's how:

- it's a simple question of geometry. Two points can only be joined in one way – with a line
- this means that any change in the relations between them can only take place along a single axis
- the conflict becomes a tug of war. George cannot gain a metre without Saddam losing a metre – and vice versa
- it's a 'zero-sum game', in which each party ultimately faces only two possibilities – victory or defeat

Escalation

If the parties to a conflict conceive of it, or *frame it*, in this way, it prepares the ground for escalation. Why? Because it becomes impossible for either to propose any change in policy which does not, clearly and unequivocally, move that party towards victory over the other. Anything else would risk being interpreted – and reported – as 'backing down'. Anything that is not 'winning' must be 'losing'. Defeat being unthinkable, each has a ready-made incentive to step up, or escalate, his efforts for victory.*

> DISCUSSION: What was the cause of this conflict, and what should be the outcome, the 'exit'? To find the answers, where should we begin looking?

Closed space, closed time; causes and exits in arena

The 'official' explanation, familiar from countless news reports about comings and goings in Washington and London as war loomed closer, was that Saddam 'threw the first stone':

- he menaced his neighbours – making war on Iran in the 1980s and Kuwait in 1990
- he used chemical weapons against his own people – the Kurds at Halabja in 1988
- he hid his programmes for building chemical, biological and even nuclear weapons from the outside world
- he refused to 'come clean' and did not seek to convince the 'international community' that he had got rid of weapons programmes banned by UN resolutions
- he was cultivating 'links' with 'international terrorism'

In this version, the cause of the conflict was located in Iraq itself – in particular the regime of Saddam Hussein. He was 'the problem'. Solutions – what the Galtung table calls 'exits' from the conflict – were also, therefore, to be found in Iraq, by bringing about 'regime change' to get rid of him.

At the same time, people around the world were talking – in bars, workplaces and their own living rooms – about an entirely different version (see the cartoon opposite).

What was really going on?

The goal of the invasion, according to the vast majority of news reports, was to remove the threat posed by Saddam Hussein and his 'weapons of mass destruction'. Later, Paul Wolfowitz, US deputy defense secretary, told an interviewer this line was chosen for public consumption for 'bureaucratic reasons', as the lowest common denominator among proponents of war.[19]

---

*War Journalism and Peace Journalism could themselves be conceived of as being in a tug of war. It is perhaps more useful to think of them as being like yin and yang – an equilibrium, requiring positive action to bring it back into balance. For a derivation of the distinction between War and Peace, as organising principles for journalism about conflict, see Chapter 7.

Cartoon by Andy Riley, originally published in the Observer Magazine, 16 February 2003[20]
Reproduced with permission of Curtis Brown Group Ltd, London, on behalf of Andy Riley
Copyright © Andy Riley 2003

In attempting to provide a reliable account of what was really going on, many journalists would have recognised as a valid aspiration this section from the BBC's *War Guidelines*, issued to its news staff shortly before the invasion: 'We must... allow the arguments to be heard and tested.' But were they?

What were the arguments for war? Consider five:

1. The crisis – later, the war – is really 'about' Iraq's WMD.
2. Iraq's WMD threaten both regional and world security.
3. Regime change is the only way to remove the threat.
4. Regime change is also the only way to improve the humanitarian situation in Iraq.
5. The only way to bring about regime change is war.

Before the war, the third of these propositions was effectively tested by being juxtaposed with an alternative – the 'coalition of the unwilling' at the UN, with their call for the inspection process to be given more time.

The Maryland study rightly pointed out that counter-propositions to the fourth and fifth in the list went largely unreported. The second took centre stage after the invasion, by which time it was, in an important sense, too late. The first remained generally unexamined and untested.

How strong was the evidence for 'the oil theory' at the time, and how important was it? War in Iraq entered the agenda at a crucial point in the geo-strategic battle for control over access to the world's remaining oil resources. In 2001, a joint task force of the Baker Institute for Public Policy and the Council on Foreign Relations issued a report[21] calculated to influence the energy and foreign policies of the incoming Bush administration:

'The American people continue to demand plentiful and cheap energy without sacrifice or inconvenience. The world is currently precariously close to utilising all of its available global oil production capacity.' Iraq was playing the role of a 'swing producer, turning its taps on and off when it has felt such action was in its strategic interest'.

The report concluded:

'The United States remains a prisoner of its energy dilemma. Iraq remains a de-stabilizing influence on... the flow of oil to international markets from the Middle East. Saddam Hussein has also demonstrated a willingness to threaten to use the oil weapon and to use his own export program to manipulate oil markets. Therefore the US should conduct an immediate policy review toward Iraq including military, energy, economic and political/diplomatic assessments.'

The report was submitted to the office of Vice-President Dick Cheney, who subsequently launched his own National Energy Plan, with the categorical statement: 'The [Persian] Gulf will be a primary focus of US international energy policy.' It agreed with the Baker report that the US is increasingly dependent on imported oil and that it may be necessary to overcome foreign resistance in order to gain access to new supplies.

Saddam Hussein's 'manipulation' of oil markets included arranging for payments to be made – under the UN oil-for-food programme – in euros instead of dollars. This offered a potential threat to the dollar's status as the global reserve currency, and, therefore, to the entire macro-economic strategy of the Bush administration of getting the world to buy cheap dollars in order to finance America's twin trade and budget deficits.

Later, Iraq even stopped pumping oil altogether in protest over the Israeli military offensive in the occupied West Bank, a deliberate echo of OPEC's embargo of the 1970s – Arab retaliation for the US sending military supplies to Israel in the Yom Kippur, or October, war.

Between them such developments, and the potential for more, amounted to a crisis, the paper said, which in turn required 'a reassessment of the role of energy in American foreign policy'.[22]

Such a reassessment was also being advocated by another source, hugely influential in Republican Washington at the time – the Project for a New American Century. According to the PNAC's 1997 *Statement of Principles*:

> 'America has a vital role in maintaining peace and security in Europe, Asia, and the Middle East. If we shirk our responsibilities, we invite challenges to our fundamental interests.'[23]

What might these 'fundamental interests' be? Before Bush entered the White House, the PNAC itself commissioned a study, which sought to frame the foreign policy agenda in such a way as to prepare the ground for the ascendancy of its supporters in appointments to the administration (Rumsfeld and Wolfowitz at the Pentagon, to name but two). It offers another clue:

> 'The United States has for decades sought to play a more permanent role in Gulf regional security. While the unresolved conflict with Iraq provides the immediate justification, the need for a substantial American force presence in the Gulf transcends the issue of the regime of Saddam Hussein.'[24]

Then consider this gloss from Donald Kagan, professor of classics and history at Yale University, chairman of the team that produced the study:

> 'When we [the US] have economic problems, it's been caused by disruptions in our oil supply. If we have a force in Iraq, there will be no disruption in oil supplies.'[25]

According to 'the oil theory':

- a modern economy has an insatiable appetite for oil
- global supplies are uncertain, with new finds dwindling – we may be at, or already past, the 'oil peak'
- China, India (expanding economically) and the European Union (expanding politically) all look, from Washington, like potential superpower rivals
- all will need much more oil if they are to emulate the lifestyle enjoyed by wealthy Americans, now widely advertised on global television

- the key to continued economic, and therefore political and military, primacy for the US will be control over access to oil supplies

Note – 'control over access'. Our friend in the bar leaves the question open – in what sense was it, is it, 'all about oil'? The responsibility of journalism was not to adopt this view, but to explore it, as in a timely contribution by business correspondent Paul Mason to the BBC's *Newsnight* programme. From his script:

'For the USA, there are arguably far more substantial spoils of war than a few oil contracts. With a pro-US regime in Iraq, it's not the future of competing oil companies that's at stake, but the future of OPEC. The oil cartel controls the price of oil by controlling its supply. Ever since 1973, when OPEC massively hiked the price of oil, policymakers have fantasised about its demise. Some believe a US-installed government in Baghdad with a seat on OPEC, and under pressure to turn on the taps to rebuild the economy, could bring the end in sight.'[26]

The point is well made, that the cost of invading and occupying Iraq – $200 billion and counting – could not possibly be recouped by selling the oil and pocketing the proceeds. Notwithstanding the suspiciously high number of supply and reconstruction contracts handed out to friends of the US administration, the counter-proposition here was not that the prime motivation behind the invasion was venal, but rather strategic.

Oil – a marginalised story

Readers and audiences in general, not just those of the BBC, would have been much better equipped to decide for themselves what was going on had Mason's efforts been emulated and followed up elsewhere. Instead, the 'oil theory' remained confined to the margins of reporting. According to one empirical study:[27]

'In the first five weeks or so of 2003... the number of articles in UK newspapers in which the words Iraq, war and either Bush or Blair – or both of course – appeared together [was] 4,657, or about 130 a day. Of those, just over one in five – 967 – also contained the word, oil.

Put a hundred of those under the microscope, as a sample, and we can get a more detailed picture. 41 made just glancing references either to oil prices or to the UN oil-for-food programme, leaving 59. Of those 59, nine referred to calculations over future oil contracts as motivating factors in diplomatic manoeuvrings by France and Russia, not the US or UK – leaving 50.

Of those 50, 13 were readers' letters, leaving 37. Of those 37, 12 were accounted for by the allegation from Saddam Hussein in reports of his interview with Tony Benn, leaving 25.

Of those 25, seven raised the idea that oil might have something to do with US or UK policy, only to dismiss it as fanciful – leaving 18. Of those 18, none contained anything more than a glancing reference to the fact that – in a phrase that crops up in several of them – '*many people think* it's all about oil' [emphasis added]. It's an analytical factor used, in other words, more for support than for illumination...

There is a 'disconnect' here... Opinion polls suggest large numbers of people in Britain believe that oil has at least some part to play in setting an agenda for war. The Pew Research Center, in one of its global opinion surveys, late last year [2002], put the proportion of Britons taking that view at 44%.

A couple of months earlier, Channel 4 Television commissioned a poll that presented respondents with a menu of options as to what they thought George W Bush was really up to. Taking action to snuff out a threat to global security – the official explanation – came top with 22%, but a grab for Iraq's oil was close behind with 21%.'

The bigger strategic picture

It's important to note that the conflation of energy and security considerations in US strategic planning is conceived, at least partly, in defensive terms. The 1982 Military Posture Statement by the Joint Chiefs of Staff, the first of the Reagan era, painted a gloomy picture of the economic risks to America from its exposure to imported resources, including a long list of essential minerals, but primarily oil.

Two months before the 2004 election, President Bush set out to the Republican National Committee his plans for a second term:[28]

> 'Osama bin Laden would like to overthrow the Saudis... then we're in trouble. Because they have a weapon. They have the oil'.

This reminds us of the underlying security concept, of the world as a field of competition for economic, political and military primacy. If the US does not guard its primacy, the argument goes, by maintaining 'full spectrum dominance', then others will take advantage, and may subjugate US interests to their own. In this sense, control over access to oil resources can be seen as a symbol and instrument of still larger strategic considerations.

The US National Security Strategy (NSS) resolves to impose on the world 'a single sustainable model for national success'. Any who beg to differ may find themselves regarded as a threat and the target of a pre-emptive strike – 'America will act against such emerging threats before they are fully formed'.[29]

The section of the NSS headed 'Develop Agendas for Cooperative Action with the other Main Centers of Global Power' opens with the sentence: 'America will implement its strategies by organizing coalitions – as broad as practicable – of states able and willing to promote a balance of power that favors freedom.'

Elsewhere the NSS gives a concise statement of the rationale for increasing military spending: 'Our forces will be strong enough to dissuade potential adversaries from pursuing a military build-up in hopes of surpassing, or equalling, the power of the United States.'[30]

Many look to *The Grand Chessboard* by Zbigniew Brzezinski – a veteran Washington insider with national security service under presidents of both parties – for a frank assessment of how *ad hoc*, US-organised coalitions of the willing, defined on a mission-by-mission basis, are intended to undermine any alternative centre of power:

> 'To put it in a terminology that harkens back to the more brutal age of ancient empires, the three grand imperatives of imperial geostrategy are to prevent collusion and maintain security dependence among the vassals, to keep tributaries pliant and protected, and to keep the barbarians from coming together.'[31]

Casualties of the invasion of Iraq, whether by accident or design, included various forms of collusion among vassals, or underlings – such as a common European Union foreign policy and, ultimately perhaps, OPEC's grip on global oil supplies.

Others put it still less politely. Here is Michael Ledeen, of the American Enterprise Institute, another think-tank highly influential in Republican Washington: 'Every ten years or so, the US needs to pick up some small, crappy little country and throw it against the wall, just to show the world we mean business.'[32]

American primacy in the wider world is to be cemented in place by winning arguments at home, Brzezinski says. Discussions are to be shaped, and realities created, by building perceptions of hidden dangers:

> 'As America becomes an increasingly multi-cultural society, it may find it more difficult to fashion a consensus on foreign policy issues, except in the circumstance of a truly massive and *widely perceived* direct external threat [emphasis added].'[33]

Causes and exits

It's worth examining 'the oil theory' in some depth because its omission or marginalisation in reporting of the conflict at the time is itself noteworthy – requiring an explanation, beyond mere happenstance, of a discernible pattern in the coverage.

It may not necessarily be 'right', at least not by itself, but it had strong and well-documented claims to be considered at least as large and salient a part of the explanation (for what was really at stake in the conflict) as the 'weapons of mass destruction' familiar from official propaganda.

It was part of the story about this conflict which could have been brought much more clearly into focus through Peace Journalism, by applying what is known and has been observed about conflict *per se*.

Above all, the insights of Conflict Analysis and Peace Research would direct us to identify and treat the US and its allies as parties to conflict, pursuing their own goals and interests – necessary if we are to examine and assess, from the outside, their habitual self-presentation as disinterested mediators, or, in this case, global policemen brought reluctantly to intervene to restore the peace, when all else has failed.

Properly testing the first and most basic argument about the war – what it was really 'all about' – would have required an awareness that causes are to be found not just in the conflict arena, but also in the broader conflict formation.

So are the solutions or 'exits', therefore – another part of the story routinely missing at the time and deserving of more attention and exploration. One imaginative way of highlighting long-term solutions came from The Detroit Project – Americans for fuel-efficient cars, which commissioned a series of TV advertisements to make its point. Here's the script for one of them:

[Music from *Once in a Lifetime* by Talking Heads.

Picture shows a car in the desert covered with a silver cloth. Camera pans around it.

Then from some distance away the camera tracks and zooms towards it. As it approaches, the silver cloth is removed to reveal – empty space. The twist is – the car underneath does not exist.]

'The first car built for the road and the world around it... it can take America to work in the morning without sending it to war in the afternoon... with a sophisticated braking system that stops our dependence on foreign oil... it does 40 miles to every gallon and thousands of thousands of dollars saved at the pump... the only problem is, Detroit won't build it... same as it ever was... same as it ever was...'[34]

A further possibility was offered by a report from the Centre for Oil Depletion Analysis, released in November 2002, illustrating the competitive advantage to be gained by taking control of Iraqi resources, with supplies elsewhere likely to be rapidly exhausted by soaring demand in the coming decades. It was notable for suggesting that Iraqi oil reserves, for various reasons, might be much more strategically important than had hitherto been generally appreciated.[35]

Then Lord Browne, Chairman of BP and a close business friend of British Prime Minister Tony Blair, used his company's presentation of half-year results to complain that, six months before the invasion, British companies were not encountering 'a level playing field' in the jostling already under way for contracts to develop and reconstruct Iraq's oil industry after the Saddam Hussein regime was ousted.

Such developments are familiar, in form if not content, from many other stories – engaging slices of Americana, surprising think-tank reports and controversial claims by leading industrialists have supplied many a 'page lead', substantial filmed report or studio discussion point for UK media over the years. In this case, though, they made hardly a ripple.

The 'oil theory' also begins to show us how a number of other countries could be seen as parties to the conflict, including Iraq's neighbours as well as potential strategic rivals to the US such as China, India and the EU. With all these other players on the map, the conflict ceases to resemble a tug of war, and becomes more like a cat's cradle:

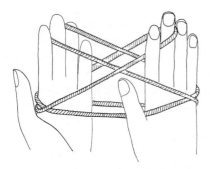

'The Cradle' from Pull the other one! *by Michael Taylor. Published by Hawthorn Press, 2000 p 25*

This represents a decisive break with War Journalism, the zero-sum game. Notice how the connections change, too. Suddenly it makes less sense to talk about 'victory' and 'defeat' and more sense to look at ways of managing and mediating, balancing and sharing.

Truth- vs Propaganda-orientated

The 'widely perceived external threat' in this case – instrumental, apparently from the ICM findings, in fashioning a foreign policy consensus by the time of the invasion – was, of course, from Saddam Hussein's supposed 'weapons of mass destruction'.

As ICM and others recorded growing public scepticism, supporters of the war, confronted by the stubborn refusal of any such weapons to turn up in Iraq, clutched at straws:

'It was the consensus of the intelligence community, and of successive administrations of both political parties, and of the Congress, that reviewed the same intelligence, and much of the international community, I might add, that Saddam Hussein was pursuing weapons of mass destruction.'[36]

Yes, France, Germany and even Russia shared much of the same intelligence on Iraq's weapons programmes; the difference, glossed over in this statement, is that they viewed it as sporadic and patchy – not 'trustworthy', President Vladimir Putin commented, as he stood next to Blair in a London news conference.[37] Further investigation was warranted, he and his fellow sceptics believed – a pre-emptive strike was not. Hence their assent to UN Security Council Resolution 1441, with its provision for a tough inspection regime, but not for 'all necessary means'.

It subsequently turned out that political rhetoric had raced far ahead of professional assessment:

- 'sporadic and patchy' was the description actually used in a report by Britain's Joint Intelligence Committee (JIC); after receiving it, Tony Blair described the intelligence on Iraq's weapons as 'extensive, detailed and authoritative'[38]
- Blair: Iraq had 'stockpiles of major amounts of chemical and biological weapons'[39]
- JIC: Iraq 'may have hidden small quantities of agents and weapons'
- Blair: Saddam had 'enough chemical and biological weapons remaining to devastate the entire Gulf region'[40]
- JIC: 'Saddam has not succeeded in seriously threatening his neighbours'
- on suggestions that Iraq might hand deadly weapons to non-state actors such as al Qaeda, the JIC, in an assessment in February 2003, said invasion would make this more likely, not less

The categorical claims about active weapons programmes came from a single source whose reliability, the British Secret Intelligence Service explicitly warned the Prime Minister at the time, remained unproven. Work with this source was at a 'developmental' stage, and was discontinued, after the war, when the source was found to be unreliable. Reliable sources were much more equivocal and vague.

These original assessments by British Intelligence were not made public until well over a year after the invasion.

How strong was the evidence available *beforehand*, both for and against the case being made by proponents of the invasion? What were the contra-indications? Did they receive sufficient prominence at the time?

The defector: 'we destroyed all the weapons'

The most prominent defector from Iraq was Hussein Kamel, Saddam Hussein's son-in-law and director of Iraq's Military Industrialization Corporation, who ran Iraq's weapons programmes throughout the 1980s and the first half of the 1990s.

Kamel was interviewed in Jordan by UN weapons inspectors in 1995, but the full transcript was not released until 26 February 2003, to two British academics. The contemporary edition of *Newsweek* carried the gist of his comments, made under interrogation over seven years earlier, but only now entering the light of day:

> 'I ordered the destruction of all chemical weapons. All weapons – biological, chemical, missile, nuclear were destroyed.'

This was the guy in charge, remember, and saying something his handlers would not necessarily have wanted to hear. It would, in a sense, have been much easier for him to do as later defectors did – the ones relied on, to its subsequent chagrin, by the *New York Times* – and exaggerate Iraq's continuing capabilities, thereby increasing his own value.

The inspectors: the dossier's claims disproved

After UN inspectors re-entered Iraq in November 2002, claims in the British government's dossier on 'Iraq's weapons of mass destruction', published two months earlier, began to be disproved, as the facilities it accused of producing weapons or weapons-related material were visited one by one. Here are a few from many examples cited in

reports by the inspectors, published well before the war:

- *Dossier:* Al-Sharqat site in northern Iraq 'rebuilt' and producing nitric acid for the purification of uranium
- *Inspectors:* 'There is no indication of resumed nuclear activities in those buildings… nor any indication of nuclear-related prohibited activities'[41]
- *Dossier:* Fallujah II plant engaged in production of chlorine for chemical weapons
- *Inspectors:* 'The chlorine plant is currently inoperative'[42]
- *Dossier:* Iraq's biological weapons programme centred on al-Dawra Foot and Mouth Disease Vaccine Institute
- *Inspectors:* the plant had been 'abandoned since 1996'[43]

These findings, and the Kamel interview transcript, came on top of assessments going back several years, and discussed in Chapter 4, that Iraq's weapons programmes had long been a 'busted flush'.

Between them, they raise an important question – and this is why it's worth going over them in some degree of detail – *why* were they not more widely reported?

The day after the UNMOVIC inspectors issued a press release with their findings about the Fallujah chlorine plant, the *only* mention of 'chlorine' in *any* UK newspaper came in a piece in the *Times* about prescription swimming goggles, allowing users to swim in chlorinated pools, and see where they were going without wearing contact lenses.

Had the media on both sides of the Atlantic been more attentive to the inspection process and its findings, they might have had less to apologise for. Instead, at the *New York Times*, 'having a reputable name, either as an organization or an individual, was apparently a liability in terms of being a source on Iraqi WMD. Certainly the *New York Times* ignored identifiable sources that might have cast doubt on the administration's Iraqi WMD claims, while featuring unidentified sources that supported the claims.'[44]

And where the *New York Times* led, many other media – including most in the UK – surely followed.

How would Peace Journalism have helped?

By enabling us to think our way on to the outside of war propaganda: through understanding the part it plays in conflict *per se*, we can find a more reliable anchorage for acknowledging, identifying and naming it.

An informed understanding of conflict leads us to *expect* that statements put out by parties to a conflict will also be part of that conflict. Without this expectation, we remain stuck in what the White House aide called 'the reality-based community', oblivious to the way realities are being created around us, and indeed to our own part in creating them:

> 'The absence of well-defined policies [for interpreting developments in conflict] might increase manipulation, and enhance "self-manipulation" – the priority given by international news-editors (more than their field reporters) to incoming items that fit their own state-of-mind, psychological pre-dispositions and news-value expectations, rather than to accept evidence from the field.'[45]

Secondly, the omission or marginalisation of contra-indications on Iraq's weapons may be partly attributed to a preparedness to believe Saddam Hussein capable of fiendish lengths of evil and cunning – way beyond even his well-documented excesses and cruelties.

So much so that a poll for the Pew Research Center found that, by the eve of war, 66 per cent of Americans believed Saddam Hussein was involved in the

Cartoon by Fiona Katauskas (www.fionakatauskas) first published in The Walkley Magazine, *issue 21, Winter 2003 (www. walkleys.com)*

September 11th attacks, while 79 per cent believed Iraq already possessed, or was close to possessing, nuclear weapons.[46]

Again, there is more detailed discussion to follow, but long before the period under discussion, Iraq had been falsely accused of:

- tipping babies out of hospital incubators, leaving them to die on the floor
- massing on the border of Saudi Arabia, preparing to invade
- possessing 'drone' aircraft capable of menacing London, New York and Sydney with deadly biological weapons

At the time, the authors of all these propaganda lines found many journalists in 'stenographer mode'. 'Curious incuriousness' about such claims is another key characteristic of War Journalism, and connected, in important ways, with the others. The Galtung table calls it 'dehumanization of "them"'; more so the worse the weapon'.

This grows out of the initial decision to frame the conflict as a zero-sum game of two parties. If each faces only two possibilities – victory or defeat – then each has an incentive to escalate his efforts for victory. That has to be justified in some way: the worse the weapon you propose to use, in pursuit of those efforts, the more justification is needed.

Planning an assault on Fallujah? Smear the city's inhabitants as 'thugs' and 'terrorists'. Preparing for genocide in Rwanda?

* *Step One*: whip up fears about invading Tutsi warriors or *inkotanyi*.
* *Step Two*: demonise all Tutsis as *inyenzi*, or 'cockroaches'.
* *Step Three*: start running the two terms into one – *inyenzi-inkotanyi* – in countless radio broadcasts, to collapse any inconvenient distinctions between combatants and civilians.

('Worse' weapons, in this case, did not mean hi-tech weapons. The last act of many victims of the genocide was to hand over all their worldly possessions in exchange for a quick, painless bullet to spare themselves a more drawn-out death.)

Dualism leads inexorably to Manicheism – us good, them bad – and to demonisation and dehumanisation of the 'Other'. Many journalists, in British media and elsewhere, did take steps to resist being co-opted in this process. Their efforts can be seen as important examples of Peace Journalism. At one Reporting the World discussion,[47] Alan Rusbridger, editor of the London *Guardian*, remarked:

'In every war you try and depersonalise the enemy and dehumanise them, but I think having someone like Suzanne Goldenberg's quality inside Baghdad [the *Guardian*'s own reporter], talking to ordinary Iraqis and making them terribly human, I think is a new element in war, and you can see why politicians don't like it. But it also makes it extremely difficult to go to war on a nation when you are getting that kind of image, and I think the humanity of her reporting and Lindsey's [Hilsum, *Channel 4 News*']

correspondent in Baghdad] was just of a different calibre and texture from the reporting we'd seen before, and I think that will in some way make fundamental changes in how war is seen.'

The *Guardian* was prepared, on several occasions, to break with convention and clear its lead front-page slot for a feature piece by Goldenberg, chronicling the war through the eyes of the citizens of Baghdad, rather than automatically lead on political or military developments. An example:

Front cover of the Guardian *on 9 April 2003, reproduced with permission. Copyright © Guardian Newspapers Limited 2003*

Elite- v People-orientated

What does it mean to say, in the terms of Galtung's table, that War Journalism is 'elite-orientated'? Consider this recollection by Mary Dejevsky, a senior journalist on the London *Independent*:

'I think we probably all do a lot of breast-beating in retrospect as to why didn't we challenge them [the UK government's dossiers on Iraq's weapons]. Well, from somebody who did challenge them to the Foreign Office, the context was very different because then there was always the risk that, the very next day, they were going to find piles of the stuff all over Iraq in the very places where they said would do, so you were at a great disadvantage expressing the scepticism that I was doing. It was a high-risk thing to do and it was also very difficult for editors, because they were very reluctant to pursue that line as a reporting line. They were happy to pursue it in editorials, columns – fine; but reporting – you had to go with what you were told [by the government].'[48]

This, remember, from an experienced reporter working for a newspaper which had already adopted a bold anti-war line in its editorial columns. The point is 'official sources' in one's own country, or in Washington, are often misconceived [in War Journalism] as neutral, or at least passive. So, for instance, 'asking the right questions of the right officials' is presented as a journalistic method for uncovering what they 'really think' – a way of piercing the diplomatic niceties of statements on the record.

However, as we suggest in Chapter 6, those sources may not be, as it were, reluctantly divulging their true intentions – they may instead be asking themselves, what would it be useful for us to give to this political editor or diplomatic correspondent for his or her live 'two-way' on tonight's news? We owe that newspaper a favour – what line can we give them as an exclusive for Sunday, to add something to the debate that might help us, too?

This is where journalism founders for a lack of reflexivity. It's as if everyone else besides the journalist is in on the secret, that what is really going on here is reality-creation, discussion-shaping, world-construction – as writ large in the dossiers themselves. This is what is meant by the 'elite orientation' of War Journalism.

The remedy could be to adopt a reflex cynicism, asking oneself 'why is this lying bastard lying to me?' – the advice, according to legend, of one famous editor to his reporters when interviewing politicians. The Peace Journalism remedy is to reconceptualise official sources as a party to the conflict – as sources, indeed, of important claims, perspectives and representations, worthy of serious and respectful treatment, but not different in kind from those of alternative sources.

Alternative sources

> DISCUSSION: Does Peace Journalism mean journalists 'resolving conflicts'; or becoming advocates for particular solutions or initiatives?
>
> (HINT – 'NO!')

Peace Journalism entails picking up on suggestions for non-violent responses from whatever quarter, and remitting them into the public sphere. There is never, in any conflict, any shortage of them. In the words of the distinguished peace researcher, John Paul Lederach:

'I have not experienced any situation of conflict, no matter how protracted or severe, from Central America to the Philippines to the Horn of Africa, where there have not been people who had a vision for peace, emerging often from their own experience of pain. Far too often, however, these same people are overlooked and disempowered either because they do not represent "official" power, whether on the side of government or the various militias, or because they are written off as biased and too personally affected by the conflict.'[49]

It means their omission or marginalisation in representations of conflict – perhaps the most noticeable characteristic of War Journalism - is a serious and systemic factual inaccuracy.

'Alternative sources' or a 'people

orientation' does not mean, or at least does not need to mean, 'vox pops' with protestors on demonstrations. One example, from the lead-up to the invasion of Iraq, was a proposal from Hans von Sponeck, who resigned in 2000 as UN Humanitarian Co-ordinator for Iraq, in protest at the effect of sanctions on the Iraqi people. It was submitted as a comment to the *International Herald Tribune (IHT)*.

In order to expand the available means to bring about change in Iraq, the European Union and other countries should take matters into their own hands; and he put forward a 14-point plan of recommendations to governments, including:

- 'Move towards re-establishing embassies. It is a scandal that many governments do not have any representation and, thus, cannot collect first-hand facts and impressions and make their own independent analyses on which to base their policies.
- Encourage trade and investments with Iraq first inside the sanctions framework, and later outside it, should the United States and others uphold the sanctions regime *ad absurdum*.
- Establish a contact group, perhaps in liaison with China, Russia, and others who want to prevent war and find peaceful solutions. Work for a just peace in the Middle East in general and in the Israeli-Palestinian conflict. The Iraq issue is not unrelated to it. Acknowledge that US initiatives have failed and that we need other completely impartial mediators in that process.
- Develop a new security regime for the whole region and honour, finally, UN Security Council Resolution 687 that requires that the Middle East shall become a zone free of weapons of mass destruction. On a more general level, it is time to realise that the threat of WMD will only increase as long as holders of nuclear weapons ignore their obligations to completely disarm their nuclear arsenals

according to the Non-Proliferation Treaty of 1968. Full compliance and access to nuclear sites everywhere would be a natural corollary to preventing new states from acquiring WMD.
- Develop a new security regime that would include economic, political, environmental, and other essential aspects of security and prohibit new military trade and establishment of bases in this already grotesquely over-militarised region.'

Von Sponeck's proposals were finally published online by the Transnational Futures Foundation (TFF), a Swedish-based NGO, in February 2003; but they were initially offered to the *IHT* the previous December. TFF director Jan Oberg takes up the story:

> 'This comprehensive peace proposal was submitted to Features Editor Robert Donahue, of the *International Herald Tribune*, on December 5, 2002. On December 19, Donahue accepted the article for publication by e-mail. Then nothing happened. On February 6, however, Mr Donahue told us that he had let another editor read the article. This editor 'didn't like the article and thought that many of its points were unrealistic – and I respect my colleague', he said over the phone. So the *International Herald Tribune* changed its mind and hoped we would accept their apology. On February 17, the European Council of the EU came together and began formulating a common foreign policy in relation to the Iraq crisis.
>
> The *International Herald Tribune* made a politically motivated turnaround [from the initial indication it gave that the piece would be published in its pages] and effectively wasted exactly two months of this proposal's life in the public debate.'[50]

This last point is the salient one. 'As long as war is the only plan in town,' von Sponeck argued, 'there is a grave danger that war will be seen as a solution'; whereas, in truth, 'violence will only replace one authoritarian elite with another'. The only prospect for real improvements lay in bringing about 'democracy with democratic means'. Such initiatives will remain 'unrealistic' as long as they are left outside the frame of reporting. To pick them up, as TFF did, is inevitably to promulgate and encourage them, shaping the issues under discussion and helping to make suggested non-violent, developmental responses more 'realistic' in the process. However:

> 'To ignore them is not to remain "neutral". Not only does it give a distorted picture, it's also to collude in concealing them from view.'[51]

In the film from which this quote is taken, Uri Avnery, veteran leader of Israel's peace movement, observes:

> 'The citizen is completely helpless. He does not hear any other voice; and if everybody says the same, it must be true.'

Solution- v Victory-orientated

Another example of how the constituent parts of War Journalism grow out of and sustain each other. The remedy for a problem, in conflict as in medicine, depends on diagnosis. Start off with a tug of war, and dehumanise one party, and the remedy is a military victory, to get rid of that party. Locate the problem wholly in the conflict arena, and you can easily convince yourself that a limited, pre-emptive, surgical strike can remove the 'cancer'.

How do you diagnose the problem differently, in the context of a news report? How do you highlight the need and potential for non-violent responses? Let's switch the focus to another conflict arena, prominent in the agenda for international news – the struggle involving Israel and the Palestinians. The following scripts show two contrasting treatments of the same violent incident – a suicide bombing in Jerusalem, in August 2003.

Exercise One
Identifying War Journalism and Peace Journalism

Read the following scripts from two television news reports on a suicide bombing in Jerusalem.[52]
In the first, can you identify at least two characteristics of War Journalism?
In the second, can you identify at least two characteristics of Peace Journalism?

Questions
- How is the violence explained?
- Who or what is to blame for the violence?
- What might we therefore expect the solution to be?

TV News Script: Version 1

(Duration: 2'40") Please note the script was written for use as an exercise. It is put together with material from various news organisations. The left-hand column indicates what the pictures show the viewer. The right-hand column tells you what the reporter and others say to accompany the pictures.

Pictures 1

"Suicide Bombing" – Standard Version
Reporter: Jake Lynch

Voice 1

Voice-over: Carnage on the streets of Jerusalem – the worst suicide bombing here in more than a year. Israelis in despair that they can ever be safe in their homes. Members of this Orthodox Jewish community already raising calls for Arabs to be forcibly moved out of East Jerusalem, the border just a few hundred yards from the scene of the blast. Rescue workers pulling survivors from the wreckage and collecting whatever pieces they could find of the dead.

Pictures 2

Voice 2

Voice-over: This, the man responsible for the horror – a 29-year-old school teacher from Hebron. The extremist group, Hamas, sent him out to kill, in revenge, they said, for Israeli attacks on their leaders. And to send a message – no compromise in peace talks with the Israelis.

Pictures 3

Ismail Abu Shanab
Hamas Spokesman

Voice 3

Ismail Abu Shanab, Hamas spokesman: The dialogue among the Palestinians is the key element of our strength and nobody can stop this dialogue unless he is intending to break the Palestinian unity.

Pictures 4

Voice 4

Voice-over: Today, the numbingly familiar routines of mourning. They're calling this the massacre of the children. A high proportion of those killed were under 10 years old, returning from the Old City where they'd gone to pray with their parents. Their killer had disguised himself as one of them. He was strapped in to a massive bomb, packed with fragments of metal to inflict the maximum deadly effect.

Pictures 5

Avi Pazner
Israeli Government Spokesman

Voice 5

Avi Pazner, Israeli government spokesman: There is no doubt that decisions will be made today. Already we have closed the Palestinian areas and we will postpone the transfer of Palestinian cities to the Palestinian Authority. But the Israeli government will have to decide how to further react to this wanton act of terrorism.

Pictures 6

Voice 6

Voice-over: Israel's president, Moshe Katzav, visiting the wounded in hospital. Israel has already announced a suspension of all contacts with the Palestinians as she mulls over possible military reprisals.

Pictures 7

Pictures 8

Voice 7

Reporter Jake Lynch, piece to camera: This devastating blow shattered a period of relative calm here, when progress on the latest peace plan, the American-sponsored Road Map began to seem possible. Now any prospect of peace between Israelis and Palestinians appears as faint and distant as it's ever been.

Voice 8

Voice-over: It all leaves Abu Mazen, the beleaguered Palestinian prime minister, unsure which way to turn. He's facing renewed demands to crack down on militant groups. Whether he's strong enough to do it, many here doubt.

TV News Script: Version 2

(Duration: 3'00") The following report gives a different version of events on 19 August 2003. Please note the script was written for use as an exercise. It is put together with material from various news organisations. The left-hand column describes what the pictures show the viewer. The right-hand column tells you what the reporter and others say to accompany the pictures.

Pictures 1

"Suicide Bombing" – Alternative Version
Reporter: Annabel McGoldrick

Voice 1

Voice-over: Another day of mourning in Jerusalem. A bus carrying families back from a prayer visit to the Old City, when the bomb went off. A high proportion of those killed were children – as if to emphasise the indiscriminate power of this conflict to destroy the lives and hopes of young and old alike.

Pictures 2

Voice 2

Voice-over: The blast confirmed the end of a ceasefire by the militant groups, Islamic Jihad and Hamas, who've admitted carrying out the bombing. The six-week truce was supposed to create space for political progress on the latest peace plan, the American-sponsored Road Map, but progress has been slow, and now risks going into reverse.

Pictures 3

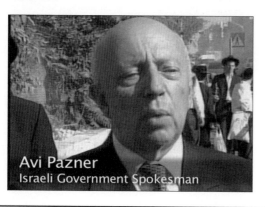

Avi Pazner
Israeli Government Spokesman

Voice 3

Avi Pazner, Israeli government spokesman: There is no doubt that decisions will be made today. Already we have closed the Palestinian areas and we will postpone the transfer of Palestinian cities to the Palestinian Authority. But the Israeli government will have to decide how to further react to this wanton act of terrorism.

Pictures 4

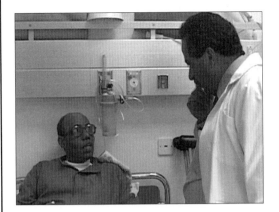

Voice 4

Voice-over: Palestinians today, dreading renewed military action like this tank raid in Gaza recently that killed eight civilians. Even after last night's attack, the Palestinian death toll, from the violence of recent years, is three times that among Israelis – with 21 killed in the ceasefire period alone. This hospital at Qalqilya is one that's had to pick up the pieces.

Pictures 5

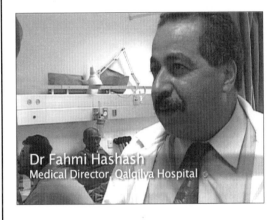

Dr Fahmi Hashash
Medical Director, Qalqilya Hospital

Voice 5

Dr Fahmi Hashash, medical director, Qalqilya Hospital: Live bullets injury, explosive bullets injury, even some injuries from explosions. We are obliged to deal with all of these cases even if the trauma and injury is too difficult for us.

Pictures 6

Voice 6

Reporter Annabel McGoldrick, piece to camera: Israelis and Palestinians are now trapped in a cycle of violence. The elaborate security and military apparatus designed to protect Israel inflicts a steady trickle of casualties on Palestinians. And every time the Palestinians lash out, as one did here, there's a crackdown, making the conditions in which they live still more onerous.

Pictures 7

Voice 7

Voice-over: Many of those deaths and injuries come in shooting incidents at army checkpoints, here to enforce Israel's occupation of Palestinian territory. These Israeli women from Checkpoint Watch carry out daily monitoring visits. Without any effective oversight, they say, shootings take place with impunity.

Pictures 8

Hannah Barag
Checkpoint Watch

Voice 8

Hannah Barag, checkpoint watch: The army claims that the youngster, the 14-year-old fellow, threw a stone at them, or talked to them in a rude way or something. We left 10 minutes earlier and they shot the fellow, it's a boy, he's 14 years old, it's a child, they shot him and killed him.

Pictures 9

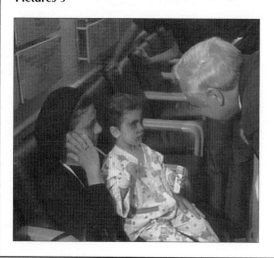

Voice 9

Voice-over: Israel's government has responded to the suicide bombing by breaking off talks with the Palestinians. But many here are calling for a renewed urgency in the political process as the only way to remove the causes of violence.

Commentary

Explanation for violence – who or what is to blame?

The first of these reports illustrates another important feature of War Journalism – violence is presented as its own cause, part of a 'tit-for-tat' series of exchanges. In the terms of the Galtung table, it concentrates on 'who threw the first stone'. It is 'reactive – waiting for violence before reporting'. In this case, it leaves us to conclude that the Palestinians are to blame, in particular the bomber 'sent out to kill' by Hamas on a revenge mission.

Crucially, the second report shows other aspects of the conflict, besides violence: the conditions of daily life in which Palestinians are routinely blocked and frustrated; the impunity surrounding shooting incidents at checkpoints, which encourages a 'shoot first, ask questions later' approach. In an important sense, it is the conflict, the system of relations shared by Israelis and Palestinians, that is to blame.

There are high stakes here:

'The attack was widely reported in the US and British media as "bringing to an end a period of calm", in which progress on the road map to peace began to seem possible. But this was not strictly accurate... throughout the ceasefire period, the Palestinians endured a daily trickle of casualties.

This [the suicide bombing featured in these reports] has since been identified as a significant turning point in Washington politics – the moment advocates of a more openly pro-Israeli stance, led by [then] National Security Advisor Condoleezza Rice, gained the upper hand.'[53]

According to Middle East envoy, John Wolf, 'the bombing on August 19 was a bombing that not only killed Israelis, but did a lot of damage to the process'.[54]

The solution

The first report suggests the solution is to 'crack down on militant groups'. The second report gives an insight into how crackdowns may increase the likelihood of further violence. Any solution, we now understand, would have to address itself to alleviating the conditions for Palestinians under military occupation.

The first report frames the conflict as a tug of war between two aggregated parties – Israelis and Palestinians. Everyone is on one side or the other; the only sources are political leaders and men with guns. The second effectively disaggregates the parties, simply by showing a Palestinian doctor – a man of healing – and Israeli peace activists. Not everyone, we are reminded, thinks, responds or behaves in the same way.

Exercise Two
Creating a PJ/WJ Table

Compile a War Journalism/Peace Journalism Table on a conflict of your choice.

How is the reporting of this conflict, in general:

- War/violence-orientated?
- Propaganda-orientated?
- Elite-orientated?
- Victory-orientated?

In what ways could it be reported in order to be:

- Peace/conflict-orientated?
- Truth-orientated?
- People-orientated?
- Solution-orientated?

Avoiding War Journalism

These examples show how the elements of War Journalism slot together, following the fundamental decision, contained in the *Newsweek* cover, to frame the conflict as bipolar, like a tug of war, underpinning all the others.

Readers and audiences are led – or left, by crucial omissions, from the reporting – to overvalue violent responses to conflict issues, and undervalue non-violent ones. They are also left unaware of contra-indications to claims made in support of violence, or they are led to attach too little importance to them. As the Glasgow Media Group findings quoted earlier suggest, they are left in the dark on basic facts.

In this case, the conflict involving Israel and the Palestinians, the same study produced strong anecdotal evidence, from scores of focus groups, of confusion and frustration among news audiences:

> 'Philo and Berry find a strong appetite for such material, among members of their focus groups. "They never really tell you the in-depth reasons behind it", one man complained. "This guy went in to bomb a pizza restaurant – why? The Israelis are going to attack – why?" "What pushes them to that extreme?" another wondered.'[55]

To avoid sliding into these patterns of omission and marginalisation, a deliberate creative strategy is needed. We have suggested how Peace Journalism is both an explanation of, and a solution to, these problems, in the context of two important stories about conflict. Is it possible at this stage to infer some general principles?

> DISCUSSION: Looking back at the Galtung table, come up with a checklist of simple recommendations to avoid slipping into War Journalism.

A 17-point plan for practical Peace Journalism

The following 17 points are practical suggestions for devising and applying such a strategy to re-balance the reporting of conflicts, countering the distorting influence of unexamined War Journalism.

1. AVOID portraying a conflict as consisting of only two parties contesting the same goal(s). The logical outcome is for one to win and the other to lose.
    INSTEAD *try to DISAGGREGATE the two parties* into many smaller groups, with many needs and interests, pursuing many goals, opening up more creative potential for a range of outcomes. *And ask yourself* – who else is involved, and how?

2. AVOID accepting stark distinctions between 'self' and 'other'. These can be used to build the sense that another party is a 'threat' or 'beyond the pale' of civilised behaviour. Both are key justifications for violence.
    INSTEAD *seek the 'other' in the 'self' and vice versa*. If a party is presenting itself as 'the goodies', ask questions about how different its behaviour really is to that it ascribes to the other – isn't it ashamed of itself?

3. AVOID treating a conflict as if it is only going on in the place and at the time that violence is occurring.
    INSTEAD *try to trace the links and consequences* for people in other places now and in the future. Ask:
    - Who are all the people with a stake in the outcome?
    - How do these stakeholders relate to each other?
    - Who gains from the conflict?
    - What are they doing to influence the conflict?
    - What will happen if...?
    - What lessons will people draw from watching these events unfold as part of a global audience? How will they enter

the calculations of parties to future conflicts near and far?

4. AVOID assessing the merits of a violent action or policy of violence in terms of its visible effects only.
    INSTEAD *try to find ways of reporting on the invisible effects*, eg the long-term consequences of psychological damage and trauma, perhaps increasing the likelihood that those affected will be violent in future, either against other people or, as a group, against other groups or other countries.

5. AVOID letting parties define themselves by simply quoting their leaders' restatements of familiar demands or positions.
    INSTEAD *enquire for yourself into goals, needs and interests*:
    • How are people on the ground affected by the conflict in everyday life?
    • What do they want changed?
    • Who else is speaking up for them besides their political leaders? Answers to this are often surprisingly accessible, as even many small grassroots organisations now have websites.
    • Is the position stated by their leaders the only way or the best way to achieve the changes they want?
    • This may help to empower parties to clarify their needs and interests and articulate their goals, making creative outcomes more likely.

6. AVOID concentrating always on what divides the parties, on the differences between what each say they want.
    INSTEAD *try asking questions which may reveal areas of common ground*, and leading your report with answers which suggest that at least some goals, needs and interests may be compatible, or shared.

7. AVOID only reporting the violent acts and describing 'the horror'. If you exclude everything else, you suggest that the only explanation for violence is previous violence (revenge); the only remedy, more violence (coercion/ punishment).
    INSTEAD *show how people have been blocked and frustrated or deprived* in everyday life as a way of explaining how the conditions for violence are being produced.

8. AVOID blaming someone for 'starting it'.
    INSTEAD *try looking at how shared problems and issues* are leading to consequences which all the parties say they never intended.

9. AVOID focusing exclusively on the suffering, fears and grievances of only one party. This divides the parties into 'villains' and 'victims' and suggests that coercing or punishing the villains represents a solution.
    INSTEAD *treat as equally newsworthy* the suffering, fears and grievances of all parties.

10. AVOID 'victimising' language like 'devastated', 'defenceless', 'pathetic', 'tragedy' which only tells us what has been done to and could be done for a group of people by others. This is dis-empowering and limits the options for change.
    INSTEAD *report on what has been done and could be done by the people*. Don't just ask them how they feel; also ask them how they are coping and what they think. Can they suggest any solutions?

11. AVOID the imprecise use of emotive words to describe what has happened to people, such as the following:
    • 'Tragedy' is a form of drama, originally Greek, in which someone's fault or weakness ultimately proves his or her undoing.
    • 'Assassination' is the murder of a head of state.

- 'Massacre' is the deliberate killing of people known to be unarmed and defenceless. Are we sure? Or do we not know? Might these people have died in battle?
- 'Systematic' – eg raping, or forcing people from their homes. Has it really been organised in a deliberate pattern, or have there been a number of unrelated, albeit extremely nasty, incidents?

INSTEAD *always be precise about what we know*. Do not minimise suffering but reserve the strongest language for the gravest situations or you will beggar the language and help to justify disproportionate responses which escalate the violence.

12. AVOID demonising adjectives like 'vicious', 'cruel', 'brutal', 'barbaric'. These always describe one party's view of what another party has done. To use them puts the journalist on that side and helps to justify an escalation of violence. INSTEAD *report what you know about the wrongdoing* and give as much information as you can about the reliability of other people's reports or descriptions of it. If it is still being investigated, say so, as a caution that the truth may not yet be known.

13. AVOID demonising labels like 'terrorist', 'extremist', 'fanatic', 'fundamentalist'. These are always given by 'us' to 'them'. No one ever uses them to describe himself or herself. And they are difficult, if not impossible, to apply impartially in every instance where they would be warranted. (What, for instance, is a 'fundamentalist regime'? A working definition might be – an unelected government with leaders avowedly guided by religious belief. But many journalists would have found it very difficult, in practice, so to describe the first George W Bush administration, appointed to power by the US Supreme Court, in 2000, despite garnering half a million fewer votes than the Democrat, Al Gore.)

In practice, therefore, to use such labels is always to take sides. They also generally mean the people labelled are unreasonable, which weakens the case for reasoning (negotiating) with them. INSTEAD *try calling people by the names they give themselves.* Or be more precise in your descriptions – eg 'bombers' and, for the attacks of September 11th, 'suicide hijackers' are both less partisan and give more information than 'terrorists'.

14. AVOID focusing exclusively on the human rights abuses, misdemeanours and wrongdoings of *only* one side. INSTEAD *try to name ALL wrongdoers*, and treat allegations made by all parties in a conflict equally seriously. This means, not taking at face value, but instead making equal efforts to establish whether any evidence exists to back them up, treating the victims with equal respect and the finding and punishing of all wrongdoers as being of equal importance.

15. AVOID making an opinion or claim seem like an established fact. This is how propaganda works – eg the campaign, primarily aimed at US and UK media, to link Saddam Hussein to 'international terrorism' in early 2002. Under a headline linking Iraq to the Taliban and al-Qaeda, came the claim that 'Iraqi military intelligence officers are *said to be* assisting extreme Palestinian groups in attacks on Israel... [emphasis added]'.[56] 'Said to be' obscures the question of who is doing the saying. See also 'thought to be', 'it's being seen as', etc. INSTEAD *tell your readers or your audience who said what.* That way you avoid implicitly signing up yourself and your news service to the allegations made by one party in the conflict against another.

16. AVOID greeting the signing of documents by leaders which bring about military victory or a ceasefire as necessarily creating peace.
INSTEAD try to report on the issues which remain, and on the needs and interests of those affected. What has to happen in order to remove incentives for further acts of violence?
Ask what is being done to strengthen the means on the ground to handle and resolve conflict non-violently, to address development or structural needs in the society and to create a culture of peace?

17. AVOID waiting for leaders on 'our' side to suggest or offer solutions.
INSTEAD *pick up and explore peace initiatives wherever they come from.* Ask questions of politicians – eg about ideas put forward by grassroots organisations. Assess peace perspectives against what you know about the issues the parties are really trying to address; do not simply ignore them because they don't coincide with established positions. Include images of a solution, however partial or fragmentary – they may help to stimulate dialogue.

✳

Endnotes for Chapter 1

1. Mark Steyn, 'The President's Brain', London *Sunday Telegraph*, 24 October 2004.
2. National Public Radio, *Morning Edition*, 17 September 2002.
3. Steve Bell, *Apes of Wrath*, Methuen, London, 2004.
4. John Kampfner, *Blair's Wars*, Free Press, an imprint of Simon & Schuster, London, 2003, p 168.
5. Michael Smith, 'Failure Is Not an Option', London *Sunday Telegraph*, 19 September 2004.
6. Commissioned by London *Guardian*.
7. Ed Pilkington, London *Guardian*, quoted in Jake Lynch, 'Reporting Iraq – What Went Right? What Went Wrong?' in Anita Biressi and Heather Nunn (eds), *Mediawar, Mediactive* No 3, Barefoot Publications, an imprint of Lawrence & Wishart, London, 2004, p 114.
8. Ibid, p 109.
9. Susan D Moeller, *WMD: Media Get Failing Grade*, Philip Merrill College of Journalism, University of Maryland, 9 March 2004.
10. Greg Mitchell, editor and publisher, 'Mea Culpa', *New York Times*, 26 May 2004.
11. Professor Justin Lewis, 'Biased Broadcasting Corporation', London *Guardian*, 4 July 2003.
12. Ibid.
13. From BBC *Producer Guidelines*.
14. Greg Philo and Mike Berry, *Bad News from Israel*, Pluto Press, London, 2004, p 217.
15. Greg Philo speaking in Jake Lynch and Annabel McGoldrick, *News from the Holy Land* (video), Hawthorn Press, Stroud, 2004.
16. Jake Lynch, 'Reporting Iraq – What Went Right? What Went Wrong?' in Anita Biressi and Heather Nunn (eds), *Mediawar, Mediactive* No 3, Barefoot Publications, an imprint of Lawrence & Wishart, London, 2004, p 110.
17. Quoted in Jake Lynch, *The Peace Journalism Option*, Conflict and Peace Forums, Taplow, 1998, p 44.
18. 30 September 2002.
19. 'Wolfowitz Comments Revive Doubts over Iraq's WMD', Associated Press, Brussels, 30 May 2003.
20. Cartoon from London *Observer* Magazine, 16 February 2003.
21. Baker Institute for Public Policy, *Strategic Energy Policy Challenges for the 21st Century* (Report submitted to Vice-President's office), April 2001.
22. Ibid.
23. http://www.newamericancentury.org/statementofprinciples.htm.
24. PNAC, *Rebuilding America's Defenses*, September 2000.

25. Quoted in Jay Bookman, 'The President's Real Goal in Iraq', *Atlanta Journal-Constitution*, 29 September 2002.

26. Paul Mason, 'Is It All about Oil?', BBC TV *Newsnight*, 13 January 2003.

27. Jake Lynch, *Iraq – Broadening the Agenda*, for www.iraqconflict.org, 20 February 2003.

28. Quoted in Niall Ferguson, 'The Depressing Reality of This Messianic President's New Empire', London *Independent*, 4 November 2004.

29. National Security Council, *US National Security Strategy* (from the opening section, 'Overview'), 17 September 2002.

30. Ibid.

31. Zbigniew Brzezinkski, *The Grand Chessboard – American Primacy and Its Geostrategic Imperatives*, Basic Books, New York, 1997, p 40.

32. Quoted in Michael Parenti, 'The Arrogance of Empire', Alternative Radio, 13 October 2003.

33. Zbigniew Brzezinkski, op cit, p 211.

34. To view the advert in RealPlayer, visit www.detroitproject.com.

35. John Humphrys, 'We're planning a war, but don't mention the oil', London, *Sunday Times*, 8 December 2002.

36. Donald Rumsfeld, testifying before US Senate Armed Services Committee, 4 February 2004.

37. Steven Lee Myers, 'Russia May Support New UN Efforts on Iraq', *New York Times*, 12 October 2002.

38. Speech to Parliament, 24 September 2002.

39. Interviewed on *NBC News*, 3 April 2002.

40. Speech to Trades Union Congress, 12 September 2002.

41. Mohamed El Baradei, statement to UN Security Council, 7 March 2003.

42. UNMOVIC Daily Inspection Activities Report, 17 January 2003.

43. John Burns, 'Inspectors Find Only Ruins at Old Iraqi Site', *New York Times*, 29 November 2002.

44. Howard Friel and Richard Falk, *The Record of the Paper – How the* New York Times *Misreports US Foreign Policy*, Verso, London & New York, 2004, p 101.

45. Dov Shinar, 'Media Peace Discourse: Constraints, Concepts and Building Blocks', paper circulated to Toda Institute for Peace and Policy, group working on Peace Journalism courses, p 4.

46. Quoted in Sheldon Rampton and John Stauber, *Weapons of Mass Deception*, Robinson, London, 2003.

47. Transcript of discussion 'Reporting Iraq – What Went Right? What Went Wrong?', Reporting the World, 15 July 2003, www.reportingtheworld.org.uk.

48. Quoted in Jake Lynch, 'Reporting Iraq – What Went Right? What Went Wrong?' in Anita Biressi and Heather Nunn (eds), *Mediawar, Mediactive* No 3, Barefoot Publications, an imprint of Lawrence & Wishart, London, 2004, p 119.

49. John Paul Lederach, *Building Peace – Sustainable Reconciliation in Divided Societies*, United States Institute of Peace Press, Washington, 1997, p 94.

50. Jan Oberg, 'Pressinfo 170', Transnational Futures Foundation, 18 February 2003, at www.transnational.org.

51. Jake Lynch and Annabel McGoldrick, *News from the Holy Land* (video), Hawthorn Press, Stroud, 2004.

52. Ibid.

53. Jake Lynch and Annabel McGoldrick, 'Losing the War on News', *UK Press Gazette*, 4 June 2004.

54. Ibid.

55. Jake Lynch and Annabel McGoldrick, 'Peace Journalism in the Holy Land', *Media Development*, World Association for Christian Communication, January 2005.

56. David Graves and Neil Tweedie, 'Allied Dossier Links Saddam to Al Qaeda', London *Daily Telegraph*, 9 March 2002.

Chapter 2

Conflict Analysis – Anchorage for Journalists

This chapter introduces and explains some basic concepts of Conflict Analysis – the firm ground beneath the journalist's feet in the torrent of competing claims, perspectives and representations.

We suggest how to go beyond the familiar dualism of War Journalism, to examine what conflicts are about and how they work. The focus is on connections between the way conflicts are reported and the limits and extent of what can be seen as appropriate and feasible responses. What are we led, or left, to expect will happen next?

This chapter:

- Presents some basic Conflict Analysis concepts and shows why each is useful to journalists
- Considers what conflict is, and theories about the causes of conflict
- Looks at ways of mapping conflict – what it is about, who is involved, how they relate to each other, and what their goals are
- Applies the principles of Conflict Analysis to the reporting of a violent incident
- Shows how partisan perceptions can be reinforced or revised by different ways of reporting
- Distinguishes between *demands* and *positions* of parties to conflict, as given by leaders on each side; and their needs, interests and goals
- Asks what is meant by peace

By the end of the chapter, the reader will be able to:

- Identify Attitudes, Behaviour and Contradictions – the ABC of conflict – and understand how they drive conflicts, sometimes into violence
- See how the choices journalists make, in reporting conflicts, can affect the understanding given to readers and audiences, and how this, in turn, conditions our expectations of what will happen next
- Discriminate between different definitions to discern what constitutes a sustainable lasting peace

Why study conflict?

Few journalists have been trained in conflict theory and analysis, a subject developed in universities and institutes during the second half of the 20th century, often known as Peace Studies or Peace Research.

There is a substantial body of work about conflict *per se* – its dynamics, what causes it and how it works. There are plentiful empirical findings and abundant theoretical material to explain them.

This work means developments or interventions in a conflict can be assessed against what is known and what has been observed about conflicts, both in particular and, crucially, in general. There is a sturdy and well-established analytical framework within which to predict their likely impact.

In common with research and fieldwork methodologies in other branches of social science, Peace Research acknowledges the principle of the 'participant-observer' – as soon as you start to observe something, you enter into relationships which inevitably impact upon it.

Perhaps the crucial precept of Peace Journalism is that journalists covering conflict are *inescapably involved* in the events and processes they are reporting on – whether they like it, seek it or not.

Skills

The skills of Conflict Analysis and 'resolution' can be applied to try to reduce violence, thus enabling the application of viable strategies for change. 'Change', in this context, has the specific meaning of social and structural transformation that alters the dynamics of conflict.

Conflict Analysis skills are not a 'given'. We are not born with them ready-made: as with any science or art form, they have to be learned and practised. Some are traditional, developed and passed on within communities; others are managerial, purposely designed as forms of intervention to help those directly affected by a conflict to bring about change. The growing field of 'media and conflict' is based on the proposition that equipping journalists with appropriate skills makes them more effective professionals, capable of:

- reporting conflicts more accurately
- identifying and restoring parts of stories about conflict routinely omitted or marginalised
- taking responsibility for their inescapable involvement in the events and processes on which they report

It is worth emphasising the 'newness' of Peace Research. It offers insights into conflict quite different from those of other, apparently related fields such as Politics or International Relations. Journalists covering conflicts cannot necessarily be content with 'common sense' or 'general knowledge' as the basis for their understanding.

One persuasive analogy is between Conflict Analysis and Information Technology. We did not all grasp instantly its true importance. It

took some practice and imagination to comprehend its constructive potential for all our lives; but now it has both demanded and enabled a rethink on how we go about all forms of communication.[1]

What is conflict?

'Conflict is a relationship between two or more parties (individuals or groups) who have, or think they have, incompatible goals, needs and interests.'[2]

> DISCUSSION: Read the following two quotes from newspaper articles. Consider the difference between this definition – basic to the study of Peace Research – and the notion of conflict written into the two typical pieces of news reporting below.

'Before the conflict is a week old, the game has changed. By adopting guerrilla tactics, Saddam's loyalists are forcing the Allies to be far more heavy-handed than they envisaged…'[3]

'Opposition to the Iraq war has risen again after the publication of the Hutton report and the row over the use of intelligence before the conflict…'[4]

The first was written during the invasion of Iraq, the other, nearly a year later. Both use the word 'conflict' to mean 'war'. But this conflict – this relationship – was much more than a week old by the time the US-led troops invaded.

From the definition we are suggesting, it follows that, by the time anyone started gathering and using intelligence, the conflict, as opposed to a particular episode of violence, must already have been under way.

The distinction is not purely semantic – collapsing the meanings of conflict and violence into one squeezes out the space to consider several questions vital to understanding what is going on and why. Consider what we would need to know, in order to be sure of what is meant by 'before the conflict':

- Who were the parties to the conflict?
- What were their goals?
- When did they start thinking of those goals as incompatible?

The answers provide you with the starting-point of 'the conflict', as distinct from a particular episode of violence.

So when did this conflict begin? 2003? 2001? 2000? 1998? 1992? 1991? 1990? 1988? 1982? 1980? 1979? 1978? 1968? 1967? 1953? 1948? 1932? 1920? 1916? 1915? 1096?

> DISCUSSION: What happened on each of these dates? How might they be relevant to the conflict of today?

2003 – US-led invasion of Iraq

2001 – Suicide hijackings of US airliners, attacks on World Trade Center and Pentagon

2000 – US Supreme Court appoints George W Bush as President following dispute over election outcome

1998 – UN weapons inspectors leave Iraq; 'Operation Desert Fox' bombing by US and British warplanes

1992 – Rio Earth Summit. President Bush the elder declares 'the American way of life [based on unlimited oil consumption] is not up for negotiation'

1991 – 'Operation Desert Storm' ejects Iraqi forces from Kuwait

1990 – Iraqi forces invade neighbouring Gulf state of Kuwait

1988 – Saddam Hussein orders chemical weapons to be used against his own people – the Kurds at Halabja

1982 – Military Posture Review of the US Joint Chiefs of Staff says exposure to foreign resources, especially oil, is biggest US security issue

1980 – Start of Iran-Iraq war; lasts till 1988. US and allies support Iraq

1979 – Islamic Revolution overthrows US-backed regime of the Shah in Iran

1978 – Saddam Hussein becomes President of Iraq

1968 – Ba'ath Party coup d'etat in Iraq

1967 – 'Six Days War' sees Israel, with US backing, occupy more Arab land – West Bank, Gaza Strip and Golan Heights

1953 – CIA-backed coup removes democratically elected Mossadeq government in Iran which had nationalised the country's oil industry; Shah begins despotic rule

1948 – Foundation of the State of Israel on land formerly ruled by British Mandate in Palestine

1932 – Iraq founded as independent state under British influence

1920 – British colonial rule in Iraq, including use of warplanes to bomb resisting villages with chemical weapons; Balfour Declaration gives British support to a Jewish homeland in Palestine

1916 – The Sykes-Picot agreement between the British and French foreign ministers, a plan to divide Arab lands into spheres of influence, thereby reneging on…

1915 – … the promise given, by Britain via Lawrence of Arabia, to Sheriff Hussayn of Mecca, that the Arabs would be allowed to rule themselves after the First World War and the end of the Ottoman Empire

1096 – The First Crusade of Christian Europe, bent on conquest and conversion of Muslim lands

These are just a few 'highlights' (or perhaps 'lowlights') from the history shared by Iraqi people and those in the main belligerent countries of the 2003 invasion – the US and Britain.

The academic study of UK television news, quoted in Chapter 1, found that Iraqis were nearly always shown greeting western invaders as 'liberators'. Incorporated in that narrative is an assessment that historical grievances such as the Crusades and the Sykes-Picot treachery can safely be ignored as factors affecting the way each party to the conflict is likely to see the actions and motivations of the other. Later, an independent Washington think-tank, the Center for Strategic and International Studies, said this assumption was part of 'fantasyland' – the view of 'ideologues [who] were fundamentally wrong about how the Iraqi people would view the United States invasion'.[5]

Our list of dates also brings several other parties – Iran, Israel and the Palestinians – directly into the conflict 'frame', together with several others by implication, particularly other big countries with oil-dependent economies such as China and India. How relevant each is to the conflict of today depends on where you think conflict comes from and what causes it.

Above all, the list raises the question of what conflict is really 'about'.

Conflict theories and terminology

The terms 'Conflict Analysis' and 'Peace Research' cover a multitude of theories and approaches – different *explanations for conflict*, different practical tools to use in *responding to conflict* and different ways of *overcoming conflict*.[6]

Explanations for conflict

- *Communications theory:*
  - **Community relations theory** assumes the conflict is caused by mistrust between the parties. Responses therefore include building tolerance, improving communication, and an acceptance of diversity.
  - **Intercultural miscommunication theory** assumes the conflict is caused by incompatibility between different styles and systems of cultural communication. Work focuses on understanding 'the other', by breaking down stereotypes, exploring each other's culture, and improving communication.

- *Human needs theory* assumes the conflict is based on unmet human needs – physical, social and psychological. It helps parties on all sides to identify and meet these needs.

- *Negotiation theory* assumes the conflict is about incompatible demands. It attempts to uncover the deeper goals of the parties and bring them to an agreement that offers mutual gain for all.

- *Identity theory* assumes the conflict is about threatened identity, perhaps rooted in an unresolved loss from the past. Work is on agreements that recognise the identity of both parties and which achieve some reconciliation between the groups.

- *Abuse of power or denial of human rights* is recognised by the Universal Declaration of Human Rights adopted by the UN General Assembly in 1948 as a minimum guarantee for each human being on the planet. The Declaration is an accepted global standard for justice, and a cause of conflict when violated; the intended response being to restore and protect human rights.

Responding to conflict

- *Conflict management* means strategies to limit further violence when resolution of a conflict is assumed to be unrealistic.

- *Conflict prevention* is, strictly speaking, a *non-sequitur*, but is widely used by policy-makers, especially in western governments. It really means ways of preventing a conflict from turning to violence.

- *Bridge-building* is work to build trust and communication between different parties in a conflict.

- *Mediation* promotes dialogue between parties in a conflict. It does not have to be face to face: a mediator can meet with groups/parties separately – or the parties can have one mediator each, with the mediators then meeting and comparing notes.

- *Peace agreement* means a signed peace agreement between political leaders. It does not have to mean a 'final settlement', but can be an important stage in the process.

- *Peacekeeping* is enforcement action, usually by troops either sent or mandated by the UN to maintain physical security after an agreement has been signed.

- *Reconciliation* means the restoration of workable relations. After violence, it may involve healing through a process like the South African Truth and Reconciliation Commission.

- *Reconstruction* is the rebuilding of a society's systems and structures, both physical and institutional.

Overcoming conflict

- *Conflict resolution* is a mediated dialogue process to deal with the causes of a conflict and build constructive relations between opposing parties.[7]

- *Conflict settlement* is a signed peace agreement between political leaders. It is often seen, not as the 'final act', but as an important stage in the process.

- *Peace-building* is a complex and extensive process of helping a society recover from collective violence. It is often seen as having four 'pillars': physical security, socio-economic development, building political institutions, and reconciliation to build relationships and psychological security.[8]

- *Conflict transformation* embraces all the processes required to bring about

peace with justice, in both the short term and the long term. It transforms underlying issues into sources of unity, not division.

Diagnosis and remedy

What makes people respond to conflict differently in different circumstances? It depends on how they themselves frame the conflict and what they see as being at stake for them. Two people can look at the same thing, disagree about what they are seeing, and both be right: 'It's not logical; it's psychological.'[9] Look at the famous Gestalt drawing below to see what this means. Does it show a young woman – or an old woman?

The way a problem is seen, or diagnosed, conditions what we are prepared to see as an appropriate remedy. (So, a doctor confronted with a swollen ankle might diagnose severe bruising and prescribe an analgesic cream. A better doctor might consider the possibility that the ankle is a warning sign of circulation problems, and end up prescribing pills or injections to ward off blood clots.)

Clearly, the 'deeper' the explanation for the causes of conflict, the more radical the solution has to be. According to one pioneer of Peace Research, conflict is: 'A ubiquitous phenomenon in human and social reality, a major *force motrice*.'[10]

Conflict can be destructive, but it can also be creative – a force for change, alive in debate, artistic expression and struggles for justice. Remember Orson Welles' famous speech in the 1949 movie, *The Third Man*:

> 'You know what the fellow said: In Italy for 30 years under the Borgias they had warfare, terror, murder and bloodshed, but they produced Michelangelo, Leonardo da Vinci and the Renaissance. In Switzerland they had brotherly love, they had 500 years of democracy and peace, and what did that produce? The cuckoo clock.'

Conflict is not a synonym for violence, however. Violence is only one possible *response* to conflict – a collective expression, or political tool to achieve ends. It can easily be self-defeating, in the long term nullifying any gains or even killing those who would have benefited from the achievement.

DISCUSSION: Go back to the definition of conflict given here and ask yourself – how many conflicts are you involved in? In your family? Your workplace? Your community? How do you respond to them?

A team of mathematicians and psychologists from Washington University say they now have a formula for predicting with 94 per cent accuracy whether married couples will stay together. It is based not on 'harmony' or expecting them to agree all the time, but on the way they respond to *disagreements*.

Monitoring this aspect of their relationship shows that successful couples keep up a 4:1 ratio of positive to negative interactions. Those who manage, in 80 per cent or more of their arguments, to keep their tempers and

consider each other's point of view, stand a chance of celebrating their golden wedding. Those who fall below this ratio might as well dial the lawyers, or at least the marriage guidance counsellors.[11]

Conflicts as you experience them in your own life can ultimately deliver something that you otherwise would not have. Hence, 'conflict the creator'. Only by acknowledging conflicts, and devising different responses to them, can a society make progress.

The course of development in a conflict depends on the interaction between the underlying issues, the incompatible needs, interests and goals – known as the Contradiction – and two aspects of response, Attitude and Behaviour.

The ABC conflict triangle[12]

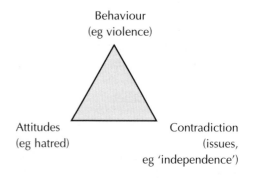

Behaviour
(eg violence)

Attitudes
(eg hatred)

Contradiction
(issues,
eg 'independence')

DISCUSSION: What will happen if only one aspect of a conflict is dealt with?

A ceasefire, perhaps greeted as a military 'victory', can leave resentments and underlying issues intact, and is therefore likely to prove only temporary. To build on a ceasefire, by working on issues and underlying attitudes, may remove the causes of violence.
The best example? The respective responses by the victor nations to the defeat of Germany in the First and Second World Wars. The Armistice of 1918 was followed by the imposition of harsh reparations, which created conditions in which Fascism arose and

thrived. It left the system of competitive nation-states intact. The late 1940s saw a very different response:

- The United Nations was created as a multilateral body to mediate global conflicts.
- The Marshall Plan brought huge aid payments from the US to rebuild the shattered European economy.
- The European Coal and Steel Community, forerunner of the European Union, was formed – a long-term political project to bind France and Germany together as allies, not enemies.
- The Universal Declaration of Human Rights, adopted by the UN General Assembly as an international norm, meant that protecting minorities from abuses, such as those meted out under the Nazis, would henceforth be an international responsibility.
- The Bretton Woods financial institutions would avert see-sawing exchange rates such as those which bankrupted the German Weimar Republic.

DISCUSSION: What influences the way people are likely to respond to conflict? In what circumstances do conflicts arise and what factors make parties more – or less – likely to respond violently? Or non-violently?

Conflict situations

Contradictions likely to cause conflict arise typically in circumstances where:

- resources are scarce (employment, income, housing, water)
- power is unevenly distributed
- unresolved grievances exist from the past

Conflict may be exacerbated by the parties' Attitudes to each other, especially if:

- poor or no communication exists between them
- parties have incorrect or biased perceptions of each other
- there is a lack of trust
- parties do not value the relationship between them[13]

A combination of these factors will create conditions in which people can be mobilised for violent behaviour – which may, in turn, harden attitudes and deepen contradictions.

The conflict orange[14]

This classic and apparently simple exercise, often presented to students of conflict and conflict resolution, can illuminate some quite complex processes and dynamics that are applicable to real conflicts.

Consider this situation: an orange is growing on a tree with its roots in one garden, but on a branch overhanging the neighbouring garden. Neighbour A has the garden where the tree is rooted; Neighbour B lives next door. This is the Contradiction – both A and B believe the orange is rightfully theirs.

It's worth noting at this stage that the biggest influence on people's responses to a conflict may be the perceived range of options. If there are clear laws and grievance procedures, viewed by everyone as legitimate, then it becomes a 'no-brainer' – they are likely to prove the first resort.

It's when laws and procedures are unclear, or lack legitimacy – at least in the eyes of some – that a greater range of responses is evident. If laws and procedures are inadequate to resolve this dispute over the orange, why might they lack clarity? How and why might they have lost legitimacy? You may want to bear those issues in mind as you tackle the following questions:

Exercise One
The Conflict Orange

- What happens next? How do the parties behave? How might their Attitudes to each other influence their Behaviour? List as many different outcomes to this conflict as you can.
- Can you give a 'score' for each of these outcomes?
  (Example: where the two neighbours fight, and A overpowers B and picks the orange for himself, A wins 1-0.)
- Of particular interest is the fact that many who do this exercise suggest cutting the orange in two, as a compromise solution. What score does this give? 1-1? Are you sure? What does it tell us about the problems of compromising?
- What might be better than compromise? What does it take to create something better than compromise?

Kinds of outcome

It is possible to classify the outcomes in four main categories:

1. *One party prevails (score: 1-0 or 0-1)*
   The Rule of Man – the pair fight for the orange. Might is right.
   The Rule of Law – adjudicate on some principle (eg tradition, need, taste).
   The Rule of Chance – some random method (eg roll a die to settle who wins the orange).
   Compensation – broadening, deepening (neighbour A gets the orange, neighbour B something else).

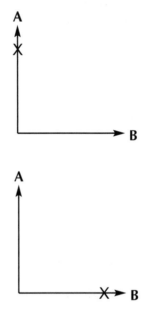

2. *Withdrawal (score: 0-0)*
   Walk away from the situation
   Destroy or give away the orange
   Just watch the orange
   Put it in the freezer

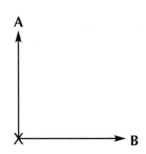

3. *Compromise (score: 1/2-1/2)*
   Cut the orange
   Squeeze the orange
   Peel the orange and divide the slices
   Any other division

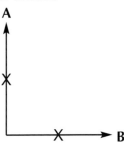

4. *Transcendence (scores: 1-1, 2-2, 3-3, etc)*
   Get one more orange
   Get more people to share the orange
   Bake an orange cake, raffle it and divide
   the proceeds
   Sow the seeds, make a plantation, take
   over the market

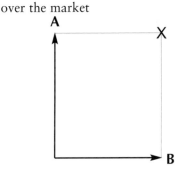

Basic thesis: the more alternatives, the less
likely the violence.[15]

What is the problem?

Some participants in this exercise, during
workshops, suggest cutting down the tree or
cutting off the branch. When asked why, they
often say, 'Because the tree/branch is the
problem'. Is it? Look again at the picture.
What else is there that might be the problem?
How might it be removed?

The real problem here may be the fence,
not the tree or the branch – in other words, a
division between people, made by people.
'Good fences make good neighbours,' it is
sometimes said – but the orange problem may
indicate a bad fence. Some of the interplay of
characters may hold a clue as to one way to
overcome this problem.

If the children of Mr A and Mr B marry,
then in one sense the fence between the two
families has been removed – part of the reason
why so many societies around the world have a
tradition of arranged marriage. The same effect
might be brought about indirectly if the parties
can be persuaded somehow to see themselves as
members of one community, all of whose
members have a stake in the outcome.

It may be possible, in other words, to
work on the relations between people in order
to address the underlying contradiction.

The other lesson, for a journalist covering
conflict, is that the issues the parties themselves
present as the bones of contention may not be
the real, or underlying, issues. As with the 'oil
agenda' for the invasion of Iraq, discussed in

Exercise Two
Reporting the Orange Conflict

Now imagine you are a journalist, sent to cover this dispute:

• How could you help the neighbours, and their village, region or even their country, to think
  about the conflict in such a way as to make a non-violent outcome more likely?
• Who would you interview, what would you ask them, and why?
• You can invent as many complications as you like to make it more interesting. For example – what
  if A is a member of ethnic group C, and B is a member of ethnic group D?
• What if group C is in the majority locally, but the next-door province or republic has a majority
  of group D?

the last chapter, exposing or illuminating these issues may be the key to conveying an understanding of the situation conducive to creating opportunities to consider and value non-violent responses.

The snag with compromising

The 'score' in each of the compromise outcomes is usually 'half-half'. It means each 'side' ends up with less than one orange, and nothing else. Each party gets less than it set out to get of the thing it knew it wanted at the outset.

The problem with this is that it may feel less attractive when compared with the option of 'one last push' to get the whole for oneself. The parties may accept compromise through war-weariness, or a prudent reluctance to risk defeat or the sustaining of any further damage; not out of any sense of enthusiasm.

It may prove less durable than is hoped – memories of hardship, during times of violence, can fade, leaving the next generation, for instance, with an incentive to 'sort it out once and for all.'

Unequal power

There is also an obvious problem in applying this classic exercise to real conflicts – it assumes the neighbours are equal in the first place. However:

- One neighbour may be powerful enough to circumvent any discussion by the mere hint of force.
- There may need to be a process of empowerment for the other neighbour before any of the other outcomes can become a realistic option. This may have to take the form of *intensification* of the conflict, especially if the powerful come to feel they can afford to overlook the legitimate claims and grievances of the less powerful.

One important liberal critique of affluent western societies is that they inhabit a 'culture of contentment' in which two-thirds feel sufficiently comfortable, in economic terms, not to have to worry about the other one-third who cannot get access to many of the material benefits they themselves enjoy.[16]

Getting the political wherewithal for action to mitigate this unequal distribution of resources may depend on the powerful finding that the problems of the powerless are, in fact, unignorable, and for this, some form of intensification may be necessary.

What about Transcendence?

To transcend means, literally, to *go beyond* – to see the contradictions in a conflict in a new light, using them as a springboard to create something different, something *more* than any one party had envisaged at the outset.

It really refers to a creative, problem-solving approach. Crucially, it enables Conflict Transformation – getting at the underlying issues and transforming them into sources of unity, not division.

Negotiated outcome

The conflicts journalists cover sometimes lead to a negotiated outcome, often called a 'peace agreement'. For journalists covering peace agreements, the insights gleaned from the orange exercise, and the discussion points arising from it, may be useful in reporting.

How far the underlying issues are addressed and transformed, to bring about transcendence, will tell readers and audiences how far they should expect the agreement to work.

Elements of withdrawal, shelving contentious issues, may store up trouble for the future.

So, too, may compromise, because it may feel inherently less attractive than the option of re-opening certain points in a bid to resolve them in one's favour. (For a fuller set of recommended questions when covering peace agreements, see Chapter 5.)

Mapping a conflict

Recall the discussion in the last chapter, about the tug of war between Saddam Hussein and George W Bush? We saw how any new development immediately begs to be assessed in terms of whether it means a side is 'winning' – if so, the other side must, at the same time, be 'losing'. It's what is called a 'zero-sum game'.

Ultimately, each faces either victory or defeat. Defeat being unthinkable, each steps up its efforts for victory. In other words, thinking of, or *framing*, a conflict as consisting of only two parties is bound to escalate it. Here we suggest ways to go beyond this bipolar model using conflict mapping.

This is a useful tool used by conflict analysts to unravel what a situation is really about and who has a stake. For journalists this concept opens up a whole new avenue of whom to interview and what questions to ask them. The more parties we can put on the conflict 'map', the further we go from the destructive bipolar model.

There is a variety of different ways to do this. We have summarised some of the basic tools. Of course, real conflict situations are often neither basic nor easily summarised – the point here is not to ignore or minimise complexities, but to offer possible starting points for thinking them through in novel and creative ways.

Tool 1: Mapping the stakeholders

We expanded the picture beyond the two presidents, Bush and Saddam, to a multi-party pattern simply by asking who has a stake in the outcome.

Do not be limited by space and time or by who is being violent. Think globally and go back or forward as far in time as you like.

Tool 2: Needs and Fears Mapping[17]

Step 1: List the different parties to the conflict
Include all who have a stake or involvement in it. In social or political conflicts, parties are often not united, but have factions, leaders and followers, core members and supporters, *et al.*[18]

Step 2: Current positions
Write down the current positions of all these parties – the demands they are making or their stated goals.

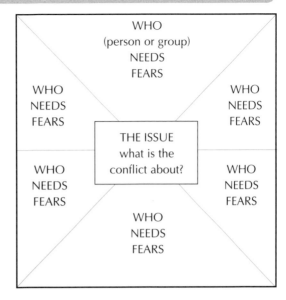

Step 3: Define the issue
You often find that defining the issue is difficult because to do so is really what the conflict is all about. In these circumstances, it is necessary to write down a number of definitions. When this is the case, the exercise has the merit of reminding us of the complexities of a conflict. This is especially useful for journalists, since it means they have to find creative ways to convey the complexity, or risk siding with one party over the other(s).

Step 4: What are the needs and fears of each party?
Needs could include the right to fish or grow crops; earnings from mineral deposits; the right to speak and be educated in the language of an ethnic group; or a guaranteed secure supply of water – or oil. This is a useful opportunity to list hidden agendas as 'needs' and 'concerns' on the map.

As for fears, this is an exercise, not in deciding what *we* think is reasonable, but in listening to what people in a particular group are afraid of. It is useful to air fears that usually go unstated but still influence people's behaviour.

Do not get bogged down in solutions. They may sometimes look like needs ('we need independence'), but go behind that and keep asking the question *Why?* – why do you need independence, what will it give you?

Try to put yourself in someone else's shoes, and beware accounts of conflict which do not show us the needs of all the parties.

> DISCUSSION: What do you think is useful in needs and fears mapping, for journalism about conflict?

- *Common ground* – it is interesting to see how some groups have overlapping needs or interests. This could be useful to a journalist for opening up a more constructive line of questioning.
- *Common visions* – seek out the values and ideas that are common to all by asking different spokespeople for the groups about them.
- *A guard against bias* – because it asks you to put yourself in the shoes of another group. This is particularly important for a journalist who belongs to one of the stakeholder groups in the conflict (one of the 'who' in the table) and must therefore be constantly finding ways to stop his/her journalism from being biased.
- *Story ideas* – this approach could open up a whole new avenue of stories for such a journalist in reporting on *the other* – exploring the needs and fears of another group in the conflict, thus creating empathy and humanising them.
- *Opportunity for dialogue* – it goes beyond slogans, demands and positions to look deeper into what people need, and so could open up new avenues for dialogue in a conflict that is stuck at a stalemate over slogans – like 'independence', 'separatism', 'self-determination' and 'territorial integrity'.
- *Hidden agendas* – a very interesting line of enquiry for journalists to clarify, particularly if a peace deal is in the offing.

Tool 3: The Onion[19]

Sometimes a conflict can be so well entrenched as to seem dominated by familiar slogans and demands.

The slogans and demands on each side make up platforms, or positions. The trouble with positions is that they are inherently divisive – the end-product of a process of *polarisation*.

Demands are really goals formulated by each side in such a way as to divide and distinguish it from the other(s).

Slogans to express these demands are most enthusiastically taken up by extremists – who often get most attention from media.

A more creative approach for journalists would be to 'peel the onion' – find ways to uncover the original goals from underneath the mass of hardened conflict discourse. Goals can, according to this approach, take the form of interests and needs:

POSITIONS
what we SAY we want
what is usually reported in the news

INTERESTS
what we REALLY want

NEEDS
what we MUST HAVE

Example: Britain and Ireland

For many years, the Britain/Ireland conflict was dominated by two slogans – 'Brits Out' on the one hand, and 'Keep Ulster British' on the other. These encapsulated the positions of parties on either end of a tug of war – a recipe for escalation, as we have seen.

At one end, the constitution of Ireland contained an historical claim to re-unification, meaning the removal of British rule from Northern Ireland. In the province itself,

Nationalists wanted a united Ireland by consent of the population; Republicans wanted to force the British out by a combination of, as another of their slogans put it, 'the Armalite and the ballot box'.

At the other end, Britain maintained a huge troop presence in Northern Ireland, vouchsafing its determination not to *be* forced out. In the province itself, Unionists representing Protestant communities said they should be able to choose to live in the UK, rather than be 'ruled from Dublin' – capital of the Catholic south. Loyalists took up arms, they said, to 'defend their communities' against Republican violence.

The key to transcending this tug of war was to unravel the positions by asking why the parties wanted what they said they wanted. What were their real interests and their real needs?

For instance, people in Catholic communities complained that the British state in Northern Ireland, as they experienced it at a grassroots level, discriminated against them. The police service, the Royal Ulster Constabulary, was 90 per cent Protestant, and was in charge of drawing up security assessments on individual citizens.

Young men in particular were likely to experience what they called 'harassment'. Secretly, they would be assessed as a 'terrorist suspect' – they never knew on what evidence it was based. They would then find themselves repeatedly stopped and searched, especially at army checkpoints, as they went about their daily business: one important reason for wanting the 'Brits out'.

The Good Friday Agreement between most of the Northern Ireland parties and the two governments provided for the British state to stay in the province, on condition that it took a new, changed form. A new police service was instituted – the Police Service of Northern Ireland (PSNI), obliged to recruit in proportion from each section of the community.

A power-sharing executive, proofed against becoming dominated by Unionists on the one hand, or Nationalists and Republicans on the other, was created to take over many devolved powers from London.

The Irish people voted, in a referendum, to drop the historical claim to re-unification from their country's constitution. One of the milestones in the process was Britain's announcement that it had 'no selfish interest' in retaining sovereignty over Northern Ireland.

As paramilitary groups decommissioned their weapons, Britain was to withdraw its troops, and cross-border co-operation on economic and security matters was to proceed – freed, as it now was, from any suspicion of a Dublin plot to 'win back' Northern Ireland, in accordance with its constitution, by stealth.

Britain agreed to appoint an international judge to look into incidents where people were killed amid allegations of collusion between Loyalist paramilitaries and branches of the British state – the police and army.

In other words, the various parties, previously lined up on one side or the other of a divide echoing with sterile slogans, all found they had to give a little to, in order to get a little from, each of the others.

The tug of war had been replaced by a cat's-cradle.

Transcendence
This was an example of transcendence. The provisions of the Good Friday Agreement went beyond adjudicating between claims by Unionists, Nationalists and Republicans, or between Protestants and Catholics.

It has been described as:

'A new modus operandi for joined-up governance, more defined and determined than anywhere else in these islands, inscribing equality in the duties of public authorities – including the police... The final text extended the equality duties to cover other ethnic minorities, age, sex, sexual orientation and disability – unthinkable in England.'[20]

Later, campaigners for racial equality and minority rights in Britain began to look to the

Good Friday Agreement for inspiration in their struggles to transform their own conflicts. The lessons fed into a successful attempt to legislate against racism in policing in Britain, not just Northern Ireland. To get this unexpected benefit from the process, the layers of the onion had first to be peeled back. Some journalists made their own contribution to this, by asking the simple question, *Why?*

It's important not to paint too rosy a picture. The Peace Process is still fraught with frustrations, contradictions and delays. But it is equally important to be specific about what grew out of the act of reframing.

In so far as there is still a 'Northern Ireland problem', it is the *conflict* that is generally now seen as the problem, whereas for a long time each side saw the other as the problem. As a result, virtually everyone agrees there is little or no prospect of a slide back into the large-scale violence of the past.

Tool 4: Partisan perceptions

An important factor in any conflict is the perceptions people have about the goals of others. ('What do they want and what does it mean for me?') One important tool for conflict transformation is to help the parties to re-examine these perceptions in the light of new information – an opportunity for Peace Journalism.

Consider an imaginary example. As antagonistic parties in a conflict, a country, Downland, and one of its provinces, Upland, have their own important 'facts' and their own ways of seeing the important 'facts' of the other side. These form the basis of their Partisan Perceptions about each other. To see where new information would be most helpful, one useful technique is to begin by drawing up a Partisan Perceptions Table:[21]

Partisan Perceptions Table	
IMPORTANT 'FACTS' THAT UPLAND SEES AS CRUCIAL	*HOW DOWNLAND SEES THE IMPORTANT 'FACTS' OF UPLAND*
This is our land	They chose to become part of Downland
It belonged to our ancestors	A primitive belief, now offered as an excuse
All Upland's resources belong to us	A selfish attitude, against our laws
Our culture and religion are under threat	Upland's culture and religion cannot be allowed to stand in the way of development
We have a right to independence	We are prepared to give you self-government within Downland
IMPORTANT 'FACTS' DOWNLAND SEES AS CRUCIAL	*HOW UPLAND SEES THE IMPORTANT 'FACTS' OF DOWNLAND*
We are all one nation	They brought us into Downland against our will
All Downland's resources belong to all Downlanders	They are stealing our resources
We need to keep Upland to ensure our national and regional security	That is not our problem
We need to settle people from overcrowded areas to where there is more space	They are trying to crowd us out
All Downlanders have the right to live in a modern country where diverse cultures and religions flourish	They want to stop us living in our own way

There is an important clue in the difference between the Uplanders' view of independence – something they have the right to take – and the Downlanders' willingness to give them self-government. Anything given may be seen as tainted; it is likely to work only if the Uplanders themselves are involved in drawing up plans for how Upland is to be run.

Cartoon 'We want peace!' by Fahim Hakim from Working with Conflict *by Simon Fisher et al, p 12. Published by Zed Books, 2000 Copyright © Responding to Conflict (RTC), Birmingham and Zed Books, London*[22]

**Exercise Three
Partisan Perceptions**

Choose a conflict situation of which you have some detailed knowledge, perhaps involving groups A and B.

Draw up a table and ask:

- What are the important 'facts' as seen by group A?
- What does group B think of these 'facts'?
- What are the important 'facts' for group B?
- What does group A think of these 'facts'?

Think about how the answers would help a Peace Journalist in knowing what to look for, and what to ask about, in any development of the conflict?

Devise plans for news stories which convey each side's perceptions of each issue.

What do we mean by Peace?

In Johan Galtung's original Peace Journalism table, reproduced in the last chapter, you will have noticed there are alternative formulae for peace:

Peace = non-violence + creativity (PJ)

Peace = victory + ceasefire (WJ)

DISCUSSION: What does each formula mean, how would it work and what would each look like in practice? What is likely to happen next, after each different kind of peace?

Stopping people from fighting does not bring a sudden outbreak of harmonious relations; nor does it mean that the root of the conflict, the issue they were fighting over, has been resolved.

- The absence of war – a change in Behaviour – is often described as 'cold' or 'negative' peace.
- A peace containing elements that also deal with Attitudes and Contradictions is a 'warm' or 'positive' peace.[23]

From the first ever Peace Journalism publication, *The Peace Journalism Option*, by editor Indra Adnan, Director of Conflict & Peace Forums:

'A society genuinely at peace is not one where there is never any conflict. Just as inner conflict leads us to examine and bring out the best of ourselves, so social conflict is useful for putting existing policies to the test and allowing constant evolution. A society capable of living peacefully is one which is good at handling these conflicts non-violently.'[24]

Non-violence stands for something most people engage in every day – self-assertion, trying to reach goals without violence, without intending to harm or hurt anybody. Non-violence entails more than just not being violent (which could include being passive, doing nothing, resigning to one's fate).

To handle conflicts without violence needs positive non-violence in thought, speech and action, together with creativity, meaning the development of new ideas. (For a fuller discussion of violence and non-violence, see Chapter 3.)

Some definitions of peace

- *Martin Luther King Jnr:* 'Peace is not the absence of war: it is the presence of justice.'

- *Albert Einstein:* 'Peace is not merely the absence of war but the presence of justice, of law, of order – in short, of government.'

- *Mahatma Gandhi:* 'Justice lived by unarmed nations in the face of odds.'

- *Judith Large:* 'A condition in which there is no direct or collective violence and there is the possibility for all to fulfil their potential. It is a state of being as well as a process.'

Exercise Four
Using Conflict Analysis in Reporting

Read the following two articles about the bombings in the Moroccan city of Casablanca in May 2003.

What understanding of key concepts from Conflict Analysis does each contain?

The first article is adapted from material filed from the scene for London-based broadsheet newspapers at the time, the second is from the London *Guardian*.

AL-QAEDA BLAMED FOR DEADLY ATTACKS ON CASABLANCA

The lowest guest rooms of the Hotel Mauritania stand fifteen metres off the ground, but their gleaming whitewashed balconies were mottled with a dull, ominous red yesterday – dried bloodstains from the deadliest of five suicide bomb explosions that ripped through Casablanca on Friday night.

Morocco's biggest city had been out celebrating the birth of King Mohammed VI's first son. Hours after the fireworks were spent, five separate blasts, timed to within minutes of each other, scattered body parts across the country's main commercial centre.

At least 41 people, including 10 bombers, died in the attack, which left dozens more injured. Four of the targets were connected with Casablanca's Jewish community or Israeli visitors.

The hotel faces the exclusive Casa de Espana club and restaurant in the city centre, a playground for European expatriates.

Rafael Bermudez, the club president, choked back tears as he recalled the traumatic events of the previous night. The Spanish businessman had been chatting over drinks on the terrace when two loud blasts interrupted the conversation. He first attributed them to short-circuits in the city's notoriously unreliable power grid – until he heard the cries of the wounded and dying.

The Casa de Espana was the worst hit because the bombers managed to make their way into the building before detonating what are believed to have been belts of explosives. On the way in, they were intercepted by Haj, the 52-year-old doorman. 'Haj asked for their membership card,

so they slit his throat,' said a neighbour, Abdul Saafi, drawing a line across his windpipe.

Many of the victims were blown to pieces. Rescue workers spent most of the night and morning retrieving body parts, some of which had been hurled on to neighbouring rooftops. 'It was like being on a battlefield,' said local journalist Hassan Alawi, who was among the first to reach the scene. 'There was debris everywhere, broken glass, cars destroyed, flashing lights.'

Yesterday, the terrace remained a charred jumble of wreckage, ripped clothing and congealed blood. A team of French police forensic staff in orange boiler suits picked carefully through the debris around the hotel entrance and foyer.

Most of the victims were Moroccans, although the overall death toll is also believed to include at least two Spaniards, two French nationals and two Italians. Lamia Haffi, a club employee, said simply: 'Inside there was flesh; flesh everywhere.'

Within 30 minutes suicide bombers also attacked the five-star Hotel Safir – where four Britons who were among the guests escaped injury – as well as a Jewish community centre, the Jewish cemetery and the Belgian consulate, which stands next to a Jewish-owned restaurant.

As governments around the world ordered security to be tightened, Paul Wolfowitz, the US deputy defense secretary, said that the blasts in Casablanca were not a surprise. 'The terrorists are still there. They are still dangerous,' he said. 'They want to take Arab Muslim people backward… but I do not believe that that is where the great majority of Arabs and Muslims want to go.'

There has been no claim of responsibility for the attacks, but suspicion fell immediately on a North African cell of al-Qaeda. The Moroccan Interior Minister,

Mustapha Sahel, said the attacks bore 'the hallmark of international terrorism'.

And it emerged yesterday that a senior member of the Islamic fundamentalist Salafi movement in Morocco had speculated about a possible attack by Osama bin Laden's followers in a magazine article published earlier on Friday.

Abu Seif al-Islam, whose movement is considered sympathetic to bin Laden, told *al-Majalla*, a Saudi-owned weekly magazine, that it was time to 'globalise' the jihad, or holy war.

'After September 11, the jihad has become open everywhere,' he said. 'I think that when the conditions are right al-Qaeda will not hesitate to hit Morocco. The current tendency is not to let the enemy feel safe anywhere.'

As a moderate Muslim state and ally of America, Morocco has long been reviled by Islamic extremists. Fearful of the sort of violent Islamic insurgency that has torn apart neighbouring Algeria, the government delayed local elections scheduled for last month because of its concern at the rise of fundamentalism.

It is believed that Casablanca, a cosmopolitan city where many women wear Western clothes and most people follow a liberal interpretation of Islam, has been targeted by hardliners for its 'decadence'. Many locals stayed home last night, steering clear of normally popular street cafés. Some criticised Morocco's crackdown on Islamic fundamentalists, believing that it may have prompted fresh fervour among extremists.

In February, in a tape recording widely believed to carry the voice of bin Laden, the Saudi-born terrorist leader described Morocco as an 'apostate' Arab country. In the same month, three Saudi men arrested in Casablanca last year were sentenced to 10 years in jail for plotting attacks on British and American warships in the Strait of Gibraltar.

CASABLANCA'S SHANTY TOWN POVERTY THAT SPAWNED ATTACKERS

Giles Tremlett in Casablanca

As Moroccan police swept through some of the poorest shanty towns of Casablanca yesterday, hunting Islamist radicals who helped suicide bombers kill 41 people on Friday, Khalid Aits was worrying not about fanaticism but about work, food and poverty.

Loitering on the corner of a litter-strewn, dirt alleyway in the Sidi Moumen shanty town, from where most of the 33 young radicals picked up over the weekend came, he shrugged his shoulders at the idea of an Islamist revolution in his neighbourhood.

'People want work. They want to earn money. That is what they really care about here,' the 23-year-old said.

A walk through Sidi Moumen, past washing lines, barefoot children, and colourful rugs set out in the sun, reveals the poverty and desperation. Khalid shares the tiny rooms of his brickshack with 16 relatives. There is no running water, and bony mules and horses add their waste to the human detritus. 'It is just as bad as a village in the countryside,' Khalid said, indicating an even poorer Morocco beyond these slums.

The divide here, in a country with a long tradition of religious tolerance and co-existence with Judaism, is not between Islamists and non-Islamists, but between rich and poor.

It finds its other expression in the huge, green-tiled mansions of the Ain Diab neighbourhood that look out over the elegant Atlantic beaches of La Corniche and the designer-clad people who gather to play.

While authorities yesterday blamed the influence of al-Qaeda and Osama bin Laden for the attacks by 14 suicide bombers on five foreign and Jewish targets, Casablancans were still surprised the perpetrators had been Moroccans.

Most believed that Morocco, where even the powerful, banned Islamist movement known as Justice and Charity is relatively moderate and against violence, would remain unshaken by the radicalism that brought a 10-year civil war to neighbouring Algeria.

In February three Saudis in an al-Qaeda cell planning attacks on US and British ships were sentenced in Casablanca. But that was considered an example of foreign militants.

There had, however, been other warnings. Police last year arrested 11 radicals from a Salafist sect after a series of punishment killings of those deemed apostates, including one man reeling drunkenly out of a bar in the middle-class playground of La Corniche.

The leader of the so-called Serat Al Mustaquin, or Direct Path, Salafist group, Youssef Fikir, wrote a letter before his trial a few months ago to the *As Sahifa* newspaper in which he warned that 'other things will happen', according to its publisher, Aboubakr Jamai.

Al-Qaeda itself, in a recent tape released to al-Jazeera, named Morocco as one of six Muslim states 'most eligible for liberation'.

The attacks would have been far worse if, with their cheap clothes, the attackers, some little more than teenagers, had not been so obviously from the poor end of town. Stopped by doormen and guards at the Hotel Farah, the Jewish Alliance club, and at a Jewish-owned Italian restaurant outside the Belgian consulate, they only managed to make their way past 52-year-old Haj, the doorman at the Casa de Espana, exploding their bombs at the doorways of the other targets. Most of the dead were in the Spanish club.

'Haj asked for their membership card, so they slit his throat,' said a neighbour, Abdul Saafi, drawing a line across his throat. 'The unemployed people here, the ones with no money and nothing to eat, will do anything.'

Security remained tight yesterday. Soldiers and police appeared to be guarding every tree along the route to the Hotel Farah, popularly known as the Hotel Safir and possibly targeted because it housed a night-club popular with many prostitutes, where the king, Mohamed VI, was expected to visit during the day.

A team of French police forensic staff in orange boiler suits picked carefully through the debris around the hotel entrance and foyer yesterday.

Mohammed Darif, a professor of political science at Mohamedia University, said that armed Salafism had arrived via Moroccans who had fought for al-Qaeda in Afghanistan.

Mr Darif said that King Mohammed faced a dilemma: there was pressure for a crackdown, and also pressure to legalise more Islamic groups. In the palace in the capital Rabat, an influential royal adviser, Andre Azoulay, claimed the king was building a form of democracy suitable for a Muslim country.

'We've done our best to build a democracy. Our vision is fought by those who want to bring the ideology of hate, and use God as a reason to kill,' he said.

There was much confusion yesterday. Among obscure groups named as possible perpetrators were Salafia Jihadia and Attafkir wal Hajira. What nobody doubted was which global group was, ultimately, behind the coordinated attacks. 'They have the signature of al-Qaeda,' said Mr Darif.

Commentary

Attitude, Behaviour, Contradiction

The first half of the first piece concentrates on behaviour – a violent incident and its aftermath. It dwells at length on the gory consequences of the bombings.

The second half tells more about attitudes – the labelling of the alleged perpetrators as 'fundamentalist' and 'extremist' speaks from the Partisan Perception that they are motivated by 'fervour' alone, and that therefore there is no 'rational' way to deal with them except by 'order[ing] security to be tightened'.

The quote from Paul Wolfowitz is also a Partisan Perception – that westernisation, for Muslim countries, represents 'progress'; the 'enemy' wants to take them 'backward'.

From the other side, the descriptions of Morocco as a 'decadent' and 'apostate' country allude to another Partisan Perception – that choices people make about how to live their own lives constitute a 'betrayal of Islam', and evidence of a western-inspired plot to subjugate Muslims.

Unravelling Partisan Perceptions

Recall the case, discussed earlier, of the Britain/Ireland conflict and how journalists could unravel the Partisan Perceptions, to get at the real needs and interests of the parties, by asking the question, *Why?*

Why might some people in Morocco want to carry out such an attack? From this article, the answer appears to be, because they are 'Islamic fundamentalists' and 'followers of Osama bin Laden'.

It begs the important question of what makes them receptive to violent political ideas in the first place. What gives 'Islamic fundamentalism' its appeal to people in Morocco? What might be wrong with the existing 'order' in the country, which might make some people go to extreme lengths to try to overthrow it?

There are one or two small clues. Casablanca is evidently home to rich 'European expatriates' and its political system is headed by a monarchy. Elections have been cancelled, but we only have the reporter's opinion, based apparently on word from the government, that this was because of their 'concern at the rise of fundamentalism'.

The same government, in the person of its interior minister, was quick to blame 'international terrorism' for the violence, rather than home-grown discontents.

The second report supplies some of the answers to these questions, or at least gives us some important clues. It is from this report that some of the details for the first article were taken, but, juxtaposed with different material, they take on a different complexion. We learn that many Moroccans live in terrible conditions, while across the city, the rich disport themselves in designer clothes. A non-violent Islamic movement committed to working among and for the poor – Justice and Charity – has been banned by the authorities.

The reference here to an al-Qaeda tape is to the word 'liberation' – which takes on some resonance now that we know more about the economic and political conditions of the Moroccan people.

What are the contradictions?

The idea that it is a sufficient explanation for people's behaviour to attribute it to 'religious fundamentalism' and 'fervour' is an example of what is called Orientalism – a name for a set of assumptions made by westerners about people from the East, particularly in Arab countries.

This western way of constructing the East is imbricated with a specific history of political, economic and cultural subjugation, as the following famous passage, from *Orientalism* by Edward Said, suggests:

> 'To feel oneself as a European in command, almost at will, of Oriental history, time, and geography; to institute new areas of specialisation; to establish new disciplines; to divide, deploy, schematise, tabulate, index, and record everything in sight (and out of sight); to make out of every observable detail a generalisation and out of every

generalisation an immutable law about the Oriental nature, temperament, mentality, custom, or type; and, above all, to transmute living reality into the stuff of texts, to possess (or think one possesses) actuality mainly because nothing in the Orient seems to resist one's powers: these are the features of Orientalist projection.'[25]

Said identifies three important elements of Orientalism:

- 'The Orient is "the other" for the West, which means the existence of the Orient is to be the "contrasting image, idea, personality, experience".'
- 'Orientalism is a Western style for dominating, reconstructing and having authority over the Orient.'
- Orientalism is what gives rise to 'notions about bringing civilization to primitive or barbaric peoples, the disturbingly familiar ideas about flogging or death or punishment being required when "they" misbehaved or became rebellious, because "they" mainly understood force or violence best.'

The first of the two articles, about the bombing in Morocco, contains nothing about the contradictions underlying the conflict. In the absence of any other explanation, an Orientalist view of the attacks and their perpetrators – irrational, actuated by 'fervour' – tends to prevail by default. As Said suggests in the statements quoted here, it may lead us – or leave us – to conclude that force or violence is the only viable response.

The second article gives us the opportunity to look again at some of these partisan perceptions, by setting aside the notion of Moroccans as 'other' and inviting us to match their experience against our own.

If you had no job, no money and no sure way of getting the next meal, you might look to a group like Justice and Charity for help. If it was banned, what would you do?

DISCUSSION: Go back to the theories about what causes conflict, given in the earlier part of this chapter.

- What theories can you find in each of these articles?
- What do they suggest is 'the problem' here?
- What do they lead you – or leave you – to infer would be an appropriate remedy?

In the first, we get only hints of Community relations theory or Intercultural miscommunication theory; the second gives us these plus Human needs theory, Negotiation theory, Identity theory and Human rights. In a sense, therefore, the kind of reporting in the second must be more accurate than the first. It gives us more of the explanation for conflict.

The first only really suggests Conflict Management and Conflict (meaning violence) Prevention – but more likely a 'crackdown'. The second contains some indications of what would have to be in a Peace Agreement and what would be needed to bring about Reconciliation and Reconstruction.

What about overcoming conflict? Because there is nothing in the first article about contradictions, or the needs or interests of parties, there is no pointer to possible conflict resolution or transformation.

The second does the job described in the table of Peace Journalism characteristics in the last chapter – making the conflict transparent, in the sense that we can see what would need to change for the underlying issues to be transformed.

Osama bin Laden

DISCUSSION: What is Osama bin Laden's view of the issues underlying al-Qaeda's conflict with the US in particular, and the West in general?

Consider the following section from one of his broadcasts, made shortly after the suicide hijacking attacks on the World Trade Center and the Pentagon in 2001:

'What America is tasting now is something insignificant compared to what we have tasted for scores of years. Our nation has been tasting this humiliation and this degradation for more than 80 years.'

What might the reference to 'more than 80 years' mean? Go back to the list of significant dates in the conflict involving the US, Britain and Iraq. In 1915, the Arabs were promised self-government by the British in return for rising up against the Ottoman Empire, which had ruled over their lands for centuries.

Then, in 1916, the British and French went back on this assurance, agreeing instead, in the Sykes-Picot agreement, to divide up Arab territory into areas of colonial control. From 1920, therefore, Arabs came under the dominion of Christian Europe, re-opening old wounds from the Crusades, centuries earlier.[26]

Later, Britain and France kept control or influence by dividing Arab territory into nation-states. Iraq was under British influence; Morocco, French.

The conditions described by the *Guardian* report may feel, to those living in them, like 'humiliation and degradation'. That may go some way to explaining why the message of al-Qaeda may have some appeal to the young dispossessed of Morocco, especially if they link their condition to the influence of the West in the political and economic settlement in their country – as manifest by the privileged, perhaps decadent existence of those westerners in the Hotel Mauritania.

The constrained horizons of young people in the Arab world are widely recognised – and not just by al-Qaeda and its followers. From the *Human Development Report on the Arab World* prepared by Arab scholars for the UN in 2002:[27]

'Arab countries have made significant strides in more than one area of human development in the last three decades. Life expectancy has increased by about 15 years, adult literacy has almost doubled and women's literacy has tripled. Nevertheless, the predominant characteristic of the current Arab reality seems to be the existence of deeply rooted shortcomings in the Arab institutional structure – freedom, empowerment of women, and knowledge.

No generation of young Arabs has been as large as today. For that reason, the report is especially mindful of the children of marginalized and oppressed Arabs, not excluding the Palestinian children. For that reason, the Report team has dedicated this first issue to "coming generations".'

Other recommendations for reporting based on applying the insights of Conflict Analysis

Rosemarie Schmidt's Five Ws[28]
WHO
- Who is affected by this conflict; who has a distinct stake in its outcome?
- What is their relationship to one another, including relative power, influence, affluence?

WHAT
- What triggered the dispute; what drew it to your attention at this time?
- What issues do the parties need to resolve?

WHEN
- When did this conflict begin; how long have the circumstances existed that gave rise to this dispute?

WHERE
- What geographical or political jurisdictions are affected by this dispute?
- How has this kind of thing been handled in other places?

WHY
- Why do the parties hold the positions they do; what needs, interests, fears and concerns are the positions intended to address?

HOW
- How are they going to resolve this, eg negotiation, mediation, arbitration, administrative hearing, court, armed warfare; what are the costs/benefits of the chosen method?

OPTIONS
- What options have the parties explored; how do the various options relate to the interests identified?

COMMON GROUND
- What common ground is there between the parties; what have they agreed to so far?

Press Institute of India's guide to 'Reporting Communal and Ethnic Tensions and Violence'[29]

1. *Factual accuracy in a single story is no substitute for the total truth.* A single story, which is factually accurate, can nonetheless be misleading.

   Example: During the Bhivandi riots a weekly newspaper reported that: 'two dozen innocent Hindus were murdered, more than five thousand Hindu houses and over a thousand shops destroyed, more than ten thousand Hindus turned refugees.'

   These figures may be factually correct but they are misleading. The report gives the impression that the Hindus alone suffered losses, whereas in fact, an equal number of Muslims were killed and made homeless.

2. *Avoid feeding, by selective reporting, common prejudicial stereotypes about groups.* Generalisations based on the behaviour of an individual, or a small number of individuals, are inevitably unjust.

   Example: Before the Ahmedabad riots some Gujarati newspapers branded Muslims as 'communal', 'backward', and 'conservative'.

   Suggestion: There should be a deliberate attempt to break false stereotypes by publication of stories that run counter to common prejudice. There should, in particular, be no irrelevant identification of communal groups, especially in court or crime stories. For example, avoid this wording: 'a Brahmin boy was knocked down by a truck driven by a Muslim.'

3. *Statements and generalisations not supported by facts and figures can often mislead.*

   Example: A Delhi Hindi newspaper talked about the 'glaring naked facts' of the unprecedented genocide of Hindus in Pakistan since independence. But it failed to present data to back up its 'facts'.

   Suggestion: Evidence (in the form of facts and figures) should always be presented to support such assertions. Even when reporting speeches, newspapers should not hesitate in the form of footnotes, perhaps, to correct claims which are patently false.

4. *Be careful how you attribute comments or information.*

   Avoid vague phrases like: 'it is feared that more violence will break out soon'.
   Feared by whom? And why?
   Or: 'Rebel forces are said to be burning schools in the north-west of the province.'
   Said by whom? And why?

Endnotes for Chapter 2

1. John Paul Lederach, *Building Peace – Sustainable Reconciliation in Divided Societies*, United States Institute of Peace Press, Washington, 1997, p 88.

2. Chris Mitchell, *The Structure of International Conflict*, Macmillan, London, 1981, Chapter 1, quoted in Simon Fisher et al, *Working with Conflict*, Zed Books, London, 2000, p 4.

3. Keith Dovkants, 'Soldiers Face Sniper Raids in Basra's Bandit Country', London *Evening Standard*, 25 March 2003.

4. Peter Riddell, 'Hostility to Iraq War Nears Peak Level', London *Times*, 11 February 2004.

5. Quoted in Dan Glaister, 'US Strategy Based in "Fantasyland"', London *Guardian*, 23 December 2004.

6. Adapted from two lists in Simon Fisher et al, op cit, 2000, pp 7 and 8.

7. Diana Francis, *People, Peace and Power*, Pluto Press, London, 2002, p 24.

8. Dan Smith, *The Atlas of War and Peace*, Earthscan, London, 2003 p 107.

9. Stephen Covey, *The 7 Habits of Highly Effective People*, Simon & Schuster, London, 1989, 2004, p 27.

10. Johan Galtung, quoted in Jake Lynch, *Reporting the World*, Conflict and Peace Forums, Taplow, 2002, p 29.

11. Tim Radford, 'Psychologists Say Maths Can Predict Chances of Divorce', London *Guardian*, 13 February, 2004.

12. Johan Galtung, *Conflict Transformation by Peaceful Means: The TRANSCEND Method*, United Nations, Geneva, 2000, p 14.

13. Fiona Lloyd and Peter du Toit, *Reporting for Peace*, Vol II, Internews, Indonesia, 1999.

14. Drawing by Annabel McGoldrick, 2002.

15. Johan Galtung, *Conflict Transformation by Peaceful Means: The TRANSCEND Method*, United Nations, Geneva, 2000, p 22.

16. John Kenneth Galbraith, *Culture of Contentment*, Houghton Mifflin, New York, 1992.

17. H Cornelius and S Faire, *Everyone Can Win: How to Resolve Conflict*, Simon & Schuster, Sydney, 1996 p 117.

18. Diana Francis, *People, Peace and Power*, Pluto Press, London, 2002, p 128.

19. Simon Fisher et al, op cit, 2000 p 27.

20. Beatrix Campbell, 'Straw's Redemption: The Home Secretary's U-Turn over Racism in the Police Can Be Traced to the Influence of Ireland', London *Guardian*, 24 February 2000.

21. Adapted from Conflict Management Group, Harvard University, quoted in Melissa Baumann, 'Reporting Conflict – Skills for Conflict Analysis', in Melissa Baumann (ed), *Media & Conflict, Track Two*, Vol 7, No 4, Centre for Conflict Resolution and Media Peace Centre, Cape Town, December 1998, p 44.

22. 'We want Peace!' Cartoon by Fahim Hakim, Simon Fisher et al., *Working with Conflict*, Zed Books, London, 2000, p 12.

23. Ibid, p 12.

24. Indra Adnan, 'Afterword' in Jake Lynch, *The Peace Journalism Option*, Conflict and Peace Forums, Taplow, 1998.

25. Edward Said, *Orientalism*, Vintage, New York, 1979, p 86.

26. Johan Galtung, *September 11, October 7 2001 and Aftermath – Three Discourses*, http://www.transnational.org/forum/meet/2002/Galtung_11SeptandAftermath.htm.

27. UN, 'Creating Opportunities for Future Generations', *Arab Human Development Report*, http://www.un.org/Pubs/whatsnew/e02175.htm.

28. Rosemarie Schmidt, 'Working with Journalists to Enhance Conflict Coverage', *The Canadian Conflict Resolution Network's Media Program*, 1994, www.crnetwork.ca.

29. Quoted in Fiona Lloyd and Peter du Toit, *Reporting for Peace*, Vol II, Internews, Indonesia, 1999.

Chapter 3

Reporting and Understanding Violence

A common misconception about Peace Journalism is that it means not reporting violence. Not so – this is a case where 'it ain't what you do, it's the way that you do it'. This chapter explores issues around the representation of violence, especially *context* and *juxtaposition*, and how the explanation for violence arises out of the way the story is reported.

Once again, we'll show how insights from the overlapping fields of Conflict Analysis and Peace Research can provide anchorage for journalists – this time in coming to grips with the all-important questions about violence. This chapter:

- Looks at different ways of responding to a single violent incident
- Divides the concept of violence into two component parts – the *effect it has* and the *form it takes*
- Discusses three distinct and different forms – direct, structural and cultural violence – and their importance in reporting conflicts
- Distinguishes between explaining violence and excusing or justifying it
- Applies Conflict Analysis to two 'hard cases' – murders of children by children, and suicide bombings against Israeli civilians
- Gives a brief history of non-violence as a powerful force for change
- Highlights the role of creativity in devising non-violent interventions
- Counterposes Realism and the Cycle of Violence as alternative models of change in conflict
- Introduces the concept of 'change agents' and their potential for broadening the range of legitimate sources for journalists

By the end of this chapter the reader will be able to:

- Respond sensitively and discerningly in reporting individual violent incidents
- Develop an analytical understanding of violence, separating the effect it has from the form it takes
- See how reporting on cultural and, in particular, structural violence can transform War Journalism into Peace Journalism
- Approach stories involving violence with a new set of tools to illuminate these often hidden aspects
- Identify the workings of the Cycle of Violence and appreciate how interventions to interrupt it can amount to significant – and newsworthy – processes of change
- Begin to develop an awareness of non-violence and a fluency in building it into everyday editing and reporting

Reporting violence

Remember the apology by the *New York Times*, about its reporting on Iraq's supposed weapons of mass destruction? To refresh your memory:

> 'Editors at several levels who should have been challenging reporters and pressing for more scepticism were perhaps too intent on rushing scoops into the paper.'

A journalist would not be a journalist without the instinct to rush scoops into the paper. And not just scoops, but dramatic and important new developments – never more so, it could be argued, than when covering violence. The cliché 'If it bleeds it leads' did not become a cliché by accident.

Peace Journalism, to repeat, does not mean not reporting violence. But there are different ways to cover any violent incident. By way of brief introduction, take a look at this report of violence in the former Yugoslav republic of Macedonia in 2001.[1]

MASSACRE RUINS HOPES FOR PEACE IN MACEDONIA

Peace talks aimed at ending the conflict in Macedonia lay in ruins last night after the massacre of eight soldiers and policemen by Albanian rebels who then mutilated their bodies.

The atrocity took place in an ambush just outside the mountain village of Vejce, near the border with Kosovo, when a joint army and police patrol was attacked with machine guns and rocket-propelled grenades, a Macedonian government spokesman said. Six men were wounded, and three vehicles destroyed.

The bodies appeared to have been cut with knives after they died, he added. One man's skull had been smashed in, probably with the butt of a rifle.

The attack was believed to be the work of guerrilla fighters from the National Liberation Army, which occupied hills overlooking Macedonia's second city of Tetovo, until it was forced out last month. Ali Ahmeti, a political leader of the NLA, denied that his men had attacked the patrol, saying they may have fired in 'self-defence'...

Now look at this alternative version.

MACEDONIAN PARTIES CONDEMN VIOLENCE AFTER GUNMEN KILL EIGHT POLICE AND SOLDIERS

There was condemnation across the political spectrum in Macedonia last night after a joint police and army patrol was ambushed near the Kosovo border, with the loss of eight men and six others wounded.

Both the main parties representing the country's minority Albanians distanced themselves from the killings, almost certainly the work of guerrillas from the self-styled National Liberation Army. Ali Ahmeti, a political leader of the NLA, denied that his men had attacked the patrol, saying they may have fired in 'self-defence'.

But the Macedonian government said the soldiers and policemen had done nothing to provoke the volley of machine gun fire and rocket-propelled grenades which also destroyed three vehicles. A spokesman added that the bodies had been cut with knives and one man's skull caved in, apparently with a rifle butt, before they could be recovered...

These two versions are quoted in a training manual,[2] from a major international media support agency, used extensively in Nepal and Sri Lanka among other places. It goes on:

'See the difference?

Traditional reporting

- The news is all bad, it is violent news and it does not seek other sides or points of view. It declares the worst: 'peace talks... lay in ruins'.

- It uses emotional and unnecessary words: massacre, mutilated, atrocity. It emphasises the violence with words such as 'mutilated bodies'.
- The traditional reporting takes sides: it describes the event from the point of view of the army spokesman. He says the patrol was attacked.

Conflict sensitive reporting

- The report goes further than violence and it reports people who condemn the violence.
- The news is balanced quickly: the NLA denies it attacked the patrol, but admits there was a battle.
- The other side is given the name it calls itself: the National Liberation Army.
- The violence is not hidden or ignored. But it is stated as a claim and not a fact.'

In other words, the violence and those interested in talking it up do not have to be allowed to eclipse the rest of the conflict picture, including those, in this case, committed to a political process to resolve differences.

The equivalent, in *New York Times* stories about Iraq's supposed stocks of weapons, might have been to give greater prominence to sources with what the paper called, in the same apology, 'misgivings' about the claims – sources that were, in practice, either omitted altogether or left 'too deep' in the offending articles.

Reports of conflict will inevitably include reports of violence – but the picture of the conflict constructed by these reports can be very different, as even the brief accounts of the Macedonian incident show, depending on juxtaposition and context.

DISCUSSION: What do we mean by violence?

Understanding violence

We all know the answer – don't we? Hitting, shooting, bombing and shelling, all involving physical contact, whether person-to-person or by using tools – weapons – to convey force to a target.

But hang on. Aren't we all familiar with other kinds of violence as well, like 'violent language' or 'psychological violence'? What about violence being 'bred', or 'incubated' in certain conditions?

There must, then, be more to violence than physical contact. What links these phenomena under the same heading of 'violence' is not the *form* they take, but the *effect* they have on individuals and society.

According to a classic definition in Peace Research, the word 'violence' can be used to describe anything that brings about a situation where:

'Human beings are being influenced so that their actual somatic and mental realizations are below their potential.'[3]

The name given to the notion of violence familiar from everyday conversation – involving physical contact – is *direct violence* or *visible violence*.[4] It's obvious how someone's potential is denied if they are hit or shot.

But this effect can also be wrought by *structural* and *cultural violence* – important component parts of the 'conflict picture' that can easily be blotted out by concentrating only on incidents of direct violence.

Structural violence is where a structure, usually understood as a *system* of political, social or economic relations, creates barriers that people cannot remove – barriers to attaining food, shelter, education, jobs, security, or whatever. It may take visible forms such as 'whites-only' buses in Apartheid South Africa or in the US under Segregation, but it is usually thought of as an *invisible form* of violence, *built into* ways of doing and ways of thinking.

Cultural violence means cultural forms that justify or glorify violence. Visible manifestations would include the statues of military heroes all over central London. But it exists as ideas and images carried in people's minds so that it, too, is usually thought of as an invisible form of violence.

> ### Exercise One
> ### Thinking about Violence
>
> Take a conflict you know:
>
> • List five examples of structural violence.
> • List five examples of cultural violence.

Typology of violence[5]

This diagram shows how the typology corresponds roughly to the three points of the ABC conflict triangle of Attitude, Behaviour and Contradictions.

• Vertical structural violence includes economic exploitation, political repression and cultural alienation.

• Horizontal structural violence may keep people together who want to live apart; or keep people apart who want to live together (like Romeo and Juliet).

DIRECT/PHYSICAL VIOLENCE (BEHAVIOUR)
hitting, beating, stabbing, shooting, bombing, raping, torture

VISIBLE
VIOLENCE

INVISIBLE
VIOLENCE
(under the surface)

CULTURAL VIOLENCE
(ATTITUDE)
hate speech, persecution complex,
myths and legends of war heroes,
religious justifications for war,
'chosenness' – being 'the chosen people', civilisational arrogance

STRUCTURAL VIOLENCE
(CONTRADICTIONS)
colonialism, apartheid, slavery,
military occupation,
corruption-collusion-nepotism,
impunity,
patriarchy,
economic injustice

The concepts of structural and cultural violence are useful in helping parties to a conflict think their way through to reconciliation:

'A structure-oriented perspective converts the relation from inter-personal, or inter-state/nation, to a relation between two positions in a deficient structure. If the parties can agree that the structure was/is deficient and that their behaviour was an enactment of structural positions rather than anything more personal, then turning together against the common problem, the structural violence, should be possible. A culture-oriented perspective also converts the relation from inter-personal, or inter-state/nation, to a relation spurred by a deficient culture.'[6]

What does this mean? The point is that structural and cultural violence cannot be seen as the fault, or at least entirely the fault, of particular individuals. They are built in to ways of doing and ways of thinking that people *inhabit*, as they do their physical surroundings, often without stopping to ask themselves why.

Equipped with this understanding, parties to a conflict can at least partly blame the structure or culture, instead of wholly blaming each other. Instead of one individual party being 'the problem', the *conflict* can be seen as the problem.

You can tell that a particular practice is part of structural violence when people say things like:

- 'We've always done it this way.'
- 'Everybody does it this way.'
- 'It's just the way things are.'

The Rwandan genocide

In 1994, Rwanda saw one of the most extreme episodes of social violence even in a century scarred by death and destruction. As many as 800,000 people may have been killed in just three months or so – a statistic that, by itself, beggars the imagination.

'To understand the number of dead, look at it this way; imagine that every single word in this book is the name of a victim. This entire volume would then list only 110,000 or so of the dead, or only about one-seventh of the likely death toll. More than seven volumes of this book would be required just to list the first names of every victim. Look at every word, and think of someone you know.'[7]

DISCUSSION: During the Rwandan genocide:

- What was the direct violence?
- What was the structural violence?
- What was the cultural violence?

Direct violence

Perhaps the most profoundly disturbing aspect of the genocide was its 'subaltern and "popular" character'.[8] Those who took part also numbered in the tens, if not hundreds, of thousands, and used a wide range of weapons and methods:

'Physicians for Human Rights identified machetes; *massues* (clubs studded with nails); small axes; knives; grenades; guns and fragmentation grenades. Victims were treated with unimaginable cruelty, beaten to death, limbs amputated, buried alive, drowned. Achilles tendons were cut so victims could not run away; pregnant women had their wombs slashed open, people were thrown alive into pit latrines, children forced to watch murders of their parents, those who hid in the attic had the house burnt down.'[9]

Cultural violence

Why were so many people prepared to inflict these atrocities – often on their neighbours and even former friends?

Those who would perpetrate the genocide were brought to see their victims in a new light, by a form of cultural violence. According to propaganda made familiar by ceaseless repetition in 'hate media' outlets –

chiefly Radio Television Libre des Mille Collines – the violence was 'not a violence against one who is seen as a neighbour but against one who is seen as a foreigner; not a violence that targets a transgression across a boundary into home but one that seeks to eliminate a foreign presence from home soil, literally and physically'.[10]

On one notorious occasion, *Kangura*, a Kigali newspaper run in the early 1990s by Hutu Power activists with strong official connections, published 'Ten Commandments to the Hutu'. They began with a warning about miscegenation and the dangerously seductive qualities of Tutsi women:

'"1. Each Hutu man must know that the Tutsi woman, no matter whom, works in solidarity with her Tutsi race. In consequence, every Hutu man is a traitor:
- who marries a Tutsi woman
- who makes a Tutsi woman his concubine
- who makes a Tutsi woman his secretary or protegée

2. Every Hutu man must know that our Hutu girls are more dignified and more conscientious in their roles as woman, wife, and mother. Aren't they pretty, good secretaries, and more honest!

3. Hutu women, be vigilant and bring your husbands, and sons to reason!"

Women, in other words, constituted a secret, sexual weapon that Tutsi leaders used cynically to seduce and weaken Hutu men... *Kangura*, which frequently ran pornographic cartoons featuring Tutsi women, explained: "The *inkotanyi* [members of the Tutsi Rwandan Patriotic Front] will not hesitate to transform their sisters, wives, and mothers into pistols to conquer Rwanda". The conclusion was irresistible: only when no Tutsi women were left could Hutu men be safe from their wicked wiles.'[11]

This was an extreme form of a narrative that has been called one of 'natives and settlers'; inscribed in definitions of 'self' and 'other' among colonised peoples in Africa and elsewhere:

'The great crime of colonialism went beyond expropriating the native, the name it gave to the indigenous population. The greater crime was to politicise indigeneity in the first place: first negatively, as a settler libel of the native; but then positively, as a native response, as a self-assertion...

It is in this context that Tutsi, a group with a privileged relationship to power before [and during] colonialism, got constructed as a privileged alien settler presence, first by the great nativist revolution of 1959, then by Hutu Power propaganda after 1990.'[12]

Structural violence

The Rwandan revolution of 1959 reversed the precedence of 'natives' and 'settlers' but left the categories themselves intact. Many Tutsis now fled to neighbouring Uganda, but they faced another problem. Because their ancestry was not Ugandan, they found themselves excluded from 'ethnic citizenship':

'Ethnic citizenship... is the source of a different category of rights, mainly social and economic. Further, these rights are not accessed individually but by virtue of group membership, the group being the ethnic community. The key socioeconomic right is the right to use land as a source of livelihood.'[13]

The refugees sought to challenge this system by redefining the basis of socioeconomic rights from ethnicity to citizenship, throwing in their lot with the National Resistance Movement led by Yoweri Museveni, who seized power in Kampala in a *coup d'état* in 1986.

Museveni duly changed the basis for civic citizenship, from two generations' to 10 years' residence, and replaced ethnic citizenship with a system of residence-based rights within local council areas throughout Uganda. But the reforms were swiftly rescinded, and 'the exiles of 1959 found their new citizenship no more than a paper promise'.[14]

The Tutsi guerrilla fighters who had helped bring the new regime to power then turned their attention to their own homeland. By now, the Second Republic in Rwanda had established civic citizenship for those Tutsi who had remained, and introduced quotas to allow their participation in professional and public life. But the provisions specifically excluded the refugees.

Therefore when Paul Kagame, Museveni's head of intelligence, founded the Rwandan Patriotic Front and invaded Rwanda in 1990, it represented an 'attempt to escape the closing scissors of a postcolonial citizenship crisis in Rwanda and Uganda'.[15]

Rwanda was known as the 'land of a thousand hills', but it was also the most densely populated country in Africa. A new influx of population, with their own citizenship claims, could mean there was not enough cultivable land to go round. And, as we suggest in Chapter 5, changes in the international political and economic climate contributed to a situation where there was not enough money, public services, jobs or security to go round either.

The ruling elite in Rwanda scared people with the prospect of a return to the 'bad old days' when the system for sharing benefits and resources was based on privilege and subjugation. The Hutu majority were told, over and over again, that they faced stark choices:

- fight for your land, and with it the means to feed yourself and your family, or lose it
- fight for your freedom or be enslaved by the old subalterns of colonialism, as before independence
- kill or be killed

Structural violence, both present and historical, took the form of barriers in people's way that they could not remove. It was present in systems of relations between people that defined some as the 'in-group' and others as the 'out-group'.

This was coterminous with cultural violence, demonising the 'out-group' as a threat, both to the 'in-group' and to the very system that kept the two in their respective places. No explanation for the direct violence is complete, or, indeed, correct without taking these other two forms into account.

'Explanation' without context – a note on 'evil'

We have already seen how particular incidents of violence can be reported in different ways – the ambush in Macedonia in 2001, the suicide bombing in Jerusalem in August 2003 (Chapter 1), and the bombings in Casablanca in May 2003 (Chapter 2).

In each case, there are practical ways of telling the story which convey some concept of structural and/or cultural violence as part of the explanation for direct violence. But it takes a *deliberate* effort to do this.

What if no such effort is made? Does a stripped-down, 'blow-by-blow' account amount to being 'neutral'? This is the view firmly held in many US newsrooms, where 'context' can be a synonym for 'bias'. As a result, the media produce 'cryptic texts [which] obfuscate important realities of power'.[16] How come?

The point is that an absence of explicit contextualising material does not mean there is no explanation for violence: instead, an explanation prevails by default. Readers and audiences are shown no intelligible reason why parties to a conflict are fighting each other. We are left to infer, therefore, that they must be actuated by some form of *unreason* – 'ancient hatreds', 'religious fanaticism' or 'tribal anarchy'. To ascribe such motives to 'the other' is part of the political discourse of Orientalism, examined in the last chapter.

Once upon a time, a BBC reporter – let us call him 'John Smith' – would file reports on the Israeli-Palestinian conflict which, according to wags in the newsroom, could all be boiled down to the same simple formula: 'Arabs and Jews hate each other's guts. They always have; they always will. John Smith, BBC News, in the Middle East.'

This is the kind of underlying narrative that remains undisturbed when the public are misled over basic facts – as shown by the poll findings quoted in Chapter 1, that many Britons believe the Occupied Territories are occupied by the Palestinians, not the Israelis; and that most believe the settlers are Palestinian, not Israeli, and the refugees come from Afghanistan. Important realities of power are being obfuscated, in our living rooms, night after night.

This kind of obfuscation has left a space into which the concept of 'evil' – as an explanation for the Attitudes and Behaviour of people who do not see the world as it appears from official Washington – has been inserted. Iraq, Iran and North Korea were

'the axis of evil'; in 2003, British Prime Minister Tony Blair received the Congressional Medal of Honor for his steadfastness 'against evil'.

These are *essentialist* explanations for violence. They come with a built-in suggestion that the perpetrators are just 'like that', acting out attitudes and hatreds that come welling up from within. A dictionary definition:

'Essentialism involves defining a group of people by a small set of fixed properties, while ignoring the conditions under which such identities emerged. In the process, it discounts any possibility of change or variation within the group.'[18]

DISCUSSION: Where does evil 'come from'? Are some people born evil or are they 'made that way' by the conditions in which they find themselves?

Political, *copyright © Tom Lubbock 2002*

What if 'evil' is not a 'fixed property' at all, but a label for a set of behaviours which arise, at least to some extent, from a response to certain circumstances, whether by individuals, communities or nations?

A famous experiment, led by Philip Zimbardo at Stanford University in 1971, tried to find out why prisons are such nasty places:[19]

- Did nasty people make prisons nasty or was a nasty environment making people nasty?
- Researchers created a mock prison in basement of University psychology building, including a solitary confinement cell.
- 21 of the 75 applicants chosen as the 'most normal' – stable personalities.
- At random, half the group chosen as guards, given uniform, dark glasses and told to keep order; the other half were prisoners.
- Prisoners were 'arrested' at home (by real local police) and brought to the basement prison.
- Prisoners stripped and given uniform.
- Number on front and back was only means of identifying prisoners.

The results were shocking, and after six days the experiment was stopped:

'The prison quickly became unsanitary and inhospitable. Bathroom privileges became a right which could be, and frequently was, denied. Some prisoners were made to clean toilets using their bare hands. Mattresses were removed from the "bad" cell, and prisoners were forced to sleep on the concrete floor without clothing. Food was also frequently denied as a means of punishment. Prisoners

endured forced nudity and even homosexual acts of humiliation.'[20]

People who were gentle and considerate in everyday life became authoritarian and, in some cases, sadistic, when put into the role of guards. Prisoners described losing their identity: 'I was really my number,' one said.

Conclusion: 'There are specific situations so powerful that they can overwhelm our inherent predispositions.'[21]

As a piece of scientific research, the Stanford Prison Experiment has been as much criticised as praised. But it does suggest that roles prescribed for us by our respective positions in a system – especially if there is a gradient of power relations – do, at least to some extent, *shape* our actions and motivations.

For obvious reasons, this surfaced in the discussions of 2004 about the prisoner abuses at Abu Ghraib jail in Iraq – abuses blamed by the US military on 'a few bad apples'. Zimbardo himself said the system of relations at the jail was more like:

'A bad barrel converting good apples into bad apples... When people are de-individualized, they are usually put in herds, or groups, and given numbers. Their identity is taken away... [In Abu Ghraib] the guards had a mob mentality, a group mindset. You

Cartoon copyright © Alan Moir, first published in the Sydney Morning Herald

start to do things because other people in your group are doing them.'[22]

Later, a paper published by experts from Princeton University in the leading journal, *Science*, surveyed results from more than 25,000 separate psychological studies, involving eight million participants, in light of the Abu Ghraib experience. The conclusion according to one of the authors? 'Could any average eighteen-year-old have tortured these prisoners? I would have to answer yes.'[23]

The struggle for context

In the Broadway musical *West Side Story* – written nearly 50 years ago – one of the young tearaways, in a spoken aside in the song 'Gee, Officer Krupke', tells the sergeant, 'I'm depraved on accounta I'm deprived.'

It's a satire on liberal interpretations of juvenile delinquency – or, at least, on the half-baked variants that give criminology a bad name. Clearly, much in this argument depends on retaining the space and opportunity to explain violence without seeming to excuse or justify it. The Princeton group emphasised, equally, that 'situationism' cannot expunge individual responsibility.

At the other extreme, neo-conservative guru Richard Perle says we need to 'decontextualize terror... any attempt to discuss the roots of terrorism is an attempt to justify it. It simply needs to be fought and destroyed.'[24]

This is a useful quote because it emphasises the connection between the way a problem is diagnosed and what can be presented as an appropriate remedy. An essentialist explanation for people's behaviour, as an expression of 'fixed properties', is used to justify violence.

The present authors flew into a brief 'media war' over this very issue in October 2001. The scene: a transatlantic flight with United Airlines, the passenger cabin darkened as the plane circled New York's JFK airport, ready to land. A voice over the intercom: the pilot announcing that US bombers had begun pounding Afghanistan – greeted by cheers from those on board.

On the ground, newsstands featured the brand-new editions of the weeklies *Time* and *Newsweek*, publications both local to New York, of course, and global. Each essayed some coherent explanation for the traumatic events of September 11th, less than a month earlier.

The contemporary issue of *New York Magazine* was running a lengthy analysis by media writer Michael Wolff, in which US media were criticised for presenting the suicide hijackings as 'some pure spasm of apocalyptic irrationality' – stripped of context and, indeed, content.

Newsweek set out to rectify this, its front cover[25] promising to answer the question of 'Why they hate us'. Inside, international editor Fareed Zakaria contributed a hefty piece examining 'The roots of rage'. This covered the chequered past of US intervention in the Middle East as well as the Arab world's home-grown political stagnation and dysfunction.

Time[26] commissioned a 'Viewpoint' from Hazem Saghiyeh, lamenting 'the bias shown

Front cover of Newsweek, *15 October 2001*
reproduced with permission
Original photograph used on cover copyright © AFP

by the US to Israel and America's cruel insistence on continued sanctions against Iraq'.

Plus, for historical reasons, 'Muslims and Arabs can always feel bitterness towards America' for installing and propping up the Shah in Iran, he wrote, and for leaving Afghanistan in such a mess after helping the Mujahideen win what turned out to be the decisive battle of the Cold War.

But Saghiyeh, a columnist for the London-based Arabic newspaper *al-Hayat*, also blamed the failures of both political and religious reform movements within Islamic societies for perpetuating their impotence and subjugation.

Time urged an understanding that Osama bin Laden, the chief suspect, had 'a well-articulated plan of action' to expel the US from the Islamic world. The problem had been that so few were prepared to listen, or to analyse the processes contributing to a context in which such a strategy might be thought feasible.

The backlash

When the two newsweeklies hit the streets, Rupert Murdoch's *New York Post*, in its lead editorial,[27] attacked them for indulging in 'Dubiously Deep Thoughts'. The paper chided 'talking heads' busy looking for 'root causes… How they so miss the point. And at America's peril.' The right response, the editorial continued, when someone asks 'why bloody-handed killers like Osama bin Laden hate America, is: "Who cares?":

'… There's no explanation needed – or possible – as to why "holy warriors" are out to destroy Western civilization. Suffice to know that they are. And that they must be stopped.

Rather than ask – corrosively – why they hate us, it might be better to think about how they came to believe they could get away with their acts of savagery. Part of that answer, at least, lies in the very self-doubt and hesitating nature of the West that is so exposed by searches for "understanding".'

The *New York Post* and Richard Perle spent the ensuing few years very much in the ascendant in US politics, of course. One important assessment has the world in this period gravitating towards opposite poles of rival 'fundamentalisms':

'With George Bush's use of "you are either with us or with the terrorists", and bin Laden's distinction between believers and infidels, both justifying violence, they can be classified as fundamentalists. The "war against terrorism" is between hard Christian (Baptist/ Presbyterian), and hard Islamic (Wahhabite) fundamentalisms. The reinforcing dialectic between the two is obvious, as in "my terrorism is good, theirs is bad".'[28]

The *New York Post*/Perle approach to political violence is fundamentalist, in the sense of being a denial of social science – just as 'creationism', another political touchstone for the Christian Right of US politics, is a denial of science, in the form of evolutionary theory.

Ibn Khaldun, the fourteenth-century Arab scholar, is credited as the world's first social scientist, precisely because he acknowledged that people's apparently 'fixed properties' are actually altered by their interaction with the world around them: 'Conditions within nations and races change with the change of periods and the passage of time.'[29]

The struggle for context is one that puts journalists where many least like to be – on the spot. Attempt, as *Time* and *Newsweek* did, to contextualise political violence and you inescapably arouse the ire of the neo-conservative Right and their cheerleaders like the *Post*.

To do so, in a news milieu, invariably takes a special effort. Context consists of processes, and a process is inevitably less newsworthy than an event. Something happens – it's a story. Something continues to happen – it's not. Yet to 'keep one's head down' and stick to what have been called 'safe stories – big bangs and the agenda set by political leaders'[30] is not to be neutral, but to take the 'other side' of the struggle.

What's at stake? Essentialist explanations

for violence eclipse those furnished by social science, which entail examining the processes by which people's perceptions, actions and motivations are constructed by their experience of everyday life, including the deep sense of humiliation arising from historical injustice and subjugation. This, in turn, raises questions about how the *conditions* of everyday life, and the historical reality, may have been influenced by, for instance, aspects of US foreign policy – as Saghiyeh suggested.

Reporting that leaves a gap where these factors rightfully belong invites propaganda to take its place – notably the self-serving analysis of the 9/11 hijackings: 'They hate us for who we are, not what we do.'

The remedy depends on the diagnosis – James Rubin, assistant secretary of state under President Clinton, told a television news audience, on the evening of September 11th, 'this is not a time to change our foreign policy'.[31]

Understanding and condemning

One of the hardest cases for journalists covering violence, and concerned to allow for invisible, structural and cultural factors as part of the explanation, came with the murder of two-year-old James Bulger in Liverpool, England, in February 1993.

Two other boys, both aged 10 at the time, abducted James from a shopping centre, brutally attacked him, then tied him to a railway line, where a train ran over his body.

Here are some of the headlines in UK newspapers from the time:

HOW CAN ORDINARY JUSTICE BE ENOUGH IN A CASE LIKE THIS?

Daily Mail, 16 February 1993

A CASE FOR REVENGE

London Evening Standard, 17 February 1993

MOB FURY FOLLOWS ARRESTS

London Evening Standard, 17 February 1993

80,000 CALL TV TO SAY BULGER KILLERS MUST ROT IN JAIL

Sun[32]

EVIL BEHIND PICTURE OF INNOCENCE

Herald (Glasgow), 18 February 1993

BEAST THAT HIDES IN THE INFANT BREAST

Times, 18 February 1993

Feelings of anger and revulsion at this incident were widely shared. Security cameras in the shopping centre captured little James being led away by the hand by two bigger boys – pictures that were played over and over again on the news, in what became one of the most powerful televised images of the 1990s, shocking in its grainy banality.

Journalists covering the story, when they came to address the question of *why* it had happened, often fell back on the trope of 'evil monsters' – the beast that hides in the infant breast. In the year from the beginning of February 1993, the name 'Bulger' appeared in 1,444 articles in the British press; the word 'evil' featured in 230 of them, almost one in six.[33]

Politicians played to the public gallery the media coverage had created. It's that connection again, between diagnosis and remedy.

Prime Minister John Major used a newspaper interview to trail a new system of secure units to incarcerate young offenders. He had this to say about juvenile crime, just weeks after the Bulger killing had taken place:

'We must condemn a little more, and understand a little less.'[34]

Later, it emerged that the two boys who killed James, Robert Thompson and Jon Venables, were known to various care agencies in Liverpool.

Notes of confidential case conferences, held after the murder but not disclosed to the trial, documented a catalogue of warning signs.

Physical abuse, poverty, alcoholism and family breakdown formed a context within which Education and Social Services officials had regularly noted and passed on their concerns, but no effective action took place to interrupt what was, in fact, a long sequence of incidents of a kind which might have triggered multi-agency intervention.

'Condemning' the two boys, in Major's word, was an alternative to confronting the shared responsibility of society at large for various forms of direct and structural violence which overshadowed their lives.

This is what is meant by demonisation – finding *sufficient* explanation for violence in the 'evil' nature of individuals, whether Saddam Hussein as discussed in Chapter 1, Osama bin Laden in the New York 'media war' of October 2001, or these boys.

The account of the trial which exposed the secret evidence about the case conferences speculates that, had they seen it, defence barristers for the boys 'could argue that Robert's family made him violent... and that he doesn't understand right from wrong. Or that Jon is such a strange, explosive child that at the time of his offence he wasn't responsible for his actions.'[35]

Instead, 'the law is arranged so that this knowledge, this Why, must be repressed... the intricacies of responsibility are not an issue.' The space for explanation had been squeezed out, in part by the strident media coverage, so that any attempt to provide one risked being interpreted as excusing the violent act.

Another murder – another way

Stuart Rees, founding director of the Centre for Peace and Conflict Studies at Sydney University, contrasts the Bulger case and the response to it with a strikingly similar incident, about 18 months later, when a five-year-old Norwegian girl was murdered by her playmates. Silje Marie Redegaard was found kicked to death in the snow in a playground outside a Trondheim housing estate. She was killed by three small boys, only a little older than her, after they had all shared a game of snowballs.

Memories of the Bulger killing were still fresh, but this time the headlines were very different, commonly highlighting calls for restraint and forgiveness by the girl's mother. The British had arraigned the killers of James Bulger before an adult court and locked them away. Norwegian psychologists and social workers planned a healing process to generate understanding within the community and forgiveness towards the boys.

There was a dialogue involving police, media, parents, the social workers and community representatives, which focused on preventing the one *act* of violence being compounded by stigmatisation and community breakdown.

Seeking to explain this trauma, the better to overcome it, did not entail excusing it, however: 'The Norwegians' attitude did not mean they were trying to forget. Rather, they seemed to know that forgiveness affected peace in their community as well as in the hearts of the individuals directly affected.'[36]

This key insight, and the response from those involved, shows an awareness of non-violence in contrast with the equivalent discourse in Britain.

Exercise Two
Explaining or excusing violence?

The script overleaf is for a television report conceived as one of a series of follow-ups to the issues raised by the bombing in Jerusalem covered in Chapter 1. It's based on the story of a suicide bomber's brother.[37] Read it and answer the following questions:

- How does it explain violence?
- Does it excuse violence?
- If not, how does it avoid doing so?
- Does it demonise the perpetrators of violence?
- If not, how does it avoid doing so?

Introduction (read by studio presenter): The Palestinian Prime Minister, Abu Mazen, is meeting the leaders of militant groups today, trying to persuade them to call a ceasefire. He believes that will give him a chance to pursue peace talks with Israel. The groups are responsible for sending hundreds of suicide bombers to kill Israelis. But who are the young men and women who carry out the attacks? What motivates them and what chance is there of stopping them? Jake Lynch went to find out.

Pictures 1	Voice 1

Voice-over: Recycling broken glass into art. A rare creative outlet for young people in Bethlehem. The organiser – Amer Daraghmeh, a peace and community activist, whose group is called, simply, Palestinian Vision.

Pictures 2	Voice 2

Amer Daraghmeh
Peace Activist

Voice-over: 'This is the way we work here,' he says. 'We share everything, and we try to create something out of nothing.'

Pictures 3	Voice 3

Voice-over: The destructive face of Palestinian youth – a suicide bombing in Jerusalem. This attack in March last year claimed 10 Israeli lives. Pictures of the perpetrator appeared on posters from the al Aqsa martyrs brigade. And one of them is on the wall in the home Amer shares with his wife and baby son, because the bomber, Mohammed, was his 18-year-old brother. How did he come to follow such a different path?

Pictures 4

Voice 4

Actor's voice reads translation: Each stage of the struggle has its own different form of resistance. Once it meant retaliation for Israeli attacks on us. But violence just creates more violence. We want a different future, and that's why we're working, that's the reason why I exist, so as to help create a better future for the kids here.

Pictures 5

Voice 5

Voice-over: At the time, refugee camps like the one where Amer lives were under attack by Israeli tanks and jets which killed 30 Palestinians. Over the years, he told me, he'd seen too many people killed and the grief of those left behind. For Mohammed, the violence brought back a terrible memory of when his best friend was shot and died in his arms.

Pictures 6

Voice 6

Actor's voice reads translation: It's the death of his friend, next to him – that really was the turning-point in Mohammed's life.

Pictures 7

Voice 7

Voice-over: Amer and the boys' mother described a mild young man who loved children and graduated successfully from technical school. Certainly not the stereotyped religious fanatic. I challenged them – did they ever think of Mohammed's victims?

Pictures 8

Ibtisan Daraghmeh
Mother

Voice 8

Actor's voice reads translation: Anyone's child is precious to its parents. The way my children are precious to me, theirs are precious to them as well. I didn't expect my son to do this, or I would have tried to stop him.

Pictures 9

Voice 9

Reporter Jake Lynch, piece to camera: Shocking as it may seem to outsiders, many Palestinians see suicide bombers like Mohammed as heroes of the struggle. Amer offers a very different role model – trying to bring hope to young people in Bethlehem of a future and a life worth living.

Pictures 10

Voice 10

Voice-over: Opinion polls show Palestinians are now in favour of a ceasefire, as long as there's no return of Israeli heavy armour to their streets. And they're keen for some renewed prospect of political progress. As for Amer himself, he's just raised his stake in a peaceful tomorrow.

Commentary

The key to maintaining the distinctions here is to show *differential* responses to similar circumstances. To be deprived is not *necessarily* to be 'depraved'.

OK, Amer had not endured the traumatic episode of his friend dying in his arms; but he and his brother had been brought up in the same place at the same time, and shared many of the same experiences of life under Israeli military occupation. The interesting thing is *why* he ended up following such a different path.

(In a similar way, in the discussion in the last chapter about coverage of the bombings in Casablanca, the *Guardian*'s version mentions Justice and Charity – a banned Islamic movement, committed to a struggle against poverty and political repression, but opposed to violence. That means the account given, of the conditions in which the bombers lived, could remain a valid part of the *explanation* for violence without being vulnerable to complaints about *excusing* it. Violence, the piece showed clearly, was not the only response.)

In the report from Bethlehem, it was also important to challenge either Amer or his mother, on camera, about their feelings for the people killed by Mohammed's violent act. This tactic, along with the piece-to-camera restoring some outside perspective, is important in order to avoid seeming to excuse it.

At the same time, there was a risk of demonising the perpetrator of violence. Giving an account of the circumstances in which he lived – including the friend who was killed and Israeli military incursions into Palestinian refugee camps – is essential to avoiding this.

We can also surmise, from the answers Amer gives, that he is reluctant to be cast as 'the good brother' and Mohammed 'the bad brother'. Hence the decision to draw attention to the paradox of the poster on the wall, the camera tilting down and zooming out to reveal the happy family scene below.

It allows for the workings of sociology and psychology – the interaction with circumstances – as part of the explanation for violence, without suggesting that our behaviour is determined by them. There is still room for the exercise of conscience.

Perhaps it raises a little higher in our minds the question – if we found ourselves in a similar situation, how would we react? That would be a good first step to empathy and understanding – the antidote both to excusing violence and to hiding the real causes beneath a clamour of demonisation.

About shapes

What is at stake in any one news story might be the implied shape of the rest. A small segment of a straight line is straight. A small segment of a circle is curved.

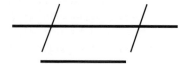

If the line represents the full story and its history, then telling part of the story in a two-minute TV or radio news item or a 500-word newspaper story would be a short segment of a straight line.

If the curved line represents the full story, its complex background and history, then telling part of the story in a two-minute TV or radio news item or a 500-word newspaper story would be a short segment of a circle.

A key characteristic of War Journalism is its *linearity*. Visualise the twin triangles – the ABC of conflict and the three forms of violence. In War Journalism, the C – the Contradictions, or issues dividing the parties – is often missed out in reports concentrating on Attitude and Behaviour. Structural violence is also generally absent, with a noticeable bias in favour of direct violence, and some weakly conceptualised cultural violence (close-ups of

flag-burning on demonstrations in the occupied Palestinian territories would be an example).

Remove one point from each triangle and you are left with the two remaining points, joined by a line. It fits with the bipolar conflict model, or tug of war, exemplified in the *Newsweek* cover showing the heads of Presidents George W Bush and Saddam Hussein.

War Journalism offers a blow-by-blow account, a series of tit-for-tat exchanges. It tells us the way it is without providing any real clues as to how it comes to be that way. Its explanations for conflict and for violence are *linear* ones.

Peace Journalism restores the missing points of the triangles, to offer us some insights into how things come to be the way they are, which is essential if we are to form any idea of how to change them.

We will discuss, later in this chapter, the Cycle of Violence – how people affected by conflict experience a number of different stages, such as grief turning to anger, or anger hardening into bitterness, *between* incidents of violence.

The point is that War Journalism is linear in its thinking and Peace Journalism is *extra-linear*, or multi-dimensional.

Other hard cases

The nature/nurture debate is too big to be settled in a news report, or even a book. There is no suggestion here that structural violence and situationism can absolve individuals from responsibility. As in the Bulger case, however, we should be suspicious when violence is presented as a 'bolt from the blue', requiring condemnation without explanation.

We have argued that a fair representation of violence must always try to illuminate the intelligible, if dysfunctional, processes that form the context for particular incidents. But how far does this hold? How does it stand up when put to the test in hard cases?

'Pure terrorism'

Old-fashioned liberation movements would turn to violence in response to injustice, and in pursuit of easily identifiable goals. Where they targeted civilians, their actions would be called 'terrorism'. Think Provisional IRA, think Hezbollah in Lebanon during Israel's occupation from 1982 to 2000.

By contrast, the September 11th attacks in the US can be seen as an example of 'pure terrorism'[38] or 'nihilism'. To draw this distinction has become commonplace in debates about political violence. But is it a useful one?

We suggested in the last chapter that Osama bin Laden's communiqué, following the attacks, did indeed identify a specific historical injustice to be avenged. What is new about 'international terrorism' is to conflate this with *ongoing* injustice on a global scale – a world apparently ordered in such a way as to relegate Muslims to a subservient position, a perception inscribed in bin Laden's own word, 'humiliation'.

The Arab world has its inchoate masses, like the poor of Morocco's shanty towns. Some attacks attributed to al-Qaeda are connected, in a linear way, with their subjugation and marginalisation – one way of becoming choate. This appears to have been the case with the Casablanca bombings, discussed in the last chapter, but they may be unusual.

One US expert who studied intelligence on 382 al-Qaeda suspects found:

> '... 17.6 per cent were upper class, 54.9 per cent middle class, and 27.5 per cent lower class. The highest number of upper- or middle-class individuals was among the Core Arabs (from Saudi Arabia, Egypt, Yemen and Kuwait), and the highest number of lower-class individuals was among the Maghreb Arabs from north Africa.'[39]

Most of the '9/11' hijackers were middle-class Saudis, but they grew up in a society where average real incomes halved in the 20 years to 2001, while the proliferating princelings of America's client regime, the House of Saud, continued to pocket a million dollars apiece just for existing. The grim prognosis for the life chances of the rising Arab generation must feel, in the most oil-rich country on earth, like proof positive of the injustice of the New World Order.

It is US economic, military and political hegemony that holds this world order in place, so the suicide hijackings can be read as a statement in a 'language of buildings' – the respective concrete symbols of each of these forms of power (assuming the downed plane was headed for Capitol Hill or the White House).

They also had clearly articulated dual goals – the ejection of 'infidels' from the 'land of the two holy places', now achieved with the withdrawal of US troops, and the downfall of the regime that invited them in:

> '[In this discourse] September 11 is seen as an Act of Justice, bringing Justice to the US essence, its economic and strategic centres, to force them to submit to stay off dar-al-Islam, Allah's lands.'[40]

How does this diagnosis affect what can be presented, and reported, as an appropriate remedy? Paul Rogers, Professor of Peace Studies at Bradford University, has coined the term 'liddism' for the belief that discontents thrown up by the existing economic and political order can be safely contained within it. But the '9/11' attack:

> '... showed that it might be impossible to maintain control of a potentially unstable world system, that keeping the lid on dissent, 'liddism', might be singularly inappropriate, contriving to increase violence and insecurity rather than diminish them.
>
> If this analysis was correct, then it suggested that the Western security paradigm should best evolve into a posture that encouraged the addressing of core problems, seeking to aid economic

cooperation for sustainable development, coupled with global environmental management and decreased reliance on military approaches.'[41]

None of this is to say that what is called 'international terrorism' is not significantly different from 'traditional terrorism'. But according to Alastair Crooke, an unusually close western observer from his service as a special envoy to Hamas for UK intelligence, they are more accurately seen as different in degree than in kind:

> 'A small proportion of Islamists, the extreme jihadists, are marginal, and have alienated many Muslims by their capricious use of violence. But for both, this is a struggle to restore the standing of Muslim societies; to assert Muslim identity and autonomy from western imposition, and to find the transition to modernity of their economies and society on Muslim terms – not on western secular ones.'[42]

The Bali bomb

Indonesia, in the years following the fall of the Suharto regime in 1998, was beset by a number of regional conflicts, some of which, like those centred on the cities of Ambon and Poso, set Christians against Muslims.

Many of those directly involved felt they faced a struggle for their own survival and that of their community, a situation so powerful that it overwhelmed predispositions – developed through several generations – towards amicable coexistence.

So what did they have to do with the Bali bomb? Here, after all, was an aberration – an attack aimed at western tourists in a hitherto peaceful part of the archipelago where the predominant local religion is Hinduism. Responsibility was quickly pinned on Jemaah Islamiya (JI), an al-Qaeda affiliate whose aim was to establish an Islamic republic across a large tranche of south-east Asia.

The absence of *direct* connections with the Bali bomb does not mean there are no connections at all. Through a chain of cause and effect, the conflicts besetting Indonesia, and the country's 'multi-dimensional crisis', formed an indispensable context for understanding the attack. According to a report by Human Rights Watch:[43] 'Indonesia's regional conflicts... create the chaos and radicalization that terrorist networks seek out.'

The report criticised the authorities for failing to bring law and order to Poso, where al-Qaeda operatives were filmed on military training, in a video discovered at one of the network's camps in Afghanistan.

Journalists investigate the ruins of a house burnt in violence, Poso, 2000

Another report noted that recruits to JI were sent to Poso and the North Moluccas, another province wracked by conflict, as 'easily accessible places where [they] could gain practical combat experience'. Recruitment drives were often accompanied by 'discussions about the Moluccas and Poso or the showing of videos about the killings taking place there. Those conflicts... served to give concrete meaning to the concept of *jihad*, a key element of JI's ideology'.

The report identified 'curious links between associates of the outlawed regional terrorist group JI and the Indonesian military (TNI)' – a connection 'strong enough to raise the question of how much the TNI knew about JI before the October 12 Bali bombing'.[44]

Consider the Bali atrocity against the history and pattern of bombings as terror tactics in Indonesia, and this element of context firms up still further:

'There is no possibility that [this] can be considered a type of criminal activity without extremely serious interests forming the background... terror in the form of bombing has occurred repeatedly in Indonesia... unfortunately there have been no efforts to clearly expose the motives or interests of the perpetrators.

This lack of clarity raises questions. Did the institution lack the capacity to examine these incidents? Or did the institution not want to investigate thoroughly because they were under pressure, or to avoid dealing with certain parties that have strong positions in the political constellation, that were presumed to be responsible?'[45]

On this view, regional conflicts form an echo chamber in which political rivalries are played out, and are kept going by a steady trickle of *provokasi* – provocations – typically, 'mysterious' bombings or shootings. The pattern could still be discerned long after the Bali attack:

'The gunshooting... at a church during Easter [2004], in Poso, Central Sulawesi, has intensified provocation and violence... it seems that the central and regional governments have been unfair and intentionally let the conflicts continue to happen.'[46]

This implies that the Bali bombing was constructed, at least in part, by the tangle of interests bound up in these regional conflicts, which in turn are rooted in structural issues affecting people's economic, political and psychological security.

Literacy in non-violence

- *An activist's view:* 'Media report things that happen. If you do not kill somebody, you are not news.' – Uri Avnery, veteran activist and leader of the Israeli peace bloc, Gush Shalom.[47]
- *A journalist's view:* 'When peace is the story it has been properly reported.' – David Loyn, BBC Developing World correspondent.[48]

In one important sense, news is about change. We pick up today's paper to find out what's changed since we read it yesterday. When a reporter pitches a story, the editor wants to know what's new about it – what has changed since precious page or programme space was last allocated to this subject.

In news about conflict, therefore, who and what gets reported depends to a certain extent on who and what are seen as bringing about, or promising, significant change.

We can all see how violence can be a source of significant change. What about non-violence? When we talk about non-violent responses to conflict, it is important to realise we are not talking about passivity:

'Non-violence stands for something most people engage in every day – self-assertion, trying to reach goals without violence, without intending to harm or hurt anybody.

Non-violence entails more than just not being violent. That could include being passive, doing nothing, resigning to one's fate. To handle conflicts without violence needs *positive non-violence* in thought, speech and action and *creativity*, meaning to develop new ideas.'[49]

Stuart Rees on the media and non-violence:

'Non-violent direct action seems to have been replaced by anything-goes direct action, in part because such violence is regarded by the media as very newsworthy. The media also needs to become more literate about non-violence, to cover and to analyse peaceful protest, to see it as educative as well as civilising.'[50]

This concept of *literacy* in non-violence is the key. To see it in its proper context is to realise its potential for bringing about significant change. One element of this literacy is to appreciate the history of significant change brought about by non-violence.

> DISCUSSION: Who are the heroes of non-violent struggle? How many can you name?

Many people can name the Mahatma Gandhi and, in some cases, Nelson Mandela. But such figures are under-represented in cultural forms most people would encounter. For instance, one study found that in 75 per cent of American TV programmes shown during hours when children are most likely to be watching, the hero either kills people or beats them up.[51]

Perhaps because of such cultural phenomena, to name a few of the heroes of non-violence is to begin to appreciate how incomplete is most people's understanding of how significant changes in our lives have actually been brought about, changes such as the end of colonialism in some cases, and the fall of state communism.

Heroes of non-violence[52]

GEORGII GAPON – a Russian orthodox priest who, in 1905, persuaded 150,000 workers to walk the icy streets of Russia's ancient capital in the century's first public challenge to autocratic power. He ignited mass action nationwide that led to the country's first popularly elected national parliament.

MARTIN LUTHER KING[53] – leader of the US civil rights movement, assassinated in 1968. Affirmed that non-violence was an active, not a passive idea, and focused on structural violence in the US. Respected the law but highlighted a moral obligation to challenge unjust laws. Led Americans on a 15-year campaign of marches and boycotts to overthrow racial segregation in the American South.

LECH WALESA[54] – the former shipyard electrician who became President of Poland in 1990 after several years in prison. He was arrested in 1981 along with other leaders of the Solidarity movement for challenging communist power in Poland by occupying factories and staging strikes.

MADRES DE LA PLAZA MAYO (MOTHERS OF MAY SQUARE) – outraged at the Argentine government's silence about the disappearance of their sons, a group of mothers started holding marches and vigils in the central plaza of Buenos Aires. They did not stop until the legitimacy of the country's military junta was undermined, leading to its downfall after the debacle of the Malvinas/Falklands War.

NELSON MANDELA – the icon of South Africa's struggle against Apartheid. Although first imprisoned for violent resistance to the state, Mandela is renowned for the kindness and forgiveness he showed his prison guards, and his calls for reconciliation between whites and blacks.

Decades of global non-violent action by boycott organisers, trade unions and religious leaders contributed firstly to international sanctions, then ultimately to Mandela's release after 27 years and negotiations for a democratic future.

LEIPZIG DEMONSTRATORS – in 1989, a non-violent demonstration in Leipzig of more than 70,000 people, mostly women, presaged the fall of the Berlin Wall. They risked brutal reprisals by the state, but none came, emboldening others to follow their lead.

AUNG SAN SUU KYI – the Burmese democracy leader, currently (July 2005) under house arrest by the brutal military regime in charge of Burma since it seized control of the country following a majority vote in favour of Suu Kyi's party. She advocates non-violence as the only pragmatic route to achieve democracy:

'I do not want to encourage and to perpetuate this tradition of bringing about change through violence. Because I'm afraid that if we achieve democracy in this way we will never be able to get rid of the idea that you bring about necessary changes through violence... it would simply not assist us in building a strong democracy.'[55]

This quote provides an important clue to the respective credentials of violence and non-violence as forces for change, and for different kinds of change. Just think for a moment about what happens after violence. Do people pick up the threads of a peaceful life? Is this what recent violent interventions have delivered?

The effects of violence cannot be measured by assessing physical damage, death and destruction alone. This is what Gandhi meant when he said: 'I object to violence because when it appears to do good, the good is only temporary. The harm it does is permanent.'

The legacy of violence
In Kosovo

The next chapter deals in some depth with propaganda claims made to justify NATO's bombing of Yugoslavia in 1999. The overall tone and effect of these was to promise a better future – 'Operation Allied Force' was a regrettable necessity if 'civilised behaviour' was to triumph over barbarism.

Five years later, the auguries were clouded, however. Renewed violence by ethnic Albanian mobs against the few remaining Serbs in the province was an unwelcome reminder that latent conflict issues remained unaddressed. It was effectively bought off by the 'international community' as awkward questions were raised, in the context of war on Iraq, about the merits of armed 'humanitarian intervention' *per se*:

'The [Kosovo Albanian] mafia recognised how desperate NATO is to avoid trouble on the Balkan front, and the rioting in March [2004] was its classic way of upping the price for quiet. And it is being paid. After a tailing-off in aid supplies over the past five years, now, each day, a mile-long queue of trucks waits to enter Kosovo from Macedonia... for Albanians, Kosovo has become a cargo cult that actually delivers.'[56]

But the flow of money into Kosovo, a palliative to keep violence in check, distorted the economy and brought unwanted side-effects such as a boom in prostitution, both in the province itself and as a means of entry into the European Union for women from all over eastern Europe and the former Soviet Union:

'Women and girls are being trafficked out of Kosovo into EU countries including Italy, the Netherlands and the UK... More than 36,000 soldiers from EU countries serve in UN and NATO forces in Kosovo, and it is the presence of this international force that Amnesty International fingers for the increasing exploitation of women. The report charges that 20 per cent of those using the services of trafficked women and girls are members of the international community and that some are even involved in trafficking itself.'[57]

The prospects for Kosovo to make a conventional and honest living are blighted by political stalemate. As we suggest in the next chapter, NATO's increasing desperation to find a pretext to bring its bombing campaign to an end, one capable of being presented as a 'victory', caused the issue of Kosovo's political future to be kicked into the long grass. This political uncertainty deters investment and economic development.

Future political arrangements will only be sustainable if they are settled amicably, as Richard Holbrooke, one of the chief architects of Washington's policy in the Balkans throughout the 1990s, later averred. And the possibility of an amicable settlement has been set far, far back by the dropping of bombs, the vicious counter-attack they triggered 15,000 feet below, and the legacy these actions left behind.

In Afghanistan

The overthrow of the Taliban was welcomed by many Afghans, and triggered a belated influx of humanitarian and development aid. However, at the time of writing (2005):

- the writ of the government of Hamid Karzai runs only as far as the outskirts of Kabul
- security situation uncertain in the rest of the country, with aid workers as well as locals vulnerable to attack – even Médecins sans Frontières have pulled out
- US paying regional militia leaders or 'warlords' to help in fighting remnants of the Taliban
- a renewal of the heroin trade that was effectively eliminated before the attack on Afghanistan in 2001

- US support for regimes across former Soviet central Asia – trading their willingness to host US military bases for Washington's complaisance in human rights abuses
- thousands of Afghan civilians have been killed – tallied, at least in the first few months of the intervention, by an ongoing academic study:

'What causes the documented high level of civilian casualties – 3,000 to 3,400 [7 October 2001 to March 2002] civilian deaths – in the US air war upon Afghanistan? The explanation is the apparent willingness of US military strategists to fire missiles into and drop bombs upon, heavily populated areas of Afghanistan.'[58]

In October 2004, pictures of Afghans queuing at polling stations, and ballot boxes being transported by donkey, seemed to herald the start of a new and more hopeful era. By now, President George W Bush was himself preparing to face the electorate; he hailed the vote in Afghanistan, in a televised candidates' debate with Senator John Kerry, as vindication of his policies: 'freedom is on the march'.

But a UN report then detailed the revival of Afghanistan's heroin trade, involving as many as one in 10 of the country's entire population and bringing in $2.8 billion a year, nearly 60 per cent of the gross domestic product. It was in imminent danger of becoming a 'narco-state', the report warned.[59]

The picture is one of latent conflicts being palliated by allowing regional power-brokers to remain in place, and letting them grow rich on poppy harvests, albeit at massive social and economic cost in Europe, where most Afghan heroin ends up – and in terms of civil liberties for the population at large.

The Taliban and the West
David Loyn, an award-winning BBC correspondent who has reported from

Afghanistan over many years, has written:
'The West's mistake was not engaging with
this movement [the Taliban] in any
meaningful way.'

The Taliban committed horrific war crimes
and their policies evinced a flagrant disregard
for the rights of women, Loyn acknowledges.
However, they successfully brought law and
order to the country; and there was a
'moderate wing' which could have been
encouraged and strengthened, with aid among
other gestures, and which offered the best
hope of drawing Afghanistan into the family
of nations. Loyn continues:

'I watched the splits and divisions among
international NGOs as they tried to
continue effective aid programmes faced
by the Taliban's severe restrictions on how
they worked. But at least most found a
way to work. In contrast, western
governments led by America turned their
back on the Taliban, and once demonised,
they became demons, acting as hosts to
those who would do the west the most
harm...
        [This] alienation of the Taliban by
the west led directly to the events of 11
September.'[60]

There is another version of the process by
which war against the Taliban grew out of
previous contacts from the west. French
intelligence sources supplied much of the
information for a book[61] – rushed out in
November 2001 as the US-allied Northern
Alliance was taking control in Kabul –
according to which this particular 'regime
change' was part of the same 'great game' to
control access to strategic oil reserves as the
later war on Iraq (see Chapter 1).

The Taliban had initially proved receptive
to a deal for the US oil company, Unocal, to
build a pipeline across Afghanistan and
Pakistan to bring oil from central Asia out
into the Indian Ocean. According to the
authors, considerable inducements were on
offer in the form of international aid:

'At one moment during the negotiations,
the US representatives told the Taliban,
"either you accept our offer of a carpet of
gold, or we bury you under a carpet of
bombs."'[62]

Eventually the Taliban demurred, and the deal
was halted. Plan B – the bombs – then moved
to the top of the agenda.

Another source, Pakistan's former foreign
minister Naif Naik, told the authors that
meetings between the Taliban, a number of
neighbouring states plus representatives of
Russia and the US, had continued up to
August of that year – just weeks before the
suicide hijackers hit New York and
Washington:

'Naik said... the discussions turned
around "the formation of a government of
national unity. If the Taliban had accepted
this coalition, they would have
immediately received international
economic aid."
        "And the [oil] pipelines from
Kazakhstan and Uzbekistan would have
come [through Afghanistan]," he added.
Naik also claimed that Tom Simons, the
US representative at these meetings, openly
threatened the Taliban and Pakistan.
        Simons said, "either the Taliban
behave as they ought to, or Pakistan
convinces them to do so, or we will use
another option." The words Simons used
were "a military operation", Naik said.'[63]

In Iraq

The invasion of Iraq brought two immediate
benefits to its people – the removal of a brutal
regime, and the lifting of punitive sanctions,
blamed by a UNICEF report for the deaths of
more than half a million children.[64]

Did it also bring democracy? A big
question, and one much in vogue at the time
of writing (2005). The answer depends on
what is meant by 'democracy'. A literal
translation is 'rule by the people'. In
representative democracy, of course, the

wishes of the majority of people are carried out by government on their behalf.

What did Iraqis wish for, going into the election of 30 January, and would the representatives they elected have the power to deliver on their wishes? Opinion polls throughout 2003 and 2004 repeatedly showed most Iraqis wanted the US-led occupying forces to leave their country,[65] as a necessary step in restoring some semblance of physical security to everyday life.

Not only were these forces perceived as an alien presence, menacing ordinary Iraqis with impunity; they were also the focus for violent resistance, and likely to be so for as long as they remained.

However, a US withdrawal was one item ruled off the agenda in advance. Building work continued throughout the election period on a number of permanent military bases, at the cost of billions of dollars. To expect them to be dismantled, simply because the Iraqi people wished it and voted for it, was to misread the essential conflict dynamics:

> 'Allowing Iraq to develop as a fully independent state could well lead to it requiring an end to US influence and involvement in the country. This would be entirely unacceptable to the United States given that the establishment of a client regime controlling Iraq's very large oil resources has been an underlying motive for destroying the Saddam Hussein regime from the start.'[66]

A demand for an early date for US troop withdrawal was common currency among the embryonic political parties contesting the elections – essential if they were to carry any credibility among voters. On the day after the results were announced, the *Financial Times*, alone among the London dailies, picked up on indications that the winners, the United Iraqi Alliance (UIA), had already quietly traded away this key commitment, in advance of the election:

> 'Another contentious issue is likely to be calls for the US-led coalition to withdraw from Iraq, or at least name a timetable for withdrawal. The Alliance campaigned on this issue, and an Alliance brochure from January 10 lists "setting a schedule for the multi-national forces to withdraw from Iraq" in between "providing security" and "respecting human rights" as key points of their political platform.
>
> The sentence was, however, later watered down – suggesting there may be more leeway in discussions between the US and the incoming Iraqi administration.'[67]

As it was, after the new government took office, one Iraqi writer, a former prisoner of the Saddam Hussein regime, complained:

> 'For ordinary Iraqis, simply venturing into the streets brings the possibility of attack. Most killings go unreported... following the US and British governments' line on human rights, members of the Iraqi government have sought to play down the violations committed by occupation troops... so much for illusions.' [68]

Other key planks of the UIA's manifesto included:

> '"Adopting a social security system under which the state guarantees a job for every fit Iraqi... and offers facilities to citizens to build homes"; the Alliance also pledged "to write off Iraq's debts, cancel reparations and use the oil wealth for economic development projects."'[69]

These, too, were ruled out in advance, however – in this case by the free-market policies imposed on Iraq by pro-consul Paul Bremer, and enshrined in agreements with the Paris Club and International Monetary Fund.

Bremer's other legacy was a set of election rules giving Washington's most reliable ally, the Kurds, 27 per cent of seats in the national assembly, despite accounting for only 15 per cent of the population. The US-authored interim constitution, requiring a majority of two-thirds or, in some cases, three-quarters to take any major decision, gave them an effective power of veto, should the other parties wish to overturn any aspect of the military or economic dispensation bequeathed by the Americans.

'What follows military action could be apocalyptic'

If the record of intervention is properly assessed, then one key analytical factor in coverage of post-invasion Iraq takes on a different complexion. It is not that 'nation-building' turned out to be more tricky than proponents of regime change expected. The proposition that violence could lead on to a genuinely democratic, orderly society warranted far closer scrutiny when it was first made.

Before the invasion, Faleh Abdel Jabar, a distinguished Iraqi social scientist exiled in London, sounded a resonant warning, largely vindicated by subsequent events:

'There is a grossly over-simplified view of Iraqi society, conveniently divided into categories such as Sunnis and Shias, PUK and KDP. As a result we are not really getting any idea of the extent of social upheaval that could follow an attempt to bring about wholesale change by violent means.

What follows military action could be apocalyptic, with the need to re-establish law and order very fast. There has been too little discussion of how this is to be done, and too little discussion of alternative political strategies for solving the problem of Iraq and Saddam Hussein.'[70]

Had the reporting at the time paid more attention to such warnings, readers and audiences would have received a more reliable account of what was really going on. Much later, it emerged that a 'big stack' of 'intelligence reports compiled in January 2003 predicted that an American invasion would result in a divided Iraq prone to internal violence, and increased sympathy in the Islamic world for some terrorist objectives.'[71]

Consequences for reporting

The point is not that journalists should necessarily *set out* to oppose violence. Some editors and reporters, in some countries, may make that choice, finding it entirely compatible with the traditions and assumptions influencing their perceived role and professional ethos. In 1999, an exhaustive consultation with senior journalists from 11 countries in sub-Saharan Africa found:

'Whether employed by state-controlled broadcasting corporations or editing weekly or daily newspapers surviving on street-corner sales, most of the journalists involved said that they believe they have a vital role to play in the prevention and resolution of conflict. For many, the question was not whether they should be fulfilling that role, but rather how they could do so.'[72]

Others, particularly in mainstream media in the west, will likely want to make a different choice, based on the old maxim: 'we just report the facts'. But, as we have seen, this has to be accompanied by *reflexivity* – an acknowledgement that reporting conventions lead to certain kinds of facts being routinely omitted or marginalised, and to imbalances in the understanding conveyed to the public.

One of the chief imbalances in most coverage of conflict is the concentration on visible damage and destruction. The damage to psychology, structure and culture, which is the *invisible* legacy of violence, is routinely omitted. To allow this pattern to accumulate amounts to War Journalism – journalism which leads us to overvalue violent responses to conflict and undervalue non-violent responses.

To revisit recent former interventions, examining them, as we do here, in light of Gandhi's famous dictum, and restoring the missing elements to the picture, is a necessary corrective to this imbalance.

The criteria for assessing proposed violent responses to conflict should also include the cost, in terms of weapons and wages, when balanced against the costs and benefits of alternative, non-violent responses – another exercise essential to fair and informed public debate.

Facts and figures[73]

'• £32 billion: the British government defence budget.

• £600 million: the amount allocated by the British government to conflict prevention and resolution, including peace-keeping.

• The UK currently has 232 Eurofighter jet aircraft on order. One Eurofighter will cost £80 million. For that amount we could:
  – put another 1,000 peace-keepers into Afghanistan, organise negotiations with warlords to bring militias and opium production under control, and support local initiatives to restore law and order outside Kabul
  – set up liaison centres all over Iraq to enable people to get help with the daily traumas – murdered civilians, destroyed homes, arrested relatives, lack of food and employment (which engender hatred for the occupying forces)

• People are currently being killed in 37 armed conflicts in different parts of the world.

• The British government currently provides subsidies to arms exporters of £426 million per annum. For that amount we could:
  – support the setting up of gun collection schemes in every single country where there is local killing, including Sudan,

the Democratic Republic of the Congo, Colombia, Indonesia, Somalia, Afghanistan, Nepal, Sri Lanka, Uganda, Rwanda, Burundi, Angola, and Nigeria
  – introduce effective boundary controls on gun-running, with severe and enforceable penalties
  – fully support the EU commitment to develop a "Civilian Crisis Management Capacity" by providing training for civilians ready to join.'

Creativity – the essence of non-violence

Martin Luther King once said violence was 'the antithesis of creativity'.[74] We are all familiar – from some of the stories most cherished and most deeply embedded in the culture of different peoples around the world – with the kind of creativity needed for effective non-violent intervention.

Some examples from the lives of the Prophets:[75]

• *Mohammed* intervened in a dispute between families involved in rebuilding the Ka'ba at Mecca. They each wanted the honour of carrying a sacred black stone back to its place. The Prophet thought for a while, and laid down his cloak on the floor, then placed the stone on top of it. Everyone could lift a corner of the cloak with the stone in the middle.

• *Christ* intervened to prevent the stoning of an adulteress, saying: 'Let him who is without sin cast the first stone.'

• *The Buddha* intervened to prevent a war over water breaking out. He reminded the parties that the water was worth very little, whereas the lives of their warriors were 'beyond price'.

The *creativity* in each of these cases lay in finding and suggesting a new way of looking at the situation in hand. In the story about

Mohammed, for example, the families involved in the dispute expected him to find some basis for *adjudicating* between their competing claims. They had assumed that either one or the other would have the honour they sought.

The Prophet's suggestion allowed them both to have it – a form of transcendence. The important thing to note is that it started with a willingness to look again at a criterion each party had thought was fixed. This is the key to creativity.

Realism versus the Cycle of Violence

The challenge is, how to convey such acts of creativity and the potential they hold for conflict management, resolution and transformation, in the news? As noted earlier, news is, in a sense, *about* change – anyone, or anything seen as bringing about change is, in principle, newsworthy.

What is at stake, therefore, is where we believe change comes from. Individual opinions, among journalists and even editors, on this question, are, in a sense, incidental to the argument. The *institutional* view of the news industry is clear. Most news resources tend to be deployed in clusters around the official decision-making centres of national states. Built into this pattern of deployment is a view of conflicts, and how they change, known as Realism.

Realism is the view that 'there is no authority over the nation-state, nor, for the realist, should there be.'[76]

There is, therefore, no legitimate source of rules governing the relations between nation states, except such temporary *ad hoc* arrangements as they may choose to enter into, between themselves. International relations are essentially anarchic, and it is up to each nation state to look after its own security.

Realism is what kindled the Bush administration's bonfire of international treaties, including the Biological Weapons and Chemical Weapons Conventions, the International Criminal Court and the Kyoto Protocol. A book by former policy aide Robert Kagan, *Paradise and Power: America and Europe in the new world order*, purporting to detect a new mid-Atlantic divide over these issues, briefly became required reading for the political class in London and Washington alike.

Where Realism's claims look threadbare is when they are tested as an explanation for what is actually going on. In the Realist schema, as one critical account puts it, 'change is only brought about by states, governments and (other) armed men.'[77]

Consider this review of Kagan's book by Mark Leonard, director of the London Foreign Policy Centre:

> 'One could fill entire libraries with books on how the biggest threats to our citizens come not from invading armies, but terrorists, climate change, drug-trafficking, population movement, or the erratic flows of the $1.5trn traded daily on the foreign exchange markets...'

> 'The campaign against al-Qaeda in Afghanistan may have been military, but to eliminate the cells of terrorists in Hamburg, Madrid or London will rely more on diplomacy than precision bombing. In this world, the weakness of American coercion will contrast with the power of European attraction. One need look no further than European and US policies towards neighbouring countries. The dangers are similar – drug-trafficking, large flows of migrants across hard-to-police borders, criminal networks – but the European response of encouraging political and economic reform by holding out the possibility of integration into the EU has had more enduring success than the swift military interventions of the Monroe doctrine.'[78]

The political, economic and social relations between people caught up in conflicts are influenced by *systems*; outside and between nation states but – far from being anarchic – characterised by predictable patterns of cause and effect. The exponential growth in car traffic in many countries contributes to the build-up of greenhouse gases, with effects on climate and geography which, in turn, intensify migratory pressures. The relentless downward drive on industrial wages can be attributed to the interplay of several systems – global financial flows, the lowering of tariff barriers and containerisation of freight traffic among them.

There is a broad range, in other words, of what are called *conflict drivers*, creating contradictions and affecting attitudes and behaviour in conflicts, from local to global. It means there is an equally broad range of possible interventions in conflict, any of which could also be the source of significant change and, therefore, worthy of being reported.

Where would we look for them? One way is by peering further into a concept familiar from news reports of conflict – the 'Cycle of Violence'. This is usually taken to mean an exchange of blows – a linear model of 'tit-for-tat'. Dr Scilla Elworthy, founder of the UK-based NGO, Peace Direct, provides us with an extra-linear model:[79]

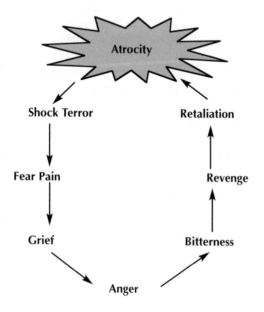

Breaking the cycle

According to Dr Elworthy:

'Intervention is needed at the point before anger hardens into bitterness, revenge and retaliation. To be effective it must address the physical, the political and the psychological security of people trapped in violence; all are equally important, and one without the others is insufficiently strong to break the cycle. In every case, the people involved in situations of violence must be supported in the development of their own resources for transformation.'

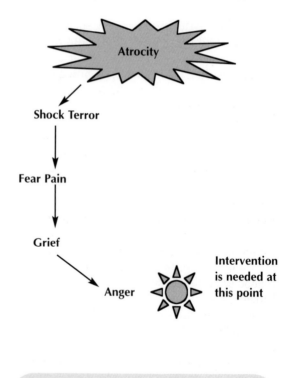

DISCUSSION: Why do we need an intervention at the point of anger?

Just imagine trying to urge someone who has suffered a grievous loss *not* to feel shock, fear, grief and anger. What can be stopped is anger hardening to *bitterness*.

Bitterness is *anger with memory* – it makes sense to say 'I was angry for five minutes when my team let in a soft goal'. It makes no sense to say 'I was bitter for five minutes'.

Another writer, Dan Smith, identifies four pillars of peace-building – a way of classifying different and complementary interventions to interrupt the Cycle of Violence:[80]

DISCUSSION: Can you think of any similar projects, particularly grassroots initiatives, that have made a tangible difference in a conflict zone?

POLITICAL FRAMEWORK or political security	RECONCILIATION or psychological security	PHYSICAL SECURITY	SOCIO-ECONOMIC
Democratization: organizing and monitoring elections Human Rights: respect for international law, development of monitoring and reporting of abuses Rule of Law: improving the drafting of laws, judicial reforms, police reform Good governance: transparency, accountability, anti-corruption Building political institutions	Dialogue: between political leaders, among political activists, NGOs Building mutual understanding: work on education curricula, especially history Avoidance of hate speech and hostile rhetoric: ethical standards for the news media or Peace Journalism Truth Commissions Bearing Witness: hearing testimonies of traumatised victims and relatives	Securing peace, monitoring, ceasefires etc Disarmament, demobilization and reintegration of combatants in ordinary society Care for child soldiers Humanitarian mine clearance Security sector reform Controls on the trade in small arms and light weapons	Physical reconstruction Investment in utilities and economic infra-structure Anti-corruption laws Schools Hospitals Return of refugees Micro investment schemes

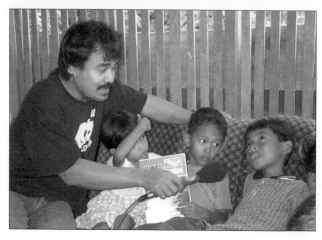

Interviewing children in Poso

understanding to their followers. Then there are relief agencies working to prevent the trauma imported into North Sulawesi in recent years, in the minds of thousands of refugees from North Maluku, from festering, and potentially inflaming religious sensibilities in Manado itself.

The Peace Journalists will never forget the sight and sound of Christian children, singing Christian songs in a refugee camp, led by a Muslim teacher wearing a jilbab. You will find their activities well reported here. In the hands of the more creative reporters,

Indonesian journalists have been at the forefront of experiments in Peace Journalism. For them, the stories of grassroots peace actors intervening to interrupt the Cycle of Violence have become important and welcome additions to the news agenda. From the introduction to a collection of Peace Journalism articles from the city of Manado:

> 'Peace, in Manado, is something that many people are actively working at, all the time. Religious leaders, for instance, come together to give messages of tolerance and mutual

Muslim teacher in jilbab, Christian children

Jake Lynch reporting from Manado

interviews with the children, about their hopes and experiences, became the basis for wonderful stories, full of imaginative connections and arresting images, which contain much of the music of today's Indonesia.'[81]

Intervention for physical security

Protection: When civilians are threatened, driven from their homes, or under attack, they can be protected in a number of ways – including civilian protection, pioneered and practised in many places around the world by Peace Brigades International. Trained volunteers accompany local NGO staff when going about their daily tasks, providing a witness to any threats of violence and intimidation.

One Indonesian example was in Tentena, the mainly Christian town on the shores of Lake Poso which has been caught up in the intercommunal clashes of recent years. The *Sintuwo Maroso* Youth Convoy (Amsimar) was a group of mainly university graduates providing protection to the 30 or so Muslims who stayed in their homes rather than flee to become refugees. They stood guard over the local mosque as well as the market-place to protect them from destructive mobs.

Intervention for political security

Control of militias: Armed militias or paramilitaries have to be brought to the negotiating table. This is not necessarily best done by armed forces; in many instances NGOs or respected civilians have succeeded, or it has been carried out under UN auspices.

In Mozambique, after years of civil war:

'The Community of Saint Egidio, supported by the Vatican, became involved in a series of meetings with leaders of FRELIMO and RENAMO culminating in October 1992 in the signing of a comprehensive peace accord. This provided for the demobilisation and reintegration of combatants, the creation of a new Mozambican Defence Force, the creation of political parties, and freedom of the press. The United Nations was given the responsibility of overseeing the transition from war to peace which led to the first free elections in October 1994.'[82]

Intervention for psychological security

Witness: The traumas experienced by victims of atrocity need attention and, if possible, healing. One way in which this is done simply and effectively is by a technique called 'active listening', whereby an independent witness or witnesses gives the traumatised person their full attention for as long as necessary to discharge their fear, grief and anger. Done well, it prevents anger hardening into bitterness and retaliation.

There are many examples of this across Indonesia. In Manado, refugee children were helped to process their trauma by singing songs, writing poems and drawing pictures of their experiences during the bitter fighting in North Maluku. Organisers found there was a profound change of subjects in children's drawings and paintings over the life of the project, from knives and weapons at the start to normal childhood scenes of houses, gardens and families.

Relief workers in Liberia have used similar techniques to help children exposed to traumatic experiences in the country's bloody civil war. These examples show how pictures of violent scenes give way to images from everyday life with the right support and opportunities.

Pictures by Amos Ndorbor aged 13 from Lofa County, Liberia, who fled the attack of Kolahun in early 2001. He worked with Sarah Elliott, a nurse with Médicins Sans Frontières

A framework of understanding

The introduction to the collection of Indonesian Peace Journalism articles, quoted above, also notes:

> 'If there is one real skill in Peace Journalism it lies in tracing connections between the stories of people like these, and the big issues and eyecatching events of the day – showing how the actions and concerns of individuals bear indirectly on the personal fortunes of every reader, listener or viewer. To do that, journalists need to be able to draw upon a deep understanding of how conflicts develop and how people can respond to them in ways likely to reduce the risk of violence.'

It involves, in other words, creating what we have called elsewhere a 'framework of understanding'[83] in which the relevance of grassroots peace initiatives can be made clear. It is important to note one thing before we leave this subject – in tracing the connections mentioned here, you unavoidably strengthen them. By communicating to others the very fact that there are people working to interrupt the Cycle of Violence and towards managing, resolving and transforming conflict, you are bound to contribute to 'a widespread sense of shared responsibility for the larger, systemic dimension of contemporary conflict.'[84]

To choose *not* to report the connections and interventions is, to repeat, not to be neutral, but to collude in concealing them from view beneath an undeclared Realist analysis of conflict and the process of change.

Ultimately it depends on whether you see the people caught up in conflict as a problem (obdurately hating those on the 'other side', or demanding aid) or as a resource, offering individual and collective courage and wisdom when responding to conflict.

Endnotes for Chapter 3

1. Jake Lynch, *Reporting the World*, Conflict and Peace Forums, Taplow, 2002, p 70.
2. Ross Howard, *Conflict Sensitive Journalism*, International Media Support, Copenhagen, 2003, p 17.
3. Johan Galtung, 'Violence, Peace and Peace Research', *Journal of Peace Research*, Vol 6, No 3, 1969.
4. Lynch, op cit, p. 29.
5. Johan Galtung, 'Cultural Violence', *Journal of Peace Research*, Vol 27, No 3, 1990.
6. Johan Galtung, '3Rs – Resolution, Reconstruction and Reconciliation', TRANSCEND http://www.transcend.org/TRRECBAS.HTM, p 65.
7. Adapted from Scott Peterson, *Me Against My Brother – At War in Somalia, Sudan and Rwanda*, Routledge, London, 2000, p 314.
8. Mahmood Mamdani, *When Victims Become Killers – Colonialism, Nativism and the Genocide in Rwanda*, Princeton University Press, Princeton, 2002, p 8.
9. Gerald Caplan, *Rwanda – The Preventable Genocide*, Report of the International Panel of Eminent Personalities to Investigate the 1994 Genocide in Rwanda and the Surrounding Events, IPEP, the Organisation of African Unity, July 2000, p 118.
10. Mahmood Mamdani, op cit, p 14.
11. Gerald Caplan, op cit, p 155.
12. Mahmood Mamdani, op cit, p 14.
13. Ibid, p 29.
14. Ibi., p 38.
15. Ibid, p 38.
16. Mark Pedelty, *War Stories*, Routledge, New York, 1995, p 15.
17. Tom Lubbock, London *Independent*, 23 February 2002.
18. From *The Free Dictionary*, http://encyclopedia.thefreedictionary.com/Essentialist.

19. C Haney, WC Banks and PG Zimbardo, 'Study of Prisoners and Guards in a Simulated Prison', *Naval Research Reviews*, 9, 1-17, Washington DC: Office of Naval Research, 1973.

20. Wikipedia reference: http://en.wikipedia.org/wiki/Stanford_Prison_Experiment.

21. Malcolm Gladwell, *Tipping Point*, Little, Brown & Company, New York, 2000, p 152.

22. Nastassia Lopez, 'Abuse at Iraqi Prison Predictable, Decades-Old Study Shows', *MTV News*, 27 May 2004.

23. Susan Fiske, Princeton University, quoted in Mark Henderson, 'Anybody Can Be Persuaded To Be a Torturer, Says Abu Ghraib Study', London *Times*, 26 November 2004.

24. Quoted in Johann Hari, 'Beheaded Hostages, Slaughtered Children, and the Misguided "War On Global Terror"', London *Independent*, 22 September 2004.

25. Edition dated 15 October 2001.

26. Edition dated 15 October 2001.

27. Edition dated 9 October 2001.

28. Quoted in Johan Galtung, 'September 11, 2001 – Diagnosis, Prognosis, Therapy', in Johan Galtung, Carl G Jacobsen and Kai Frithjof Brand-Jacobsen, *Searching for Peace – The Road to TRANSCEND*, Pluto Press, London, 2002, p 89.

29. Ibn Khaldun, *The Muqaddimah*, trans Franz Rosenthal, ed and abridged by NJ Dawood, Princeton, 1969, p 24.

30. Jake Lynch and Annabel McGoldrick, *News from the Holy Land* (video), Hawthorn Press, Stroud, 2004.

31. Interviewed on *Channel 4 News*, 11 September 2001.

32. Quoted in Blake Morrison, *As If*, Granta Books, London, 1997, p 234.

33. Search engine Lexis Nexis – selection of UK publications: NB excludes 'downmarket' tabloids such as the *Sun* and *Daily Star*.

34. Jonathan Holborow, 'We Should Condemn a Little More, Understand a Little Less', *Mail on Sunday*, London, 21 February 1993.

35. Blake Morrison, op cit.

36. Stuart Rees, *Passion for Peace*, University of New South Wales Press, Sydney, 2003, p 180.

37. Broadcast on BBC *Breakfast*, 1 December 2003.

38. Brendan O'Neill, deputy editor, *Spiked online*, speaking at 'The Error in Terrorism' conference at Southampton Institute, 11 November 2004.

39. Brendan O'Neill, 'Meet the Al Qaeda Archetype', *Spiked online*, 13 July 2004.

40. Johan Galtung, *From September 11, October 7 2001 and Aftermath – Three Discourses*, http://www.transnational.org/forum/meet/2002/Galtung_11SeptandAftermath.html.

41. Paul Rogers, *Losing Control – Global Security in the 21st Century*, 2nd ed, Pluto Press, London, 2002, p 133.

42. Alastair Crooke, 'It is Essential to Talk to the "Terrorists"', London *Guardian*, 10 December 2004.

43. *Indonesia: Violence Unchecked in Central Sulawesi, Militias May Continue to Threaten Peace in Indonesia*, Human Rights Watch, New York, 4 December 2002.

44. Catherine Munro, 'Bali Group, Indonesian Army had "Curious Link"', *The Age*, online edition, 12 December 2002.

45. Aguswandi, 'Politics of Terror in Indonesia', paper presented to CODEP event at St Ethelburga's Centre for Reconciliation and Peace, London, 25 October 2002.

46. *Sinar Harapan* editorial, quoted by BBC Monitoring, 14 April 2004.

47. Jake Lynch and Annabel McGoldrick, op cit (video), 2004.

48. David Loyn, 'Witnessing the Truth', *Open Democracy*, 20 February 2003, http://www.OpenDemocracy.net/debates/article-8-92-993.jsp.

49. Jake Lynch and Annabel McGoldrick, *Peace Journalism Manual*, written for British Council training workshops in Indonesia, October 2000, p 15.

50. Stuart Rees, op cit, p 177.

51. Marshall Rosenberg, *Nonviolent Communication – A Language of Compassion*, PuddleDancer Press, Del Mar, California, 1999, p 15.

52. Peter Acherman and Jack Duvall, *A Force More Powerful – A Century of Non-Violent Struggle*, Palgrave, London, 2000.

53. Stuart Rees, op cit, p 166.

54. Peter Acherman and Jack Duvall, op cit, p 113.

55. Aung San Suu Kyi, *The Voice of Hope* pp 112-13, Penguin, London, 1995.

56. Mark Almond, 'A Housing Boom with No Buyers', *New Statesman*, 31 May 2004.

57. Amnesty International report, May 2004, http://news.amnesty.org/library/Index/EN GEUR700132004.

58. Marc Herold, 'A Dossier on Civilian Victims of US Aerial Bombing of Afghanistan' – details at http://www.cursor.org/stories/civilian_dea ths.htm.

59. 'UN Warns of Afghan "Drug State"', *BBC News* website, 18 November 2004.

60. David Loyn, 'Recognising the Taliban', *Open Democracy*, www.opendemocracy.net , 4 April 2002.

61. Jean-Charles Brisard and Guillaume Dasquie, trans Lucy Rounds, *Forbidden Truth – US-Taliban Secret Oil Diplomacy and the Failed Hunt for Bin Laden*, Thunder's Mouth Press, an imprint of Nation Books, New York, 2001.

62. Julio Godoy, 'US Policy towards Taliban Influenced by Oil', Inter Press Service, 15 November 2001.

63. Ibid.

64. 'Iraq Surveys Show Humanitarian Emergency', *UNICEF Information Newsline*, 12 August 1999.

65. Tom Regan, 'New Iraq Poll: US Seen As "An Occupying Force"', *Christian Science Monitor*, 29 April 2004.

66. Paul Rogers, *Iraq and the War on Terror*, Oxford Research Group, Oxford, 2004, p 35.

67. Charles Clover, 'Power-Sharing Key to Iraq's Political Future', London *Financial Times*, 14 February 2005.

68. Haifa Zangana, 'So Much for Illusions', London *Guardian*, 7 March 2005.

69. Naomi Klein, 'Sorry, George, But Iraq Has Given You the Purple Finger', London *Guardian*, 12 February 2005.

70. Faleh Abdel Jabar, speaking at 'Iraq – Broadening the Agenda', Reporting The World event, London, 20 February 2003.

71. Tabassum Zakaria, 'US Prewar Intelligence Saw Possible Iraq Insurgency', Reuters, 28 September 2004.

72. Abiodun Onadipe and David Lord, *African Media and Conflict*, Conciliation Resources, London, 1999, p 2.

73. Peace Direct website www.peacedirect.org, February 2004.

74. Quoted in Stuart Rees, op cit, p 233.

75. Chaiwat Satha-Anand and Michael True, *The Frontiers of Non-Violence*, International Peace Research Association, Bangkok, p 83.

76. Vincent Ferraro, Ruth C. Lawson Professor of International Politics, Mount Holyoke College – see 'Vinnie's Home Page' at http://www.mtholyoke.edu/acad/intrel/pol 116/realism.htm.

77. Jake Lynch, op cit, 2002, p 16.

78. Mark Leonard, 'Life on Mars' – review of *Paradise and Power: America and Europe in the New World Order* by Robert Kagan (Atlantic Books), *New Statesman*, 17 March 2003.

79. Scilla Elworthy and Paul Rogers, *The 'War On Terrorism': 12-Month Audit and Future Strategy Options*, Oxford Research Group, September 2002, p 15.

80. Dan Smith, *The Atlas of War and Peace*, Earthscan, London, 2003, p 106.

81. Sidik Pramono et al, *Kabar dari Manado*, British Council, Jakarta, 2002.

82. Dylan Mathews, *War Prevention Works*, Oxford Research Group, Oxford, 2001, p 40.

83. Jake Lynch, *The Peace Journalism Option*, Conflict and Peace Forums, Taplow, 1998, p 24.

84. John Paul Lederach, *Building Peace – Sustainable Reconciliation in Divided Societies*, United States Institute of Peace Press, Washington, 1997, p 89.

Chapter 4

War Propaganda

'The first casualty, when war comes, is truth.'[1]

Senator Hiram Johnson's maxim is well known, but does it still hold good? Is 'propaganda' just a longer word for 'lies'? What forms does war propaganda commonly take? How does it articulate with War Journalism and how would Peace Journalism provide an effective counter-strategy in favour of a reliable account of what is really going on?

Topics include:

- The tell-tale signs of propaganda – six reliable indicators
- A case study of propaganda in action – NATO's war on Yugoslavia, 1999
- Lessons learned – techniques for resisting war propaganda
- Whose words are they anyway? How can journalists plot a course through the linguistic swamp of competing propaganda strategies?
- The dangers of accusing someone of 'lying'
- 'Below the intellect' – the psychological dimension of propaganda

By the end of this chapter the reader will be able to:

- Recognise propaganda in War Journalism
- Pick up potential propaganda lines being spun by parties in a conflict
- Apply new tools to overcome propaganda in stories about war
- Understand how propaganda is working in any conflict

War propaganda – how to recognise it

There are a number of key claims in war propaganda which tend to recur in any conflict where media representations and public perceptions may be assumed – by any of the parties – to have some bearing on the outcome:

'We are under threat'

A classic example is the suggestion, discussed in Chapter 1, that Saddam Hussein was equipped and poised to strike with chemical and biological weapons – or to pass them on to others who would.

'We have the support of ...'

- our allies
- the 'international community' or 'the civilised world'
- ordinary people on the 'other side'

'We are taking on "evil-doers"'

Saddam gassed his own people; Milosevic sent paramilitary death squads to do his dirty work. Enemies are often likened to Hitler (the 'Axis of Evil' is reminiscent of the 'Axis Powers' of World War II).

Propaganda occludes important questions about the nature and extent of the danger posed by such figures, and evidence that 'regime change' is not best brought about through violent means.

'We are left with no alternative'

All diplomatic overtures have failed; the enemy will not see reason; the choice is, 'we must deal with this' or 'turn a blind eye'.

'We must save them'

Intervention is presented as humanitarian, the only way of protecting people against their own rulers or the depredations of armed groups.

'We must act *now*'

For example: Saddam Hussein is seeking the ingredients for a nuclear weapon – 'we cannot wait for the final proof to be a mushroom cloud',[2] we must act *now*: non-military means would take too long.

Why are these the staples of war propaganda?

Remember we raised, in the Prologue, the question of whether *meanings* in media are generated at the moment of production, or the moment of reception. One of the most important contributions to reception theory was by the British sociologist, Stuart Hall, in a famous essay called *Encoding/decoding*.[3]

It's a landmark rejection of 'textual determinism', noting that 'decodings do not follow inevitably from encodings'.[4] That would, on the face of it, represent bad news for the authors of propaganda, since it means they cannot control the way their messages are used or interpreted. This part of the process – decoding – is influenced by cultural conditioning from a range of sources, chiefly, Hall argues, the socio-economic position of the reader or viewer.

The dominant ideology is typically inscribed as the 'preferred reading' in a media text, but this is not necessarily the way it is received. 'Dominant' readings, Hall says, are produced by those whose social situation favours the preferred reading; 'negotiated' readings, by those who *inflect* the preferred reading to take account of their social position, and 'oppositional' readings are produced by those whose social position puts them into direct conflict with the preferred reading.

Imagine a car plant, for instance, and it's easy to see how production-line workers on the shop floor might read the business pages of a newspaper very differently from executives in the boardroom above. Readings can be readily negotiated by measuring media messages against individual and social experience. When it comes to 'rogue dictators' with 'weapons of mass destruction', or 'international terrorism', this is much harder to do, however (and socio-economic interests may, in these stories, be divided and contradictory – for a fuller discussion, see Chapter 7).

It means the basis for reception, and any negotiation of the preferred reading, is more clearly *textual*, or perhaps inter-textual. The staples of propaganda, listed here, make up, between them, a *narrative* – one familiar, it so happens, from Hollywood's portrayal of 'how the West was won'. In one classic example, Burt Lancaster's Wyatt Earp gathered allies – notably Kirk Douglas as Doc Holliday – and, when all else had failed, went to the OK Corral for a shoot-out with the ruthless Clanton gang. This was the only way to protect local people, and could no longer be delayed, since the bad guys were gathering for an attack. It ushered in the golden age we know today...

This narrative arc is discernible in US war propaganda at the encoding stage, and, it seems, is highly influential on the way it is decoded by American public opinion. (Not only in America – the entertainment industry is one of the most powerful and pervasive US influences on the rest of the world, including, at least potentially, key conflict arenas such as Iraq. Before the invasion, Hollywood executives served on a White House 'brains trust',[5] conferring with administration officials on ways to help spread the US message at home and abroad.

After it, a veteran commentator on military affairs ruminated:

'Even if the insurgents are successful in forcing the US to abandon its armed struggle, they have much less chance of prevailing against Tom Hanks, Julia Roberts and their kind, who can sustain an occupation of Iraqi homes effortlessly now that satellite TV is almost universally available'.[6])

Cartoon copyright ©Steve Bell/ All Rights Reserved, originally published in the Guardian

The Americans Talk Issues Foundation specialises in detailed Public Interest Polling, prompting respondents to weigh alternatives on a variety of policy issues, rather than just giving a facile yes/no response. The foundation's director, Alan Kay, said he 'fell in love with the American people' when he spent time 'learning what they really thought'.

Kay's findings[7] suggest that Americans do not go to war lightly – he has identified six 'screens' that need to be passed before the public will condone the US use of force:

- rogue leaders
- evidence tying them to heinous crimes
- non-military means exhausted
- military allies (to share the risk and cost)
- a visionary objective (eg turn an enemy into an ally or bring long-term peace to a region)
- early non-military intervention

Kay has shown that if most or all of these stipulations are fully met, support for the use of force can reach a 'consensus level' of 80-90 per cent approval. Between them, Kay's 'screens' describe a narrative of heroic, selfless struggles, gathering and leading a posse of 'good guys' against the 'bad guys', culminating in a happy ending. As a six-point opinion poll test, it seems to hold good across a number of conflicts.

Take, for instance, the 'posse provision' that if the US is to act as Sheriff, it must be seen as leader of a group of allies.

One poll in 2002, when President George W Bush was beginning to make the case for invading Iraq, asked the US public if they supported 'taking military action in Iraq to end Saddam Hussein's rule, even if it meant that US forces might suffer thousands of casualties'. Those who agreed with this proposition comprised 42 per cent of the sample. They were then asked another question about allies. The number still in favour of military action 'even if allies won't join' went down to 18 per cent.[8]

The durability of such factors in swaying public opinion means that propaganda in wartime, at least for the US and its traditional allies, tends to concentrate on Kay's six 'screens'.

Why is it important to recognise propaganda?

It is important for journalists to recognise propaganda, to be able to decode it for themselves, not only in order to offer a reliable account of what is really going on, but also because a 'state of unknowing' may incentivise the provision of more propaganda:

'The media are subject to massive propaganda from the parties involved, and are often without their own knowledge representing the necessary link between the propaganda machinery and the audience. If they are not aware of this potential role themselves, the danger of playing the role as a catalyst for propaganda will be even bigger.'[9]

War propaganda articulates with the reporting conventions of War Journalism, something we can appreciate by considering a propaganda strategy in the round, comparing it with the media view at the time and examining the hidden issues – bits the propaganda was designed to blot out.

A propaganda strategy in action – NATO's war on Yugoslavia, 1999

This extended case study shows how propaganda in NATO's war on Yugoslavia in 1999 was calibrated to mesh with each part of Kay's opinion poll test. We look back at some key propositions at the time:

- Yugoslavia's President, Slobodan Milosevic, was a 'rogue leader'
- he was guilty of ordering Serb forces to commit atrocities against ethnic Albanian civilians
- honest attempts by a 'Contact Group' of governments to broker a diplomatic solution between two antagonists had failed
- US firepower was backed by contributions from allies
- the operation would help to bring the last remaining European redoubt of state socialism 'in from the cold' – establishing a free, democratic order in Serbia and Kosovo
- the Organisation for Security and Co-operation in Europe, the OSCE, had tried an early non-military intervention, the Kosovo Verification Mission, but that proved insufficient
- how NATO won – if it did – and how the bombing achieved its effect

In each case, we examine the contemporary media view of these propositions, along with some issues that remained hidden by the propaganda.

Exercise One
Test the Propaganda

How effective was the propaganda? Can you remember, at this distance:

- Why NATO went to war?
- Why diplomacy failed?
- Whether NATO won?
- Whether its initial aims were achieved in the final agreement?
- How NATO won and how the bombing achieved its effect?

Propaganda: 'military action a last resort'

When British Prime Minister Tony Blair visited NATO HQ in April 1999, he told a press conference:

> 'We took this action after months of political and diplomatic activity in which we tried to persuade Milosevic that he should do the decent civilised thing, stop this repression in Kosovo, get his forces out of there and allow these people to live in peace. It was his decision to refuse that agreement; it was our decision inevitably then to take the military action upon which we are now engaged.'

The media view: blame 'the Serbs'

The media context for this 'political and diplomatic activity', at least in the US and UK, was shadowed by experiences of the Bosnian civil war some years earlier. According to one account, by BBC World presenter Nik Gowing:

'In Bosnia, above all, there is more evidence than many media personnel care to admit that journalists embarked on crusades and became partial. They empathised with the Bosnian government because of personal outrage at Serb aggression. *Prima facie*, this partiality distorted the reporting and led either to a refusal to include certain qualifying facts in stories or to distorting the overall impression.'[10]

The 'crusade' many joined was to try to 'shame' the US into leading a military intervention against 'the Serbs' – the Bosnian Serb forces in Bosnia and their allies in Belgrade – whom they blamed for the conflict. The most dramatic episode was a live satellite link-up in 1994 in which CNN's star reporter, Christiane Amanpour, challenged President Clinton over what she called 'flip-flops' in his administration's policy.

Some set out to correct what they saw as the 'consensus', that all sides were to blame for the war – an analysis they tended to interpret as a claim that 'it was nobody's fault. It was just, somehow, the nature of the region. It was a lie that western governments at that time liked. It got the western world off the hook.'[11]

Other accounts see this as a misrepresentation of the position taken by most 'Western governments':

'Western policy-makers had blamed the Serbs for the war from the start... Yugoslavia was already subject to international sanctions and diplomatic censure, while the Croatian and Bosnian governments enjoyed the support of powerful Western states... US policy throughout the 1990s was ruled by a simplistic dogma that blames one nation, the Serbs, as the origin of evil in the Balkans.'[12]

'An illustration of this is provided by former UN commander General Sir Michael Rose, who describes an aerial tour of Bosnia on which he and an American officer were accompanied by a woman from the US Embassy. Flying toward Tuzla by helicopter, the woman "exclaimed excitedly": "Look at what the criminal Serbs have done." Rose pointed out that the scene below was of Croat villages razed by Bosnian Muslim forces. Arriving later at Mostar, she cried out: "Well, at least this was done by the criminal Serbs", and nearly burst into tears when Rose pointed out that the Croats had been to blame.'[13]

Precisely where this Manichean analysis originated is a moot point, however, and one with substantial implications for our discussion in Chapter 7. There were some in Western governments who tried to convey a more nuanced reality to journalists at the time, but they found it an uphill task, likely to be construed as 'backsliding' in a tug of war. Jenny Ranson, a senior information officer at the UK Foreign Office in the 1990s, recalled:

'The media said very early on that the Croats wore the white hats and the Serbs wore the black hats.

I'm not saying the Serbs were good or bad, but anybody that was there knows that there were atrocities and equal amounts of nationalism on both sides. Yet the government found it very difficult, once the media had got this simplification angle, to say too much that was bad of either the Croats or Muslims, and the Muslims were seen throughout as victims...

The media want to be able to say this is bad, this is good and we're on the side of the good, that's a great danger and that can happen in any number of conflicts.'[14]

War propaganda works because it fits or articulates with the established conventions of War Journalism; where it does not, it is much less effective.

A few years later, the same pattern of events seemed to be unfolding again: 'Kosovo

was viewed... as a fulfilment of hopes that had remained frustrated during most of the Bosnian conflict.'[15]

In this context, media reports of the Contact Group's manoeuvrings over Kosovo tended to be viewed either as a tedious but necessary precursor to 'real' (ie military) action to resolve the situation, or with suspicion, as evading responsibility to confront the villain of the piece, Milosevic. Sheila McVicar, then a senior correspondent with ABC TV, later CNN, characterised it as 'the international community, putzing around, wondering what the hell to do about Kosovo'.[16]

The story was one of a reluctant 'international community' being pushed, regretfully, into disinterested military action, having been left with no choice by the intransigence of 'the Serbs'.

Hidden issues: cultivation of the KLA

At the time both Blair and McVicar were referring to, in 1998, elements, at least, of the international community knew exactly what they wanted to do and were already pursuing a strategy to bring it about. In the process, prospects for diplomacy to deliver a satisfactory outcome were undermined, then destroyed.

Officially, the hopes of the Contact Group for 'decent civilised' behaviour to prevail between Yugoslavia and the Albanian Kosovars were invested in the Kosovo Verification Mission (KVM), sent into the province, in its distinctive bright orange four-wheel-drives, by the OSCE.

This came after a spring offensive by the Kosovo Liberation Army (KLA) and heavy-handed reprisals by the Yugoslav Army, the VJ. Hundreds of thousands of ethnic Albanian civilians left their homes as refugees.

The KVM successfully oversaw the withdrawal of army units, and nearly all the refugees returned to their villages. But the initiative was not even-handed. The monitors were not briefed to do anything about the KLA. Indeed, it subsequently turned out that

the mission had been infiltrated by the CIA, who were training, equipping and preparing the KLA for war.

'It [the KVM] was a CIA front, gathering intelligence on the KLA's arms and leadership', said one [CIA agent]... The KLA has admitted its long-standing links with American and European intelligence organisations. Shaban Shala, a KLA commander now involved in attempts to destabilise majority Albanian villages beyond Kosovo's border in Serbia proper, claimed he had met British, American and Swiss agents in northern Albania in 1996.'[17]

The guerrillas swarmed forward to take over the VJ's revetted positions, from where they intensified their campaign of harassment against Serb targets such as police patrols. In Brussels, NATO's governing body, the North Atlantic Council of ambassadors, was briefed by the KVM that most truce violations were coming from the KLA.

This fact was uncovered long after the war by a major BBC investigation;[18] at the time, it was kept deadly secret, since it risked contradicting the basic propaganda narrative of Serb 'repression' of a defenceless population.

The VJ were sent back into Kosovo to face an opponent gathering strength, with predictable results – a major escalation of what had been, by international standards, a relatively low-intensity civil war. It also enabled the KLA to displace, as internationally recognised representatives of Kosovo's majority population, long-time advocates of non-violence and a negotiated settlement, led by Ibrahim Rugova.

Propaganda: 'It was all Milosevic's fault'

According to the war propaganda, Milosevic brought the bombing on himself by refusing, unreasonably, to sign up for a peace plan devised by the international community – the Rambouillet Accord.

The Milosevic government was brought by ultimatum to Chateau Rambouillet outside Paris to agree an accord under which Kosovo would win autonomy within Serbia and 28,000 NATO troops would police the agreement. The trigger – or pretext – for war came, as Blair averred at NATO, when they refused to sign it.

On 19 March 1999, days before the start of NATO bombing, James B Foley, a State Department media briefing officer, was asked about the prospects for war. He replied:

'The critical factor here is... whether President Milosevic reverses course. We are seeing quite the opposite. He's digging in his heels; he's digging in his forces; he's refusing to negotiate. He's putting himself in a position where he will bear the consequences of his obstinacy.'

The media view: bombing justified

In the UK, the bombing enjoyed editorial support from virtually the entire mainstream written press. Perhaps the most surprising recruit was the *Guardian*, albeit with plenty of dissenting voices on its Op-Ed pages – notably that of veteran war correspondent John Pilger. Pilger's contributions drew a withering counterblast from the paper's diplomatic editor, Ian Black, who reported on the negotiations both from Rambouillet and when they later reconvened in Paris.

The argument between them was about a key plank of the propaganda strategy – was it fair and accurate to see the refusal by President Milosevic to sign up to the draft accord as 'obstinacy', or 'digging in his heels'?

Hidden issues: the Rambouillet text

As Pilger pointed out, the answer depended on what, precisely, Milosevic was being asked to sign up to. He highlighted two provisions in the Rambouillet draft text.

One was, effectively, a mandate for occupation – NATO troops were to enjoy unfettered access not merely to Kosovo but also into and across the whole of the territory of Yugoslavia, where they would, moreover, be immune from local criminal and civil laws. The other was that Kosovo should have an economy run 'in accordance with free market principles'.

Black used a *Guardian* column to accuse Pilger of downright invention. The notion that NATO's real agenda was occupation and what Black called 'unreconstructed international vampire capitalism' was, he declared, 'a canard now circulating among Serb apologists'. But the facts were on Pilger's side. Both provisions were categorically stated in the draft accord. Black – the man responsible for bringing *Guardian* readers their news of the crucial diplomatic exchanges – eventually 'refused to confirm or deny whether he had read the full text' while reporting on the negotiations.[19]

Actually, neither delegation at Rambouillet was prepared to sign up to the accord. The KLA refused because it would have meant them giving up both their arms and their demand for full independence.

By the time the parties came back together in Paris, however, another draft was on the table. This new document contained key concessions to the KLA, who had spent the intervening period in talks with the US State Department. One was that provisions in the original draft for demilitarising Kosovo, including across-the-board disarmament, would not apply to weapons in the hands of Albanian Kosovars, which would instead be classed as private property.

The other concession was in code, albeit a fairly transparent one – that within three years there would be a referendum on Kosovo's final political status, one certain to result in a vote for independence and, therefore, a redrawing of international borders.

This brought the KLA onside but ensured that no Serbian leader could possibly sign up to the accord, as it would have meant losing sovereignty over Kosovo and, with it, historic sites viewed as the cradle of Serb national identity.

It would also have meant Serbs in Kosovo being ruled by a people instrumentalised by the Nazis as their oppressors in World War II – a fear enthusiastically played upon by the baleful narratives of Serb nationalism, in Kosovo no less than in Croatia and Bosnia.

So the propaganda strategy before and during the war concentrated on the areas indicated by Alan Kay's 'six screens' – painting Slobodan Milosevic as a rogue leader, solely or mainly responsible for violence, dogmatically refusing to accede to reasonable demands.

The US was seen to be acting in concert with allies, with whom the cost, both monetary and political, could be shared. Diplomacy – leading to the Rambouillet process – and non-violent intervention, in the shape of the Kosovo Verification Mission, were portrayed as well-intentioned 'honest brokerage', aimed at resolving the conflict but foundering on Serb intransigence.

Propaganda: 'NATO won'

This was the key propaganda claim *after* the war. The ethnic Albanian riots in Kosovo in early 2004 – discussed in the last chapter – led to renewed questioning, notably during a news conference at the British Foreign Office, held as the fifth anniversary of the start of bombing loomed.[20] From the transcript:

Question: 'On Kosovo, is this a sign that the first war that this government has embarked on has actually been less successful in nation-building and peace-making than you expected?'

Foreign Secretary: 'No it is not, it is a sign that there are deep historic divisions going back centuries right across the Balkans, and many of these historic pressures are represented in the divided communities in Kosovo... I would just ask colleagues here to think about the state the Balkans were in and what would have happened if we in our back yard had allowed that kind of ethnic cleansing, brutal genocidal slaughter

to go on unchecked. There was in practice no alternative to us intervening in Kosovo, we were right to do it and were right to stay there.'

The media view: a picture is worth a thousand words

As in the euphoric interlude following the invasion of Iraq, detailed examination of whether the Kosovo campaign could be described as a 'victory' was eclipsed by the powerful images saturating television coverage in particular.

In 2003, the main image was the toppling of Saddam Hussein's statue, conveniently right in front of the hotel used by most international media – prompting a front-page headline in the London *Times* which was typical of many: 'Victory – now win the peace'.

Photograph copyright © Kael Alford/Panos Pictures
A statue of Saddam Hussein in Firdaus Square, Baghdad, is prepared to be toppled

Four years earlier, countless pictures of Kosovo Albanians making victory salutes as NATO troops entered the province seemed to cement in media discourse the notion that NATO had 'won' the war.

Hidden issues: cause and effect

In a statement to Parliament about the Kosovo bombing campaign, Prime Minister Tony Blair told MPs: 'It will have as its minimum objective to curb continued Serbian repression in Kosovo in order to avert a humanitarian disaster.'[21]

But that was before the bombing *triggered* an incipient humanitarian disaster, with hundreds of thousands of Kosovo Albanian refugees on the move into neighbouring Albania and Macedonia. Disaster was only averted when aid resources were diverted from other disasters, notably in sub-Saharan Africa, with consequences that also rightly belong in any humanitarian 'balance of advantage' to be taken into account when testing the arguments for military action:

'The Kosovo toll is now being counted. Urgent relief programmes everywhere else are being crippled; many voluntary repatriation programmes are being cut back for lack of funding; aid boats are being diverted from Africa to the Adriatic; and programmes aimed to prevent future crises are being slashed.'[22]

'Between March and June 1999, the UN High Commission for Refugees (UNHCR) received funds from donor countries equivalent to a weekly budget of US$10 million for an estimated 800,000 Kosovar refugees. At the same time, UNHCR was able to raise only US$1.3 million of an annual US$8 million appeal for nearly half a million Sierra Leonean refugees in Guinea and Liberia, most of whom have fled almost unimaginable atrocities.

In other words, in 1999 UNHCR spent about 11 cents per refugee per day in Africa. The average of US$1.23 spent

per refugee per day in the Balkans was ten times the amount spent on African refugees.'[23]

Many of the Kosovo refugees brought with them harrowing tales of 'ethnic cleansing' at the hands of Serbian paramilitaries. Warplanes on the attack three miles above were, effectively, unassailable. The predictable – and predicted – result was for Belgrade to strike, with its trademark lack of discrimination, at those it blamed for calling down NATO's bombs on Serb heads.

While some refugee stories were doubtless true (no one leaves home and flees to an uncertain future without good reason) other claims, and the extrapolations built upon them by supporters of the war, were false, as later investigations showed.

There was no 'herding' of thousands of people into the sports stadium at Pristina. Bodies were not taken to be burned in the blast furnaces of a local mine. There were no 'gang rape houses'. All these claims were peddled and repeated in media reports as part of the propaganda barrage.

The estimate given by US Defense Secretary William Cohen, that as many as 100,000 men 'may have been killed'[24] was at least one order of magnitude too high, and perhaps two. There was also plenty of evidence – albeit, at best, a marginal factor in most reporting – that some refugees were fleeing the bombing itself:

'The hundreds of thousands of Serbs who fled the bombing were... determinedly ignored by British journalists', though there were exceptions. 'A report in the *Sunday Times* (28 March), for example, noted that some refugees had fled "the threat of NATO attacks", interviewing one woman who "looked bewildered when asked if Serbian troops had driven her out. 'There were no Serbs,' she said. 'We were frightened of the bombs'."

The *Telegraph*... reported that "most residents [of Pristina] say they are fleeing of their own accord and are not being forced out at gunpoint" (1 April). This revelation was buried in the 22nd paragraph of an article headed: "Thousands expelled at gunpoint"[25].'

A US Congressional delegation, led by senior Republican Jim Saxton, visited Yugoslavia with the express purpose of piercing the fog of media coverage and evaluating the situation for themselves. They found that 'some one-third of the Albanian and other refugees appear, in fact, to be fleeing further into Serbia, to avoid the Kosovo Liberation Army... there is no doubt that NATO bombings have contributed heavily – perhaps overwhelmingly – toward the outflow'.[26]

At the outset, Blair said a 'failure to act' would have meant 'we would have to deal with hundreds of thousands of refugees'. The rationale for the bombing had been to avert this, remember – a cause that was lost almost straightaway. But this brought a classic example of propaganda sleight-of-hand – the redefinition of war aims.

George Robertson spent the war as British Defence Secretary; later, ennobled as Lord Robertson of Port Ellen, he became Secretary-General of NATO. He recalled:

> 'Just two weeks ago, I went again to Kosovo, on the first anniversary of Operation Allied Force, NATO's air campaign to end and reverse the ethnic cleansing of the Albanian community.'[27]

Almost unnoticed by the watching media, 'avert' transmogrified into 'reverse'. Indeed the Albanians did eventually go back to their homes in Kosovo, but the end of the war saw the exodus of as many as 200,000 Serbs and other ethnic minorities, condemned to life as refugees, either elsewhere in Kosovo or elsewhere in Serbia.

The continuing salience and appeal of extreme nationalist politics in Serbia owes much to this injustice, and makes any progress towards political agreement on Kosovo's future correspondingly less likely – as discussed in the last chapter.

Public opinion

There are limits, notably limits of time, to the capacity of war propaganda to hold public approval for the use of force, as the ICM findings on the Iraq war, adduced in Chapter 1, suggest. There is considerable resonance in the words of one of the most enduring journalistic comic creations, Lord Copper, proprietor of the fictional *Daily Beast*:

> 'The British public has no interest in a war which drags on indecisively. A few sharp victories, some conspicuous acts of personal bravery on the Patriot side, and a colourful entry into the capital. That is the *Beast* Policy for the war... We shall expect the first victory about the middle of July.'[28]

Alastair Campbell, then Downing Street press secretary, said in a lecture after the Kosovo bombing that 'the only battle NATO might lose was the battle for hearts and minds... that would have meant NATO ending and losing the war'.[29]

The fact is that, as the bombing dragged on into a third month, this battle was indeed being lost. A Pew Research Center poll found that, in mid-April 1999, Americans approved of President Clinton's handling of foreign policy by 51 to 39 per cent. A month later, as the war dragged on indecisively, the same poll showed a much closer margin at 46 to 43 per cent.

In propaganda terms, the campaign was headed in the wrong direction. NATO needed a way out, and turned to other players, notably the Russians, to help provide it. The diplomatic initiative launched by former Russian Prime Minister Viktor Chernomyrdin and former Finnish President Mahti Ahtisaari led to the drafting of yet another version of a political framework for Kosovo and agreement for troops to police it. These were to be under UN mandate, with a Russian contingent under their own separate command in their own area – something NATO had previously resisted.

This was adopted by the G8 at Konigswinter, and the EU in Cologne, in June; and was later passed by the UN Security Council as Resolution 1244. It differed from earlier versions in one crucial respect – the provision for a referendum on independence for Kosovo was dropped. In its place was a mandate to establish 'substantial self-government', with the Rambouillet Accord taken 'into full account' – diplomatese for 'kicked into the long grass'.

This was essential to getting Belgrade's agreement to pull its forces out of Kosovo, and to avoiding a UN veto from Moscow – but it entailed NATO dropping the demand that had set the bar for any agreement too high for the Yugoslav leadership to surmount.

Propaganda: 'Bombing targeted fielded forces'

The propaganda line about the bombing itself was that it was focused on the alleged perpetrators of 'brutality' against Kosovo's ethnic Albanian population:

> 'Today is another busy day, and our operations are ongoing with even greater success against fielded forces. Our operational tempo and effectiveness continues to increase. And I believe that our momentum is building with encouraging pace.'[30]

The rival propaganda operations gave contrasting assessments as to how effective this campaign, against the 'fielded forces', really was. At one point, NATO claimed 'accuracy of 96.6%',[31] in contrast to the estimate given after the bombing by the Yugoslav commander on the ground:

> 'Lt. General Nchojsa Pavkovic... claimed that NATO only destroyed 13 tanks, six armoured personnel carriers, and 27 artillery pieces.'[32]

What nothing could quite dispel was the image of the Yugoslav army rolling out of Kosovo, its ordnance rather conspicuously intact. On NATO's own estimate, they still had '47,000 troops and nearly 800 tanks, armoured personnel carriers and artillery pieces'.[33]

Hidden issues: battering 'the Serbs' into submission

Actually, there were two, simultaneous, bombing campaigns going on. Foremost in NATO propaganda was the one mentioned, against the 'fielded forces'. But this campaign was ineffective and, in truth, never expected to be otherwise. Months, even years, of bombardment would have been necessary to be a serious threat to the ground forces of the VJ, provided they remained under cover.

The other campaign was aimed at battering the Serb population and the political leadership into submission. When NATO started hitting power stations in April, bow-tied Pentagon spokesman Kenneth Bacon told reporters: 'This is a new class of target... we think the Serbs should put pressure on their leadership to end this'.[34]

US General Michael Short, in charge of sending out the bombers from Aviano airbase in Italy, remarked later that 'most of our political leaders don't really understand air power'.[35] During the war, he briefed the *New York Times* as to the tactics which *could* be expected to work:

> 'I think no power to your refrigerator, no gas to your stove, you can't get to work because the bridge is down – the bridge on which you hold your rock concerts and you all stood with targets on your heads. That needs to disappear at three o'clock in the morning... I think you begin to ask, "Hey Slobo, what's this all about? How much more of this do we have to withstand?"'[36]

Subsequently, General Wesley Clark, who had overall command of the campaign, told the BBC's Mark Urban he had authorised the bombers to hit 'phase three' (civilian) targets – against NATO's rules which required specific advance approval from the political leaders of member states.[37]

Thousands of industrial facilities were destroyed, including oil plants and chemical works from which toxic substances were released, poisoning the environment for generations to come. Roads, railways, waterworks and power stations were on General Clark's list – causing damage estimated at $100 billion.[38]

'Why did Milosevic finally cave in?' asks Timothy Garton Ash, in a retrospective on the campaign.[39] For manifold reasons, he suggests, but one above all: 'NATO... started destroying Belgrade's electrical power grids. Not just disabling them for a few hours with graphite bombs, as they had earlier done, but demolishing them.

This damaged Milosevic's central command and control system, and the morale of his population. It also meant that patients on life-support systems and babies in hospital incubators had their power cut off'. Not an aspect the propagandists were keen to draw attention to at the time.

Lessons learned

Phillip Knightley, author of *The First Casualty*, the classic history of war reporting, laments the 'weak collective memory' which he blames for journalists' propensity to fall for the same propaganda techniques over and over again:

> 'The military, on the other hand, is an institution and goes on forever. Wars are studied, lessons are learnt, systems are devised, tested and polished. The British Ministry of Defence has a manual, updated after every war, which serves to guide the way it will handle its relationship with the media in wartime. What newspaper or television company does anything similar?'[40]

DISCUSSION: How can journalists continue to offer a reliable account of what is really going on, in the face of sophisticated and determined war propaganda?

Firstly, there needs to be an acknowledgement, as Phillip Knightley implies, that this is an issue for a whole news organisation, not just individual journalists.

We argue throughout this book (see particularly Chapter 7) that news as presently conceived and organised is *structurally* and *systematically* biased in favour of War Journalism. What is needed is a *deliberate creative strategy* to restore the discourses and perspectives that are, in the normal run of things, routinely marginalised – a strategy we call Peace Journalism. The enlightenment of a handful of individuals, even senior ones, cannot, on its own, make up for this.

In the words of Uri Avnery, a former magazine editor, now head of the Israeli peace group Gush Shalom – 'the real influence of the media is not in [individual] articles, it is in the way you write the news. The terminology of the news, the angle of reporting'.[41]

DEVELOPING STRATEGIES TO RESIST PROPAGANDA

Some suggestions and questions:

- REMIND readers and audiences of past occasions when war propaganda turned out to be misleading – perhaps keep a file on them in the newsroom.
- Have you been able to CHECK the information for yourself? If not, say so – and that what you are saying may not be true.
- Do not keep REPEATING claims that have not been independently verified.
- Explain any RESTRICTIONS that may have affected the material or information you have been able to gather.
- Be on the lookout for SHIFTING WAR AIMS.
- Be wary of claims about CAUSE AND EFFECT. For example, was the NATO bombing in Kosovo a response to the exodus of refugees, as per the propaganda, or vice versa?
- Are OUTSIDE PARTIES disinterested mediators, or (perhaps secretly) complicit actors in a conflict, with their own interests?
- Be prepared to go back and INVESTIGATE days, weeks, months and years after a CLAIM has been made.
- Check your words – are you using the LANGUAGE of the military, the authorities or a particular group to describe an event?
- Is your reporting DEMONISING – blaming one person or group for everything, or labelling them as EVIL?

• Remind readers and audiences of past war propaganda

War propaganda, because it is designed to keep hitting the same 'buttons' in public opinion, has a tendency to repeat itself. The narrative is familiar, only the details are changed.

Often, claims are made which are difficult or impossible to check. Journalists can be called on to respond to a breaking story before it can be fully investigated. In these circumstances, they cannot say the claims are false. What *can* be given is a 'health warning' about similar claims in the past that turned out to be misleading.

Nothing better exemplifies this than the history of claims, in connection with Iraq and its 'weapons of mass destruction', about drone aircraft.

1997: 'Western and Iraqi intelligence sources' told the London *Sunday Times* about an unmanned drone, originally a Polish-designed crop-spraying aircraft, adapted by Iraq to drop anthrax. The report quotes Ken Munson of *Jane's Dictionary of Unmanned Aircraft*: 'If Saddam could get such a plane over the target area, he could well just use the chemical hopper' to dispense deadly germs.

There was one crucial question Munson was never asked by the reporters, however – the range of the plane, an M18 Dromeda (335 miles or about 540 km).[42] If it managed to stop and refuel several times *en route* to London or Washington, it could be a threat to 'our cities', as the *Sunday Times* and other reports suggested. If not...

To recall this episode might have helped in unpicking subsequent propaganda claims on the same lines.

2003: In the weeks leading up to war, reporters in Baghdad demanded that their Iraqi handlers take them to see sites identified as suspect by US or British intelligence. Lindsey Hilsum, diplomatic editor of *Channel 4 News*, recalled:

> 'The Americans suddenly got very excited about a drone, which they said the weapons inspectors had hidden in their report but this drone was a terrible threat to the future of the world.
>
> Now, the drone was like something out of *Aeromodellers Monthly*, it was made out of the fuselage of an aircraft, it was done up with duct tape and it had an engine which, as one American reporter put it, "was smaller than a weed-whacker"...

We actually had pictures from the November trade fair [in Baghdad] where they were trying to sell these drones to other Arab countries and they were painted fluorescent pink, so that people would notice them. Now the Americans were telling us that this drone was a threat to the security of the world and it was only when we got to that point that we felt bold enough to say, hang on – I don't think so.'[43]

- # Have you been able to check the information for yourself?

Checking propaganda claims against information from other sources takes time, and time is at a premium in global news, when events are increasingly covered live or very shortly after they have occurred. Nik Gowing labels this 'the tyranny of real time'. He explains:

'Through an ever-expanding spectrum of delivery systems, notably satellites, we have more information coming in text, video and sound from more parts of the world than ever before. It is being delivered in real time, or as near as damn it. It is the age of *now*. Not two hours, two days or two weeks hence – but now. By the minute or by the hour – and from wherever you are – you can select which crisis you want to dip into or get an update on, and you can select from the proliferation of video or text outlets providing it.'[44]

What can be done? BBC correspondent Allan Little – one of a handful of western journalists in Baghdad during the 1991 Gulf War – spent the early months of 2003 stationed with the American military in Kuwait.

Propaganda claims were made on several occasions that an 'uprising' was taking place in Basra against the Iraqi forces holding the city. Little was, inevitably, expected to comment in real time.

But he took the opportunity to issue a warning – if this was really happening, it would be a highly significant political prize for the invading forces, and backing for the propaganda claim that they would be welcomed by Iraqis as 'liberators'. It might even help to convince other Iraqis that 'the game was up' and they should lay down their arms.

Given the obvious incentive, therefore, to *lead us to believe* Basra was rising, he said we should treat the claims with caution, at least until verified from within the city itself.

Little later recalled: 'I kept thinking to myself, we only have the British army view on this, so we have to be very careful.'[45] He had 'this feeling that so far we are all inescapably part of someone's war effort'[46] – an experience he described as 'unsettling'.

He was all too well aware, he said, of the British military concept 'Information Operational Effect' – deliberate manipulation of the media as a military tactic. 'The Coalition War plan demands that by the time the US tanks reach the gates of Baghdad, the Iraqi regime will know – because they will have seen it on satellite television – that their authority has collapsed everywhere else in the country.'

At the same time, the Iraqis were just as aware of the value of pictures and were prepared to ferry journalists around Baghdad each day to show the latest devastating effects of Coalition bombing.

Allan Little's three-point plan for dealing with propaganda:

- accept that you, the journalist, will be used by both sides
- mediate the output to put rolling news in context
- ask yourself – why is this person telling me this? What is their interest?

He raises a number of concerns about 24-hour television news,[47] notably the 'strapline' across the bottom of the screen, intended to add to the sense of urgency with which new developments are brought to the viewer, but unavoidably stripping those developments of any context.

In the example discussed here, the strapline 'Uprising in Basra' would appear. Journalists based at Centcom, the military briefing centre in Qatar, would see Sky, Fox and BBC news with the sound turned down. So they would respond to the strapline, rather than to whatever cautions were being issued, by presenters or reporters, about its veracity or the lack of any confirmation.

They would then immediately go after quotes from briefing officers, so they could file their own copy to add to what was, apparently, a breaking story. Of course, the briefing officers were – given the nature of that story and its propaganda value – happy to oblige.

• Do not repeat claims that have not been independently verified

Propaganda works in the same way as advertising, using the same techniques – association and repetition. Advertisers associate their product, service or brand with certain images, ideas or values; then the message is repeated often enough for the rest of us to make the association for ourselves.

Alastair Campbell once said it was only when 'insiders' – journalists and politicians – had become thoroughly bored with hearing about any given message that one could be sure it was getting through to the public.

Repetition is the key. Time and again, in propaganda used to justify the invasion of Iraq in 2003, its proponents would demand that Saddam Hussein 'come clean' over the whereabouts of weapons stocks produced before the Gulf War of 1991 which UN inspection teams had failed to trace. A British government 'dossier'[48] demanded that Iraq account for:

*   any remaining VX nerve agent
*   10,000 litres of anthrax
*   6,500 chemical shells

It was a list that found its way into many a

graphics 'stack' on television news – an attractive presentational device for a package or illustrated studio 'intro', and one that is fairly labour-intensive to produce. (For these reasons, graphics stacks, once commissioned and made, have a habit of reappearing at frequent intervals.)

Formulating a political message into handy 'bullet points' suggests an intention that they *be* repeated, serving as a convenient shorthand for the case against Saddam Hussein. In fact, repeating the list proved to be so convenient that the *likelihood* of any such weapons remaining, and posing a threat, was very seldom scrutinised.

The word 'litres', referring to a liquid, in the British government's list, held an important clue. Fully five years earlier, a Washington think-tank report by Anthony Cordesman, a former high-ranking soldier and Pentagon official, now an independent military analyst, had concluded:

> 'Anthrax spores are extremely hardy and can achieve 65% to 80% lethality against untreated patients for years. Fortunately, Iraq does not seem to have produced dry, storable agents and only seems to have deployed wet Anthrax agents, which have a relatively limited life...
>
> The shelf-life and lethality of Iraq's weapons is unknown, but it seems likely that the shelf-life was limited. In balance, it seems probable that any agents Iraq retained after the Gulf War [of 1991] now have very limited lethality, if any.'[49]

In one sense, the UK government's list was beside the point. The point was not that Iraq might have some chemical weapons lying around; the case being made in war propaganda – the case for war, rather than allowing more time for inspections – was that Iraq was in a position to use those weapons to pose a threat; a threat that was, in the words of President George W Bush, 'great and growing'.

Robin Cook, then Leader of the House of Commons, resigned from the British cabinet on the eve of war, with these words, to a rapt audience of MPs:

> 'Iraq probably has no weapons of mass destruction in the commonly understood sense of the term – namely a credible device capable of being delivered against a strategic city target.'[50]

On both these counts, the propaganda claims were misleading. Reporting them once brings a duty to test them against other authoritative assessments. If they are to be repeated subsequently, they must at least be accompanied by some form of words giving the gist of those assessments, in order to caution the audience that the claims may be misleading. As a minimum:

> '…but other experts say Iraq's chemical and biological weapons have almost certainly lost their deadly effect because they were made so long ago.'

Or:

> '…but other experts say, even if such weapons do still exist, it's extremely unlikely that Iraq possesses the means to use them.'

Not difficult – but much needed.

• Explain any restrictions on news-gathering

The BBC was one of a number of news organisations to draw attention to the circumstances in which news could be gathered:

> 'The movements of those reporting from Baghdad are restricted and their reports are monitored by the Iraqi authorities. Reporters with the US and British military are restricted in what they can say about precise locations or military plans.'[51]

However, this could not, by itself, make up

for the lopsidedness *built into* the pattern of news-gathering by the twin-track US military media strategy – the system of *embedding* reporters with forward units on the one hand, and of creating on the other hand a hostile environment for journalists seeking to work as so-called 'unilaterals', with media workers being killed and injured in unprecedented numbers.

The normally supine European Broadcasting Union was moved to complain, through its Secretary-General, Jean Stock:

> 'US Central Command policy is now actively restricting independent newsgathering from Southern Iraq. Reporters and camera crews who put their lives at risk have been detained by American and British troops and returned to Kuwait.'

Organisations from countries not participating in the American-led coalition appeared to be particularly subject to this treatment: 'As a result, journalists are now exposed to a much greater risk and the coalition policy targets the quality of their reporting.'[52]

Embedding as a propaganda strategy

Phillip Knightley believes the whole system of embedding was devised as a response to presentational difficulties arising from the Kosovo crisis. Bromides from Brussels, given out at daily briefings by NATO spokesman Jamie Shea, would invariably be 'trumped' by stronger visual material showing death and destruction on the ground:

> 'The military looked around and said… we don't want them writing stories about people being bombed and shot and murdered, so this time we are going get over that by embedding the correspondents with the military so that all they can write about is the activities of the troops that they are embedded with.'[53]

Above all, the embedding system provided a steady stream of compelling pictures, capable of competing with, and displacing from the top of television news bulletins, the images being sent from crews based in Baghdad, of human suffering caused by American and British bombs and shells.

Those images were, in any case, sanitised, at least in the programmes watched by 'home' audiences in the 'coalition of the willing' – thus weakening them in what was now a 24-hour competition for airtime with output from the embeds.

Such restrictions originate in considerations of 'taste and decency'. But they cannot avoid becoming a factor in political calculations about the 'saleability' of war as a policy option. If the reality of people being killed and blown apart is to be kept out of viewers' living rooms, it must become a factor to be taken into account when planning any propaganda battle for 'hearts and minds'. One prominent Australian TV newsreader reflected a widespread unease at the feeling of inescapable complicity:

'I feel coverage of, for instance, the Gulf war should reflect the brutality and horror – not skirt around the edges because some viewers might be traumatised.

Withholding the full effect of what conditions are like, presenting instead a more clinical, cleaner set of pictures, is tantamount to telling half the story.'[54]

There are signs that the arrival of non-western television news organisations, led by Al Jazeera and constrained by no such inhibitions, is leading others to think again. Mark Damazer, the BBC's deputy head of news, told a London conference, shortly after the invasion, that the now readily available contrast with BBC World television output posed a 'significant problem'. The BBC's own coverage had, in this respect, been 'too conservative':

'We've been too static and our credibility with international audiences is on the line. BBC World is showing one thing and other channels around the world are showing something different.'[55]

• Go back and investigate after a claim has been made

Journalists covering the civil war in Nepal grapple with a situation familiar to many colleagues in many countries. They receive regular reports from military authorities about violent incidents taking place 'up country'. They suspect that, in many cases, the press releases are propaganda – intended to mislead. They know they should go and check the army's account against their own information gathered first hand from the scene. But trips to the front line are difficult, dangerous and expensive.

In addition to these practical problems, editors and proprietors are aware that for any one of them to make a habit of investigating these incidents too closely would risk being seen as going 'out on a limb', and invite political repercussions.

These were some of the issues the not-for-profit Himal Association considered when establishing, in 1997, the Nepal Centre for Investigative Journalism (NCIJ). It has its own independent sources of funding from overseas grants, and its reports are open to all media to reproduce.

In 2002, one of them exposed the truth behind army claims to have killed 67 Maoists in the Kalikot district in what it termed 'encounters'. Some months later, the NCIJ director, Mohan Mainali, travelled far into remote western Nepal to speak to survivors, piecing together information to conclude:

> 'It is clear that the killing was a tragic combination of mistaken identity and other errors… proof of the senselessness of the violence that has been unleashed on the Nepali people in the name of Maoism and of the callousness of officialdom.'[56]

This particular 'encounter' had taken place when soldiers stormed a hut being used by a work gang building a civil airfield runway. The authorities stuck to the line that the 'fathers and sons' of bereaved women, interviewed by Mainali, 'were terrorists'. But they were, in fact, innocent bystanders.

Not all incidents can be so painstakingly investigated; we cannot wait to do so before reporting them. As with propaganda claims about Iraq's flock of deadly drones, however, this particular investigation now forms a *prism* through which any fresh claim can be

assessed. It makes it legitimate to remind readers and audiences that, when similar incidents have been independently investigated, the truth has sometimes proved at variance with official accounts.

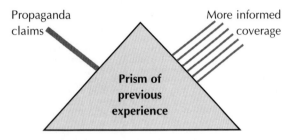

Propaganda claims ... Prism of previous experience ... More informed coverage

Mainali's findings regularly cropped up, over the next couple of years, in some highly influential international media.[57] Even though he went to press fully six months after the event, it was still worth doing.

• Check your words – whose are you using?

'Encounter' is one of a group of words characteristic of accounts, given by military authorities the world over, of incidents in which people have been killed. It encodes a key propaganda claim – that soldiers only kill people when they are legitimately engaged in battle.

One report from Baghdad, screened on BBC television news a few months after the invasion of Iraq, gave the number of US and UK troop losses since the official end of 'major combat operations' – along with 'an unknown number of Iraqis killed in crossfire and general lawlessness'.

This is pure propaganda. Firstly, the number was 'unknown' to the Coalition authorities only because, as General Tommy Franks made clear, it would be politically inconvenient to give their own estimate: 'We don't do body counts.'[58]

In response to this stance, the Iraq Body Count project was already monitoring and collating reports of Iraqi casualties, and producing regularly updated figures.[59] Later, a population survey published in the leading scientific journal, *The Lancet,* gave an estimate of 100,000 civilian deaths due to the war – most of them directly from the invasion.[60]

Secondly, the term 'crossfire' implies that those killed were unfortunates who accidentally got in the way of exchanges between US-led occupying troops and armed belligerents on the other side – not, as in most reported cases to that point, unarmed demonstrators or civilians who 'looked as if they might be about to attack'. It glosses over the calculus behind bombing and shelling raids on densely populated urban areas – that civilians, who inevitably find themselves in the firing line, are expendable.

Exercise Two
Decoding Propaganda

- Come up with your own list of propaganda terms, from a conflict you are familiar with.
- How are they misleading?
- What other words would you use in their place?
- How would you explain the facts so as to avoid misleading readers and audiences?

Nepalese journalists produced a glossary of propaganda terms with guidance as to how they should be treated. This was a useful example of a deliberate creative strategy to avoid becoming the unwitting instrument of war propaganda. Some of the words:

- *Clash* – another word sometimes used to cover up killings of civilians. Journalist needs to ask, were people armed, how many were injured, how many were killed?

- *Collateral damage* – a military term used to 'soften' language about death. If used, must always be attributed to them. Literally means killing people.

- *Crossfire* – another military term again used to 'soften' language about death. If used, must always be attributed to them. Check if people have been killed or injured, and if they were armed.

- *Freedom Fighter* – an armed group fighting for independence from the state. Implies that they are the 'good guys'. One man's freedom fighter is another man's terrorist. Better to find a more neutral term.

- *Martyr* – a word some religious groups use to describe the death or suicide of their members. Can be disrespectful to those who died in the incident. Glorifies violence and tends to immortalise the death.

- *Massacre* – one of the most misused words. Usually used by one party to demonise the other. It means the deliberate killing of people known to be unarmed and defenceless. Are we sure we have all the facts to prove both the intention and the defencelessness of those killed? Or do we not know? Might these people have died in battle?

- *Softening up...the front line* – a military term used to describe attacking the enemy. Journalists need to ask more questions – what does the military mean, what was destroyed, were people killed?

- *'Terrorism' and 'terrorists'* – special care required. The inbuilt bias in the word 'terrorist' is well known – the BBC World Service, and Reuters news agency, to name but two, do not use it, except when quoting someone. One senior Indonesian news editor gave the following account of his paper's efforts to keep open vital distinctions that risked being collapsed into the catch-all term 'terrorism':

'We don't want to generalise, using

terms like "Muslim radicals"; "Muslim fundamentalists", or "Muslim militants". Being militant or radical does not mean you're a terrorist. We have been very careful to make this distinction.'[61]

DISCUSSION: Come up with a 'neutral', dictionary-style definition of 'terrorism'. Could you apply it neutrally, so that all situations meriting this description could be reported as 'terrorism'?

Any dictionary-style definition of terrorism would have to include three elements:

- violence being used – just *thinking* you would like to, say, bomb the UN is not terrorism
- directed against civilians – shooting at an enemy soldier is not terrorism
- aiming to bring about a political effect – senseless killing, as when someone 'goes postal' with a gun in the workplace, is not terrorism either

The meaning of the term 'political effect' almost certainly includes intimidating people into doing or accepting something they could not be *persuaded* to do or accept by non-violent means.

Now compare that with the pronouncements, quoted above, from Kenneth Bacon and General Michael Short, about how they expected NATO's bombing campaign in 1999 to be effective in ejecting Yugoslavian forces from Kosovo. This was bombing of civilian infrastructure to get the Serbs to 'put pressure' on their leadership to give in.

This could be described as 'terrorist'. But could journalists get away with using the word 'terrorism' in this context? ('NATO HQ, Brussels – More terrorism by NATO today…') If not, then it cannot be applied even-handedly. And that being so, should it be applied at all?

Perhaps better to stick to descriptive terms – 'bombers', 'suicide hijackers', 'armed group' 'paramilitaries'.

Truth and lies

DISCUSSION: If you see a piece of propaganda which you believe is misleading, should you call it a 'lie'? What would you expect to happen if you did?

Have you noticed that when someone is accused of lying, there is a giant sucking noise? That's the sound of the real issues disappearing 'down the gurgler'.

This is what Andrew Gilligan of the BBC found when he said, live on air, that the British government included a claim about Iraq's weapons, in a published dossier, even though:

'We've been told by one of the senior officials in charge of drawing up that dossier that, actually, the government probably knew that 45 minute figure was wrong, even before it decided to put it in.'[62]

The claim was that Iraq could launch an attack with chemical or biological weapons within 45 minutes of an order being given. The government, at least at the level of officials, knew it was unreliable – based on a single source – and they knew it was misleading, since the dossier did not spell out that the claim only related to battlefield weapons, not to those capable of menacing any other country. But the allegation that they *probably knew it was wrong* went further: it was effectively a charge of lying.

This facilitated what Robin Cook called 'the Alastair Campbell feint'[63] – the government's then communications chief used it, with the help of friendly newspapers, to turn the tables on Gilligan, and transform the issue into one of BBC reporting and editorial governance. The feint effectively obscured the government's own responsibility for so representing the intelligence as to place on it, in the words of the later Butler report, 'more weight... than it could bear'.

Outright lies – some rare examples

Propaganda seldom depends on outright lies. But two stories used to sell the Gulf War of 1991 were, indeed, complete fabrications:

- *The 'dead babies' story:* A meeting of US Congress members heard harrowing testimony from a witness claiming to have fled her job as a nurse in the main hospital in Kuwait City. Occupying Iraqi troops, she claimed, were turning premature babies out of incubators and watching them die. It transpired that she was the daughter of the Kuwaiti ambassador to Washington, who had not been back home for several years; she had been 'put up' by the PR firm Hill and Knowlton. Investigations after the war proved her allegations groundless.

- *'Troops massing on Saudi border':* Stormin' Norman Schwarzkopf, in his autobiography *It Doesn't Take a Hero*, remembers attending a US cabinet meeting at Camp David to discuss responses to Iraq's invasion of Kuwait. Colin Powell – then his boss as chairman of the Joint Chiefs of Staff – told him: 'I think we could go to war if they invaded Saudi Arabia. I doubt if we would go to war over Kuwait.' Then came news of Pentagon satellite photographs purporting to show a quarter of a million Iraqi troops massing on the Saudi border, ready to pounce. After the war, the Pentagon said the claim had been 'mistaken'.

The influence of these stories on political debate about the war at the time bore out the comment attributed to Marie de Medici, Queen Consort of France in the 17th century: 'It is enough that a lie is believed for three days. It has then served its purpose.'

Both were later exposed by journalists.

Many reporters who visited Kuwait after the Iraqi army withdrew were keen to follow up the babies-and-incubators story; all pronounced it groundless. A reporter from a small US provincial newspaper, the *St Petersburg Times* in Florida, commissioned her own satellite pictures of the Iraqi-Saudi border from Soyuz Karta, a recently privatised agency of the Soviet military apparatus. They showed only empty desert, the roads covered with undisturbed sand.

These were exceptions in being entirely without foundation; but they are part of the record which should make us cautious about claims from similar sources in any subsequent wars.

Partial accounts

More typical is the partial account or representation which is not, on closer inspection, a lie. According to one well-known definition, propaganda is simply 'the deliberate and systematic attempt to shape perceptions, manipulate cognitions, and direct behaviour to achieve a response that furthers the desired intent of the propagandist.'[64] What does it mean, to 'manipulate cognitions'? Think of the Gestalt diagram reproduced earlier – propaganda may get us to see only the young woman, or only the old woman, depending on the desired effect. Two examples:

- *'Kosovo situation grave':* NATO Secretary-General Lord Robertson, in the speech quoted in the Kosovo case study earlier in this chapter, went on to attack what he called 'revisionism' in assessments of the Alliance's attack on Yugoslavia. He said: 'By March of 1999, Serb oppression had already driven almost 400,000 people from their homes.'

  He omitted to mention that, by March of 1999, nearly all the refugees had gone back home again. In January of that year, a report by the German Foreign Ministry found: 'The often feared humanitarian catastrophe threatening the Albanian population has been averted.' In the larger cities 'public life has since returned to relative normality'.[65]

Nothing in the speech was actually untrue – but can it have been anything other than a deliberate attempt to mislead?

- *'Iraq–al-Qaeda contacts':* George Tenet, US director of central intelligence, wrote to the Senate Intelligence Committee that Saddam Hussein and al-Qaeda had 'senior level contacts... going back a decade' – a claim subsequently repeated many times by proponents of war on Iraq, including President George W Bush and Vice-President Dick Cheney.

  The September 11th Commission subsequently found that 'while [Osama] bin Laden was in Sudan between 1991 and 1996, a senior Iraqi intelligence officer made three visits to Sudan, and that he had a meeting with bin Laden in 1994' – in other words, there were contacts, and they did go back a decade, but there they ceased. The Commission found 'no evidence of a collaborative relationship'.[66]

  Use of the words 'going back a decade' must have been intended to mislead – to make us think the contacts continued over that decade. Because the phrase can have two meanings, it is not actually untrue.

Crucially, if propaganda is not the same as 'lies', then 'reporting the facts' or 'telling the truth' will not do as a corrective. What is needed is some organised form of reflexivity, identifying cumulative patterns of omission and marginalisation – and *which* facts, which *parts* of the truth, we therefore need to confirm and bring back into the central thrust of our coverage, in order to counter distortion intended to mislead.

LM vs ITN: the lost debate

In 1992, camera crews from the British television news company ITN went to what is now the Bosnian Serb Republic, to follow up press reports about 'concentration camps'.

They visited two separate locations – Omarska and Trnopolje – between the towns of Prijedor and Banja Luka. The first was a *bona fide* prison, a former factory where hundreds of inmates – Muslim refugees from Bosnian villages and towns now under the control of Bosnian Serb forces – were held under the watchful eye of armed guards. They were locked in, and plainly terrified.

Those at Trnopolje were not under lock and key, but had been forced to come for protection. Paddy Ashdown, then leader of Britain's Liberal Democrats and later Bosnia's High Representative, wrote, after his own visit:

> 'They have gathered here because they have to go somewhere... Muslim extremists pressurise the men to join up with the guerrillas, so they have come here for safety.'[67]

It was here that one of ITN's camera crews took a famous (or infamous) picture – that of Fikret Alic, an emaciated man, stripped to the waist, with two strands of barbed wire limned against his bony chest.

DISCUSSION: Look at the picture of Fikret Alic. What does it remind you of?

The image went around the world and was used by many other media to draw a parallel with Nazi death camps in World War II.

Years later, *LM*, a small-circulation London magazine, branded it 'the picture that fooled the world'. The wire was not *encircling* the camp, the magazine said, but *adjoining* it – marking the perimeter of a yard belonging to an electricity generator, where the crews were standing. Fikret Alic was not standing inside the barbed wire, but outside it.

Fikret Alic at Trnopolje camp,
Bosnia, 1992
Photograph copyright © ITN Archive

Reaction by the world's press
Front page of the Daily Mirror *on 7 August 1992,*
used with permission, copyright © Mirrorpix

All that closed in the refugees was a low fence surrounding what had been a school playing-field. What prevented them from leaving was the fear of what would happen to them if caught, wandering in the area, by Bosnian Serb forces or paramilitary gangs (and indeed, as Paddy Ashdown commented, those gangs sometimes raided the camp by night).

In a press release to mark the magazine's re-launch, *LM* Editor Mick Hume wrote:

'Journalists who have some kind of emotional attachment in a conflict can end up seeing what they want to see, not what is really there...

The line between reportage and propaganda can be stretched thinner than a string of barbed wire... Taking sides can be an excuse for taking liberties with the facts.'

LM was right about the geography of the camp, the barbed wire and the generator, as Jake Lynch – then a Sky News reporter – was easily able to see on a visit there in 2000. The trip was spent gathering material for a 'backgrounder' on a court case in which the reporters, Penny Marshall and Ian Williams, sued *LM* and Mick Hume for libel.

They won, and were awarded substantial costs and damages. How come? In fact their own reports, played and picked over in court, had been extremely circumspect in describing what they found. They did not say these were 'concentration camps'; neither did they state categorically, in their TV reports, that the men were 'fenced in' by the barbed wire.

The iconic quality of the Alic image may, in *LM*'s words, have 'fooled the world', but if so, the jury found, it was not the fault of exaggeration or misrepresentation on the reporters' part. Speaking in court, Williams deplored the way the image 'took the story two steps ahead of the evidence' as it passed around the global media village.

Marshall and Williams said Hume's press release effectively accused them of lying, of seeing 'what they want[ed] to see, not what [was] really there'. Crucially, the press release was refuted.

Moreover, strong testimony was given on behalf of Marshall and Williams by Idris Merdzanic, the doctor at the camp, who had secretly handed the ITN crew a camera used to take photographs of fellow inmates he had been called on to treat – after they sustained serious beatings at the hands of camp guards in an interrogation room. The essential nature of Trnopolje camp, and what went on there, was not misrepresented by the reporters; it was the comparison with Auschwitz and Belsen that was fanciful, and that was a matter of interpretation by others, after the picture left their hands.

What was the issue? Where was the propaganda?

The court saw a piece run by ITN the night after the original report was screened, by a different reporter, in which world reaction was illustrated with clips from news bulletins from several other countries. In every one, a link was explicitly made with the concentration camps; the regrets expressed by Ian Williams at this exaggeration were notably absent. ITN, originators of the material, did nothing to correct the distortion as they drew it to their own viewers' attention.

The original assignment arose from a challenge, made on camera weeks earlier, to the Bosnian Serb leader Radovan Karadzic, who was in London for talks. Karadzic guaranteed ITN safe passage to investigate press reports accusing the Bosnian Serbs of running concentration camps.

The court in the eventual libel case heard that Marshall, Williams and their crews had met Karadzic twice along the way. Both times, he had urged ITN to follow up, with similar vigour, allegations against the Bosnian government side in the war. At one meeting, in Pale, he handed them a list of 24 camps in the Sarajevo area, which he said were Muslim-run concentration camps.

Ian Williams said in evidence: 'We thought these allegations of his should be investigated, and [said] we would pass them on to people in a better position to do so.'

But of course there never were any comparable reports on the conditions for those held in camps run by the Bosnian government, either by ITN or anyone else.

• Demonisation – confusing bad behaviour with blame for the conflict

A UN study in 1994 concluded that, of all the camps in the former territory of Yugoslavia, 237 were run by the Bosnian Serbs or Yugoslav government, and 170 by their enemies – the Bosnian government, Bosnian Croats and the Croatian government.

Reports abounded on all sides, it said, of these camps being used to carry out:

> '... mass executions, torture, rapes and other forms of sexual assault. They are the scene of the worst inhumane acts. These inhumane acts are committed by guards, police, special forces, and others who are allowed to come from the outside to perform such acts.'[68]

But the incidence of such acts was 'far lesser', according to the UN study, at camps run by the parties other than the Bosnian Serbs, because among the authorities only the Bosnian Serbs condoned them. By contrast: 'The government of Croatia has, since late 1993, according to information received by the Commission, condemned these violations and sought to curb their occurrences.'[69]

By late 1993, however, condemnation was an empty gesture. Parts of Croatia populated by Serbs (the Krajina and Slavonja) had been 'ethnically cleansed' – involving the biggest single movement of people in the Yugoslavian wars until the exodus of Kosovo Albanians in 1999.

Consider the statement to journalists by a Croat camp guard, Miro Bajramovic:

'Nights were worst for [our prisoners]... burning prisoners with a flame, pouring vinegar over their wounds mostly on genitalia and on the eyes. Then there is that little induction field phone, you plug a Serb onto that... The most painful is to stick little pins under the nails and to connect to the three phase current; nothing remains of a man but ashes... After all, we knew they would all be killed, so it did not matter if we hurt him more today or tomorrow.'[70]

Moreover, Bajramovic said that a paramilitary leader, Tomislav Mercep, had command responsibility: 'Mercep knew everything,' Bajramovic claimed. 'He told us several times: "Tonight you have to clean all these shits". By this he meant all the prisoners should be executed.'

Mercep, known as 'the Napoleon of Vukovar', was decorated by President Franjo Tudjman for his part in the campaign and later became an aide in the Croatian Interior Ministry and an MP. Which is likelier – that people like Bajramovic had the impression, at the time, that their actions were officially condemned, or that they were *sanctioned*, albeit tacitly, by those they recognised as leaders?

The UN report has been criticised for its apportionment of blame; and many have found it difficult to accept as definitive, not least because no one visited camps run by the Croats or Bosnians at the time. Let's say, for the sake of argument, we do accept it – where does it get us?

The behaviour of one party in a conflict can nearly always be proved worse than that of the others. In Northern Ireland, Republican paramilitaries were responsible for many more deaths in the 'troubles' than the British army and loyalists combined; Dayak gangs inflicted horrifying atrocities in communal conflicts in the Indonesian province of Kalimantan, in the late nineties and early two-thousands, while sustaining relatively little in the way of retaliation from their enemies, the Madurese.

In these and countless other cases, however, to blame the conflict itself on the party responsible for the worst behaviour would be to miss the real conflict dynamics, and to contribute to prolonging it by justifying more violence in order to 'punish' them.

In the ABC conflict triangle presented in Chapter 2, the B, the Behaviour of the parties, is part of what is called the *meta-conflict* – the complex tangle of thoughts and actions built on top of the underlying conflict, the Contradictions denoted by C.

To give a full account of these contradictions in the Bosnian war would take a chapter, if not a book all to itself. In brief, they can be brought together under five headings:

- *Political and economic upheaval* – the break-up of Yugoslavia followed the death of its 'strongman' leader, Marshal Tito, in 1980; globalised industrial production got under way during the rest of that decade, and the climax of the Cold War came at the end of it.

- *Poverty* – the country was impoverished economically, its industries were laid waste by cheap foreign competition in western markets, and it lacked legitimate state authorities.

- *Independence for some* – western countries, led by Germany through the then European Community, quickly recognised Croatia and Slovenia as independent.

- *Nationalism* – Croatian nationalists took control in Zagreb, and declared their new country a state 'for Croats' – not 'all citizens of the Croatian republic'. As one immediate effect, non-ethnic Croat police officers were dismissed.

- *Bosnian independence* – a referendum followed in which Bosnians, too, voted for independence from the Yugoslav federation.

The American deputy military commander in Europe at the time takes up the story:

'In this atmosphere of fear, uncertainty, and resurgent nationalism, first the Croatian and then the Bosnian Serbs – with Serbian support – took up arms to do what international recognition had done for the Croats of Croatia and the Muslims of Bosnia: ensure that they would not be a minority in a state they perceived to be hostile.

What is frequently referred to as rampant Serb nationalism and the creation of a greater Serbia has often been the same volatile mixture of fear, opportunism, and historical myopia that seems to motivate patriots everywhere in the Balkans. Much of what Zagreb calls the occupied territories is in fact land held by Serbs for more than three centuries.'[71]

It is when bad behaviour by one party is conflated with, or read as *blame* for, a conflict that we tip over from analysis to propaganda. This requires bad behaviour to be ascribed not mainly but *entirely* to that one side, and shades into *demonisation* – a consequence of failing 'to include certain qualifying facts in stories'. Some of the qualifying facts are given in our brief list of contradictions – not as excuses, but as part of the explanation.

No such explanation would be complete without taking into account the effect on people's behaviour of finding themselves in prison-type settings, divided into inmates and guards – as shown by the Stanford University experiment. It was the conflict that *constituted* the relationship between people in the first place; and for the conflict, many parties, both inside and outside former Yugoslavia, were co-responsible.

This would have been clearer if allegations against the Bosnian government had been followed up with equal rigour – not just by ITN but by other media as well. The image of Fikret Alic, and the use others made of it – to make the connection with Nazi concentration camps – greatly amplified the process of demonisation. This was the substantive issue *LM* magazine was seeking to raise. And, as we suggest in this chapter, it carried over into the reporting frame applied to the Kosovo crisis, in such a way as to make the media highly receptive to war propaganda:

'For the decade 1989-1999 the international community operated on a standardised, one-truth, black-and-white explanation of what the conflict was about. They blamed the Serbs in general and Slobodan Milosevic in particular for the Kosovo conflict. They ignored the complex framework in space and time of which Kosovo was a part: the dissolution mechanisms of former Yugoslavia, the wider context of the Balkans and the restructuring of the world order as well as the transition from the Cold War paradigm.'[72]

Those who take issue with the 'official' explanation for the Yugoslavian wars are often smeared as appeasers, revisionists or apologists for the 'butcher of Belgrade', ready to overlook ethnic cleansing and worse. The important contribution of Peace Journalism, attentive to the insights of Conflict Analysis and Peace Research, lies in providing anchorage – a firm basis on which to draw distinctions. To insist that the conflict should not be seen as the fault of one party – 'the Serbs' in this case – does not entail turning a blind eye to that party's bad behaviour.

The psychology of propaganda

Oscar Wilde said: 'I can stand brute force, but brute reason is quite unbearable. There is something unfair about its use. It is hitting below the intellect.'[73]

If propaganda is not the same as 'lies', perhaps, instead, this is its defining characteristic: it is a form of 'brute reason'. It works by plumbing psychological depths below the intellect, notably by constructing binary oppositions of 'us and them'. Helene Lewis, a psychologist – indeed, a self-described 'psycho-historian' – explains: 'The individual both needs and uses "enemies" as external stabilisers for a sense of identity and inner control.'[74]

Enemies can be *created* by the psychological process, first defined by C G Jung, known as 'projection', which stabilises our identity by attaching to others the bits of it we dislike:

'Projection is used by the individual to ascribe his own unacceptable thoughts, impulses or traits to someone "out there" in an effort to be rid of them. As individuals we project our own unacceptable (disowned) parts onto another person or onto another race.'

As with explanations for violence, those for demonisation still leave room for individual, and indeed social, responsibility. Projection is not the only way to script our own subjectivity:

'Over a thousand-year span, there has clearly been progress from a psycho-historical perspective – progress based on improved child-rearing. Improved child-rearing over the ages has rendered healthier individuals, healthier societies and thus less projection, more compassion and more tolerance towards others.'[75]

The likelihood that people will define and defend their identity by projection depends on circumstances, both historical and everyday. Another way of defining propaganda would be as something that lowers the barrier – perhaps, by dint of association and repetition, leading people to believe their circumstances are more parlous than they really are – thereby bringing forward the point of projection.

The centrifugal forces pulling apart the federal state of Yugoslavia were powered by a motor of 'othering', including some pretty vicious propaganda, which gathered momentum through economic and political upheaval both within its borders and without. Michael Ignatieff witnessed these forces acting upon what he called 'the narcissism of minor difference' between Serbs and Croats:

'Nationalism does not simply "express" a pre-existent identity: it "constitutes" a new one. It would be false to the history of this part of the world to maintain that ethnic antagonisms were simply waiting, like the magma beneath a volcano, for a template to shift, a fissure to split open. It is an abuse of anthropological terminology to call Serbs and Croats ethnic groups at all.'[76]

In the words of Dobrica Cosic, a writer known as the 'father of the Serbian nation', reflecting on the break-up of Yugoslavia: 'The enemies of the Serbs made Serbs Serbs.'[77]

Propaganda has no use for any enquiry into how categories and divisions came to be constructed in the first place. Propaganda, *to be* propaganda, has to hit below the intellect – to enable the 'dark, split-off sides' of one's own identity to be ascribed to someone else. It requires not analysis, but demonisation – a strict dividing line between 'us' and 'them', where *all* the blame can be loaded on to 'them'.

In the break-up of Yugoslavia, the 'demons', the Serbs, came ready-made as the recipient of projection by other parties. They became the repository for 'alterity', or otherness – from *alter ego*, to borrow another term from psychology: literally, 'other self'.

There could be no Serb victims in this discourse, only perpetrators. The 200,000 civilians ethnically cleansed, forced out by the Croatian army (with help from US mercenaries) in 1995, the Serb refugees from Kosovo, the interns in Bosnian government prison camps – all were effectively excluded from the frame.

Endnotes for Chapter 4

1. American Senator, Hiram Johnson, 1917, quoted in Phillip Knightley, *The First Casualty – The War Correspondent as Hero and Myth-maker from the Crimea to Kosovo*, Prion Books, London, 2000, p viii.
2. George W Bush, 7 October 2002, remarks made in a speech in Cincinnati.
3. Stuart Hall, 'Encoding/Decoding', *Culture, Media, Language: Working Papers in Cultural Studies*, Centre for Contemporary Cultural Studies, London, 1972-79, Hutchinson, pp 128-38
4. Ibid, p 136.
5. Laura Miller and Sheldon Rampton, 'The Pentagon's Information Warrior', *PR Watch Archives*, 4th quarter 2001, Center for Media and Democracy, Wisconsin, USA.
6. Max Hastings, 'Julia Roberts Has a Better Chance of Winning This War', London *Guardian*, 19 January 2005.
7. Alan F. Kay, 'When Americans Favor the Use of Force', *International Journal of Public Opinion Research*, Vol 12, No 2, Summer 2000, pp 182-90
8. Pew Research Center for the People and the Press mid-September omnibus poll, 19 September 2002.
9. Birgitta Hoijer, Stig Arne Nohrstedt and Rune Ottosen, 'The Kosovo War in the Media – Analysis of a Global Discursive Order', *Conflict & Communication online*, Vol 1, No 2, 2002, p 4.
10. Nik Gowing, *Media Coverage – Help or Hindrance in Resolving Deadly Conflict?*, Carnegie Corporation of New York, 1997, p 12 in online edition at http://wwics.si.edu/subsites/ccpdc/pubs/media/12.htm.
11. Allan Little, 'The West Did Not Do Enough', *BBC Online*, 29 June 2001.
12. Philip Hammond, in David Chandler (ed), *Rethinking Human Rights*, Palgrave, London, 2002, p 183.
13. David Binder quoted by Philip Hammond in ibid.
14. Quoted in Jake Lynch, *Reporting the World*, Conflict and Peace Forums, Taplow, 2002, p 43.
15. Philip Hammond, 'Third Way War – New Labour, the British Media and Kosovo', in Philip Hammond and Edward S Herman (eds), *Degraded Capability*, Pluto Press, London, 2000, p 124.
16. Speaking at the Freedom Forum European Centre, London, March 2000, launch event for new edition of Phillip Knightley, *The First Casualty* (op cit).
17. Tom Walker and Aidan Laverty, 'CIA Aided Kosovo Guerrilla Army', London *Sunday Times*, 21 March 2000.
18. Allan Little (reporter), 'Moral Combat', BBC TV *Panorama*, 21 March 2000.
19. Phillip Knightley, op cit, p 524.
20. Quoted in Jake Lynch, 'Reporting Kosovo – Violence Now Proves the Stories Missed in 1999 Were the Most Important', Transnational Futures Foundation, 22 March, 2004.
21. *Hansard*, 23 March 1999, http://www.publications.parliament.uk/pa/cm199899/cmhansrd/vo990323/debtext/90323-06.htm.
22. John Vidal, 'Blacks Need, But Only Whites Receive', London *Guardian*, 12 August 1999.
23. *Seeking Protection: Addressing Sexual and Domestic Violence in Tanzania's Refugee Camps*, Human Rights Watch report, October 2000.
24. On *Face the Nation*, CBS-TV, 16 May 1999.
25. Philip Hammond, op cit, 2000, p 127.
26. Quoted by Jake Lynch, in Peter Goff (ed), *The Kosovo News and Propaganda War*, International Press Institute, Vienna, 1999, p 51.

27. Lord Robertson of Port Ellen, Secretary-General of NATO, 'Kosovo: The Real Story', speech before the Los Angeles World Affairs Council, 6 April 2000.

28. Evelyn Waugh, *Scoop*, Penguin Modern Classics ed, London, 1937, p 42.

29. Alastair Campbell, 'J'Accuse', London *Guardian*, 10 July 1999.

30. Air Commodore David Wilby, NATO Briefing, Brussels, 8 April 1999.

31. Anthony H. Cordesman, *The Effectiveness of the Nato Tactical Air and Missile Campaign against Serbian Air and Ground Forces in Kosovo*, Center for Strategic and International Studies, Washington DC, August 2000.

32. Ibid.

33. Ibid.

34. Quoted in Alex Brummer, Martin Kettle and Martin Walker in Washington, 'Cracks in NATO Unity', London *Guardian*, 24 April 1999.

35. Interviewed by Allan Little, *Panorama* (op cit), 2000.

36. Quoted in Matthew Campbell and Stephen Grey, 'His Worst Fear', London *Sunday Times*, 16 May 1999.

37. BBC TV *Newsnight*, 20 August 1999.

38. 'Western Estimates' quoted in Professor Michel Chossudovsky, 'Impacts of NATO's "Humanitarian" Bombings – The Balance Sheet of Destruction in Yugoslavia', University of Ottawa, available at http://www.diaspora-net.org/food4thought/chossudovsky.htm.

39. Timothy Garton Ash, 'The War We Almost Lost', *New York Review of Books*, 4 September 2000.

40. Phillip Knightley, quoted in Matthew Ricketson, 'Turn Down the Volume, Turn Up the Quality', Melbourne *Age*, 31 March 2003.

41. Jake Lynch and Annabel McGoldrick, *News from the Holy Land* (video), Hawthorn Press, Stroud, 2004.

42. Quoted in Jake Lynch, *The Peace Journalism Option*, Conflict and Peace Forums, Taplow, 1998, p 6.

43. Speaking at 'Reporting Iraq – What Went Right? What Went Wrong?', Reporting the World event, London, 15 July 2003.

44. Nik Gowing, 'Information in Conflict: Who Really Commands the High Ground?', Liddell Hart Centre for Military Archives Lecture, 2 March 2000.

45. Telephone interview with authors, 16 March 2004.

46. Allan Little, 'War Reporters Face New Challenges', *BBC Online*, 24 March 2003.

47. Telephone interview with authors, 16 March 2004.

48. UK Government dossier, *Ten Questions Iraq Must Answer*, 28 January 2003.

49. Anthony H Cordesman, *Iraq's Past and Future Biological Weapons Capabilities*, Center for Strategic and International Studies, Washington DC, February 1998.

50. *Hansard*, 18 March 2003.

51. Stated in many BBC news stories, eg, *Reporters' Log*, 28 March 2003, at http://news.bbc.co.uk/1/hi/2890403.stm.

52. Quoted in 'EBU Protests against Media Restrictions in Iraq', *Broadcast Engineering*, 5 April 2003.

53. Speaking at 'Reporting Iraq – What Went Right? What Went Wrong?', Reporting the World event, London, 15 July 2003.

54. Quoted in Jake Lynch and Annabel McGoldrick, *Reporting the World Global Survey*, at www.reportingtheworld.org.uk.

55. Jason Deans, 'BBC's War Coverage Was "Too Conservative"', London *Guardian*, 25 June 2003.

56. Mohan Mainali, 'Unfriendly Fire', *Nepali Times*, 9-15 August 2002.

57. See, for instance, Bertil Lintner, 'Nepal's Maoists Prepare for Final Offensive', *Jane's Intelligence Review*, October 2002.

58. Quoted on www.iraqbodycount.org.

59. At www.iraqbodycount.org.

60. 'Iraq Death Toll "Soared Post-War"', *BBC Online*, 29 October 2004.

61. Artistides Katoppo interviewed by Mick O'Regan, broadcast on ABC Radio *National Media Watch*, Australia, 17 October 2002.

62. *Today*, BBC Radio 4, 6:07 am, 29 May 2003.

63. Quoted in Jackie Ashley, 'One Stark Truth – Blair Was Wrong and Must Admit It Now', London *Guardian*, 7 July 2003.

64. G S Jowett and V O'Donnell, *Propaganda and Persuasion*, Sage, London, 1992.

65. Quoted in David Edwards, 'Kosovo and Iraq – Same Bombs, Different Lies', Media Lens *media alert*, 31 March 2004.

66. Walter Pincus and Dana Millbank, 'Al Qaeda-Hussein Link is Dismissed', *Washington Post*, 17 June 2004.

67. Paddy Ashdown, 'We Are Making Europe's Palestinians', London *Independent*, 13 August 1992.

68. Commission of experts on the former Yugoslavia, *Final Report*, United Nations Security Council S/1994/674, 27 May 1994.

69. Ibid.

70. Chris Hedges, 'Croatian's Confession Describes Torture and Killing on Vast Scale', *New York Times*, 5 September 1997.

71. Charles G Boyd, 'Making Peace with the Guilty', *Foreign Affairs*, Vol 74, No 50, September/October 1995, pp 22-38.

72. Jan Oberg, 'Peacemaking in Kosovo Coming to an End – For Predictable Reasons', *TFF Pressinfo 197*, Transnational Futures Foundation, 29 April 2004, http://www.transnational.org/pressinf/2004/pi197_KosovoEnd.html.

73. Oscar Wilde, *The Picture of Dorian Gray*, 1891, Chapter 3 available free at http://www.classicbookshelf.com/library/oscar_wilde/the_picture_of_dorian_gray/3/.

74. Helene Lewis, 'Racism as Projection', *Rhodes Journalism Review*, 20, August 2001, Department of Journalism and Media Studies, Rhodes University and the Media Peace Centre, Cape Town, South Africa.

75. Ibid.

76. Michael Ignatieff, *The Warrior's Honor: Ethnic War and the Modern Conscience*, Vintage, London and New York, 1999, p 38.

77. Quoted in Vesna Pesic, 'Serbian Nationalism and the Origins of the Yugoslav Crisis', *PEACEWORKS 8*, United States Institute of Peace, April 1996, available at http://www.usip.org/pubs/specialreports/early/pesic/pesic3.html.

Chapter 5

Scenarios and Dilemmas

We will now apply some of the concepts we have covered so far to real life situations. All the scenarios in this chapter are couched in terms of asking 'What would you do if…?'. In other words, they are presented as a series of *dilemmas* the journalist may encounter when reporting conflicts. These can be used as exercises with groups to explore their developing views and understanding.

The scenarios include:

- 'Tension is rising'
- Deterioration – the beginnings of violence
- Early warning
- Massacre or mistake? Or crossfire?
- Reporting on refugees
- Stalemate – the conflict story that 'never changes'
- Reporting on a 'peace deal'
- Shots for shots – offers of violence to make good pictures
- Parties to conflict not talking to each other
- Reporting from one side of the line

By the end of this chapter, the reader will be able to:

- Grasp more fully how Peace Journalism applies to the real world
- Tackle some of the trickiest situations faced by journalists in the field
- Translate Peace Journalism principles into tools tough enough to be relied on when tackling difficult stories

Work through the following nine dilemmas and decide how you, as a journalist, would tackle them.

1. 'Tension is rising' – before direct violence

You are reporting in a relatively peaceful country. The society is typically multi-ethnic and/or multicultural – with potential fault lines, therefore. Perhaps the economy is deteriorating or undergoing some kind of upheaval or transition. People begin to grumble about the basis on which jobs, contracts, access to services etc are being allocated. The fault lines begin to be opened up by political extremists, using propaganda based on projection and 'othering'.

Photograph copyright © Rob Huibers/Panos Pictures
Visitors at the funeral in Nabire, West Papua, of Wellem Manimwarba (27) who bled to death after being shot by police in a demonstration about the wearing of traditional arms

The ABC of conflict is in place: an underlying Contradiction, hostile Attitudes between groups, and the beginnings of antagonistic Behaviour, but with only limited direct violence.

(It is almost never the case that this situation prevails for long without *any* violence. This example is about options for journalists to respond to a feeling that major violence is brewing.)

Symptoms can include:

• racist rhetoric and incitement
• bad-tempered demonstrations
• occasional riots
• assaults on minority groups, sometimes fatal
• allegations of partisanship by law-and-order or security forces
• rising unemployment and/or economic insecurity
• emergence of openly racist political parties or groups
• mainstream political parties playing the 'race card'
• political debate becoming dominated by the 'numbers game'
• groups beginning to organise and take up arms

Examples:

• hostility towards asylum seekers in various European countries including Britain, also in Australia
• Macedonia 2001-present
• parts of Indonesia – such as Ambon, Poso and West Papua – where conflicts escalated into violence after the fall of the Suharto regime in 1998
• former Yugoslavia after the death of Marshal Tito in 1980
• racism and discrimination in the US in the 1960s, or Britain in the 1990s

DISCUSSION: Do you:

a) Talk it down – ignore the story?
b) Talk it up – sensationalise the story?
c) Devise a Peace Journalism approach?

a) Talk it down – ignore the story

This is what the media did before the fall of the dictatorships in Yugoslavia (with its official ideology of 'Brotherhood and Unity') and Indonesia:

'There was a particular sensitivity to any story highlighting splits and divisions among the many nations, races and religious groups of the archipelago. Television journalists laboured under specific regulations against covering "issues that might give rise to SARA conflicts" (*Suku* – ethnicity; *Agama* – religion; *Ras* – race; and *Antar golongan* – social class). Those on other media, too, if they entered such contentious territory, could expect a summons from the Ministry of Information.'[1]

PROBLEM: People with genuine grievances may become frustrated if they feel no one is listening to them. They may escalate their actions until someone does listen.

Example: In the 1960s, institutionalised racism, discrimination and under-development kept black Americans at the bottom of the socio-economic pile. But this was seldom reported:

'Newspapers, and later broadcasters, wanted all potential *affluent* consumers regardless of their personal political interests. Consequently, if a group as a whole were poor, as was true of some minorities, papers wished to avoid news of them and their issues. Problems affecting lower-income communities generally did not become news until they affected affluent consumers.'[2]

In Britain, unrest involving members of black inner-city communities was born of frustration over a number of grievances – among them, the treatment of young black men at the hands of some police officers. This included a number of deaths while in police custody – deaths which, local people felt, were not being properly investigated. In the coverage of one disturbance, in 1996:

> '[One] report mentioned the grievance over Wayne Douglas's death and carried a still picture of him. But there was no humanising interview with his family; the concentration was on the violence and its immediate consequences, evidence of damage etc. Police officers injured in the trouble gave victim testimony from their hospital beds.
>
> The custody death itself had not been reported at the time, and [Patrick] Younge [a BBC executive, then editor of the corporation's *Black Britain* programme] suggested the implicit message to local activists was that to get attention for their grievances, they should riot.'[3]

In Indonesia and Yugoslavia, the pressures keeping such grievances out of the news – the threat of censorship and official reprisals if conventions were breached – were different, but the effect was, arguably, the same. It left fault lines to be exploited later by those intent on violence – in some cases, as a smokescreen behind which to pursue their own interests. Gerry van Klinken, editor of *Inside Indonesia* magazine, offered just such an analysis of the conflict in Ambon, in the province of Maluku, from 1999:

> 'I'd like to suggest a better explanation than that such conflicts are triggered by pure bigotry. It is based on the idea that people often identify with a particular religious community for quite worldly reasons. In Ambon at least, joining the Protestant or the Muslim community means being part of a network that not only worships God in a certain way but does practical things for its members – provide access to friends in powerful places for example, or protection when things get tough. These networks extend up the social ladder to influential circles in Jakarta. And they extend downward to street level, where gangs of young men provide the protective muscle that an inefficient police force cannot provide.'[4]

In either case, the media were complicit in concealing these problems from view, preventing them from becoming seen as a political imperative – something decision-makers, from local police chiefs to government ministers, could be seen as being under pressure to resolve.

b) Talk it up – sensationalise the story

> PROBLEM: There are two challenges frequently encountered at this stage of a conflict – *over-reporting*, and the *causative fallacy*. Both are visible in coverage of the 'asylum seeker' issue in countries like the UK.

Over-reporting may lead people to suppose the issue at hand is bigger and more important than it really is. After a year in which it dominated the headlines of several tabloid newspapers, one opinion poll on the asylum issue contained a 'multiple choice' question, asking British people to estimate what proportion of the world's asylum seekers ended up in their country. The most popular estimate was between 25 and 30 per cent (the true figure at the time was 1.98 per cent[5]).

Many of the headlines drew attention to the money spent by various branches of government on public services used by asylum seekers – GP and dental surgeries, public transport and, above all, housing.

This came at a time when these services were all under pressure, but the origin of this pressure was seldom spelt out in the coverage. Instead, it was submerged in the words chosen to convey the numbers of asylum seekers entering Britain. Some examples: 'swamped', 'rising tide', 'flood of people'.

These inundation metaphors constructed a causative fallacy – that people's experience of trying to access public services under pressure, such as queuing for social housing, could be *blamed on* the arrival of asylum seekers; even that provision of such services for incomers was placing an 'intolerable strain' on the UK economy.

In fact, shortages in public services could be more accurately attributed to spending decisions made by governments of different stripes over many years. Fewer new houses were being built in Britain around the turn of the 21st century than at any time since World War II.

Part of the rise in the number of asylum seekers in the 1990s could be traced to the difficulty of gaining legal access to immigration by any other means. And any overall cost/benefit analysis of immigration to Britain 'in the round', including asylum seekers, found a significant benefit to the economy as a result.

In other words, sensationalised coverage led British people to assume they had a problem when it was, arguably, a benefit. Whatever the precise extent of the 'problem', the way it was presented was out of all proportion to the numbers involved.

It contributed to the rise of far-right politics, as the openly racist British National Party began to attract votes and attention. Another disturbing development was an increase in racially motivated attacks. The Refugee Council and the Association of Chief Police Officers agreed in attributing this, both its nature and its extent, in part to media coverage of the issue.

c) Peace Journalism approach

There are two decisions to make – whether to cover a particular issue and, if so, how to cover it.

Indonesia, late 1990s

Decisions on whether to cover something often entail assessing whether it can be 'placed' in a particular narrative. Is a fight over, say, a place on a minibus just a fight, or could it portend an escalating violent conflict along fault lines already coursing with tension – as in Ambon?

This was one arena for what Indonesians called a 'horizontal conflict' – between different sections of the community at a local level – although, as van Klinken suggests, political rivalries in Jakarta may have been a shadowy presence in the background.

In the late 1990s, several 'vertical conflicts' were also on the rise – in East Timor, Aceh and West Papua. The other name for these is 'centre-periphery' conflicts. Membership of the UN comprises some 200

states. The world contains – at a conservative estimate – about 2,000 different (self-defined) nations, with many more races and tribes.

Moreover, globalising forces – including transnational capital, organised crime and global civil society networks – have led to what some commentators call a 'hollowing-out of the national state'[6] (one reason to look beyond Political Realism as an explanation for change in conflicts, as discussed in Chapter 3).

Given the resulting sense of flux – in Indonesia as elsewhere – around issues of identity and allegiance, it is perhaps no surprise that the centre-periphery formation has become steadily more salient in explaining and analysing conflict.

Consider, then, an example loosely modelled on conflicts in areas of Indonesia such as West Papua, complicated, as they are, by the phenomenon of *transmigrasi* (trans-migration – the movement of settlers, especially from Java, to outlying areas). The following is a list of questions for deciding whether and how individual developments belong in the narrative of a centre-periphery conflict involving an imaginary Province A, where there is a nascent movement for independence from Country B:[7]

- How seriously do indigenous people and settlers living in province A view the prospect of an outbreak of violence?
- How are fears, resentments and grievances being expressed?
- Are they making people shun each other, stop trading with each other, discriminate in giving people jobs/contracts etc (structural violence), or insult and slander each other (cultural violence)?
- Are there individuals working at the grass roots to promote understanding, break down stereotypes and foster a dialogue about ways of living together?
- Could they appear in your coverage as 'heroes in the community'?

If these questions can help in deciding *whether* to cover individual developments in a conflict, they also point towards important considerations in *how* to cover it.

Macedonia, 2001

A context where events were reported as developments in a centre-periphery conflict was that of the former Yugoslav republic of Macedonia, which was convulsed by exchanges of violence during two brief periods in 2001.

Chapter 3 gives two contrasting examples of how one particular incident could be reported. There were different ways to respond to the event and there were different ways to cover the underlying process, too. Based on the questions above, the centre-periphery narrative was a valid one for this conflict.

But representations of the conflict were highly contested, with the parties keenly aware of the power of media reports, particularly in light of the recent NATO intervention in Kosovo. Indeed, the (ethnic Albanian) National Liberation Army presented themselves as drawing attention to grievances, previously ignored, by escalating their struggle:

> 'The group's leader, Ali Ahmeti, appeared to confirm, in an interview with Mark Urban on the BBC's *Newsnight* programme on July 4th [2001], that the armed campaign by his men had indeed been, at least in part, a publicity exercise. Asked what they had gained by taking up the gun, he replied, "all the people of Europe now know about our situation"'.[8]

The following are later passages from two texts used in Chapter 3, this time illustrating different ways to report on issues of structural and cultural violence:

First version

Cartoon copyright © Jim Morin, Miami Herald,
CartoonArts International/CWS

MASSACRE RUINS HOPES FOR PEACE IN MACEDONIA (CONT.)

…But many ethnic Albanians appear ready to throw in their lot with the guerrillas. One young activist from Tetovo, who has escorted journalists to rebel strongholds, said last night: 'Nobody cares for our rights, and those who are most militant have decided the gun is the only way for their voices to be heard'.

After fierce fighting in March and April, the European Union began applying pressure to the Skopje government to accede to Albanian demands for official recognition of their language and status within the country. The Albanians in Macedonia Crisis Centre, a US-based group of émigrés, has been circulating findings from the European Commission against Racism and Intolerance, which has criticised the existing citizenship law as discriminating against minorities.

Since the NLA was driven out of the hills, the police, 93 per cent of whom are Macedonian Slavs, have been making arbitrary arrests of men in and around Tetovo on charges of aiding and supporting terrorism.

The fighting has hardened opinions on both sides. Editor-in-chief Branko Geroski complained in a recent edition of *Dnevnik*, a Skopje newspaper, 'Macedonians have always believed that politicians in power are giving far too many rights to Albanians. People feel let down. They realise that all the concessions failed to bury the Albanians' dream of creating their own state in western Macedonia'.

The government has concentrated on encouraging the two main Albanian parties to bury their differences and join together as partners in the ruling coalition, to minimise the scope for political mischief-making – a process analysts expected to become more difficult after the weekend's renewed conflict.

On the streets of the capital, a new, polarised reality is taking shape. Before the NLA crossed the border in their first offensive, the Ak Saraj tea house in the old Albanian market quarter of Skopje echoed to the tones of several languages, including the Slavic tongue of the Macedonians and the occasional strain of Turkish. Now, only Albanian is spoken there.

Second version

DISCUSSION: What are the important distinctions between these two articles?

MACEDONIAN PARTIES CONDEMN VIOLENCE AFTER GUNMEN KILL 8 POLICE AND SOLDIERS (CONT.)

...If territorial ambitions remain a minority pursuit, there is evidence of genuine causes for Albanian grievances to match the Macedonians' fears. The policemen who died were among the 93 per cent of the force drawn from the two-thirds majority Macedonian population. Albanian families in the Tetovo area have complained that their menfolk are now subject to arbitrary arrest, detention and beatings.

Some have been charged with serious terrorist offences, despite the government's repeated assertion that the NLA are a bunch of interlopers from Kosovo, not a home-grown paramilitary grouping.

Meanwhile their children even face difficulties in accessing basic services such as nursery education, according to Shpresa Sinani, president of the Tetovo Albanian Women's League. She said the city has five Macedonian-language kindergartens, but only one for Albanians, who comprise more than three-quarters of the 80,000 population.

The political reforms under discussion in Skopje include plans to empower local authorities to raise and spend their own money. Ms Sinani called for some to be allocated to provide more Albanian nursery schools. Practical help with such needs is provided, in the meantime, by aid agencies.

The Skopje office of Search for Common Ground runs interethnic kindergartens for four-to-six-year-olds. Executive director Eran Fraenkel paid tribute to parents still prepared to send their children to a cross-community group: 'In Macedonia, most people from different ethnic groups live in parallel worlds', he said, 'that very rarely intersect. The neighbourhoods are segregated. The media [are] in different languages. The kids go to different schools. These kindergartens are a way of breaking that cycle'.

International diplomats have welcomed signs of negotiated political reform. The European Commission against Racism and Intolerance, a Brussels-based human rights quango, recently commended government plans to overhaul Macedonia's citizenship laws, which it had previously criticised as discriminating against minorities.

There are Macedonians, at least in the capital, Skopje, who believe that a slide into further violence is far from inevitable. The outbreak of fighting earlier this year led to panic buying. A few days after the beginning of the crisis, sales doubled, the owner of the Kam supermarket chain recalled. One shopper laid in 100 tins of sardines but then, some days later, brought them back. 'The lady was asking to return the cans because she realised there wouldn't be a war'.

The first of these two versions refers to the Albanian population's legitimate grievances, but it collapses some important distinctions, leaving the reader to infer that:

- the 'men of violence' are the only authentic representatives of those who nurture such grievances
- the grievances can only be resolved by victory, through force of arms, in a zero-sum game – two parties in a tug of war over the same contested piece of territory
- everyone assumes that only more violence can follow

The second finds ways to open up these questions:

- Do people with grievances want them resolved by violence?
- Can the grievances be addressed by victory for one side in a zero-sum game? Are there other ways of addressing them, and who is pursuing them?
- Is violence as 'inevitable' as it seems?

As with the example of the Britain/Ireland conflict examined in Chapter 2, the key to maintaining a focus on underlying conflict issues, in a period of 'tensions on the rise', may be to keep asking the question *Why?*

- Why might an armed group, lining up behind the demand of 'independence', attain traction in this community, at this time?
- Why do people want independence? Is it the only way – or the best way – of addressing underlying issues of structural and cultural violence?

Exercise One
The British Media's Coverage of Asylum Seekers[9]

Read the scripts for two television reports about asylum seekers in Britain and ask, in each case:

- How are the asylum seekers described?
- Who are 'they' and who are 'we'?
- What are we told about the asylum seekers' reasons for coming to Britain?
- What is diagnosed as the 'problem' here?
- What are we led – or left – to infer is the 'solution'?

Asylum Seekers: Version 1[10]

This is a transcript of a piece run by a major UK-based television news channel in March 2000

Introduction by presenter in the studio
The government has announced new tougher plans to deal with the flood of people coming to Britain and seeking asylum. They'll now be placed in reception centres where their claims will be assessed before they're officially granted asylum and given permission to stay here. It comes amid concerns that asylum seekers are making false claims to enter Britain and living illegally on state benefits.

Pictures 1

Voice 1

Voice-over: Begging on the streets of Britain is a criminal offence but it is becoming a way of life for some asylum seekers who are already living rent free with hundreds of pounds a month in benefits. It is estimated that around 100,000 people who had asylum refused and should have been deported are still in the country illegally. With another 100,000 living on benefits while their cases are decided.

Pictures 2

Voice 2

Voice-over: To speed up that process the government has spent nearly five million pounds converting this former RAF base near Cambridge into a reception centre for asylum seekers. The aim is to process within seven days asylum seekers who are thought to be bogus. Up to 13,000 people a year could pass through this centre.

Pictures 3

Voice 3

Barbara Roche, Immigration Minister: If people are making genuine claims we will continue to honour our very proud record but we can't have a situation in which 70% of those claims turn out to be unfounded – that is not right to genuine asylum seekers.

Pictures 4

Voice 4

Voice-over: This is not the first time Jack Straw has tried to crack down on bogus asylum seekers. Last year the Home Secretary presented a new asylum law. But the opposition says the government's problems are of its own making.

Pictures 5

Voice 5

David Willetts, Conservative spokesman:
What we really need is for the government
to get a grip on the situation where for the
past 3 years it has steadily deteriorated
because ministers have been dangerously
complacent. They've sent out the message
that Britain is a soft touch for asylum
seekers: that's why we now have the
problem that they're having to wrestle with.

Pictures 6

Voice 6

Voice-over: The first asylum seekers will
arrive at the new reception centre
tomorrow but although cases may initially
be decided within seven days appeals
could still take months, or even years.

Commentary on Version 1

How are the asylum seekers described?
Asylum seekers do not get a chance to speak
for themselves in this piece – their actions and
motivations are characterised for them, by the
reporter and by rival politicians.

The first line of the first story describes the
asylum seekers as criminals. One of the
pictures shows a woman hiding her face and
running away from the camera as if she has
something to hide. We are told 'they' are
receiving hundreds of pounds a month in
benefits and living 'rent free'. The asylum
seekers are described as bogus.

There is a paradox in the asylum system in
Britain. People fleeing persecution have the
right to claim asylum once they arrive, but it is
very difficult to get in, to make any such claim,
especially if you have had to smuggle yourself
out of your own country for reasons of self-
protection. The Refugee Council says, in a
report on its website exploding 'media myths':[11]

'The fact that an asylum seeker may have
entered the country illegally does not mean
their case lacks credibility. It is virtually
impossible for people fleeing persecution to
reach Britain without resorting to the use of
false documents. In recognition of this fact,

Article 31 of the 1951 Convention on Refugees prohibits governments from penalising refugees who use false documents.'

How generous are the benefits? The report goes on:

'Asylum seekers are not allowed to claim mainstream welfare benefits. If they are destitute, the only option for some is to apply for support with the National Asylum Support Service (NASS), the government department responsible for supporting destitute asylum applicants. NASS support is very basic indeed. A single adult has to survive on £37.77 a week – 30% below the [official] poverty line. It is irrational to suggest that asylum seekers embark on arduous and often dangerous journeys to the UK for that amount of money.'

Who are 'they' and who are 'we'?

The basic message of this piece is: WE GIVE; THEY TAKE.

'**They**' are scroungers, always wanting a handout, whether in state benefits or by exploiting the misplaced generosity of passers-by. They are pictured thrusting their suspiciously docile babies under commuters' noses – exploiting their children for monetary gain.

'**We**' represent the opposite values. The British press campaign against asylum seekers of the early two-thousands was launched by two publications at about the same time – the London *Evening Standard* and the *Daily Mail*, both titles owned by Associated Newspapers.

There is a well-worn formula, familiar from the *Mail* in particular, to construct its own 'imagined community' – the 'us' in binary oppositions of 'us and them'. The 'we' of so many stories are, according to these papers, '*hard-working families*':

- *Concorde crash, Paris, July 2000:* Nearly all the casualties were Germans – a

problem for Britain's tabloid press with its chauvinistic attitude to Anglo-German relations. Those on board had paid for a package holiday, of which a flight on the famous supersonic airliner was a part – a line journalists spun a little further to anoint the passengers as 'hard-working family members' who'd saved up for the trip of a lifetime. A more palatable alternative than drawing attention to their nationality, which tended to be 'buried' in lower paragraphs.

- *Fatal rail accident, west London, October 1999:* In the crash the brunt of the impact was borne by those in the front carriage. Journalists speculated that, as the train was approaching the station in the morning rush hour, conscientious workers keen to reach the office may have congregated at the front to get to their destinations on time. They were, the *Mail* gushed in its front-page lead, 'among the best of us – hard-working family contributors'.

- *Zimbabwe land conflict:* Veteran reporter Ross Benson filed a feature on a white farmer married to a former model – pictured attractively around the family homestead. Benson focused on the prospects for them and their two children. 'Their plight,' he wrote, 'is one that hard-working families everywhere would recognise'.

Are we told why they come to Britain?

We are not given any explanation as to why 'they' have come to the UK. In this form of reporting, there is seldom if ever any information about conditions in the countries asylum seekers leave behind. Finally, in 2004, a group of MPs, the International Development Select Committee, released their own report[12] connecting these issues – issues that War Journalism, with its propagandistic us/them presentation, had kept separate for so long.

The Refugee Council again:

'The report highlights the links that should be made, but generally are not, between migration and issues such as the arms trade, globalisation, environmental disaster and poverty.'

What are we led – or left – to infer is the 'solution'?

If 'bogus' asylum seekers are seen as an issue of law and order, it creates a ready-made incentive to 'crack down', in the words of this reporter. That only makes sense if you ignore the reasons why they fled their homes in the first place.

The Refugee Council commented, on the Select Committee report:

'These issues can only be understood and properly managed once we view them in the round. What is required are joined-up policies in response to these findings.

The solution for Zimbabwean asylum seekers, for instance, is not to prevent them coming here, but to tackle the reasons causing them to leave their homes.

Policies must be put in place to tackle the human rights abuses that are the fundamental causes of refugee movements. At the same time asylum seekers, refugees and other migrants in Britain need to be treated more fairly and equitably, with a greater understanding of why they come and what valuable contributions they bring.'

The government and the media

Shortly after this first report went to air, and amid a strident press campaign by the *Mail*, *Evening Standard* and others, the UK government presented new legislation to 'deal with' the asylum issue. This duly took the form of a 'crackdown' – a policy devised at least partly on calculations that it would likely be reported as a solution to the perceived 'problem'.

Later, indeed, two political journalists revealed how the government had actually collaborated with Rupert Murdoch's *Sun* newspaper to manage the news on asylum. On hearing that the paper planned to run a week's worth of special reports on 'Britain's immigration crisis', Downing Street devised a cluster of announcements intended to be seen as getting on top of the problem. Then Home Secretary David Blunkett gave the *Sun* an exclusive interview in which he promised 'tough measures to crack down on asylum cheats'.[13] It's a prime example of the 'Feedback Loop' connecting journalists, their sources and audiences, discussed fully in Chapter 7.

Asylum Seekers: Version 2[14]

This is a transcript of a piece run, later in 2000, by the same major UK-based television news channel.

Introduction by the presenter in the studio
The government has today published its new Immigration and Asylum Bill. One of its provisions is for asylum seekers to be 'dispersed' around Britain instead of being allowed to gather in London and other big cities. Critics have said it will hinder new arrivals to this country as they try to pick up the threads of their lives. Jake Lynch reports.

Pictures 1

Voice 1

Voice-over: Kurdish refugees from Turkey at their community centre in North London. Of more than 5,000 members here, young and old, most are seeking asylum. They gather to follow the news from their homeland and support each other in coming to terms with the traumatic events which drove them out of it.

Pictures 2

Voice 2

Voice-over: The Turkish army have cleared hundreds of villages in the last ten years in their fight against the Kurdish separatists, with renewed clashes in recent days.

Pictures 3

Voice 3

Advice worker and asylum seeker: For these groups of people do need this type of community space, where they receive solidarity and understanding and sharing the pain – this becomes one of the key things that sticks these people together within these communities.

Pictures 4

Voice 4

Voice-over: The advice centre helps people to claim benefits but training in language and practical skills also prepares them for work.

Pictures 5

Voice 5

Yashar Ismailoglu, centre director and asylum seeker: We had about 34 people on regular attendance and after the end of the ten sessions of the catering course every one of them took employment in the catering industry and ten of them opened their own businesses.

Pictures 6

Voice 6

Reporter Jake Lynch, piece-to-camera: Ten years ago this part of Stoke Newington Road was more or less derelict. Today it is thriving thanks partly to the enterprise of Kurdish refugees who have come here over the past ten years. An example, they say, of what can be done if members of an exiled community are allowed to stick together and help each other.

Pictures 7

Voice 7

Voice-over: Instead from now the Home Office will be dispersing asylum seekers in smaller groups across Britain. Critics say that will make them dependent, like the beggars demonised in recent press coverage.

Pictures 8

Voice 8

Barbara Roche, immigration minister: We are speeding up the system taking on very many more people to process the cases in an absolutely professional way. We are also bringing in a system of dispersal so that no one part of the country has to bear an unfair share of the burden.

Pictures 9

Voice 9

Voice-over: In other parts of the new Bill, asylum seekers will have to use vouchers instead of cash to buy food, and lorry drivers with stowaways caught onboard at Britain's ports face a 2,000 pound fine.

Commentary on Version 2

Go through the same questions, on page 131, again. This report:

- draws attention to the problems in the Kurdish area of Turkey, which caused people to leave, seeking asylum, in the first place
- gives a voice to asylum seekers themselves, and their own representatives

It unravels the basic binary opposition on which the previous report is based. This one:

- takes issue with the 'us' and 'them' of the previous report, showing asylum seekers as hard-working, too – if given the chance
- shows how the stereotypes of asylum seekers have been constructed by 'recent press coverage'

It gives us another perspective to pose against the claim from the Home Office minister that asylum seekers represent a 'burden' on communities. Their efforts have effectively salvaged what had been a derelict and run-down high street in north London, but such efforts will be jeopardised if they are denied the chance to form their own supportive communities.

This second report, then, resists 'us/them' propaganda by identifying characteristics of the 'self' in the 'other'.

Some journalists – notably at the London *Independent*, see below – tackled widespread misconceptions about the subject head-on.

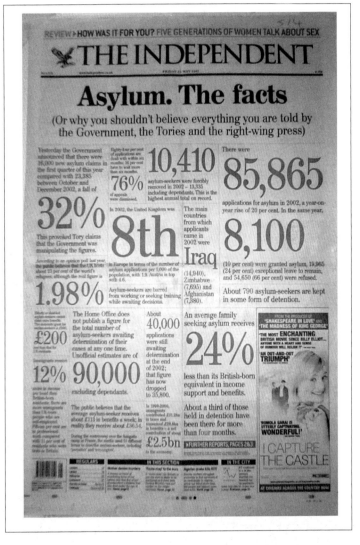

Front cover of The Independent, *23 May 2003, reproduced with permission*

2. The beginnings of violence

You are trying to persuade an editor to send you to a country where war 'may be just around the corner'. There have been sporadic incidents of violence, in particular against civilians, and political discourse is becoming increasingly polarised and strident. People tend to ask themselves 'who will protect me?' and find the only answer is 'my own kind'.[15]

One question that often underpins decisions made in international media for or against covering a story is whether such developments fit into a narrative in which some form of international intervention may ultimately enter the equation. If so, in what form?

Symptoms can include:

- massacres of civilians
- human rights abuses
- impunity for the perpetrators
- deteriorating economy with sharper economic divisions
- politicians calling increasingly openly for violence against a particular group
- media representations demonising members of minorities

Examples:

- Rwanda October 1990 – March 1994
- Cote d'Ivoire
- Kosovo 1998
- Darfur, western Sudan, 2004

> DISCUSSION: Do you:
>
> a) Say the situation is getting worse and call for international intervention to stop it?
> b) Devise a Peace Journalism approach?

Airborne patrol, Southern Philippines

a) Say the situation is getting worse

> PROBLEM: This can occlude a number of key questions:
>
> - What kinds of intervention are available?
> - What methods of conflict management have proved effective in other similar situations?
> - Might some kinds of intervention make the situation worse? How?
> - What kinds of intervention might make the situation better? How?
> - Who will intervene and what are their goals?
> - What kind of intervention is already under way and how is that affecting the conflict?

The problem can be compounded by other aspects of War Journalism. The undeclared Realist orientation in many reports of international news – arising out of Objectivity conventions – means that official sources in nation states, with their monopoly on legitimate violence, are prime sources (as discussed in Chapters 1 and 7).

The result can be that the debate over the role and responsibilities of potential third parties is collapsed into a misleading over-simplification:

'How did the Left end up on the same side as Serbia, complaining about Nato's war on Belgrade, wishing we had stuck to the alternative – namely, do[ing] nothing?

... it became one thing or the other: either the West could try to halt the greatest campaign of barbarism in Europe since 1945 – or it could do nothing.'[16]

Iraq provides another prime example: for British Prime Minister Tony Blair in 2002, it was a question of 'dealing with' Saddam Hussein or 'turning a blind eye' – a frame of reference internalised, broadly speaking, by most of the British media through the subsequent invasion of Iraq and beyond.

The other complicating factor is a lack of anchorage in Conflict Analysis. With no or limited means to explore and convey issues of structural and cultural violence, the conflict remains opaque, and media representations are more vulnerable to propaganda, since it is more likely to seem as though one party is to *blame...*

b) Peace Journalism approach

Peace Journalism can do three important jobs in this situation:

- give 'early warning' of trouble ahead
- explore peace initiatives and non-violent responses
- test stated goals of would-be intervening parties by considering possible unstated goals

Early warning – Rwanda

Could Peace Journalism have helped to prevent the Rwandan genocide?

This genocide of April-July 1994 represents one of the most traumatic and troubling episodes in the recent history of social conflict, especially given the role played by local media in this context (see Chapter 3 and Epilogue).

It's perhaps the prime example of a recurrent problem: situations arguably grave enough to warrant urgent international media and political attention, at least by the criteria evident in the responses to other conflicts, often do not receive it.

The quandary remains of how to issue an 'early warning' about potential major violence, without unwittingly fuelling calls for interventions which, as in Kosovo and Iraq, bring a huge escalation of violence and might well make underlying conflict issues more difficult to manage, resolve and transform.

Photograph copyright © Sven Torfinn/Panos Pictures
Nyamata Claudette (23), a survivor of the genocide with scars visible on her head, visits the memorial of the Rwandan genocide

DISCUSSION: What would you have done, as an editor or reporter, to try to alert the outside world to the dangers in Rwanda between 1990 and March 1994?

Some important clues were to be found in a UN report, issued in August 1993, on several massacres of Tutsi civilians after the invasion of the country by Rwandan Patriotic Front guerrillas in October 1990.

According to the report of the UN Special Rapporteur on 'Summary, Arbitrary and Extra-Judicial Killings in Rwanda', hundreds were killed on each occasion. The report specifically warned the international community that a pattern was taking hold in Rwanda of large numbers of people being killed with:

- impunity for the perpetrators
- strong indications of official complicity in, even authorship of, atrocities
- a weak judicial system unable to identify killers and bring them to account
- a sensationalist and partisan media fanning people's fears with inaccurate reporting and divisive propaganda
- no system for protecting ethnic minorities

The report goes on to make a set of strong recommendations based on the 'Principles on the Effective Prevention and Investigation of Extra-legal, Arbitrary and Summary Executions' recommended by UN Economic and Social Council resolution 1989/65 of 24 May 1989. It says:

> '**Prevention**
> Governments shall prohibit by law all extra-legal, arbitrary and summary executions and shall ensure that any such executions are recognized as offences under their criminal laws, and are punishable by appropriate penalties which take into account the seriousness of such offences...
>
> Such executions shall not be carried out under any circumstances including, but

not limited to, situations of internal armed conflict, excessive or illegal use of force by a public official or other person acting in an official capacity or by a person acting at the instigation, or with the consent or acquiescence of such person, and situations in which deaths occur in custody. This prohibition shall prevail over decrees issued by governmental authority.'

This reads as an instruction to the governments of member states to behave themselves, in their own territories, leaving aside the question of what should happen if they don't. But there's more:

> 'Governments shall make every effort to prevent extra-legal, arbitrary and summary executions through measures such as diplomatic intercession, improved access of complainants to intergovernmental and judicial bodies, and public denunciation. Intergovernmental mechanisms shall be used to investigate reports of any such executions and to take effective action against such practices.'

These prescriptions were devised for precisely the kind of situation the UN Special Rapporteur found in Rwanda, where the authorities, far from discharging their responsibility to protect their own citizens, were complicit in killing them.

There was scope for preventive Peace Journalism here, through early warning. This was a *narrative* within which individual incidents of violence could be placed. But it required an understanding of conflict dynamics which, according to some critics, was largely missing from reports of Rwanda at the time.

The duty to intervene, to prevent violence, moves up a notch when it comes to genocide.

The UN Convention defines Genocide, in Article II, as:

Any of the following acts committed with intent to destroy, in whole or in part, a national, ethnical, racial or religious group, as such:

(a) Killing members of the group;
(b) Causing serious bodily or mental harm to members of the group;
(c) Deliberately inflicting on the group conditions of life calculated to bring about its physical destruction in whole or in part;
(d) Imposing measures intended to prevent births within the group;
(e) Forcibly transferring children of the group to another group.

Article I imposes a stringent obligation on signatory states: 'genocide, whether committed in time of peace or in time of war, is a crime under international law which they [states which have signed the convention] undertake to prevent and to punish'.

The 'Principles' of 1989 mean that governments should intervene to prevent extra-judicial and summary killings; the Genocide convention means they should do something to stop any and all of the five forms a – e.

A failure of Conflict Analysis

These responsibilities placed on outside parties raise the political stakes in the way violence is represented by international media. The investigative reporter, Linda Melvern, exposed secret negotiations at the UN to prevent the word 'genocide' appearing in any official communiqué, thereby avoiding the obligation to intervene in Rwanda.[17]

A failure of Conflict Analysis meant that media reports confused the picture of what was really going on – a political plot to exterminate a section of the population – with 'a mixture of fiction and half-truths'. In effect, Melvern argues, this made them complicit in efforts by the US and UK governments to shirk their duties:

'News reports described a frenzy of bloodletting, the killings anarchic, chaotic and tribal. And the media's failure to report that genocide was taking place, and thereby generate public pressure for something to be done to stop it, contributed to indifference and inaction. This is of vital importance in explaining the failure to intervene in Rwanda's hour of need. In 1994, with no moral outcry about genocide, it was easier for politicians to claim that the hatred in Rwanda was impervious to outside help.'

What kind of help?

What 'something' could have been done? This is where a reliable account must go beyond the facile question of intervention or not, to discriminate between different kinds of intervention.

Existing interventions in Rwanda's political and economic affairs were already having a calamitous effect. The internationally brokered Arusha Accord of 1993 provided for political power-sharing, but was not backed up with sufficient determination or resources to overcome hostility from within the existing elite to the ending of one-party rule. The effect was to incentivise the elite to organise outside formal political structures, resulting in the proliferation of militias noted by the UN Special Rapporteur.

Then there was the role of IMF structural adjustment programmes, which demanded, among other things, that services such as health and education, previously free at the point of use, now had to be paid for. Moreover:

'The civil war was preceded by the flare-up of a deep-seated economic crisis. It was the restructuring of the agricultural system which precipitated the population into abject poverty and destitution. This deterioration of the economic environment, which immediately followed the collapse of the international coffee market and the imposition of sweeping macro-economic reforms by the Bretton Woods institutions, exacerbated simmering ethnic tensions and accelerated the process of political collapse.'[18]

So the 'something' could usefully have taken the form of repair work on the damage done by the interventions already underway. That could have been flagged up by more careful reporting but to do so would entail a level of understanding, of the dynamics of conflict and how it works, such as to appreciate the importance of these factors.

Then there was the famous fax, sent by Romeo Dallaire, the Canadian general in charge of UN peacekeepers, back to HQ in New York before the genocide. In it, he warned of impending bloodshed and gave an estimate that, with a mere 5,000 extra blue helmets on the ground, it could be prevented. The response was to cut back the already small size of his detachment.

Appreciation of the potential for prevention would, again, have entailed a greater degree of Conflict Analysis than was evident in much of the coverage.

The allegation made against many international media is that editors and reporters reached instinctively for what we called, in Chapter 3, an *essentialist* explanation for violence – that here was an example of a spontaneous up-welling of deep-seated 'hatreds' festering in the 'savage breast' of African tribesmen. Implicit in this was a suggestion that there was something inevitable about it, and so there was no point in trying to prevent it.

This served to obscure the *sociological* explanation – that it was a well-planned and systematically executed plot, to use violence to cement the grip on power of extremist parties under threat from dilettante international meddling. It obscured the ideological campaign to exploit fears and grievances bequeathed from colonial times and embedded in Rwandan society. It was this plot, and this campaign, that Dallaire believed he could stop in its tracks at relatively little cost.

Exercise Two
How was the Rwandan genocide characterised in news reports?

Use an Internet search engine of English language media for the period between 7 April and 30 April 1994. Enter the following pairs of search terms and see how many times they occur together (answers for UK newspapers given at the end of this chapter):

- Rwanda AND anarchy.
- Rwanda AND chaos.
- Rwanda AND tribal.
- Rwanda AND savage OR savagery.
- Rwanda AND genocide.

Peace initiatives in the 'Kosovo crisis'
A Peace Journalism approach reports and explores a variety of potential peace initiatives and solutions. The point is not to adopt or advocate them, but to help readers and audiences assess for themselves the claim that there are only two possibilities – violence or inaction.

In 1999, the Yugoslav government were blamed for bringing NATO bombs on their own heads when they refused to sign up to the Rambouillet Accord, with its provision for a referendum on independence which would have severed the province from Serbia.

But this was far from being the only deal on the table. From 1997, the Serbian Orthodox Church had called for a federal cantonisation plan, in which Serb enclaves would be empowered to run some of their own affairs, as would the Albanian majority.

This plan could have been adopted along with later proposals, approved by the Serbian National Assembly, for the UN and OSCE to police a solution based on autonomy for Kosovo.

Cantonisation under UN auspices would have offered a way to restore the self-government removed in 1989, and to insure it against any further meddling from Belgrade; while obviating the need for a change in internationally recognised borders.

These notions never figured in discussions involving the 'contact group' of governments, led by the US, that worked on the issue through 1998; but following the violence of March 2004, there were signs that an attenuated form was taking shape on the ground:

> 'Belgrade dreams of a Bosnian solution here, with a Kosovo Serb entity created on the same lines as Republika Srpska. This strategy is already being discussed, with a cantonisation plan floated a couple of weeks ago by the Serbian prime minister Vojislav Kostunica and recently echoed by Miroljub Labus, the deputy prime minister.
>
> With the strong support of the Serbian Orthodox Church, Belgrade will do everything to keep the remaining Serbs in the north. The strategy of building parallel institutions that was already in place in northern Mitrovica, and which has infuriated the Albanians over the last few years, will continue. The Serbian state will continue to issue documents to the people of the northern Serbian enclave, building up a Serbian health and educational system there, paying pensions and so on.'[19]

NATO could have had that deal at the outset, without the death and destruction and enormous further damage to structure and culture inflicted by the bombing and the retaliation on the ground. Instead, five years on, it was being forced to settle for it.

Goals of would-be intervening parties – stated and unstated

Of the three 'deliverables' of Peace Journalism, in this scenario where violence is beginning, the two we have already discussed – giving early warning, and highlighting peace initiatives – may be thought of as relatively benign and uncontentious. Not so, necessarily, with the third, since it often entails taking issue with the self-presentation, in war propaganda, by powerful third parties.

As in Chapter 1, in the discussion on the invasion of Iraq, an awareness of conflict dynamics leads us to take claims by certain parties to be acting as disinterested mediators, or 'policemen', and test them against other possibilities, that they may be more accurately seen as pursuing their own goals and interests.

Why did the US, leaders of the contact group, find nothing to interest them in the Kosovo cantonisation plan? American pre-eminence is chiefly in the military field, of course, rather than the political. If a problem on European soil is political in nature, then European institutions are best placed to deal with it and guarantee a solution. If, on the other hand, it ceases to be purely political and begins to be military as well, then it is the US that suddenly appears the prime candidate to rectify it.

A conspiracy theory? Not really – just going by well-documented strategic priorities. Consider the famous Pentagon Paper leaked to the *New York Times* in 1992, as Washington's interest in the Balkans began to increase:

> 'It is of fundamental importance to preserve NATO as the primary instrument of Western defense and security... We must seek to prevent the emergence of European-only security arrangements which would undermine Nato.'[20]

NATO presented itself as the saviour of Kosovo; but, as the London *Independent*'s Robert Fisk pointed out, Kosovo effectively saved NATO as the instrument of continued US involvement in European affairs.

This is, after all, what Zbigniew Brzezinski, in *The Grand Chessboard*, called 'the Eurasian Balkans' – Eurasia being the 'centre of world power':

> 'It is imperative that no Eurasian challenger emerges, capable of dominating Eurasia and thus of also challenging America...'[21]

'How America "manages" Eurasia is critical. A power that dominates Eurasia would control two of the world's three most advanced and economically productive regions. A mere glance at the map also suggests that control over Eurasia would almost automatically entail Africa's subordination, rendering the Western Hemisphere and Oceania geopolitically peripheral to the world's central continent.'[22]

Today, perhaps the most enduring legacy of the US role in Kosovo is Camp Bondsteel, the largest purpose-built American military base outside America.

3. Parties not communicating

You are sent by your editor to 'get both sides' of a story. You speak to a leader from one party, listen to the familiar demands and positions, then, hopefully, probe a little deeper in order to understand real interests and needs. You casually ask whether he has tried putting his position to 'the other side' and, if so, how they respond. You are met by a blank look, and then it hits you. You are not going to be reporting on a process of communication between parties; you *are* the process of communication.

> DISCUSSION: What is your responsibility as a journalist if parties to a conflict are not communicating?

Reporters who contact each side in turn for comments or stories may be among the only messengers between different groups. Here are some examples of what journalists have done in such situations.

Natal, South Africa, 1994

Three black nurses, shopping at a white-owned supermarket, were wrongly accused of shoplifting by the manager, and thrown out. They came to Khaba Mkhize, an editor on the *Natal Witness*, to complain.[23]

He wrote up their story and contacted the store manager for a comment. The reply he received was 'rude and insulting'.

Mkhize sent the story – as yet unpublished – to the head office of the supermarket chain. Straight away the provincial manager set up a meeting with the journalist, the local manager and the three nurses.

They received an apology, and the supermarket avoided damaging publicity: 'in mediating the nurses' grievance, Khaba has communicated to a supermarket manager some lessons that he will not forget – lessons about respect, and about changes in the nature of social power'.

Northern Ireland, 1994

In a key phase of the Northern Ireland peace process, journalists were 'instrumental in facilitating an indirect dialogue between their governments and the Irish Republican movement about the terms on which Sinn Fein, the political wing of the Irish Republican Army, could be admitted into political talks.'[24]

This 'megaphone diplomacy' worked through parties to the conflict using the media as 'a notice board where it is possible to post messages to the other side by presenting them to journalists in newsworthy formats'.

This was in a context where either Republicans or the British government could encounter media hostility and political difficulties if they were seen to speak directly to the other side.

One key 'newsworthy format' was used by Sinn Fein when asking, via the media, for 'clarifications' to the Downing Street Declaration, which kick-started the 'official' peace process in 1994. Journalists would report their statements and go to the government for a response – a response which would be calibrated to send a message to the Republicans without appearing to breach the British government's policy of 'never talking to terrorists'.

For journalists to play this role, it was not necessary to make a conscious break from their normal function in the way that, perhaps, Khaba Mkhize did in the example from South Africa. Those from UK-based media, at least, remained blissfully unaware of the mediating role they were playing. For them, the statements from either side were facts created in order to be reported.

Queensland, Australia, 1998

Farmers rallied to oppose 'native title' – a recognition of Aboriginal land rights which, they feared, would see them driven off their farms. *Australian Story*, a weekly TV documentary programme by the ABC, focused on one of them – Camilla Cowley:

'The saga starts with her anger and dismay when she and her family first received a document in the mail notifying them that a native title claim had been lodged on their property by the Goongarrie people.

"We believed thoroughly that we were in terrible danger of losing title to our property" she says'[25]

Camilla went to meet local Aboriginal women to find out more about what they really wanted – which led to her being ostracised by the Queensland farming community in which she lived.

The programme team set up, and filmed, re-enactments of these meetings. *Camilla's Conversion*, the name given to this episode, shows her realising that the Goongarrie did not want her to lose her property, but wished merely to be able to exercise rights on it such as hunting and fishing. They could *co-exist* on the land.

At the time of the broadcast, this was not widely appreciated among farming communities. Because the parties to this conflict were not communicating, they assumed their goals were incompatible. Thanks to the programme, many more of them realised this was wrong. To many the conflict, which had appeared as a tug of war, now seemed capable of resolution and transformation.

Camilla Cowley and Gladys Tybingoompa at Parliament House, Canberra, 1997

4. What if you can only report on one party?

You are assigned to the army HQ of one of the parties in a conflict. Your job is to attend all of their press conferences and report on their military statements.

Their job is to justify the violence to themselves and the outside world. All their statements minimise any reference to the impact on civilians. You have limited access to other sources of information. What do you do?

Symptoms include:

Philippines camera crews gather for a military press conference

- a huge amount of propaganda in facts and figures
- staged events for you to film and photograph

Examples:

- NATO HQ, Brussels, during Kosovo Crisis, 1999
- embedded journalists during Iraq War, 2003
- Indonesian media reporting on military action in Aceh, 2003-04
- Philippines journalists assigned to the military

DISCUSSION: Do you:

a) Accept and reproduce claims that the violence is all in the pursuit of a greater good?
b) Ridicule and scorn claims that the violence is all in the pursuit of a greater good?
c) Devise a Peace Journalism approach?

---

a) Accept and reproduce the claims

Questions focusing on the need to step up violence to achieve stated aims can include suggesting escalations (egging them on).

NATO HQ, Brussels, 1999

During NATO's bombing of Yugoslavia, some reporters stationed at the alliance's HQ would ask questions apparently regretting what they detected as 'squeamishness' in holding back from targets of particular political significance, or with a high risk of incurring civilian losses. Notable among this group – the 'frothers', Fisk called them – was the BBC's Mark Laity, who subsequently left to become a NATO spokesman. An example from the transcripts:

> '*Mark Laity, BBC:* One of the issues now is that you're attacking, if you like, strategic targets – the top targets – but it's the front line troops who are driving through the Kosovo villages, it's the tanks that are there. How soon can you get to attacking the actual targets, the actual Serb concentrations that are doing the damage in Kosovo?
>
> *Air Commodore Wilby:* Thanks for your question, Mark, it's a good question.'
> (26 March 1999)

And from another occasion:

> '*Mark Laity:* Has there been any change in NATO targeting? Clearly, the intensity is there but you don't seem to be going for Belgrade and things like that.'
>
> (4 June 1999)

PROBLEM: In this book (see Chapter 7), we argue that a Feedback Loop of cause and effect is discernible in the interaction of media and conflict, which makes journalists' reporting of what is happening now at least partly responsible for what happens next. At some times, such as those above, it's more visible than at others – providing an incentive to violence with the promise of being reported as right and justified, even suggesting new ways of being violent.

b) Ridicule and scorn the claims

Example: a UK newspaper headed one critical piece on the same conflict: 'Morality? Don't make me laugh!'

PROBLEM: This is an alternative to accepting at face value the justification put forward by a party involved in violence; one likely to prove gratifying to those who are already convinced it is false. But what of those who remain to be convinced, either way?

Acceptance at face value means leaving key propaganda propositions about the purpose and conduct of the war untested. But ridiculing their justification may have the same effect. If you decide, at the outset, that stated aspirations about 'the greater good' are mendacious, you cut off the possibility of exploring whether the means proposed, or being used, are likely to bring it about.

In another example, it was necessary, but not sufficient, to raise questions over whether the invasion plan for Iraq was really about liberating people from Saddam Hussein, or was, instead, 'all about oil' – as discussed in Chapter 1. It was also necessary to take the former, not at face value, but *on its merits*, thus making room to hear about alternative means to bring about regime change and to improve the human and civil rights of the Iraqi people.

Only in this way can readers and audiences be equipped to make an informed judgement as to whether the position of a party to a conflict is really the best way to secure their stated goals. If the *position* cannot be satisfactorily explained as a means of securing the stated goals, the next question might be to consider what their *unstated* goals are, as a way of opening up that question with people who are *not* already convinced about them.

c) Peace Journalism approach

First, focus on likely outcomes of violence:

- take the stated purpose on its merits
- then ask whether they are storing up trouble for the future, including a likely recurrence of the same problem

Second, introduce creativity.

You can bring in new ideas by asking questions which raise them with the party concerned.

For example, this question, at NATO HQ in Brussels, during the same conflict in 1999 – the occasion was a news conference given by the British Prime Minister, Tony Blair:

> '*Jake Lynch, Sky News:* Prime Minister, as I am sure you know, the European country with the highest number of refugees is – even now – not Albania or Macedonia, but Serbia itself. If it is right that Kosovan refugees be allowed back to their homes in Kosovo, is it not also right for Serbian refugees to be allowed back to their homes in, say, the Krajina? And if you were

prepared to take that on board, perhaps *alongside* NATO's five objectives, might that be a basis for an outcome, seen by both NATO and Yugoslavia to be fair and even-handed – the kind of outcome you yourself have championed in Northern Ireland for example?'

(20 April 1999)

Preventative – the 'road to Basra' question. In 1991, a column of Iraqi tanks, lorries and various other vehicles was attacked by the US air force while retreating from Kuwait City to Basra in southern Iraq. One officer described it as a 'turkey shoot' and hundreds were killed. As they were withdrawing in defeat and disarray when attacked – and effectively defenceless against US air power – it could be described as a massacre.

Then in 1999 NATO said it would only stop bombing Yugoslavia when a 'verifiable withdrawal' of army units from Kosovo was already under way.

The preventive Peace Journalism question at NATO headquarters was: 'At what point in moving along a road does, say, a column of Yugoslav army tanks cease to be a legitimate target for bombing and become the start of a verifiable withdrawal? You'll have to sort it out because after all, we don't want another "Road to Basra" do we?'

Eventually NATO changed its policy, and stopped the bombing *before* the start of the withdrawal, perhaps mindful that 'turkey shoots' would be greeted, at least by some journalists, as unacceptable from a party presenting itself as 'the goodies'.

Talking to killers

It's become commonplace, in analyses of the so-called 'War on Terrorism', that the 'other side' cannot be talked to or negotiated with. In the traditional sense of getting leaders round a table, to 'deliver' their people to a 'deal', that may be true. But that does not mean there is no scope for what has been called *social negotiation*; no point in understanding 'what makes them tick' or

discussing steps to alleviate the structural and cultural factors which may be creating conditions in which people can be more easily mobilised for violence.

The Palestinian legislator, Hanan Ashrawi, once told an interviewer that suicide bombers, for instance, 'are not born that way – they are being made that way'.[26] There is no way back for them, of course, but her general point is proved by people who *were* that way, then changed. One particularly impressive story in the London *Daily Mirror* was a feature piece, in the aftermath of the '9/11' attacks, based on an interview with a former paramilitary from Northern Ireland.[27]

In it, Alistair Little recounts his experiences in the loyalist Ulster Volunteer Force:

'Since September 11, Alistair Little has been watching the young men flocking to join extremist Islamic organisations closely.

"My experience is that people are easily engaged in violence when they are hurting, or their voices aren't being heard, or they feel under threat," he says. "It is a human response to pain and hurt".'

Recent developments included the bombing of Afghanistan and the arrest of Richard Reid, the would-be 'shoe bomber' who boarded a transatlantic flight with high explosives in the sole of his training shoe. Little tells interviewer Ros Wynne-Jones:

'While I can understand America's response, I think it is creating other young men who will join the al-Qaeda organisation... to understand what is happening in the minds of these people, we need to look much deeper.'

He speaks frankly about his own history of violence. His friend's father was shot dead by Republicans, and Little joined the UVF to carry out a revenge killing. He was sent to the Maze prison, where, as the years passed, it began to occur to him that he had more in common with Republican fellow inmates – predominantly young working-class men like himself – than with politicians on the outside, 'talking about fighting and dying for Ulster'.

Such people carry a unique authority to speak about violence, what makes it happen and how it can be prevented. In another example, the *Jakarta Post* newspaper ran a feature piece[28] from the troubled city of Ambon, on Baihajar Tualeka, a young woman presented as a 'bomb-maker turned peace-maker':

> 'Like everybody else in Ambon, she saw the conflict as a crusade, believing that if they got killed, they would go straight to heaven. "Every one of us, men, women, adults and children, were so overpowered by that overzealous perception that we would do dangerous things like making crude bombs, guns and Molotov cocktails".'

Now, she has joined a group of peace activists, with both Christian and Muslim members, 'trying to build awareness in the community that the conflict has been engineered by outside forces' – turning together against a deficient structure in which heavy-handed military deployments succeed only in exacerbating the situation, to the benefit of economic and political profiteers.

5. Reporting on massacres

Reports begin filtering through of a massacre of civilians. The location is remote and there is no immediate, practical way of reaching it yourself. What do you do?

Symptoms include:

- risk of escalating violence through revenge attacks or calls to 'punish' the party held responsible
- poor communications to the area at the centre of the story
- people afraid to talk to the media

Richard Bulane, survivor of a massacre by Philippines army troops which killed three members of his family, Davao del Sur, Mindanao, February 2005

Examples:

- Nepalese government military and Maoist rebels, 1996 onwards (see Chapter 4)
- Kosovo Albanians during the NATO bombing campaign, 1999
- Aceh, Indonesia, 2003/4

DISCUSSION: Do you:

a) Splash it as an atrocity, demanding urgent action, likely to change the course of war?
b) Ignore or downplay it?
c) Devise a Peace Journalism approach?

a) Splash it as an atrocity

PROBLEM: Massacres do take place; they are horrific and all too real. But there is also a long and nasty history of what are claimed as massacres turning out to be either made up or, if based on the truth, looking very different when the full picture is finally revealed.

Crucially, a 'massacre' must entail the killing of defenceless people. And the killers must act deliberately, knowing them to be defenceless at the time.

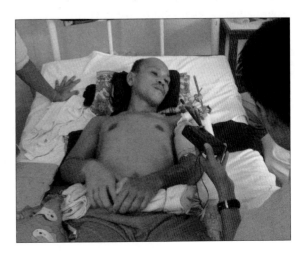

b) Ignore or downplay it

> PROBLEM: Not practical since other reporters will be filing on it and your editor will want to know why you are not following suit!

You risk the party that originated the reports stepping up its efforts to get your attention, perhaps with more extreme or more violent means.

c) Peace Journalism approach

Report the reports, ensuring that your audience knows as much as you can tell them about:

- who originated the reports, whom they told, how and in what circumstances
- any areas of continuing uncertainty
- whether any police, forensic or other independent investigation is under way
- whether there is any particular aspect the investigation is looking at
- whether anyone else was there at the time, besides the people who originated the reports you've seen. What do they say about it? If this is unknown, say in your story, 'We are still waiting to hear from them'

Sometimes massacres can be invented for propaganda purposes. In World War I, the British spread stories of German soldiers bayoneting Belgian babies. We have already mentioned the 'babies-in-incubators' story used to justify Operation Desert Storm.

On some occasions, incidents get labelled as 'massacres' when they are in fact battles between *bona fide* combatants – or even mistakes, albeit ghastly ones.

Mahehle, KwaZulu/Natal, South Africa
In the run-up to South Africa's first democratic election, a 'massacre' took place as part of ongoing violence between the African National Congress (ANC) and the rival Inkatha Freedom Party (IFP) in 1994.[29]

A group of teenagers camping in a disused hut on the outskirts of a village were shot dead late one night. It turned out that their campfire had caused some locals to panic, thinking an attack on the village was being planned, and they alerted vigilantes from the IFP.

A police investigation concluded that the guns had been fired from a considerable distance, not something one would expect if the killers knew those inside the hut were unarmed. A picture emerged of fear among villagers that the shadowy figures around the campfire were ANC raiders come to threaten them in their homes.

In this case the information, reported in the *Natal Witness* by Khaba Mkhize, switched the focus away from blame – ie seeing the violent acts of one party as 'the problem' – to the whole conflict, in which errors of judgement occurred with consequences no one intended, including the killing of children.

In your report of such events, you could always remind readers, listeners or viewers of past 'massacres'– like the ones discussed here – which turned out to be either contrived or, on the basis of a genuine misunderstanding, misdescribed. A useful caution, perhaps, against jumping to conclusions.

6. Reporting on refugees

You are sent to a border crossing just inside an independent republic abutting a province where tens of thousands of indigenous people have appeared as refugees – fleeing, they say, the brutality of that country's armed forces. Children are crying, there is a shortage of clean water and aid agencies are having difficulty feeding everyone.

First, there is a question about the accuracy of the refugees' stories. Symptoms include:

- people traumatised, living in misery and squalor
- horror stories of appalling human rights abuses
- aid agencies talking up the atrocities to get media attention

Examples:

- Borders of Macedonia and Albania with the province of Kosovo, 1999
- Border of Chad with Sudan, from 2004
- Border of Thailand with Burma, from 1989

DISCUSSION: Do you:

a) Seek out the most extreme horror stories?
b) Play it down?
c) Devise a Peace Journalism approach?

Ethnic Karen refugees in Kawthoolei, Burma

a) Seek extreme horror stories

This is an approach observed by the journalist Edward Behr as long ago as the first Congo civil war of 1962 – a TV cameraman in a camp of Belgian civilians called out: 'Anyone here been raped and speak English?' Get people to tell you the most heart-rending stories and to give the most graphic descriptions of the violence they endured.

PROBLEM: People do not leave their homes except for serious reasons. But history tells us that some refugees almost invariably give exaggerated and/or confused accounts of the situation which forced them to flee.

By reproducing such accounts you risk spreading alarm among other people in the same territory who may then leave their homes. You also risk providing 'justification' for a disproportionate analysis of the situation and for a violent response against the supposed perpetrators.

b) Play it down

Approach the assignment determined to disbelieve refugee stories unless they can provide forensic proof.

PROBLEM: Proof to back up true stories to a standard required in a court of law only ever comes to hand much later. Your editor is unlikely to want to wait that long!

c) Peace Journalism approach

- Seek out refugees who can tell you what happened to them – personally.
- Look for interviewees who can say what they saw with their own eyes.
- *Beware:* reporting things people have only heard about is the way rumours begin to be exaggerated.
- *Be careful* not to report as '*fact*' estimates, extrapolations and suppositions by aid agencies.
- *Be careful:* some people from province A have an interest in talking things up.
- *Beware:* NGOs may talk up the figures/atrocities because they want money to provide for the refugees.

- You may meet refugees under the guidance or protection of an aid agency or NGO, who may, in turn, have an interest in talking up the seriousness of the situation and the privations endured by the people you're talking to. The refugees themselves may very well realise this. If they are depending on the agency or NGO for food and shelter, they may feel they have to 'come up with the goods' in the stories they tell you.
- Try to suggest some of the factors which may be leading country B to behave badly towards civilians in province A.
- Be frank about *all* wrongdoing and do not seek to excuse it.
- *Always* seek the underlying explanation for wrongdoing.[30]

7. Stalemate

You know of a country or province where people are enduring desperate humanitarian suffering, brutality at the hands of the army or other armed groups etc. Over time this situation loses its news value – nothing seems to change, and the story becomes 'ossified'. You are uncomfortably aware that silence on your part could amount to complicity. What can you do to help people get some attention, to keep their situation 'on the map'? How can you sell this story to your editor?

Symptoms can include:

- low-level guerrilla fighting by rebel group(s)
- human rights abuses against civilians and the opposition by government forces

- email communication by activists on the ground, documenting atrocities
- sanctions by the international community that impact on the civilian population causing starvation and severe health problems
- widespread poverty

Examples:

- Burma under successive military dictatorships
- Iraq under sanctions before the 2003 invasion
- West Papua, disputed province of Indonesia from 1969 onwards

DISCUSSION: Do you:

a) Ignore it?
b) Sensationalise it and say the situation is about to explode into all-out war?
c) Devise a Peace Journalism approach?

KNLA fighters plan guerrilla tactics in Burmese jungle

a) Ignore it

> PROBLEM: You risk sending the message that the only way you will cover something is if there is an escalation in violence.

b) Sensationalise it

> PROBLEM: 'Crying wolf' only works once. Your editor and the public will not trust you in the future.

c) Peace Journalism approach

- Seek out the moderates within the regime. Do they have any ideas for change or dialogue?
- Discuss with peace groups what alternative solutions they have which could open up a new angle and enable you to return to document the human rights abuses.
- Wait for a political development – no matter how small – to use as a peg to enable you to return to document the human rights abuses again.
- Look for entry points which could change the balance of incentives for continuing the human rights abuses, perhaps drawing on the lessons of the Helsinki process from the 1970s and its eventual dividend of helping to bring down the Iron Curtain across eastern Europe.

Burma/Myanmar March, 1999

The present authors went on a filming trip inside Burma, on a facility with the Karen National Liberation Army (KNLA). By the time the material was presented to editors, they were too preoccupied with the KLA in Kosovo to take much interest in the KNLA.

Months later, however, two 'pegs' did materialise. First, a group of armed Burmese exiles stormed the Burmese embassy in Bangkok – one of Asia's main media capitals. Pictures of the stand-off went straight on to satellite feeds supplied by the main international news agencies.

This may well have been an example where the general indifference of the outside world drove desperate people to desperate measures, to get some attention for their plight. Our KNLA material focused on their armed struggle, but also on their call for autonomous self-government within a federated Burma (a change from their traditional demand of independence) and the practical steps they were taking to alleviate the situation of internally displaced people. Then, some weeks later, a British activist, James Mawdsley, was arrested by the Burmese authorities. It became a story of a 'Brit in trouble abroad'; but this, too, offered a peg for another story, using the rest of our material.

Annabel McGoldrick reporting on KNLA fighters in Burmese jungle

Both reports by Annabel McGoldrick were broadcast by Sky News, which, to its credit, has kept on drawing viewers' attention to the situation inside Burma whenever an opportunity has arisen.

Another example: when Burma's military rulers opened talks on a new constitution in May 2004, the *Insight* programme on CNN used it as a peg for visiting Mae Sot, in northern Thailand, to interview refugees and aid workers.

So there are many ways to keep in the news a situation which merits concern. As so often, this requires a deliberate, creative strategy, based on a recognition that if we wait for developments in the traditional 'news diary', then the situation may not receive the attention it deserves.

8. Peace proposals

The leaders of two parties to a conflict have been negotiating – let us call them A and B. At a government press conference, you are given details of a peace plan which Party A say they have tabled in the talks. Party B are refusing to comment, then later say they cannot accept the proposals.

Symptoms include:

- the plan is described as a peace deal
- there has been no real negotiation – or public consultation – about the content of the plan
- contained in the small print are elements which are unacceptable to the other side
- the plan omits elements important to the other side

Examples:

- Camp David summit, involving Ehud Barak and Yasser Arafat, 2000
- Rambouillet agreement drawn up by NATO in 1999

DISCUSSION: Do you:

a) Report this as an important offer?
b) Describe it as 'Peace in our Time!'?
c) Devise a Peace Journalism approach?

a) Report it as an important offer

Do you suggest that it is only B's intransigence preventing a peace agreement?

PROBLEM: There may be nothing in the text you have been given which you think B should object to, but how do you know you have been shown the full text, or the same text as them?

Are you part of a media strategy to prepare us to blame B for the imminent breakdown of negotiations?

Misunderstanding between Yasser Arafat and Ehud Barak, as President Clinton looks on, Camp David, July 2000
Photograph copyright © REUTERS/Win McNamee

b) Describe it as 'Peace in our Time!'

Some tentative signs emerge that B may be ready to sign up to the deal. You report the text you have received as a solution to the conflict.

> PROBLEM: Leaders may have many reasons for signing an agreement, but their respective peoples may find it does not address the real issues affecting them. So in time the violence recurs and the cycle continues.

c) Peace Journalism approach

Suggested questions a reporter could ask of any peace plan:

1. What was the method behind the plan? Dialogue with parties and in that case with all the parties? Some trial negotiation? Analogy with other conflicts? Intuition?
2. To what extent is the plan acceptable to all parties? If not, what can be done about it?
3. To what extent is the plan, if realised, self-sustainable? If not, what can be done about it?
4. Is the plan based on autonomous action by the conflict parties, or does it depend on outsiders?
5. To what extent is there a process in the plan, about who shall do what, how, when and where, or is it the only outcome?
6. To what extent is the plan based on what only elites can do, what only people can do or on what both can do?
7. Does the plan foresee an ongoing conflict resolution or is the idea a single-shot agreement?
8. Is peace/conflict-transformation education for people, for elites or for both, built in to the plan?
9. If there has been violence, to what extent does the plan contain elements of reconciliation?
10. If there has been violence, to what extent does the plan contain elements of rehabilitation/reconstruction?
11. If the plan doesn't work, is the plan reversible?
12. Even if the plan does work for this conflict, does it create new conflicts or problems?[31]

Camp David talks, 2000

The talks between Israeli Prime Minister Ehud Barak and Palestinian Authority Chairman Yasser Arafat were a classic case of the intransigence of one side – Arafat – being blamed for squandering a chance for peace, turning down a generous offer, etc.

This rapidly attained the status of a media myth, setting the scene for the escalation of subsequent years. Actually, some accounts, including by some involved in the talks, doubt whether actual proposals were ever tabled by the Israelis at all – despite plentiful 'mood music' to suggest they had been.

West Bank settlement activity greatly expanded under Barak's ministry, and he proved unwilling to make interim concessions agreed in previous rounds of the peace process. This, he calculated, would allow him to be seen at home as negotiating the 'big step' to final status talks from a position of strength, husbanding his cards for the crucial power play. However:

> 'The intended recipients of his tough statements – the domestic constituency he was seeking to carry with him – barely listened, while their unintended recipients – the Palestinians he would sway with his final offer – listened only too well. Never convinced that Barak was ready to go far at all, the Palestinians were not about to believe that he was holding on to his assets in order to go far enough. For them, his goals were to pressure the Palestinians, lower their expectations and worsen their alternatives.'[32]

Others point out that, from what we know of Barak's proposals, even assuming they were really tabled at Camp David, they would have fallen far short of the minimum Arafat could have accepted. Gush Shalom, the Israeli peace bloc, has found a particularly effective way to illustrate this on its website, with its map showing the 'amazing disappearing Palestine',[33] with the West Bank divided and reticulated by Israeli settlements and associated infrastructure.

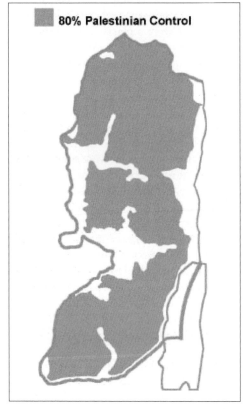

Map from Gush Shalom
(Israeli Peace Bloc) website
info@gush-shalom.org

Gush Shalom comments:

'No nation in the world would accept this as a "peacetime" solution... the "generous offer" is a fig leaf for those who justify this war against the Palestinians.'[34]

9. A facility with the men of violence

*Sudan People's Liberation Army,
Southern Sudan, 1998*

DISCUSSION: You are offered a facility with a local militia group, the Sudan People's Liberation Army, to film them 'on the move'. Do you:

• Accept the invitation?
• Decline?
• Wonder what your editor might say if you turn them down?
• Have an excuse if a rival reporter accepts the offer?

You decide to accept. The men are patrolling near the frontline. They offer to fire their artillery pieces to make a good picture for you. Do you:

• Accept?
• Decline?
• Have an explanation if you do decline?

What are the journalist's responsibilities in this situation?

- If they are firing their guns just to make a picture for you, do you explain to the viewer that it's just for show? Would your editor be happy with that?
- If they are firing their guns at real targets, can you be sure they would have fired them, at this time and place, even if you were not there to film them?
- What responsibility do you bear, therefore, for the consequences, ie whatever happens when the shells fall?
- If your choice, as to how to represent the conflict, is to base it on armed men and their comings and goings, what understanding will you project?
- How might this understanding feed in to political calculations about the conflict and the prospects for interventions of different kinds?
- What influence will you have on the behaviour of the parties themselves?
- How else could you convey the reality of the conflict?

Answers from page 144
The Rwanda results

Search results from the UK publications section of lexis-nexis, between 7 and 30 April 1994:

Rwanda AND anarchy: 23
Rwanda AND chaos: 18
Rwanda AND tribal: 84
Rwanda AND savage OR savagery: 25
Rwanda AND genocide: 15

---

*

Endnotes for Chapter 5

1. Jake Lynch and Annabel McGoldrick, 'Reporting Conflict – An Introduction to Peace Journalism', in Thomas Hanitzsch, Martin Loffelholz and Ronny Mustamu (eds), *Agents of Peace – Public Communication and Conflict Resolution in an Asian Setting*, Friedrich Ebert Stiftung, Jakarta, 2004, p 120.
2. Ben Bagdikian, *The Media Monopoly*, 6th ed, Beacon Press, Boston, 2000, pp 178-9.
3. Quoted in Jake Lynch, *The Peace Journalism Option*, Conflict and Peace Forums, Taplow, 1998, p 25.
4. Gerry van Klinken, 'What Caused the Ambon Violence?', *Inside Indonesia*, No 60, October-December 1999.
5. MORI poll for the UK Refugee Council, June 2002.
6. Stephen Cope, Frank Leishman and Peter Starie, *Law-and-Order Policy-Making in the 1990s*, University of Portsmouth, www.psa.ac.uk/cps/1995%5Ccope.pdf.
7. Jake Lynch and Annabel McGoldrick, *Peace Journalism Manual*, prepared for British Council training workshops in Indonesia, October 2000.
8. Jake Lynch, *Reporting the World*, Conflict and Peace Forums, Taplow, 2002, p 22.
9. Loosely based on Jake Lynch, 'Responding to Difference', *Rhodes Journalism Review*, No. 20, August 2001, Department of Journalism and Media Studies, Rhodes University and the Media Peace Centre, Cape Town, South Africa.
10. *Sky News*, 19 March 2000.
11. *Mythbuster*, UK Refugee Council, December 2002, available at http://www.refugeecouncil.org.uk/news/myths/myth001.htm.
12. 'How to Make Migration Work for Poverty Reduction', *Migration and Development*, House of Commons International Development Committee, 8 July 2004.

13. Simon Walters and Peter Oborne, *Inside Blair's Bunker*, quoted in Michael White, 'No 10 "Worked with *Sun* to Manage News"', London *Guardian*, 24 May 2004.
14. *Sky News*, 3 April 2000
15. Michael Ignatieff, *The Warrior's Honor*, Vintage, London and New York, 1999, p 45.
16. Jonathan Freedland, 'The Left Needs to Wake Up to the Real World: This War Is a Just One', London *Guardian*, 26 March 1999.
17. Linda Melvern, *A People Betrayed: The Role of the West in Rwanda's Genocide*, Zed Books, London, 2000.
18. Michel Chossudovsky, 'IMF-World Bank Policies and the Rwandan Holocaust', *Third World Network Features*, 26 January 1995.
19. Gordana Igric, 'Albanians Lose the Plot', *Balkan Crisis Report*, No 488, Institute for War and Peace Reporting, 23 March 2004.
20. 'Excerpts from Pentagon's Plan: Prevent the Re-emergence of a New Rival', *New York Times*, 8 March 1992.
21. Zbigniew Brzezinkski, *The Grand Chessboard – American Primacy and Its Geostrategic Imperatives*, Basic Books, New York, 1997, p xiv.
22. Ibid, p 31.
23. Lesley Fordred, 'Presence and Absence – Journalists as Facilitators', in Melissa Baumann (ed), *Media & Conflict, Track Two*, Vol 7, No 4, December 1998, Centre for Conflict Resolution and Media Peace Centre, Cape Town, pp 28-31.
24. Kirsten Sparre, 'Megaphone Diplomacy in the Northern Irish Peace Process – Squaring the Circle by Talking to Terrorists through Journalists', *Press & Politics*, Harvard University, 20 April 2000.
25. John Millard (producer), 'Camilla's Conversion', *Australian Story*, ABC Television, Australia, 5 March 1998.
26. *Channel 4 News*, London.
27. Ros Wynne-Jones, 'I Was Only 17 But I Asked to Fire the Gun...', London *Daily Mirror*, 13 February 2002.
28. Pandaya, 'Ex-bombmaker Turns Peacemaker', *Jakarta Post*, 17 September 2002.
29. Related in Lesley Fordred, 'Natal Cockroaches Fly: Khaba Mkhze and Communitarian Journalism in KwaZulu-Natal, South Africa', in George E. Marcus (ed) *Late Editions: Cultural Producers in Perilous States*, Chicago University Press, Chicago, 1997.
30. Jake Lynch and Annabel McGoldrick, op cit, 2000.
31. Johan Galtung, *Conflict Transformation by Peaceful Means – The TRANSCEND Method*, United Nations, Geneva, 2000, p 173.
32. Hussein Agha & Robert Malley, 'Camp David – The Tragedy of Errors', *New York Review of Books*, 9 August 2001. Viewable at http://www.gush-shalom.org/media/barak_eng.swf.
33. Quote and map from http://www.gush-shalom.org/generous/generous.html.

Chapter 6

Doing Peace Journalism

This chapter will examine, in depth, Peace Journalism treatments of three kinds of important story – a single violent incident, follow-ups to a violent incident, and a complex international political story. It will show how practical reporting options fit in to a sliding scale from War Journalism to Peace Journalism.

By the end of this chapter the reader will be able to:

- Identify missing Peace Journalism elements in accounts of violent incidents
- Devise effective tactics to re-conceive, re-source, reconstruct and rewrite them as Peace Journalism
- See how a newspaper or programme could carry out a creative strategy, through follow-up reports, to counter the ignorance and misunderstandings left behind by War Journalism
- Identify missing Peace Journalism elements in a complex international political story
- Devise effective tactics to re-conceive, re-source, reconstruct and rewrite it as Peace Journalism

A violent incident – the Palu bomb, Indonesia

Exercise One
Writing Peace Journalism

- Read the following news story from the *Jakarta Post* about a violent incident.
- Imagine you are the *Post*'s Palu correspondent.
- Rewrite the article as an on-the-day story, transforming it into Peace Journalism.
- Word limit – 800 words.
- Read the steps that follow the article before you begin your task.

Indonesian journalists interview refugee children, Palu

BOMBS TERRORISE PALU, POLICE TIGHTEN UP SECURITY[1]

Unexploded bombs were discovered in several places in the Central Sulawesi capital of Palu on Friday, frightening locals further after a bomb blast one day earlier seriously injured three people outside the city's Marantha Bible School.

The bombs were discovered separately at the Palu Mitra Utama shopping center, the Bala Keselamatan Hospital, a government office on Jl. Cendrawasih and a kiosk on Jl. Tanjung Harapan.

The discoveries forced local authorities to tighten security in Palu, particularly at houses of worship and other public places, to prevent the situation from worsening.

Meanwhile, a suspected bomb found at Eklesia Pantekosta Church on Jl. ThYulianton turned out to be a hoax.

Members of the provincial police's Mobile Brigade managed to defuse the homemade bombs at each place in the morning. However, the discovery of the bombs caused panic among local residents.

'Our life is not really safe', a woman on Jl. Tanjung Harapan told the *Jakarta Post*.

Central Sulawesi Police chief Brig. Gen. Zainal Abidin Ishak said the bomb scares showed the security situation in Palu was 'extremely vulnerable'.

'I ask police in districts and regency administrations to organize patrols. Anybody out after midnight needs to be questioned', he said.

Zainal said his office would soon set up a special team to deal with the terrorism in the city and hunt for the perpetrators and other culprits.

Asked whether rioters were moving to Palu as the nearby conflict-torn town of Poso was under tight security, he said the provincial police were investigating possible links between the two incidents.

Poso has been the site of religious fighting since 2000, with thousands of people killed in clashes. Muslim and Christian leaders signed a peace deal last December but it appeared to be ineffective with the renewed outbreaks of violence.

Zainal called the bombing in front of the Marantha Bible School on Thursday 'inhuman'. The blast left two civilians and a policeman severely wounded.

Activities at the school returned to normal on Thursday, said its principal Rafles Loke. 'May God forgive the bombers', he said, commenting on the incident.

Since early this year, Palu has had numerous bomb threats. The first bombs exploded at four churches on New Year's Eve, but no casualties were reported.

Three suspects, including Yono, who was a signatory to the peace deal, have been put on trial.

In June, another bomb blast damaged a roadside kiosk in Palu. No suspects were arrested in the incident.

Before you write consider:

- Do you report the bomb?
- Do you say it was planted outside a Christian school?
- Why – or why not?
- What effect do you think the bombers intended?
- Do you raise or explore that in your report?
- How can you avoid 'doing their work for them'?
- Who else will you quote in your report?
- How will you establish their relevance to the story?
- How will you create a framework of understanding in which other sources will be clearly seen as relevant to the incident?

Indonesian TV covers refugee children in Palu

The aim of the bomb is provocation

Remember you are the Palu correspondent, so the editor is bound to want the discovery of the bombs to be the 'top line' of your report. What are the likely consequences? What would be the likely consequences of not reporting it?

The planting of these bombs might very well be facts created in order to be reported – what has been called, in another context, 'staging propaganda by deeds'.[2] The aim? What Indonesians call *provokasi* – provocation. It refers to ill-intentioned outsiders stirring up trouble, trying to scare people into taking sides against each other in what are called 'horizontal conflicts' – in this case, between followers of different religions in the same place.

Could you illuminate this issue in your article, to enable readers to inspect and assess from the outside the possible calculations behind the propaganda? Could you offer your own judgement? What would be stronger than your own judgement? Could you find an analyst to quote?

You can't stop people finding out

Any editor with a reporter in Palu is going to want these bombs covered. It would be impossible to prevent people from finding out about this incident. Ignoring it could bring difficulties, as we saw in the last chapter; if one act of violence has been perpetrated to get the media's attention, and that is not forthcoming, it may incentivise more and bigger acts of violence to the point where they become unignorable.

Everyone knows it was a Christian school

Likewise, it would be impossible, in practice, to prevent people from finding out the bomb was planted outside a Christian school. This is pretty clearly intended to convince people that a religious war is just around the corner, so they had better prepare for it by grouping together with 'their own kind', obtaining weapons, paying for protection etc – a process Indonesians call *pangkelompokan*

(literally, 'group formation'). It is intended, in short, to escalate conflict.

One destructive factor in these situations is the power of rumour, leading people to give credence to suggestions of hidden developments and conspiracies. Journalism can be an antidote to this. If people are confident that anything of real importance will be professionally reported, then rumours, which do not appear in reputable media, can be discounted with equal confidence.

Media as a force for moderation

People's trust is based on confidence that facts are not being withheld:

> 'Journalists can only be forces for moderation if they have the trust of their audience, and therefore attempts by governments to censor accurate reports, or attempts by journalists themselves to suppress facts in order to reduce conflict are misplaced and counterproductive. We know that suppressing news about conflicts only creates a greater public appetite for information...
>
> Within every community there are extremists and moderates. By censoring the facts, journalists do not hurt the hot-heads, for censorship only makes their interpretation of the story and statement of 'the facts' (in print, audio and video) seem more credible. Censorship hurts the moderates, by taking away from them the information which they need to convince others in their community that the outside threats are not so bad as to warrant the policies advocated by extremists.'[3]

Some media in Indonesia sometimes omit, from their reporting of developments in 'horizontal conflicts', any mention of the religious identity of locations, victims or perpetrators. They believe that, by doing so, they can avoid inflaming readers or audiences. But they may, in the process, be unwittingly undermining the media's ability to proof communities against rumours, put about by those with an interest in escalating the conflict.

The question, therefore, is how you report

this incident frankly and honestly, while avoiding getting trapped into doing the bombers' work for them. For this, we need to find some additional sources to the ones quoted in the *Jakarta Post*.

Other sources – interview other characters

A role-play for two people

Instructions:

- Begin with person A playing the role of one of the two characters described below.
- Person B is the interviewing journalist.
- Conduct the interview to reveal the character's part in breaking or diverting the cycle of violence (see Chapter 3).
- Then person B assumes the role of the other character, and person A, that of the interviewing journalist.
- Each journalist must then write the story of the Palu bombs, drawing on the notes about their own character and their interview with the other character.

The interview characters, and the experiences they relate, are closely based on real people and real events. Don't make it too difficult for the journalist to get the information from you – but don't make it too easy either!

Jotje Yulianto

Jotje Yulianto is a religious leader – a priest and head of a regional Christian lay association in Palu, Central Sulawesi.

Someone came to his office a few days ago and left a large brown envelope for him. Mr Yulianto was out. The man would not give his name, but just left the envelope with Mr Yulianto's secretary.

It contained a sinister calendar, with each month of 2003 illustrated with a photograph of a prominent local Christian from the Palu and Poso areas of Central Sulawesi. Each photograph had a

red skull and crossbones on it.

It was clear, Mr Yulianto says, that these people were being earmarked to be killed, one per month.

The envelope also contained a letter claiming that 3,000 local Muslim men had signed up for a revenge mission against the Christians of Poso, in response to thousands of Muslims having been attacked, killed and driven from their homes in riots in 2001.

He recalls an incident at Kilometre Nine, a tiny village on the road from Poso to Tentena, where Muslims were attacked in the local mosque, which was then burned down. 'Some Muslims in this area find it very difficult to forgive or forget the sacrilege,' he says.

Mr Yulianto has been collecting examples of where Christians and Muslims have helped each other and where religious leaders have helped to defuse tension.

One local Imam organised a group of Muslim men, not for revenge, but to help clean and rebuild churches where Christian refugees had returned to their homes.

Mr Yulianto himself welcomed Muslim refugees into the area where his church is situated. The local Christian people kept pigs in the neighbouring field to eat, and he realised this might be insensitive to their new Muslim neighbours. So he arranged for the pigs to be moved to a field at the far end of the village, out of sight of where the refugees were housed.

Mr Yulianto has shown the calendar to the police and received a letter from the local police chief promising to provide extra security.

He has also alerted the *Sintuwo Maroso* Youth Convoy, a group of civilian monitors, who have promised to watch over the named people in the months concerned.

On the claim about the revenge mission, he says so many weapons have now been handed in to the authorities and destroyed, under the Malino peace agreement, that the situation has become safer. There are no longer hordes of people running around armed, spreading fear and alarm among residents.

Mrs Hidayat

Mrs Hidayat is a Muslim woman, originally from Poso.

Her husband was killed in violence between local Muslims and Christians in 2000. She is now living in a house in a village near Palu, as a refugee, with her two boys, Husai, now aged 15, and Agus, 13.

Her other child, a girl of seven, was killed when she ran back to their home to get her favourite doll. Their house had been set on fire and, when the girl went in, it collapsed on top of her.

Also, Mrs Hidayat has been shown great kindness and generosity by the local people. This helps reduce her anger about what has happened to her.

Local farmers and residents in Nunu where she lives have organised themselves into a local grassroots NGO, *Bantaya*, to loan land to the refugees.

Mrs Hidayat works on this land to grow food for the family, but also sells some of the surplus such as chillis, corn and pepper to earn money for them.

Mrs Hidayat joined a local women's group developing strategies for peace. The group share ideas on how to prevent their children from joining in the violence. When one of them finds a 'line of argument' which appears particularly persuasive, she shares it with the others.

Mrs Hidayat does not want revenge. She wants to see the men who killed her husband and burned down her house brought to justice. But she realises that for people to take the law into their own hands is counter-productive.

Mrs Hidayat tells her two sons not to turn to violence or seek revenge for the deaths of their father and sister or the rape of their mother. 'You will need to grow up to a future where people in this place can all trust each other', she says to them. 'Revenge and bitterness will trap you in the past – it's hard, but we must move on. I can, even with what happened to me – you should too.'

Reporting on work opportunities for refugees, Palu

What the characters add to the story

Above all, each of these characters shows that not everyone in the Palu/Poso area is prepared to interpret incidents such as the bombs as a cue for *pangkelompokan*. This proves to readers that the one does not automatically follow from the other. Provocations like the calendar – another fact created, possibly, in order to be reported – do not have to provoke.

Along the way we hear about several groups – *Bantaya*, the *Sintuwo Maroso* Youth Convoy, as well as individuals like the religious leaders from either faith – taking positive action to protect their shared community against a descent into factional fighting.

They are providing physical, psychological and political security as ways to interrupt the cycle of violence.

The challenge is to convey their *connection* with the conflict, and the outlook for its likely development, in the course of a news story. At some point you have to *turn the corner* from details about the bomb and the response of the authorities, to material about these two individuals and what they have told you.

The police chief, for example, is the kind of source readers would expect to see quoted in a story such as this – the formula becomes familiar through constant use. To work in the likes of Mr Yulianto and Mrs Hidayat automatically makes such a story less familiar.

You need, therefore, to construct a *framework of understanding* in which the relevance of new perspectives to the story about the bomb can be made clear.

Examples based on adapting the existing story (new bits in italics)

Central Sulawesi Police chief Brig. Gen. Zainal Abidin Ishak said the bomb scares showed the security situation in Palu was 'extremely vulnerable'.

'I ask police in districts and regency administrations to organize patrols. Anybody out after midnight needs to be questioned,' he said.

Police have also been asked to keep an eye out for copies of a sinister calendar, being circulated in the Palu area, which appears to show prominent Christian figures earmarked for execution, one per month.

Jotje Yulianto, a local priest and leader of a Christian lay organisation, had one delivered to his office when he was out. It was clearly aimed

at scaring people into 'taking sides' in a religious war, he said – but he and fellow religious leaders were taking their own actions to forestall tensions between residents and refugees from both the Muslim and the Christian faith...

And:

Asked whether rioters were moving to Palu as the nearby conflict-torn town of Poso was under tight security, he said the provincial police were investigating possible links between the two incidents.

Poso has been the site of religious fighting since 2000, with thousands of people killed in clashes. Muslim and Christian leaders signed a peace deal last December but it appeared to be ineffective with the renewed outbreaks of violence.

Civic leaders have raised fears that refugees from conflict-torn areas of Indonesia might bring the contagion of inter-communal strife to Palu. One of them, Mrs Hidayat, was forced to flee her home in Poso, in 2000.

She lost her husband and one child, but despite her tragic story, she is very firm that her two teenaged sons should not seek revenge or join in the violence...

Refugee children share their experiences, Palu

Connecting words

Some words are useful to connect different elements within the same story – for example, 'as', 'amid' and 'if'. Remember, from Chapter 2, the London *Guardian* report on the Casablanca bombings. It opens:

'As Moroccan police swept through some of the poorest shanty towns of Casablanca yesterday, hunting Islamist radicals who helped suicide bombers kill 41 people on Friday, Khalid Aits was worrying not about fanaticism but about work, food and poverty'.

The essentials of the story are given, with the reporter's new contextualising material woven in from the outset. 'Amid' can fulfil a similar function – so, in this story about the Palu bombs:

'Police were last night sweeping the streets of Palu, after defusing several bombs across the city, amid calls for calm by religious leaders following an earlier blast that seriously injured three people outside a bible school'.

For a gear-shift, or corner-turn, in mid-story, the word 'if' comes into its own:

'If the bombers' aim was to sow discord between followers of different faiths, however, then, according to some local religious leaders, they were destined to fail. Jotje Yulianto...'

We suspect this *was* the bombers' aim and you might, on the day, be able to find, say, a local analyst to quote to this effect. What if you can't, or you don't have time? In the linking sentence above, you can air this analysis without having to attribute it, or put it forward as your own. And it's a good way to draw in your new source.

Extra material

You could also find some background material on the underlying contradictions of the Poso conflict, and the incident said to have triggered the violence there. Good internet resources are available – one gives a brief guide to some important shared problems, including:

- a questionable political system in which the Bupati (local government leader) was appointed, not elected, and may therefore not be representative

Refugees in Palu tell their story

- no provision to protect the rights of different sections of the community
- a suggestion of corruption in the allocation of jobs and contracts
- a people deprived of land rights for 'top-down' development projects

This section is adapted from 'Peace Journalism in Poso':

'The road itself holds a clue – part of the Trans-Sulawesi highway connecting the island's main cities [including Poso and Palu], a Suharto-era project which has brought the benefits of increased commerce as well as the problems associated with transmigration and development. At the end of the school day, villagers erect tripods in the road, made from the branches of palm trees, a rather forlorn attempt to get through-traffic to slow down, to protect their children.

Virtually all the cultivable land in this part of the island is along the coastal strip, where the tropical jungle and inhospitable mountains of the interior give way to a narrow fertile littoral. The road itself gobbled up substantial chunks of it, leaving many without access to what they would have considered their birthright.

The *Pamona* people who originally settled here learned Christianity a century ago from Dutch missionaries. New arrivals, mainly *Bugis* from Makassar but also a sprinkling of Javanese, tended to be Muslims, until the groups attained roughly equal numbers.

By convention, the local government leader *(Bupati)* would be appointed alternately from one section of the community, then the other. But the road and other developments made the office a valuable bauble in terms of kickbacks and patronage. With the fall of Suharto, the Muslim incumbent, Arif Patanga, challenged the convention by proposing his brother Agfar to succeed him. The younger Patanga seems to have set out to turn religious difference into a political weapon to stir up trouble in Poso, with the object of keeping out the Christian candidate.

In the afternoon, the city is full of uniforms – local police as well as *Brimob*, but also a large number of civil servants making their way home from the office. As a main administrative centre, Poso's livelihood depends heavily on public sector jobs. Simultaneous upheavals in both national and local politics were bound to have an unsettling effect.'[4]

Another issue is raised by the incident often said to have triggered the violence in Poso – a street brawl in which a Muslim man was allegedly stabbed in the arm. Instead of going to the police, he ran to the local mosque and roused fellow Muslims to strike back. According to the account quoted here, 'the first round of house-burnings, known latterly as Poso I, ensued'.

It suggests that a lack of trust in the authorities, as neutral arbiters of people's grievances, may be another structural problem making the other problems worse and making violence more likely.

See if you can find ways to bring in one or more of these issues of structural violence into your story.

Follow-ups – Israel and the Palestinians, 2003

DISCUSSION: Go back and read the two reports of the suicide bombing in Jerusalem (Chapter 1).

- What is missing?
- What do you want to hear more about?
- Has it aroused your interest to find out?

The first of the two reports, the example of War Journalism, reiterates what many will already think of as the answers: all Arabs and Jews hate each other; violence is inevitable and more will inevitably now follow; the peace process is doomed.

Palestinian boy stands at a checkpoint in the West Bank

The second effectively raises a number of questions. Is the military occupation of Palestinian lands really a good way to ensure Israel's security? Do all Israelis agree with it? How is it connected to the suicide bombings? And more.

Missing elements:

- impact of Israeli military occupation on daily life of Palestinians
- water inequality – shortages for Palestinians
- Israeli public opinion – majority favour evacuation of illegal settlements as part of a peace deal
- Palestinian public opinion – majority favour ending the Intifada to create space and atmosphere conducive to peace talks
- ways to break the cycle of violence

- ideas on how to resolve the conflict or any image of a solution
- images of peace and co-operation between communities
- how the culture of violence is being reproduced – and challenged

Here are some notes for possible Peace Journalism follow-up stories:

Impact of Israeli military occupation

- *The Wall:* Israel's so-called 'security fence' is the most visible representation of military occupation impacting on Palestinians.

Prophetic graffiti on Israel's 'security fence', Qalqilya, occupied West Bank, 2003

- *Palestinian casualty figures:* The second version of the story incorporates these to balance the picture. But the daily roster of Palestinian casualties is usually omitted – most reports are of Israelis being killed in suicide bombings, and most omit the context.
- *The checkpoints:* Across Israel and the West Bank the checkpoints prevent Palestinians from moving from one village to the next. They frequently have to queue for hours to go shopping, keep medical appointments or visit friends. These are potential flashpoints and where many killings take place. Few if any soldiers are ever brought to book over any of these killings. In the Peace Journalism version of the suicide bombing story we met a group of Israeli women, Checkpoint Watch, who monitor what goes on there.

Water inequality – shortages for Palestinians

The figures demonstrate another aspect of structural violence experienced by Palestinians. Since 1967, Israel has confiscated 80 per cent of the West Bank's water reserves. On one estimate, for every 876 litres of water available to the settlers only one litre of water is available to each Palestinian.[5]

Is this just another problem, or could it be reported as an opportunity for creative solutions? The Alexander River conservation project is a rare story of co-operation between Israelis and Palestinians. The river flows through Nablus in the West Bank down through Israel to the estuary in the Mediterranean Sea. Like many rivers in the region, it was suffering from 50 years of heavy pollution.

'A river restoration project can serve as a bridge to overcome major conflicts between authorities, entities and even Israelis and Palestinians who want to live together in peace, on one small piece of land.' – Amos Brandeis, chief planner of the Alexander River Restoration project.

Since the Alexander River Restoration Administration was formed in 1995, it has generated a bigger restoration budget than any other river in Israel: spending reached $10 million by 2001. The project has won a host of international prizes for its 'ground breaking co-operative agreements', signed by local Israeli and Palestinian leaders.[6]

Israeli public opinion about evacuation of illegal settlements

- *Interview an opinion pollster* who asks questions about the evacuation of illegal settlements as part of a peace deal. Mina Zemach from the Dahaf Polling Institute found in 2003 that the proportion of Israelis agreeing with this proposition had risen to an all-time high of 62 per cent.[7]
- *Visit the settlements* and ask how they feel about being given back as part of a peace deal.

Israeli settler Rachel Zucker with her family, Bet El, occupied West Bank

Palestinian public opinion about ending the Intifada

- *Interview an opinion pollster* who asks questions about ending the Intifada to create space and atmosphere conducive to peace talks. Dr Nabil Kukali, of the Palestinian Centre for Public Opinion, found in 2003 that the proportion of Palestinians in favour of halting the Intifada had risen to 44.5 per cent, outstripping for the first time the proportion in favour of its continuation, at 42 per cent.[8]

Breaking the Cycle of Violence

- *The Parents Circle* is one of the best-known reconciliation groups in region. It now has more than 500 members, who have each lost a child in the conflict. Together, Israeli and Palestinian parents work to end the occupation and find a political solution. They exchange and publicise their own stories about coming to terms with the death of their child. They call, not for revenge, but for an end to violence so more children like theirs do not die.
- *Israel Palestine Centre for Research Information (IPCRI)* ran an important education programme for both Israeli and Palestinian children to explore concepts of freedom and citizenship, as a way of building up to a challenge to the dominant narratives of the conflict.
- *Israeli Committee Against House Demolitions*, as well as taking direct action, helps to rebuild demolished homes. The group calculates that 8,000 Palestinian homes have been demolished since the Occupation began in 1967.
- *International Solidarity Movement* is another grassroots group standing up to the violence. Activists from across the globe volunteer to protect Palestinian homes by standing in front of Israeli tanks and bulldozers. In March 2003 American activist Rachel Corrie died in the Rafah refugee camp in Gaza taking part in such an action.

Ideas on how to resolve the conflict, images of a solution

- *The Geneva Accord*, designed by a group of former and serving politicians – both Israeli and Palestinian – shows there are partners who are ready and willing to negotiate, and offers a detailed blueprint for a two-state solution. It also shows how the population on both sides are taking part in a dialogue about peace.

  It made the front page of the London *Independent* newspaper in 2003.[9]

Both Israelis and Palestinians feel increasingly desperate for some hope of a solution, Haifa, 2003

- *Middle East Policy Initiatives Forum* in London is one of a number of groups working on new ideas. Its chief aim is to create an international protectorate in the West Bank and Gaza to allow the Palestinians to develop effective state institutions.[10]
- *TRANSCEND* has ideas for a UN-led Conference for Security and Co-operation in the Middle East. This would involve all states in the region and consider the possibility of neighbouring states ceding some territory to a Palestinian state.[11] An attempt to emulate the success of the Helsinki Process in the 1970s – in that case, for eastern Europe – by building solidarity between civil society activists and giving them international recognition and legitimacy.
- *Neve Shalom/Wahat al-Salam*, meaning 'Oasis of Peace' in Hebrew and Arabic respectively, is a co-operative village of Jews and Arabs, demonstrating the possibility of co-existence by developing a community based on mutual acceptance. An antidote, if nothing else, to the essentialist explanation for the conflict, that Arabs and Jews simply 'hate each other's guts'. If the village itself is a real community, so the network of Israeli Jewish and Arab and Palestinian schoolteachers who join the IPCRI peace education programme is one example of a *virtual* community, also based on mutual acceptance. It means there are many

opportunities to *show* co-existence as a vision of what peace would actually be like.

Cultural violence

The story of three Palestinian children is told in a sensitive film by the British cameraman James Miller, who was shot dead by the Israeli army before the film was complete.[12] All the children lose close friends and relatives – an experience that tends to make them more receptive to war propaganda.

In the film, 12-year-old Ahmed talks about his dreams of becoming a 'martyr'. It's an important and deadly narrative of cultural violence, where killing, involving the taking of one's own life, is glorified.

We see Ahmed posing with a rocket launcher and spying for paramilitary groups on the streets of Gaza at night.

A year later, we meet the children again in a package on the UK's *Channel 4 News*, and learn how disrupted their education has been, particularly that of 16-year-old Najla, who dreamed of being a lawyer 'so I can give justice to the people'.

Now, we see, her home has been demolished, her schoolbooks lost; she finds it hard to concentrate and has missed three school exams in the Israeli-imposed curfews and 'closures'. She still dreams of becoming a lawyer, but she also thinks about becoming a 'martyr' – 'this is

Grieving Palestinian woman and child, Gaza

not a life, and they've stolen our childhood. The Jews have planted hatred in our hearts since we were little. What is there to live for? They took everything beautiful in our life.'[13]

As with the story of the two Palestinian brothers, examined in Chapter 3, it takes a lot to explain how violence is being constructed, without seeming to excuse or justify it. What this film shows is the workings of a cycle of violence: the discourse of martyrdom involves inflicting the same trauma and injury on 'the other side', overlaying the basic Contradictions with a dense and destabilising *meta-conflict* of Attitudes and Behaviour.

> DISCUSSION: How do these 'missing elements' change the framing and supplement official narratives?

These story ideas help to break down the bi-polar model of Israelis versus Palestinians by showing Israelis working to support Palestinians (Checkpoint Watch, Parents Circle, and Israeli Committee Against House Demolitions), and focusing on Palestinians who want a halt to violence and a negotiated two-state solution instead.

They give an image of a solution exploring the Geneva Accords, as well as the ideas put forward by the Middle East Policy Initiative Forum and TRANSCEND, thereby opening up new avenues for dialogue and breaking the misperception that there are no Palestinians to negotiate with.

The Wall shows the workings of structural violence and gives a people's perspective on the daily impact of this development. The Alexander River project demonstrates a collaborative response to overcome another example of structural violence.

The construction of cultural violence is explored in the stories of the Gaza children, and is a process that is challenged by the IPCRI education programme.

> ### Exercise Two
> ### Israel's Military Refuseniks
>
> In Chapter 1, the Peace Journalism treatment of the suicide bombing in Jerusalem reminded us that, in the violence since 2000, Israeli military actions have claimed three times more lives than Palestinian suicide bombings.
>
> Read the following script for a TV follow-up to such an action, and explain what it contributes to Peace Journalism.
>
> - How does it affect the model and shape of the conflict?
> - How does it add to the explanation for violence?
> - Who or what is to blame for the violence?

Reporter Annabel McGoldrick talking to students Alon Ginat and Yuli Friedman at The Charles E Smith High School of the Arts, Jerusalem

***TV News Script: Refuseniks*[14]**

Introduction read by studio presenter
Israel's policy of military occupation in the West Bank and Gaza Strip is running into opposition from its own soldiers. Growing numbers of conscripts and reservists are disobeying orders to serve in the territories – or rejecting military service altogether. Now, the army is taking six young recruits to court, apparently to deter others from following suit. Jake Lynch reports.

Pictures 1

Voice 1

Voice-over: An Israeli army checkpoint in the occupied West Bank. Soldiers checking identity papers of villagers on their way to the Palestinian city of Nablus, for shopping, to keep medical appointments or to visit friends. Israel says it needs to control people's movements, for its own security. But it's these duties that a growing number of Israelis are now refusing to carry out. Adam Maor, at home with his parents in Haifa on a weekend break from military detention, faces up to three years in jail for disobeying orders.

Pictures 2

Adam Maor
Refusenik

Voice 2

Adam Maor: Keeping checkpoints, not letting people get out to work. Getting into houses to look for armed men. You cannot do that and let the Palestinian people keep their ordinary life.

Pictures 3

Voice 3

Voice-over: Instead, Adam wants to study music at college in Jerusalem. He'd get away with it if a doctor pronounced him unfit to serve, or if he quietly objected as a pacifist. It's his highly public opposition to Israel's military occupation that's got him and five other young refuseniks into trouble.

Pictures 4

Miri Maor
Adam's Mother

Alex Maor
Adam's Father

Voices 4

Miri Maor: I think it is very bad that he is going to prison because he has the courage to say what others don't.

Alex Maor: Adam and his friends have done very brave things and their voice is being heard and it is very important. And I am very proud of him.

Pictures 5

Voice 5

Voice-over: A military court in Jaffa and the first of these cases to be decided. Yoni Ben Artzi was tried separately because he's refused all army service. Yoni's uncle is Binyamin Netanyahu, Israel's hardline former Prime Minister.

Pictures 6

Yoni Ben Artzi
Refusenik

Voice 6

Yoni Ben Artzi: I guess he also does respect a person's right to his belief and as a result to be exempt from military service.

Pictures 7

Voice 7

Voice-over: The court has yet to pass sentence, but Yoni's case has highlighted a growing divide among Israelis – the fault-line running through his own family.

Pictures 8

Matania Ben Artzi
Father

Voice 8

Matania Ben Artzi: Maybe more people will be convinced that there is another way after all. That what Yoni is talking about is a different culture, a culture of peace and a culture of compromise.

Pictures 9

Voice 9

Reporter Jake Lynch, piece-to-camera:
The army fears that hundreds, even thousands of other young soldiers could follow suit, and choose to reject their orders as well. And that could form the basis for a campaign of civil disobedience against Israel's military occupation of Palestinian territories.

Commentary

Who or what is to blame for the continuing violence?

This piece gives another insight into the culture and structure of the conflict – in this case the militarism of Israeli society. To serve as a conscript is very much the norm. Life can be made quite unpleasant for those who do not conform, as Adam Maor and Yoni ben Artzi have found.

It shifts some of the blame from the individuals on either side to the system of relations between them – an insight that might make reconciliation easier:

'An army is a very strong structure, filled with rewards and punishments, and a very strong culture associated with it, of patriotism, nationalism of all kinds, and in the Israeli case, of course, the theocratic aspect of Judaism. So if you look at all of this, it's enough to take the individual soldier off the hook; to take him or her off – and tell the Palestinians, and the

Palestinians telling themselves, this may still be a good guy, but there is something wrong with the structure and culture.'[15]

The story of Adam Maor and his friends also serves to problematise a standard assumption in journalism – that the military 'top brass' themselves are the only competent judges of military affairs; an assumption manifest in the preponderance of armchair generals as studio pundits when war comes on the agenda.

Peretz Kidron, a refusenik from a previous generation, observes that *selective refusal*, aimed specifically at the illegal occupation of Palestinian territory, is 'arguably the Israeli peace movement's most original contribution to the "arsenal" of anti-militarist protest'. It's a form of civil disobedience that sharpens the challenge to the authorities because those involved 'place themselves on a par with generals and politicians in judging overall policy, and arrogate to themselves the prerogative of choosing, by their own lights, which orders to obey or disobey.'[16]

An international political story – the case for war on Iraq

So far, we have seen how a Peace Journalist could respond to a single incident of violence in Indonesia; and how a creative Peace Journalism strategy could be devised and implemented over time to bring readers and audiences a better understanding of a regional conflict, in the Middle East. What about a complex international political story?

In December 2002, Iraq gave its own account of what had happened to its stocks of chemical and biological munitions and agents, in a dossier submitted to the UN.

At that time, the story was dominating the global news agenda, with significant developments taking place on many 'fronts' at the same time. What follows is a summary of the coverage offered by one major international news broadcaster – let us call it '*Globelink News*' – in its main bulletin that evening.

The job went to four senior correspondents, on the Diplomatic, Defence, Politics and Washington 'beats' respectively. Below, we reproduce sections of their actual scripts, along with transcripts of what was said by and about every source – whether speaking on or off the record – for their contributions to the programme.

Only the names have been changed to protect the innocent. For the purposes of this discussion, we will call the four reporters

Dolly Dipcorr

Dick Defcorr

Percy Polcorr

and

Wally Washcorr.

As the last notes of the signature tune fade out, the presenter, or news-anchor, says:

'Good evening. All the signals from London and Washington looked ominous today, pointing to a possible war with Iraq within months. Jack Straw, the foreign secretary, accused Saddam Hussein of lying about his weapons programme, and this evening Colin Powell, the American secretary of state, said he wasn't optimistic that Iraq would comply with international demands.

They were both giving their first assessments of the report sent recently by the Iraqis to the United Nations. That dossier denied the existence of any weapons of mass destruction. UN weapons inspectors, of course, are still at work in Iraq, and they've said today they'll be revealing their first impressions tomorrow. This report from Dolly Dipcorr:'

Dolly Dipcorr

'The omens are not good,' Dolly remarks, in her opening script. Powell appears, at a Washington news conference, to say:

> 'Our analysis of the Iraqi declaration to this point, almost two weeks into the process this weekend, shows problems with the declaration, declaration gaps, omissions, and all this is troublesome.'

Straw's comments are in a written statement – she describes it as 'tough and categorical' – reproduced, by the graphics department, on screen:

> 'This will fool no one. If Saddam persists in this obvious falsehood, it will become clear that he has rejected the pathway to peace laid down in [UN] Resolution 1441.'

'The concern in Washington and London,' Dolly adds, by way of interpreting Straw's statement, 'is not to let him [Saddam] think he might be let off the hook.'

Next, Prime Minister Tony Blair appears, speaking in the House of Commons:

> 'We will make a formal response shortly after the Christmas break. In respect of Colin Powell's remarks, I think most people who have looked at this obviously very long document are pretty sceptical about the claims that it makes, but it's important that we study it in detail and make a formal and considered response.'

Then comes opposition foreign affairs spokesman Michael Ancram, interviewed outside Parliament:

> 'The Prime Minister in the House of Commons effectively batted this away and said we're not going to take a view until after the Christmas break, and even before he said that, Jack Straw had already given a formal view on behalf of the government which said that there had been a material breach.'

Dolly closes her report with a piece-to-camera, recorded outside the Foreign Office:

> 'And the next step, say British diplomats, is to get Saddam Hussein to explain these apparent omissions in the dossier – come up with proof to prove he's destroyed weapons. Allow the Iraqi scientists to be interviewed. And if he fails that test, then, say officials, there really will be a case for war.'

Dick Defcorr

The presenter now explains that Dick is to look in more detail at military preparations for British involvement in any invasion plan. His piece opens with pictures of US troops, pointedly carrying out exercises in Kuwait, just a few miles from the Iraqi border. Dick says:

'Britain's role in all of this, still not clear. We are starting to get ready – the first cargo ship was chartered today.'

Cut to defence secretary Geoff Hoon, speaking in the House of Commons:

'These are contingency preparations aimed at increasing the readiness of a range of options. This process does not lead inexorably to military action. The use of force is not inevitable.'

This, evidently, is viewed with some suspicion by the opposition Conservatives, whose defence spokesman, Gerald Howarth, retorts:

'The House and the country are entitled to know what kind of level of military commitment the government has in mind. It is frankly bizarre that our TV screens are full of US troop manoeuvres in the Gulf, and the government so far has said virtually nothing about possible British involvement.'

Dick himself then remarks: 'The precise nature of Britain's involvement in any military campaign is still not known. A headache for the man in charge of making preparations.'

We then cut to a shot of Dick, wearing suitably resolute facial expression, in the audience of a question-and-answer session with the chief of defence staff, Admiral Sir Michael Boyce. We see him ask:

'From your point of view, how problematic or frustrating is that continued level of uncertainty?'

Boyce replies:

'Well, obviously, it's frustrating, in the sense that you always want to know exactly where you're heading, so you can actually do proper planning for it. This is not a frustration which is directed against anybody because nobody knows where we're heading.'

Percy Polcorr

The presenter now turns to Percy and Wally, on satellite links in Downing Street and Washington respectively, for a live 'down-the-line' with the pair of them. Tony Blair's relatively downbeat response in the House of Commons struck an apparent contrast with the more emphatic phrasing of Jack Straw's written statement. Which should we believe?

Percy is unequivocal:

'Jack Straw, frankly... In fact, British officials have combed through this dossier... and they've decided that the key omissions there, about the chemical weapons, and the biological weapons, *are* sufficient to start the process that leads to war.'

'People here assume', he goes on, that UN weapons inspectors will discover some trace of these weapons, or be prevented from doing so.

'Once that happens, then war is certainly inevitable' ... 'Officials tell me' that they believe Saddam Hussein has already deduced what lies in store, from the build-up of US forces in the Gulf, but 'I'm afraid the final decision will be taken in Washington, not in London.'

Wally Washcorr

A cue, to switch to our man on the Potomac. Wally opens with the observation:

'It's highly significant that Colin Powell right now is America's spokesman, because he is the leading dove in the administration.'

Tomorrow, he continues, 'we expect' Powell to say, after a Security Council briefing by chief weapons inspector Hans Blix on his team's progress so far, 'that Iraq is in serious violation of the UN resolution'.

Where did this expectation originate? A clue, perhaps, from Wally's closing contribution:

'One official saying tonight, Saddam Hussein has already put his boot through one tripwire, and he's well on his way to putting his boot through another.'

Exercise Three
Reporting on Iraq's Dossier

1. List the sources used for these reports, including those speaking:
   – on the record
   – off the record
2. What do they have in common?
3. Do these sources disagree on anything? If so, what? How would you describe the degree of disagreement between them? What views or perspectives do they all have in common?
4. What perspectives are left out of these reports?
5. Look again at how the sources are used by the reporters, especially those quoted anonymously, ie speaking off the record. What do the reporters use them to do?
6. What assumptions have the reporters made about what their sources are saying, and why?
7. Do you agree with their assumptions? What other possibilities are there?
8. What *effect* might the sources be trying to bring about:
   – on debate about the war?
   – on public opinion?

Commentary

A *restricted frame of reference*
All the sources for these reports are *officials* of some kind – members of governments, or the 'front bench' of the official opposition, whether speaking in the House of Commons or at news conferences, issuing written statements, interviewed on camera or (perhaps most interesting) briefing anonymously, off the record.

The range of opinions encompassed by these sources is very narrow. Only within this highly restricted frame of reference could Colin Powell be seen as a 'dove'. Where they disagree, they do so only about the clarity with which expectations of military action should be declared publicly.

The propositions they all agree with, explicitly or implicitly, are:

- this is 'all about' Iraq's 'weapons of mass destruction'
- these weapons pose an authentic threat to global security
- Saddam Hussein is failing to 'come clean' over 'his' weapons stocks
- if he persists in this behaviour, military action is the inevitable consequence

This was the situation lamented by a BBC editor at an influential London conference held just two months after the programme summarised here, and days after the huge anti-war demonstrations around the world:

'The BBC has an editorial policy meeting every month, which is a great thing because it is an accessible environment where you can go and debate how we are covering certain issues. We had one in January which was way before the last big demonstration but I sat there and sort of got the impression from everyone in the room that the BBC was being far too anti-war. The questions and comments were "are we giving too much space to the anti-war movement?"

Now someone needs to sit down and do a quantitative assessment of the voices that are being put on the air and say it is not like that – look at the facts: you've given Colin Powell 23 minutes this week and you've given whoever else it might be, a sum total of seven minutes.

There was a demonstration at the end of January that got no coverage. It was a symbolic invasion of RAF Fairford I think [the US military base in south-west England from where B-52 bombers flew sorties over Iraq]. Something has changed though over the past week after the massive demonstration in London but I think it would be all too easy for that to slip away.'[17]

As discussed in previous chapters, there were, at the time, plenty of people taking issue with these propositions – it was really 'all about oil'; Iraq's weapons could not possibly pose any threat; and, perhaps most importantly, the view that military action was unwarranted and would likely create more dangers than it would remove.

'Adding value'

Dolly, Dick, Percy and Wally all use material available to any reporter, from any media – officials speaking on the record. There is nothing terribly clever about this. These days, a live picture feed from parliament is available to all, and it is not difficult, with proper accreditation, to get into a news conference in London or Washington.

Frontbenchers from all parties come into the Westminster media centre at 4 Millbank and 'do the rounds' when they have something to say. Hang around in the corridor with a camera and you can get a few minutes to put your own questions to them.

But the Globelink reporters are in a highly competitive business. Why should viewers switch on the television in the evening to hear this from them, rather than tuning into one of the many 24-hour channels – which may be covering the debate or the news conference live – when they are at work, clicking on the news feeds offered by their internet service provider when they pick up their emails, or listening to the radio on the way home?

All four of our friends here add value by offering an interpretation of what the officials have said. Notice, however, that it is not *their own* interpretation, but the interpretation of other officials. They use their off-the-record sources to validate their reading of the on-the-record sources.

'Turning over stones'

In an important critique of Peace Journalism,[18] senior BBC correspondent David Loyn acknowledges that Objectivity is, strictly speaking, impossible; but 'journalists share a language and certain assumptions with their audience' and, within that framework, it remains a worthy goal. In pursuing it, journalists should, he argues, follow the philosophy of a character in the Tom Stoppard play *Night and Day*. The character, Guthrie, a professional photographer, describes his job as 'turning over stones' in a search for 'the truth'.

This assumes that reportable facts are out there, waiting to be *found*, if we look hard enough. In this edition of *Globelink News*, the implicit message from all four reporters is that somewhere, beneath the statements designed for public consumption, are the 'real thoughts' of those in officialdom about the prospects for war. Ask the right questions of the right people and these can be *uncovered*. Even if the officials really 'in the know' do not care to speak on the record, they may divulge their secrets to journalists with privileged access.

The possibility this neglects is that these *officials may have their own agenda*.

Their messages to reporters may not *express* a 'real' privately formulated position, but may instead be devised in order to *construct* something. They may represent an intervention in the 'system' of debate about the war, an attempt to shape the issues under discussion and alter the climate of expectations.

In short, Dolly, Dick, Percy and Wally all treat their sources as *passive* – revealing a reality that already exists. In a media-savvy world, what sources say and do cannot be fully understood, or accurately reported, without conceptualising them as *active* – trying to create a reality that does not yet exist, and willing and able to use the media in order to do so.

'Sequencing'

By this stage – mid-December 2002 – the position had not changed, fundamentally, since a speech Tony Blair gave to trade unionists two months earlier (see the next chapter for further analysis of this story). At the time, one newspaper commentator remarked:

'Tony Blair was at pains to soothe their [the TUC's] anxieties... as he will be next week at the Labour conference in Blackpool. The aim, he assured them, was simply to get rid of weapons of mass destruction under the auspices of the UN. If the regime changed as a by-product, so much the better. But yes, Saddam Hussein could save himself by compliance.

It's only necessary to listen briefly to the chorus of administration voices in Washington insisting on the exact opposite, however, to realise this is a fraud – and that Blair knows it. From the president downwards, they have made utterly clear that regime change remains their policy, and force their favoured method – with or without a UN resolution and whether or not Saddam complies with inspections. And they are the ones making the decisions.

What is actually happening is that Blair, as Bush's senior international salesman, is providing political cover for a policy which is opposed throughout the world, using the time-honoured New Labour methods of spin and "sequencing": drawing his government and MPs into a succession of positions intended to lock them into acceptance of the final outcome.'[19]

Wally's talk of 'tripwires' and the Jack Straw statement about Saddam Hussein 'rejecting the pathway to peace laid down in UN Resolution 1441' are classic examples of 'sequencing'. Active sources are doing their best to *present* their assumptions as 'shared' – that Iraq possesses 'weapons of mass destruction', that these constitute a threat and

that, unless Saddam 'comes clean', we are therefore locked into a path that makes war, in Percy's words, 'certainly inevitable'.

And, one might add, capable of being presented as a 'necessity', into which its proponents have been forced, regretfully, when all other measures have been tried and found wanting – as per the public opinion 'screens', examined in Chapter 4, on which war propaganda is commonly calibrated. The intention is to circumvent and damp down, for as long as possible, any discussion of whether a war *should* take place.

This method of reporting – sticking to official sources, even when they do not fundamentally disagree with each other, and conceptualising them as passive, not active – *leaves journalists open to manipulation.*

There is a feeling of circularity to the Globelink coverage, suggested by Dolly's infelicitous phrase: 'come up with proof to prove he's destroyed weapons'. Throughout this opening sequence, occupying nearly 12 minutes at the top of the show, one official is used as proof to prove what another official is saying. It all acts as a kind of echo chamber, in which the sequencing and spin of war propaganda are constantly being amplified.

It's important to emphasise, once again, that we are holding nothing back. This is a full and accurate account of the way this story was treated by a real international broadcaster – disguised because the identity of the reporters and their programme is, in a sense, immaterial. The output on this particular day typified the general patterns of omission and marginalisation, in news about Iraq from this period, discussed in Chapter 1.

Readers and audiences are misled over vital issues in conflicts, not by journalists doing what they are not supposed to do, but by journalists doing what they *are* supposed to do; not despite their best intentions but because of them.

Our four friends here, in common with their rivals in other news organisations, are *meant* to be 'adding value' to important stories by cultivating close relations with, for instance, government officials working in departments relevant to their 'beats' – here, the British Foreign Office, Ministry of Defence and Number 10 Downing Street, and the State Department and White House in Washington.

The remedy is not, therefore, for journalists to do the same, only try harder. The remedy is to do something different.

Weighing and testing the arguments for war

The *New York Times*'s post-war apology, for misleading its readers about the 'dire' nature of the 'threat' from Iraq's weapons, lamented: 'Accounts of Iraqi defectors were not always weighed against their strong desire to have Saddam Hussein ousted.'[20]

At the same time, as Robert Fisk has remarked, 'one sure sign that the US is preparing for military action is when newspaper front pages become a daily "notice board" for "sources" from within the administration. They brief journalists anonymously to float ideas and soften up the public for war.'[21]

Messages on the record, from sources such as Iraqi defectors, would be validated and amplified by messages from anonymous officials

– giving the same sense of circularity we have noticed in the coverage by *Globelink News*.

The paper calls for accounts to be 'weighed'; an echo of the BBC *War Guidelines*, issued in January 2003, which tells editors and their teams to 'allow the arguments to be heard and tested' (see Chapter 1).

Commentary

To answer these questions, you must first identify the arguments that need to be tested – the assumptions broadly shared by all the sources in the Globelink News programme. A reminder:

- this is 'all about' Iraq's 'weapons of mass destruction'
- these weapons pose an authentic threat
- Saddam Hussein is failing to 'come clean' over 'his' weapons stocks
- if he persists in this behaviour, military action is the inevitable consequence

Clearly, sources we meet elsewhere in this book could come into these contributions to the programme, as long as 'corner-turns' could be devised to establish their relevancy

---

Exercise Four
What would you do?

What would you do, in order to weigh and test, if you were one of the reporters on this bulletin:

- Dolly Dipcorr?
- Dick Defcorr?
- Wally Washcorr?
- Percy Polcorr?
- Their editor?
- The presenter/news anchor?

What alternative sources would you use? And what would they add?
Use the material from their existing packages and devise ways to 'turn the corner' into any of your alternative sources.

to the 'top line' for the day, and construct a 'framework of understanding':

- the Detroit Project campaign for cleaner, greener cars on US roads (see Chapter 1)
- the Centre for Oil Depletion Analysis study indicating that we may be at or beyond the peak of the 'oil age' (see Chapter 1)
- the Washington think-tank, the Center for Strategic and International Studies, and its authoritative 1998 assessment, by a former army general, that Iraq's weapons left over from before the 1991 Gulf War cannot possibly still be a threat (see Chapter 4)
- the Alan Simpson/Glen Rangwala independent report on Iraq's weapons (see Chapter 7)
- the ideas put forward by Hans von Sponeck to isolate the Iraqi regime, encourage civil society (backed up by smarter sanctions) and ultimately bring about regime change (see Chapter 1) – a plan released on the very day of this edition of *Globelink News*

'Corner-turns' to draw in alternative sources

The *Globelink News* editor could commission material, whether in the form of packages, with interviewees voicing alternative elements as part of the background to war, or by asking correspondents to consult such sources as well as government officials.

He or she might have a problem, however. Official sources become prolific at times like this. A party conference here, a presidential visit there; a press point today, a troop deployment tomorrow. The barrage of news events in the Downing Street or White House 'grid' is intended, in part, to blot out any alternative agenda. As Tony Blair's press secretary Alastair Campbell once said, the job of government media teams in wartime is to 'hold the public's interest on our terms'.[22]

Any or all of these developments might demand to be covered. So how is the editor to find space for material drawn from alternative sources – perhaps dealing with the oil agenda, or ideas for non-violent measures to be adopted, through forms of international and/or civil society co-operation, to bring about 'regime change' in Iraq?

One solution is to set up a connection or 'corner-turn' – starting from the 'official' agenda, but being prepared to use it as a 'peg' on which to hang one's own material. A perfect example was provided when US national security advisor Condoleezza Rice was in London.

Dr Rice had stopped off to give a news conference *en route* to the Middle East, where, it was said, she would press Washington's case for progress on the 'Road Map to Peace'. At the same time, building work on Israel's new separation wall, or 'security fence', was rather conspicuously continuing. Plenty of critics were pointing out that its construction would establish a 'fact on the ground' which would make a two-state solution – as envisaged in the 'Road Map' – much more difficult to achieve.

Channel 4 News sent presenter Jon Snow to the news conference; he'd questioned, he said, 'whether that wall is compatible with the Road Map'. The programme then ran a single clip of Dr Rice – her answer to Snow's question:

'Obviously, the Middle East that the President envisions, the two-state solution that he envisions, is one in which two democratic and stable states can live side by side in peace, in which there would be no need for any kind of physical separation, and that's certainly the world that we envision and the one that we're working toward.'

The programme then 'turned the corner' into a filmed report – a lengthy investigation by correspondent Jonathan Rugman. It covered the case made for the wall, its likely effects on the day-to-day lives of Israelis and Palestinians, and its prospective influence on the chances of peace.

Crucially, the programme had sent a very clear signal that it was setting its own agenda; its journalists were in charge of deciding which were the important questions; they were interested in the answers from official sources to those questions, but they were not going to let those sources set the questions or the agenda themselves. This was an important way of *measuring* official claims and pronouncements against evidence the programme itself had gathered about what was really going on.

To do so, *Channel 4 News* had to perform a nifty corner-turn – from the 'top line' of Condi's visit to London, where she was intent on talking about the Road Map, to its own pre-planned film about the wall.

The Sliding Scale

In practice, getting opportunities to do Peace Journalism is a study in the art of compromise. The sliding scale pictured below refers to representations of the conflict in the southern Philippines.

The more space journalists find to report on the factors in the right-hand column, the further the 'cursor' moves towards the Peace Journalism end of the scale.

To create this space often entails connecting and combining elements from the left-hand column – to hook the reader in, or to provide an arresting 'top line' for a more process-orientated story.

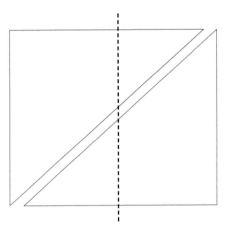

War Journalism

Concentrating on Behaviour, especially Direct Violence

Official political discourse and agenda

About 'Terrorist' plots and conspiracies

Underlying sectarianism

Peace Journalism

Focusing on Contradictions + issues of Structural Violence

Space for grassroots activism + perspectives

About rights, freedoms, power imbalances

Underlying inequalities

Exercise Five
Working with the Sliding Scale

- Spot the connections between elements from either end of the WJ/PJ sliding scale in two stories from the Philippines.
- Write the top line and opening paragraph(s) for each story.
- With further research on the background to the bombings in Manila and two southern cities – and the conflict in Mindanao – write an 800-word Peace Journalism article on each story.
- Online resources could include mindanews.com, reuters.com, pcij.org (Philippine Centre for Investigative Journalism), (*Philippines Daily Inquirer*) inq7.net.

Story 1:
Valentine's Day
bombings

Forensic teams
inspect the blown-
up bus in Manila,
14 February 2005

1. Police are investigating three bomb blasts, killing 11 people and wounding nearly 130 in different cities across the Philippines, on the evening of 14 February 2005.

2. The first device exploded in General Santos City, Mindanao. The second, shortly afterwards, hit the island's capital city of Davao. The third explosion was in a bus station in the central business district of the Philippine capital, Manila.

3. The three blasts came within an hour of each other, as people were leaving work or going out for a romantic dinner on Valentine's Day.

4. Mindanao has a long history of unrest, violence and – from the point of view of some on the island – exploitation and subjugation, both by colonial powers and latterly by the government of the Republic of the Philippines (GRP). The Moro Islamic Liberation Front (MILF), a 12,000-strong guerrilla army, is currently in peace talks with the GRP over claims for substantial autonomy in a sizeable section of the island.

5. The Abu Sayyaf Group (ASG), a small Muslim militant group linked to al-Qaeda, said it carried out the attacks.

6. An ASG spokesman, Abu Soleiman, called a radio station to claim responsibility for the attacks, in revenge for civilian deaths during military operations against its fighters on the island of Jolo, next to Mindanao to the south-west. 'This is a Valentine's Day gift to President Gloria Macapagal Arroyo,' he said.

7. A spokesman for Arroyo said she would 'not be diverted from the War on Terrorism'.

8. Hours before the bombings, a mainstream political grouping, the Suara Bangsamoro Partylist, issued its own call for complaints of human rights abuses to be properly and impartially investigated, and for a pullout of troops from Jolo to be going on with.[23]

Story 2:
Farmers' land rights

Work on new commercial development next to Mapalad farmers' land, April 2005

1. A group of farmers struggling for land rights in the Philippines form the Mapalad co-operative in the village of San Vicente, in Bukidnon Province of Northern Mindanao.

2. Years earlier they went on a hunger strike that was widely reported. They pursued their land claim all the way to the Supreme Court in Manila, successfully capturing the nation's imagination. But the judgement went against them.

3. On the other hand, the political gains included an extension of the Philippines Land Reform programme for a further 10 years, to 2008. However, Bukidnon Province was named by the Department of Land Reform as an area where redistribution has been slowest.[24]

4. The farmers eventually inherited, from the will of a local freeholder moved by their plight and determination, a small patch of land to subsist on.

5. Today they are in the early stages of another campaign, against plans by a multinational company to build a huge commercial piggery next door. According to them, the law means this patch should, instead, be classified as part of Land Reform and therefore made available to the landless.

6. **MINDANAO THE 'NEXT AFGHANISTAN'; MINDANAO A 'MECCA FOR TERRORISM'** Newspapers made much of remarks by Joseph Mussomeli, chargé d'affaires at the US Embassy in Manila, apparently labelling Mindanao as the number one 'hot spot' in the so-called 'Global War on Terrorism'.

   Interviewed on Australia's SBS Television, he declared:

   'We're not focused enough on the threat here… the threat is much more long-term; that certain portions of Mindanao are so lawless, so porous the borders that you run the risk of it becoming like an Afghanistan situation… Mindanao is, forgive the pun, the new "Mecca" of terrorism.'[25]

7. Communist rebels form a variety of groups fighting an armed struggle in rural areas – most importantly the New People's Army (NPA), which is committed to a Maoist-style People's War and is estimated to have 9,000 active members. They tend to take up grievances over poverty, land rights, logging and mining issues.

Commentary

Story 1: Valentine's Day bombings
A possible intro:

> The Abu Sayyaf group said it planted three bombs which exploded in the cities of General Santos and Davao and the Makati financial district of Manila yesterday evening, killing at least 11 people, in revenge for civilian deaths in military operations on its island stronghold of Jolo.
>
> The blasts came just hours after a Moro political group called for troops to pull back and for allegations of human rights abuses to be properly investigated.
>
> The first explosion, in General Santos, happened...'

The rest of the story could be developed as follows:

- Details of the bombings and casualties come next.
- Further paragraphs could explain the background to the imminent peace talks and make it clear that many more people besides Abu Sayyaf are concerned about issues of justice for people living in the conflict zone.
- You could quote a commentator spelling out the risk that leaving grievances over summary executions unaddressed risks creating conditions in which people can be more easily mobilised for political violence – a counterpoint to official rhetoric about the 'War on Terrorism'.

The Abu Sayyaf claim is what enables the link to issues of structural violence – impunity and a lack of justice. The drawback, for many

Mindanao journalists, of using it to make this connection is that focusing on the ASG means playing along with self-serving representations of the conflict by outsiders.

These, many feel, elevate the ASG to a much greater importance than is warranted. In the six months to the time of writing (May 2005), the group cropped up in 2,455 articles in English-language written media alone, compared with 1,402 for the much larger MILF and just 908 for the NPA.[26]

Then there is the suspicion, associated with the ASG since its emergence in the early 1990s, that it is at least partly a creature of the authorities, its activities helping to justify security 'crackdowns' as a response to conflict. The journalist who first reported on the group, Joe Torres, recalls a time when 'bandit leaders and military leaders rode together in military vehicles while ordinary soldiers and bandits killed each other in the battle zone'.[27]

The Valentine's Day bombings saw these suspicions resurface. Carolyn Arguillas, an experienced local editor and exponent of Peace Journalism, interpreted them as a spoiler, contrived perhaps by elements on either side hostile to the imminent MILF peace talks and conveniently blamed on the ASG:

> 'There are elements from both parties, from both the government and the Moro Islamic Liberation Front, for instance, that do not like the peace talks to end, to conclude in a peace agreement.'[28]

So the story and the lead-in to it are riven with compromises; but it does at least excavate some of what we recognise as the real issues, from beneath the rubble left by the act of direct violence, the bombings.

Commentary

Story 2:
Farmers' land rights

Mapalad farmers'
children look to a future
without land

A possible intro:

> Even as the senior US diplomat in the Philippines was being called on to explain recent remarks, that 'poverty and lawlessness' mean Mindanao risks becoming 'the next Afghanistan', a group of poor farmers on the island were complaining that laws passed to help them are being ignored in favour of deals with multinational companies – many American-owned.

The rest of the story could be developed as follows:

- Subsequent paragraphs would explain the farmers' case.
- It would have a delicate job to do in making it clear that such grievances, if unaddressed through non-violent and/or political means, may feed into an ongoing violent conflict instead.

The day after Mussomeli's remarks surfaced, they made a page lead for most Manila newspapers. When he was summoned to the foreign ministry to explain himself, the story acquired still greater traction, promoted, in several publications, to the next day's front-page lead.

We are using a *paradox* to lift the farmers' story on to what the PR industry calls an 'issue platform'[29] – something journalists already think of as a hot story. The paradox is that the failure to implement a law designed to protect the rights of the landless represents a different form of 'lawlessness' from the one the diplomat referred to.

Why bother? This is, potentially, a useful and important Peace Journalism story. It highlights contradictions keenly experienced by people at the grass roots, and focuses on exponents of non-violent responses.

One local writer, who visited the farmers as part of a Peace Journalism workshop,[30] began her report with the observation that theirs was 'a story one would surely wish to know'. An editor might ask, *Why?* Why would one 'surely wish to know' their story – or rather, why now? This is where the issue platform is useful, although it entails compromise, once again, in linking with War Journalism and a version of the conflict we may see as misleading.

Another connection with the 'mainstream' agenda could be explored by reminding readers of the words of one of the judges in the Supreme Court case:

'The resolution of such cases has far-reaching implications for the success of our land reform program. Indeed, their successful resolution can bring peace or rebellion in our countryside.'

These developments came shortly after the resurgent NPA were branded 'the greatest internal security threat to the country'[31] by the Philippines defense secretary. It is to oppose the NPA that the majority of troops are deployed in rural areas, particularly Mindanao, where they are accused of persistent human rights abuses – a link back to the Valentine's Day bombings.

As the judge's comments suggest, contradictions to do with land use feed directly into this conflict. What is at stake is the efficacy of alternative responses. Such issues are met with two distinctively Asian forms of struggle. On the one hand is a People's War, espoused by the NPA and claimed – however vicariously – by the ASG as justification; and, on the other, Gandhian non-violence, including hunger strikes, along with the political remedy of Land Reform. A concept for this story that connects elements from both War Journalism and Peace Journalism.

Endnotes for Chapter 6

1. 'Bombs Terrorise Palu, Police Tighten up Security', *Jakarta Post*, 21 September 2002.
2. Birgitta Hoijer, Stig Arne Nohrstedt and Rune Ottosen, 'The Kosovo War in the Media – Analysis of a Global Discursive Order', *Conflict & Communication Online*, Vol 1, No 2, 2002, p 9.
3. Harvard Conflict Management group, 1994, quoted in Jake Lynch and Annabel McGoldrick, 'Reporting Conflict – An Introduction to Peace Journalism', in Thomas Hanitzsch, Martin Loffelholz and Ronny Mustamu (eds), *Agents of Peace*, Friedrich Ebert Stiftung, Jakarta, 2004, p 132.
4. Adapted from Jake Lynch & Annabel McGoldrick, 'Peace Journalism in Poso', *Inside Indonesia*, No 66, April-June 2001, available at http://www.insideindonesia.org/edit66/peace1.htm.
5. Norman Finkelstein, *Rise and Fall of Palestine*, University of Minnesota Press, Minneapolis, 1996.
6. Alexander River project leaflet, Brisbane River Festival, 2002.
7. Speaking in Jake Lynch and Annabel McGoldrick, *News from the Holy Land* (video), Hawthorn Press, Stroud, 2004.
8. Ibid.
9. London *Independent*, 14 October 2003.
10. Jonathan Freedland, 'At Last a Fresh Idea', London *Guardian*, 15 January 2003.
11. Johan Galtung et al., *Searching for Peace*, Pluto Press, London, 2002, p 201.
12. James Miller, *Death in Gaza*, Channel 4 Television, London, 25 May 2004.
13. Lindsey Hilsum, follow-up news item on the children in Miller's documentary, *Channel 4 News*, 26 May 2004; and Lindsey Hilsum, 'Bulldozers Crush Gaza Children's Dreams and Build Its Martyrs', London *Observer*, 30 May 2004.
14. Broadcast on *Breakfast*, BBC 1, 29 November 2003.

15. Johan Galtung speaking in Jake Lynch and Annabel McGoldrick, op cit, 2004.

16. Quoted in Jake Lynch and Annabel McGoldrick, 'Peace Journalism in the Holy Land', *Caduceus*, No 65, Winter 2004.

17. Bill Hayton, then Europe regional editor, BBC World Service, speaking at 'Iraq – Broadening the Agenda', Reporting the World event, London, 20 February 2003.

18. David Loyn, 'Witnessing the Truth', *Open Democracy*, www.opendemocracy.org, 20 February 2003.

19. Seumas Milne, 'We Are Sleepwalking into a Reckless War of Aggression', London *Guardian*, 27 September 2002.

20. Greg Mitchell, editor and publisher, 'Mea Culpa', *New York Times*, 26 May 2004.

21. Quoted in Jake Lynch, 'War Reporting', *The A-Z of Free Expression*, Index on Censorship, London, January 2003, p 273.

22. Alistair Campbell, 'J'Accuse', London *Guardian*, 10 July 1999.

23. Mindanews, 14 and 15 February 2005.

24. Blanche S Rivera, 'Farmers Poorer Despite Land Reform', *Philippines Daily Inquirer*, 16 April 2005.

25. *Philippines Daily Inquirer*, 12 April 2005.

26. Figures from www.lexis-nexis.com/professional.

27. Jose Torres Jr, *Into the Mountain – Hostaged by the Abu Sayyaf*, Claretian Publications, Quezon City, Philippines, 2001, author's note.

28. Personal interview with the authors, Davao, 8 April 2005.

29. Colin Byrne, chief executive, Weber Shandwick PR, in comments at 'Becoming Media-Savvy', a workshop run by the authors for security-sector NGOs, London, 4 November 2003.

30 Peace Journalism workshop, Cagayan de Oro, Philippines, offered by British Council, Manila, in partnership with Balay Mindanaw Peace Centre and Min-Wow, Women Writers of Mindanao, 11-15 April 2005 – led by the authors.

31. Cecil Morella, 'Philippines Military Reviews Strategy to Meet Communist Threat', *Agence France Presse*, 1 April 2005.

Chapter 7

Why is News the Way it is?

Peace Journalism is being borne on a steadily rising tide into many university courses – Conflict and Peace Studies, Media and Communications Studies, Development Studies, International Relations, and of course all branches of Journalism.

It sometimes appears as an isolated 'eddy' in such disciplines, however – cut off from the mainstream and with no direct connection to other important currents of analysis. This chapter brings a 'sea change' from the others up to now. It's intended as a navigation aid, tracing some important theoretical tributaries to the body of ideas we present here as Peace Journalism, in particular:

- Gatekeeper theory
- The Propaganda Model
- The liberal theory of press freedom
- Journalistic Objectivity – the big 'O'
- Objectivity and War Journalism
- Structuralism and the Linguistic Turn
- Feedback Loops of cause and effect
- Deconstruction

As with our discussion of conflict theory in previous chapters, we will consider these concepts in the context of real issues facing real journalists covering real stories.

DISCUSSION: Consider – 'The purpose of journalism is [nothing] more than to seek meaningful facts.'[1] Can that be right? Can it be the full story? If not, what is missing?

Once you begin to think about it, it's obvious – the 'purpose of journalism' cannot be defined without first considering *which* facts it is seeking and by what criteria they qualify as 'meaningful'.

There is a curiosity here. These questions are the starting-point for any serious analysis of the media – what they are doing, why and how they are doing it – in any of the fields listed above. But many journalists (particularly in English-speaking countries such as the US and UK) never really think about them; instead, they bury their heads, ostrich-like, in the sand.

Meet Otto the Objective Ostrich:

Photograph copyright © REUTERS/Sergei Karpukhin

The curiosity is that variations on the statement 'we just report the facts' still function as the guiding principle across a broad sweep of professional activity. The claim quoted above is from a former newspaper editor, television regulator and, at the time of writing, head of a major international agency specialising in issues of media, peace and security – a senior insider. But such nostrums would not pass muster, in any examination from the outside, for longer than a few minutes.

What does 'the guiding principle... of professional activity' mean? Many *individuals* within the news industry are prepared to acknowledge that, in the words of one executive, 'there are cultural assumptions underlying all editorial decisions',[2] but there is little or no apparatus to build on this insight. News organisations and journalists do not generally *examine* the assumptions underlying the decisions they habitually make, or their impact in shaping public understanding – let alone their influence over the actions and motivations of parties to conflict.

Even when they go so far as to formulate guidelines and codes of practice, their provisions are often trumped, unnoticed, by reporting conventions held to be so self-evident as not to require ongoing justification from first principles.

There are interesting reasons for this, which we will go on to consider in this chapter. We will suggest that news is the way it is, with a dominant discourse of War Journalism, partly because it possesses no organised form of reflexivity, or critical self-awareness.

Gatekeeper theory

'The facts' is a category of practically infinite size. A famous American TV crime series introduced itself with the catchline: 'There are eight million stories in the Naked City.'[3]

Today, there are six billion stories on our planet, increasingly laid bare by the omnipresent lens of global media. Clearly, though, even the biggest newspaper and the longest news programme cannot find space for all of them. There has to be some process of selection.

Researchers began to examine this process systematically as long ago as the 1950s, when one of them – David Manning White – coined the term 'Gatekeeper theory'. In any news production process, there's a series of 'gates'. The first could be when a press release arrives in the post and an editor decides whether or not to hand it over to a reporter to check out. The next is when the reporter, having checked it out, decides whether it's a story – and so on. Some make it through, some don't. Then comes the crunch:

'The person under this theory with the ultimate power is the person at the end of the chain who can gainsay or veto all of the work by all the people who've gone before and say "No, sorry, this isn't going to go" and every journalist has had the experience of that where a story gets spiked. It's been commissioned, it's been done, it's been negotiated, been through the lawyers for defamation, etc, gets to the end of the process – gets spiked by the editor and doesn't go through.

The argument in classical gatekeeper theory is that that person is the terminal gatekeeper and the terminal gatekeeper has the most power and therefore the terminal gatekeeper is the most highly esteemed. He or she is the person to whom everybody works because they're all trying to get him or her to actually get the story through.'[4]

The Propaganda Model

Professional journalists have a name for the set of precepts guiding them in their work, as gatekeepers, to legitimate stories – *news values*. What are these news values? Who decides them, and how?

The sheer disparity in size between the facts and the space available means some bits are inevitably going to be stopped at the gate, while others go through. It is when patterns can be discerned, when the bits left out are always, or usually, the same bits, that researchers seek evidence of news values, enabling them to deduce the criteria by which the journalists must be making their gatekeeping decisions.

In Chapter 4, we examined different propaganda strategies as a factor incidental to the news, but setting out to *influence* it. Our present discussion would not be complete without considering another possibility. Noam Chomsky and Edward Herman propose that news itself is best understood *as* propaganda, 'manufacturing consent' for the way society is organised and run. Omitting important parts of important stories, or confining them to the margins of reporting, can create or perpetuate misconceptions among readers and audiences; but these misconceptions may in fact be 'necessary illusions', they say, to safeguard the interests of the powerful.

Mention the Propaganda Model to Otto and he will bury his head even deeper. Many who become journalists are attracted by the idea that news serves a useful societal purpose – telling it like it is, without fear or favour; in Chomsky and Herman's words, 'cantankerous, obstinate and ubiquitous in [its] search for truth and independence of authority'. But the image, they say, is misleading:

'[Instead] the "societal purpose" of the media is to inculcate and defend the economic, social and political agenda of privileged groups that dominate the domestic society and the state.'[5]

Chomsky and Herman, concentrating on US media, assemble a formidable weight of evidence in answer to the question we started out with, in Chapter 1. From many examples over many years, patterns of omission, marginalisation and distortion are not the exception, they argue, but the norm.

How come? Chomsky's own explanation of news values echoes Stuart Hall's model of encoding and decoding, discussed in Chapter 4. Journalists do both, of course, and when

they receive propaganda, Chomsky's model implies that they then *re-encode* it on the basis of a preferred, or dominant, reading, influenced chiefly by their own socio-economic position and the class interests of their bosses:

'Major media – particularly, the elite media that set the agenda that others generally follow – are corporations "selling" privileged audiences to other businesses. It would hardly come as a surprise if the picture of the world they present were to reflect the perspectives and interests of the sellers, the buyers, and the product...

Furthermore, those who occupy managerial positions in the media, or gain status within them as commentators, belong to the same privileged elites, and might be expected to share the perceptions, aspirations, and attitudes of their associates, reflecting their own class interests as well. Journalists entering the system are unlikely to make their way unless they conform to these ideological pressures, generally by internalizing the values; it is not easy to say one thing and believe another, and those who fail to conform will tend to be weeded out by familiar mechanisms.'[6]

DISCUSSION: Does War Journalism predominate because it is in the interests of those who own the media and their clients?

Our definition of War Journalism, remember, is that it leads us, or leaves us, to overvalue violent, reactive responses to conflict, and undervalue non-violent, developmental ones. If we decide that War Journalism predominates because it reflects the interests of the media-owning class, we must also decide that this class has a predominant interest in violence as a response to conflict. Does it?

Britain/Ireland – winners and losers

Actually, for many years in the Britain/Ireland conflict, 'Business', on both sides of the Irish border and across the water, wanted a peace settlement to bring an end to violence and create a more propitious commercial and trading environment.

Tourism, in particular, was an industry waiting for peace in order to prosper. The Irish and Northern Ireland Tourist Boards courted controversy when they pre-empted the Good Friday Agreement with a joint television campaign, selling the whole island as one destination – 'Ireland – live a different life'.

Tourism is one of the biggest clients for newspapers, radio, television and the internet alike. But while media organisations were busy mopping up tourism advertising budgets, their news coverage was, for the most part, still stuck in the groove of War Journalism.

- *The 'hierarchy of death'*[7] – research published in Britain found the killings of civilians from nationalist communities were treated, by UK media, as being of relatively little importance.
- *Story framing* – as though Republican paramilitaries were 'the problem', and 'victory' or 'putting them in their box', a solution.
- *No structural violence* – there was hardly any mention of civil rights issues, police harassment or discrimination, or their impact on the overall context of the conflict.
- *Peace work suppressed* – the diligent and broadly based work of peace activists, over many years, remained below the radar of most newsdesks and reporters, even though it was slowly and surely building trust between communities – trust measured, eventually, in the overwhelming vote by referendum in favour of the Good Friday Agreement.

This coverage meant the possibilities for a non-violent solution were neglected and undervalued for many years, the political barriers, for anyone advocating inclusive dialogue, effectively raised. It confounded the interests of some of media owners' most important clients, but that was not enough to change it.

Georgia – winners and losers

Business prospects in the former Soviet republic of Georgia are blighted by the centre-periphery conflict with the breakaway Abkhazia *oblast*. The fact that it blocks access to a choice section of Black Sea coast prohibits any real development of tourism there, too – one of the country's few potential foreign exchange earners.

Most Georgian media are owned by members of the new oligarchy, who could certainly expect rich pickings in the event of a negotiated outcome. The newspapers and television stations they own provide what is, by regional standards, a good professional service; and yet, on this story, a virulent form of War Journalism holds sway. Characteristics include:

- no context
- conflict blamed on 'meddling from Moscow'
- extremism unchallenged

A typical example of the last concerned the erection of a memorial, 10 years after the conflict, in Tbilisi, and a gathering addressed by a local politician – quoted at length, with no balancing comment or qualification of his remarks:

> 'Nothing will help this country until we re-take Abkhazia... what happened in Abkhazia affected the whole country. If anyone sipped Georgian blood there, in Abkhazia, he sipped the blood of the whole country and not that of one man. If somebody killed pregnant women he did so to wipe out the Georgian gene.'[8]

The great taboo is exploring the question of *why* Abkhazians fought for independence from Georgia, and continue to hold out. There is no room for *context* – any notion that the Abkhazians may have genuine fears and grievances of their own. Instead, when any explanation is offered, it portrays them purely as puppets of Moscow – the 'big brother' extending a malign hand to keep Georgia, the 'little brother', in his place.

It would be naïve not to see this as part of the background, but to rely on it as a complete explanation for the conflict is to avoid listening to one's enemy, a sure way to prolong it, and make violence more likely.

Invading Iraq – a high price for business

The invasion of Iraq could be interpreted as serving the interests of American business – an extension of what President Eisenhower called the US 'military-industrial complex'. Profiteering by Halliburton, the company formerly run by Vice-President Dick Cheney, came to symbolise complaints about hard-faced men in corporate boardrooms doing well out of the war. What about Britain's participation? The interests of British business, it could be argued, were more against than in favour. The war brought:

- depressed stock market performance
- meagre pickings in reconstruction
- ballooning public deficits
- a longer and deeper advertising recession

The London Stock Exchange sustained record falls as it became clear that Britain was off to war even without a second UN resolution giving legal cover.

Lord Browne, chairman of BP and one of Prime Minister Tony Blair's biggest buddies in the business world, used the presentation of his company's half-year results, about six months before the invasion, to complain that UK oil companies were not competing on a 'level playing-field' in the jostling for a share of Iraqi assets and contracts.

Intensive ministerial lobbying did eventually secure a thin slice of reconstruction and security work for UK Ltd, but not nearly enough for the profits to offset the corporate share of the extra tax burden the adventure imposed.

Then, as chancellor (finance minister) Gordon Brown struggled with a growing budget deficit for 2004-5, mounting bills for the invasion and occupation of Iraq threatened to push public spending over his target figures, to howls of protest from the City of London, worried about its potential fiscal and monetary impact.

What about the media themselves? Industry executives queued up to blame the war for prolonging and worsening a three-year advertising recession. Olivier Fleurot, chief executive officer of the *Financial Times*, wrote in the company's annual report that his paper's losses blew out in 2003 because 'advertising declines were significantly worse immediately before and during the war in Iraq'.[9]

In the US, Tony Ridder, chairman of the giant Knight Ridder newspaper group, complained that while the dip in recruitment advertising during the early two-thousands had been offset by demand from the retail sector, 'starting this past Spring, retail, too, began to falter. There are multiple causes. Among them are, firstly, the war in Iraq'.[10]

In Australia, 'just as [advertising] executives have begun to celebrate signs of a recovery, another cloud of uncertainty has appeared: the prospect of war... It's an unwelcome turn of events for an industry that very much looked forward to 2003. Most reports were predicting growth of 3-5 per cent in Australia this year, a welcome turnaround from the worst industry recession since the 1930s. But the optimism that surfaced in the last three months of 2002 has tapered... Media buyers have noticed another softening of the market in the first three months of 2003.'[11]

Despite all this, War Journalism dominated the coverage in all three countries, especially in the crucial six weeks or so when the decision was, to all intents and purposes, being taken, as we argued in Chapter 1.

In spite of the traditional view that you can always find a market for graphic accounts of violence, matters hardly improved when jaw-jaw gave way to war-war. Roy Greenslade, a former national newspaper editor now commentating on the media for the London *Guardian*, quoted circulation figures from the first weeks of hostilities showing an 'underlying public rejection of wartime papers':

'[Reporters] have risked their lives to tell what has been happening in Iraq. Back in London, editors and production staff have worked hard to fill endless pages about the conflict, devoting many unpaid hours to the task... Some newspaper journalists have been outstanding. Most papers have been excellent.'[12]

Despite all this, fewer copies were shifting than before. 'When they return to Britain, what will they think when they discover that the public were completely unappreciative of their efforts?'

Declining sales were compounded by plummeting ad revenues, Greenslade lamented: 'Some will see this as canny: you can't sell a holiday next to the picture of a wounded child.'

DISCUSSION: When the hard commercial interests of media owners and their clients are against war, or against violence, why do we not see a sudden outbreak of Peace Journalism?

Either their perceptions, aspirations and attitudes are simply not *transmitted* to the journalism of the media they own or patronise, or at least not always in the linear way Chomsky suggests.

Of course, it could be that prudent executives avoid making life too difficult for political leaders, even when particular policies are bad for the bottom line; but that would be to say that their interests should be seen as *divided* and in some ways contradictory.

(Or there's another possibility – the ruling class, they just don't know what's good for 'em! For whatever reason, the dots are not joined.)

None of this is to negate familiar observations that some do profit from some wars in some places at some times:

'Economic gains are enjoyed by warlords whose personal coffers are enriched by territorial conquest, theft and taxation. Warriors and gangs of thugs also use the power of their weapons to gain personal wealth. Arms merchants benefit from more, and more prolonged wars.'[13]

The point is that War Journalism – the patterns of omission and marginalisation we have identified in the way news organisations respond to so many conflicts – cannot be *explained* solely as a 'reflect[ion of] the perspectives and interests' of those in charge of them.

Reflecting or constructing?

We have suggested that journalism is, in any case, better understood as playing a part in *constructing* the world around it – *creating* realities, and shaping discussions. This is not just a semantic point.

Yes, the proponents of war may meet in secret to set their course, as at President Bush's Texas ranch in March 2002, and then devise a propaganda strategy to sell it. But we have also seen how war propaganda takes shape around the established conventions of reporting.

War Journalism conceives of conflict as a tug of war involving two parties – dualism, which prepares the ground for demonisation to justify escalation. When western governments cast Slobodan Milosevic as a reincarnated Hitler, they found a ready media reception. By contrast, the efforts of Jenny Ranson at the UK Foreign Office to convey a more nuanced analysis of the conflict in Yugoslavia, discussed in Chapter 4, fell flat.

The tendency of War Journalism to present

violence as its own cause, stripped of context, *invites* the presentation of more violence as an appropriate remedy. The '9/11' attacks were reported in most US media as a bolt from the blue; whereupon anyone attempting to contextualise them was shouted down, as discussed in Chapter 3.

The question of when, where and how America would 'strike back' dominated coverage over subsequent days and weeks, despite the findings of a global Gallup poll which found that most people, in most countries, favoured a judicial response over a military one.

What was unusual about this poll was that both possibilities were posed: with the choice spelt out, opinion even in the US was divided about 50-50.[14] But the possibilities were generally not posed, and indeed, history shows, seldom are.

Howard Friel and Richard Falk lament the 'persistent refusal' by the *New York Times*, in particular, over several decades, 'to consider international law arguments opposing recourse to and the conduct of war by American political leaders, and by this refusal allowing the citizenry to overlook this essential dimension of controversial foreign-policy decisions'.[15]

There is a well-established media template in other words, for such stories, and it does not include raising questions about the lawfulness or otherwise of different responses.

The public seldom hears anyone arguing for a strategy of intelligence-sharing, issuing arrest warrants and bringing individual perpetrators to justice – one the public prefers, Gallup found, when they do hear about it.

Anyone tempted to advocate responses such as this – non-violent, based on co-operation to uphold international law – would have to *reckon with* War Journalism, since it means anything which is not unequivocally 'winning' risks being reported as 'losing' or 'backing down'. To argue for a violent response – and devise a propaganda strategy to match – is, in that sense, a safer bet.

War Journalism is 'already there' – a factor in calculations by parties to conflict as

they formulate their interests and perspectives into policies and propaganda. War Journalism and war propaganda are *coterminous*. So where did these news values, these reporting conventions, come from in the first place? How did they arise, and why?

The liberal theory of press freedom

For the answer, go back to a previous question: where did we get that notion of journalism having a 'societal purpose', as Chomsky and Herman put it? Welcome to the liberal theory of press freedom. One of its most eloquent exponents was the 19th-century English philosopher John Stuart Mill:

> 'The peculiar evil of silencing an expression of opinion is that it is robbing the human race; posterity as well as the existing generation; those who dissent from the opinion, still more than those who hold it. If the opinion is right, they are deprived of the opportunity of exchanging error for truth: if wrong, they lose, what is almost as great a benefit, the clearer perception and livelier impression of truth, produced by its collision with error.'[16]

In other words, the free flow of information, especially if it brings competing perspectives into 'collision', is not only a good thing in itself, it can also be defended on a utilitarian basis, as something that helps society to work better. It is supposed to be a check on the use of political power in a democracy, since people can find out what the government of the day is doing on their behalf, and assess it against criticisms, complaints and alternative proposals, which can be freely aired.

In the words of James Madison, fourth President of the United States, about half a century before Mill was writing:

> 'A popular government without popular information, or the means of acquiring it, is but a Prologue to a Farce or a Tragedy,

or perhaps both. Knowledge will forever govern ignorance, and a people who mean to be their own Governors, must arm themselves with the power knowledge gives.'[17]

The revolution in 1776 that brought Madison and his predecessors to office can be seen as one of a series of political upheavals inspired by the ideas of the Enlightenment, or Age of Reason – including the French Revolution of 1789, Britain's Great Reform Act of 1832, and the revolutions in Europe of 1848.

What did they have in common? 'Enlightenment thinkers argued, if reason can control the natural world, it can also be used to discover the "laws" governing the social world.'[18] The exercise of power in this social world therefore requires *legitimation* through reasoning, rather than being able to sustain itself by appeal to irrational religious and social orthodoxies. On this basis, monarchies appeared less legitimate than democracy.

Hence the case for a free press: bringing readers 'the truth' equips them to function as reasoning citizens, capable of holding the authorities to account through public opinion and, ultimately, the ballot box.

In the time of Madison in the US, and Mill across the Atlantic, anyone with a modest sum of money, and a similarly modest number of like-minded supporters, could launch a publication and survive by selling it. As education reforms made literacy more widespread, so a broader range of ideas could collide and compete with all the others in a growing market-place.

This meant that any community – even quite small ones – could have their own media, equipped to consider in depth the issues of pressing local interest to their inhabitants. But in industrialised countries like Britain and America, market conditions were changing, with an increasingly urbanised population and the emergence of a consumer society.

The growth of mass media

Former *Washington Post* editor Ben Bagdikian explains what happened next:

'Pursuit of advertising... reduced the media's responsiveness to reader desires. Publishers became more dependent on advertising revenues than on reader payments. Ads swelled the size of the paper each day, requiring larger plants, more paper and ink, and bigger staffs, with the result that it was no longer easy for newcomers to enter the newspaper business.

As the country's population grew and new communities arose, the old pattern disappeared. Instead of new papers to meet changing political forces, existing papers pushed beyond their municipal boundaries to the new communities and, increasingly, reached not for all the new citizens but for the more affluent consumers.

Soon each metropolitan paper was pre-empting circulation in thousands of square miles with hundreds of communities and voting districts. The newly captured populations were inundated with ever-larger quantities of regional advertising, but the papers, and later the radio and television stations, could not possibly tell each community what it needed to understand its own problems and needs.

From 1900 to 1950 the American population doubled and the number of urban places almost tripled, to 4,700. But the number of daily newspapers dropped from 2,226 to 1,900.'[19]

All of this meant the kind of journalism needed, to ensure commercial survival, also changed. Niche marketing had given way to mass marketing. At one time, journalism had had to fire its adherents with enthusiasm, or absorb a small, local constituency in their own concerns. Now, it had to avoid putting off any of its potential consumers.

Hence the rise of what we now think of as Journalistic Objectivity as an industry standard (throughout the rest of this chapter, we denote it with a capital 'O') – a set of conventions allowing the news to be presented as all things to all people – or at least, all of those with enough money to buy it.

Journalistic Objectivity – the big 'O'

DISCUSSION: What does Objectivity mean and where does the idea come from?

Objectivity, as an ethos in journalism, was a phenomenon of the Enlightenment, and the political, economic and social changes imbricated with it:

'The popular commercial dailies developed the first version of journalistic Objectivity; an independent, universalizing stance that looked at the world and the body politic from the viewpoint of the ideal citizen: a prudent, rational, fair-minded individual, committed to individual rights, political democracy, a market economy, and progress through science and education.'[20]

Two latter-day definitions:

'It is the value of fairness, which is extremely important. It's the ethic of restraining your own biases, which is also important... It's the idea that journalism can't be the voice of any particular party or sect.'[21]

'An effort to report the facts without developing – or at least without revealing – an opinion about them.'[22]

Objectivity conferred a considerable commercial advantage on news in the consumer society. Journalism matching these criteria would avoid putting off potential consumers among the educated classes on the rise in political dispensations born of Enlightenment-inspired reforms and upheavals. It was likely to prove *unexceptionable* to rational, fair-minded readers, of all political views and none.

Radio and television depend on the use of public goods, or 'commons' – the airwaves (and later, the geostationary orbit). Each station depends on the authorities' protection to stop anyone else setting up and muscling in on its allotted frequencies, cable connections or satellite footprint. These rights are generally safeguarded by a licence to broadcast issued by the state, in exchange for which the stations generally have to make certain undertakings. For many, this involves reporting the news in such a way as to avoid allegations of bias from any quarter. Hence the principle of 'due impartiality' – of which, more later.

But it was not easy to pull off. How did journalists get round the obvious problem we have already met?

'While the rules of journalism prohibit reporters from making subjective interpretations, their task demands it.'[23]

The first decisions reporters and editors make, on any story, are in their role as gatekeepers. Why this story, and not another? Then, once they have decided that, why this source, and not another? This issue was defused, as the methods of Objective journalism hardened into industry conventions, by the habit of *indexing* – projecting such basic decisions on to an external frame of reference that was not, apparently, of the journalist's own making.

Official sources

In practice, indexing often meant tracking the agenda set by official sources – governments, the police and courts, financial authorities and so on. To lead, say, the television evening news, or the front page of the *New York Times*, with a report of a speech by President

Bush on Iraq need not be taken to mean that the programme or the paper agrees with him. His comments can be presented as newsworthy – whatever he actually says – *because he's the President*. A subjective interpretation – of what constitutes the most meaningful fact of that particular day – is still involved, but it's one chosen on a seemingly 'neutral' basis. These news values are deeply embedded in structure and practice:

> 'Journalism's criteria of newsworthiness and factuality, and its routines of newsgathering anchored in bureaucratic institutions with designated spokespeople and prescheduled routines, are mutually constitutive. Taken together, they tend to ensure routine and privileged access for bureaucrats and agency officials, who provide the "hard facts", credible claims and background information for Objective reporting.'[24]

For these reasons, a bias in favour of official sources is probably still the single most widespread convention in global news. Go to any capital city in the world, pick up a copy of the main newspaper, and there's a good chance that the deeds and pronouncements of that country's political leaders will be on or near the front page.

Anomalies and contradictions

The trusty sword of Objectivity, forged in the Enlightenment and a choice weapon in later battles for commercial and political survival, has over time ensured the primacy in news of the 'official agenda', assiduously documented by the likes of Chomsky and Herman.

But journalism, having, as it were, lived by the sword, is now in danger of dying by it, as it comes under pressure from proliferating sources of information and, indeed, misinformation, to burnish its credentials as a

reliable account of what is really going on. Objectivity rules out any form of what we have called 'anchorage' (see Prologue and Chapter 2). To map out solid ground beneath our feet; to declare, in advance, that we intend to use it, to assign meanings and draw distinctions, is to risk revealing an opinion, thereby putting off potential consumers or inviting complaints about 'bias'.

Without anchorage, however, there can be no firm basis for assessing what is important in a given story. Aspects that official sources do not care to discuss tend to drop off the edge of the news. Hence the tiny number of reports dealing with control over access to oil resources as a key strategic consideration behind the invasion of Iraq. Hence, also, the negligible coverage of any alternative means of unseating Saddam Hussein, despite the rich history of non-violent 'regime changes' discussed in Chapter 3.

Bagdikian, referring to US print media in the early decades of the last century, says: 'The safest method of reporting news was to reproduce the words of authority figures.' But this reporting method brings risks of its own – risks that have come into sharper focus as governments, even 'empires', set out to shape discussions and create realities:

> 'In the nature of public relations most authority figures issue a high quotient of imprecise and self-serving declarations.'[25]

The glaring anomalies in the story about Iraq's 'weapons of mass destruction', exposing the imprecision of claims before the war, increased the risks – as Dominic Lawson, then editor of the London *Sunday Telegraph* reflected:

> 'Our mistake was in believing what we were told. There is a sense in which we were duped. If you feel you have been duped, then you are more cynical.'

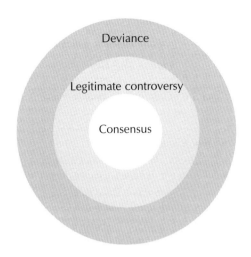

Based on The Uncensored War
by Daniel Hallin

Lawson himself commissioned the story discussed in Chapter 1, revealing that British Prime Minister Tony Blair had secretly signed up to 'regime change' long before the British people were told about it, and splashed it on his front page. It called into question Blair's self-presentation as having been brought, reluctantly, to the sticking-point after giving Saddam Hussein a last chance to 'come clean'.

This was the most notable of a series of exclusives of similar bent. Another exposed the fact that, contrary to official protestations that the chaos following the overthrow of Saddam Hussein's regime came as an unwelcome surprise, Blair had received explicit warnings long before the event that this would happen.

Lawson made it clear that these stories were commissioned in pursuit of hard-headed business interests:

'Since the middle of the year [following a takeover] there has been no proper marketing budget for the paper, so it's been important for us to produce scoops.'[26]

Mounting anomalies may expose contradictions, and herald a paradigm shift in

the sense coined by *The Structure of Scientific Revolutions* – see Prologue. Chomsky notes that it is not difficult to find critical stories in US media about conflicts, in which the US is involved, where the extent of criticism is limited to the theme of 'good intentions' frustrated by circumstance or even stymied by bad planning and preparation.

Daniel Hallin, in a major retrospective study of news about the Vietnam war,[27] called this the category of 'legitimate controversy'. What is rare is journalism that raises a more fundamental question – whether it is not more accurate to regard the actions of authorities on 'our side' as part of the problem, rather than part of the solution.

For obvious reasons, this is wormwood to official sources, and so is generally confined, in Hallin's schema, to the category of 'deviance' – ie unworthy of being taken seriously.

Peace Journalism in *The Independent*

The London *Independent*, more than any other newspaper, has been adduced in this book for examples of coverage that satisfies most if not all the criteria of Peace Journalism. It, too, has notched up a number of important scoops – notably by veteran reporter Robert Fisk, on the first weekend of 2004, concerning the brutality meted out by British soldiers to civilians in southern Iraq. A further step into the zone of deviance, compounded as the paper hammered away at its theme over succeeding weeks and months.

The Independent is owned by a PLC, which, in London's lightly regulated stock market, is open to merger or takeover at any time. Moreover, the daily and Sunday titles have the smallest readership of all national newspapers, so they could be said to feel the breath of market forces on their backs more intensely than any of their competitors, at both a corporate and a consumer level. This means they have to operate within tight marketing budgets, and so the onus is on innovation and investigation. It works – they have bucked a long-term trend in the London newspaper market by increasing sales.

Others also proved willing to maintain critical scrutiny, both of war propaganda and of the balance of advantage accruing from violence – notably the *Guardian* and *Daily Mirror*; we have mentioned the *Sunday Telegraph* and, in its careful specialist reporting of issues in the Iraqi election, the *Financial Times* (see Chapter 3).

After what President Bush called 'the end of major hostilities' in Iraq, the primary interest of media owners that was transmitted to editors and reporters – sheer commercial survival – helped to ensure that:

'The case for invading Iraq remained a matter of public concern in the aggressor countries to a greater extent [than] after any other war in recent times...

Some journalists did expose misinformation and misrepresentations in the case for war both after Operation Desert Storm in 1991 and Operation Allied Force, the NATO bombing of Kosovo, in 1999. But, on those occasions, pursuing such angles remained a minority media pursuit. In this case, they were kept firmly on the agenda as a matter of vital public interest.'[28]

**Exercise One
Testing the Big 'O'**

Read the following two newspaper reports, and say:

- Which one is Objective?
- If both are, which is more Objective?
- If neither is, which is less Objective?
- What makes them Objective – or not Objective?

In September 2002, British Prime Minister Tony Blair made a speech to trade unionists in which he gave a warning that the 'threat' from Iraq's chemical and biological weapons needed to be dealt with, lest it somehow 'engulf us'. It was exhaustively reported – the lead story in that night's television news on all the main channels and prominent in the next day's papers.

The following piece, in the London *Express*, was typical:

Photograph copyright © REUTERS/Ian Hodgson
Britain's Prime Minister Tony Blair addresses the Trades Union Congress (TUC) conference in Blackpool, 10 September 2002

WE'LL ATTACK IF YOU DEFY THE UN, SAYS BLAIR; NO MORE GAMES, SADDAM

BRITAIN and America will act against Saddam Hussein if the Iraqi dictator keeps playing 'games' in defiance of the United Nations, Tony Blair said yesterday.

A sombre Prime Minister addressed the TUC conference in Blackpool ahead of George Bush's crucial speech to the UN General Assembly tomorrow.

Apart from a lone heckler, the TUC delegates, many of whom on Monday voiced bitter opposition to the idea of a new war on Iraq, heard Mr Blair in silence.

He detailed Saddam's crimes against his own people and defiance of the UN: 'With the Taliban gone, Saddam is unrivalled as the world's worst regime: brutal, dictatorial, with a wretched human rights record.

'Given that history, to allow him to use the weapons he has or get the weapons he wants, would be an act of gross irresponsibility and we should not and we must not countenance it.'

Mr Blair said he understood concerns about 'precipitate military action' and pledged military action would only ever be a last resort.

And it was right to deal with Saddam through the UN, whose resolutions his regime was breaching: 'If the challenge to us is to work with the UN, we will respond to it.

'But if we do so, then the challenge to all of us in the UN is this: the UN must be the way to resolve the threat from Saddam not avoid it.

'Let it be clear that he must be disarmed. Let it be clear that there can be no more conditions, no more games, no more prevaricating, no more undermining of the UN's authority.

'And let it be clear that should the will of the UN be ignored, action will follow.'

Diplomacy was vital – but dictators had to know that force could be used against them.

'If we do not deal with the threat from this international outlaw and his barbaric regime, it may not erupt and engulf us this month or next; perhaps not even this year or the next. But it will at some point. And I do not want it on my conscience that we knew the threat, saw it coming and did nothing.'

Mr Blair urged critics to reflect on the case he would develop over coming weeks. And he promised Parliament would be consulted and be able to debate the matter 'before there is any question of taking military action'.

He also promised to act in a 'sensible, measured way'.

Afterwards, some union leaders said they had not been reassured, particularly on the TUC's demand that any military action must be backed by the UN.

Unison general secretary Dave Prentis said: 'He did not give us a categorical assurance that President Bush and Prime Minister Blair would not bilaterally start a war in the Middle East.'

GMB boss John Edmonds said: 'I welcome the Prime Minister's stress on the importance of the UN but he has got to start portraying the UN as the key that will solve the Iraq crisis rather than the battering ram.'

Just hours before Mr Blair's speech, Iraq's vice-president called for terrorist attacks on British and American targets if war breaks out.

Taha Yassin Ramadan said Arabs should 'confront the interests of the aggressors, their materials and humans wherever they are'.'

Another version

Days afterwards, a backbench Labour MP, Alan Simpson, and a lecturer from Cambridge University, Glen Rangwala, held a news conference at the House of Commons to launch their independent study, *The Dishonest Case for War on Iraq*.

It marshalled all the evidence that Iraq did *not*, in fact, constitute any kind of threat, and that dire warnings, however imprecise, were misplaced:

'There is no case for a war on Iraq. It has not threatened to attack the US or Europe. It is not connected to al-Qaeda. There is no evidence that it has new weapons of mass destruction, or that it possesses the means of delivering them.'

This disappeared without trace on television and radio news, however, and formed the basis for just one press report, in the *Daily Mirror*. Here it is:

WAR ON IRAQ: LABOUR MPS TORPEDO BLAIR DOSSIER ON SADDAM

By Oonagh Blackman, Deputy Political Editor

LABOUR MPs have ambushed Tony Blair with a hard-hitting dossier exposing government hypocrisy and lies over Iraq.

The document, seen by the Daily Mirror, will acutely embarrass No 10.

It has been circulated in time to torpedo the Premier's own dossier against Iraq which is due out ahead of tomorrow's emergency Commons debate.

The report is designed to give Labour MPs ammunition to blow apart Mr Blair's arguments for sending British troops into a US-led war on Saddam Hussein.

The No 10 document will contain graphic pictures of the victims of chemical warfare.

But the Labour Against The War dossier highlights a catalogue of myths and decades of hypocrisy over Britain and America's dealings with Iraq.

It says America has turned a blind eye in the past to Iraq's use of chemical weapons, experts insist there is no proof that Saddam is close to building nuclear weapons, and Iraq has only a small number of missiles.

The dossier, using intelligence and official reports from Europe and America going back 20 years, was written by MP Alan Simpson and Cambridge University lecturer Dr Glen Rangwala.

It says: 'This pamphlet separates the evidence for what we know about Iraq from the wild suppositions used as the pretext for a war.

'You cannot launch a war on the basis of unconfirmed suspicions of both weapons and intentions to use them.'

Mr Blair will today preside over one of the most turbulent Cabinet meetings since Labour came to power in 1997.

Some MPs believe International Development Secretary Clare Short and Commons Leader Robin Cook could end up resigning over the Premier's plans to back President Bush's war on Iraq.

The two Cabinet rebels risked the fury of Downing Street and spoke out over the weekend about their opposition to military strikes.

Ms Short said on GMTV: 'We cannot have another Gulf war. We cannot have the people of Iraq suffering again. They have suffered too much. That would be wrong.'

Several Labour MPs are convinced Mr Cook will quit the Cabinet if British troops join a US-led war against Iraq without UN backing. The ex-Foreign Secretary said: 'It is very important that any action taken on Iraq is one that does have international support.'

Liberal Democrats will step up pressure against war at their party conference in Brighton this week. Leader Charles Kennedy said yesterday: 'We want to see the moral as well as the political authority of the United Nations remain paramount in all of this.'

Tory leader Iain Duncan Smith backed Mr Blair, and said military action was the only way to stop Saddam breaching UN resolutions over weapons of mass destruction. Former Foreign Secretary Lord Owen said Iraq should be invaded and Saddam Hussein put on trial at a UN court for using chemical weapons on his own people, unless he complies with UN resolutions.'

Commentary

The *Daily Mirror* report clearly belongs in a paper which had, by this stage, already decided to use its pages to oppose the use of military force. The case for war, it says, is based on 'lies and hypocrisy' – only loosely attributed to its sources.

Even without these rhetorical flourishes, however, choosing the Simpson/Rangwala report as the basis for a news story would have rung alarm bells. Deciding to use sources like Simpson and Rangwala risks criticism and complaint, by immediately drawing attention to itself *as a decision*. It would invite the objection, encountered by a reporter from her editors at the *Times of India*, when she sought out 'change agents', like those discussed in Chapter 3, to report on: 'What is their claim to fame, exactly?'[29]

Why, in other words, should their perspective be any better qualified, as a 'meaningful fact', than anyone else's?

And yet the Simpson/Rangwala assessment of the 'threat' posed by Iraq and its weapons was much more accurate than that of Tony Blair. The 'games' the Prime Minister spoke of referred to Iraq's denials that it still had any operative chemical or biological weapons – denials which were, in fact, fully justified.

Reporting by the British media at this time was greeted as more Objective, by virtue of concentrating on the Prime Minister, than it would have been had they accorded more space and more airtime to a backbench MP and an academic. Only a newspaper which had already declared itself against the war took any notice.

But readers and viewers would have received a much more accurate impression of the situation if the respective proportions of news resources given over to these two versions had been reversed. Each was an assessment, essentially an opinion. The one chosen by the *Mirror* was more realistic, but the other one was more easily disguised as a 'meaningful fact' – and it was on that basis that it dominated the coverage; not despite, but in a sense because of, journalists' best intentions. The public were misled, not through a want of Objectivity, but through too much.

Objectivity and War Journalism

Under the Objectivity conventions, War Journalism is the dominant discourse in the reporting of conflict. This is not by happenstance. Three conventions of Objective reporting, in particular, are *predisposed* towards War Journalism. Their 'natural drift', as it were, is to lead us – or leave us – to overvalue violent, reactive responses to conflict, and undervalue non-violent, developmental ones. The conventions are:

* a bias in favour of official sources
* a bias in favour of event over process
* a bias in favour of 'dualism' in reporting conflicts

We have suggested in previous chapters that news is, by its very nature, preoccupied with

change. There are many ways to bring about change in a conflict, many 'levers' to pull. As we discussed in Chapter 3, anyone working to intervene in the cycle of violence, for example, can be regarded as a 'change agent'.

But the Objectivity conventions mean we hear relatively little about them, compared with official sources – a category topped by leaders of national states. The sociologist Max Weber provided a definition that has become famous: the state is a political organisation that '(successfully) claims the monopoly of the legitimate use of force within a given territory'.[30] So the levers reserved for the *exclusive* use of authority figures in national states are, ultimately, violent or coercive ones – armies and police forces.

This means that a method of reporting which relies mainly or exclusively on these authorities as sources for stories is bound to contain an inherent and general bias in favour of violent responses to conflict. In the news, proposals for multi-lateral initiatives to remove objectionable regimes, for instance – including the use of international legal apparatus, and solidarity action at the level of civil society – are bound to be marginalised, unless journalists adopt a deliberate creative strategy to keep them on the map.

A bias in favour of event over process

In other chapters, we have analysed reports of several violent events – the suicide bombing in Jerusalem, the attack on Casablanca, the Rwandan genocide.

A news story is supposed to answer six basic questions:

* Who?
* What?
* When?
* Where?
* Why?
* How?

In each of the examples, we have seen how our understanding of 'why' arises out of choices made by editors and reporters – in particular, whether and how they manage to convey issues of structural and cultural violence as part of the underlying reasons for what has happened.

That means talking about poverty and political dysfunction in Morocco, or Israel's military occupation of Palestinian territory. It involves tracing the effect of international meddling in Rwanda's economic and political dispensation. But to focus on these ongoing *processes*, as part of the explanation for violence, is to stray on to controversial ground.

The authorities in Morocco would rather attribute the attacks to ill-intentioned outsiders, stirring up trouble – it diverts attention from problems for which they are, to some degree, responsible. Israel's official view is that the occupation is a response to terrorism – not the other way round.

Leaders in the 'international community' are accustomed to presenting themselves as intervening between incorrigible warring factions. In the case of Rwanda, they sometimes 'fess up to their failure to do so, as an argument against 'doing nothing'. But official discourses generally have no room for any really critical thinking about *ongoing* interventions and the role they may play in setting factions against each other in the first place.

A journalist assigned to produce an Objective story may feel stirrings of caution. Far safer to stick to *events* – things which have, incontestably, taken place. But we have seen how reports of direct violence that don't consider structural or cultural violence as part of the explanation amount to a distorted representation of the problem. They may lead us to infer that more violence – 'the only language they understand' – is an appropriate remedy, or at least the inevitable 'next step'.

Or they may insulate from proper scrutiny the imposition, from outside, of what the US National Security Strategy calls the 'single sustainable model for national success' – multiparty democracy, with or without safeguards for minorities; and market

'reforms' in the form of IMF structural adjustment – even where, as with the case of Iraq, discussed in Chapter 3, the resulting economic strictures cut directly across the clear and democratically expressed wishes of the people.

Any who refuse to swallow the medicine, whole and without demur, may therefore appear, *ipso facto*, unreasonable (or even, in the document's own words, a 'threat') – another potential justification for violence.

A bias in favour of dualism

One safe way to insulate oneself against allegations of bias is to 'hear both sides'. It means the journalist cannot be seen as 'the voice of any particular party or sect'. Classic BBC reporting, for instance, is said to adopt the formula: 'On the one hand... on the other... in the end, only time will tell.'[31]

And this chimes with the way many other parts of occidental life are organised. Politics? Conveniently divided into Left and Right. Our personality, thoughts and dreams? Try 'conscious' and 'unconscious'. In the end, we will all be sorted into sheep and goats, in the last battle of Good and Evil.

This means that any narrative organised around two poles may appear to us as 'common sense'. A decision to tell a story in that way can slip past, unnoticed, without drawing attention to itself, because of its close resemblance, in shape and structure, to so much of the story-telling we already take for granted. Dualism is, for these reasons, a key part of Objectivity; but, as we saw in Chapter 1, with the cover of *Newsweek* counterposing the disembodied heads of Presidents George W Bush and Saddam Hussein, it is a key element of War Journalism, too.

Where does all this leave us *vis-à-vis* the Propaganda Model? There *is* a connection, after all, between the overriding class interests of the owners of commercial media – to sell audiences to advertisers – and the prevalence of reporting conventions we recognise as War Journalism.

However, the connection is not linear, as

Chomsky and Herman suggest, but structural and historical, built into the very concept of journalism inscribed in the liberal theory of press freedom, with its traditional criteria of newsworthiness and factuality. This concept arose from a complex, multi-dimensional process – economic and political, yes, but social and cultural as well.

Moreover, the connection is riven with contradictions – contradictions that come to the fore when anomalies proliferate. The London *Telegraph* newspapers are usually associated with a kneejerk bellicosity, and have been the last redoubt of War Journalism on the Britain/Ireland conflict (their editorial stance being, one wag noted, 'all we are saying is give war a chance'). And yet the glaring anomaly of Iraq's non-appearing 'weapons of mass destruction' prompted them to expose parts of the case for war seldom seen in mainstream news.

On the editor's own account, this was born of a feeling of 'cynicism'. Cynicism would be one response; Peace Journalism would be another. Remember, as we suggested in the Prologue, it is based on reflexivity – accepting that media representations are themselves part of the story – and an anchorage in Conflict Analysis, including the insight that official sources should be seen as representing parties to a conflict, pursuing their own goals and interests, no matter what their self-presentation.

As such they should be treated as a source of views and perspectives – treated respectfully, sure, but not as being different in kind from other sources. To call these views and perspectives 'self-serving' should not necessarily be seen as pejorative: all parties, to all conflicts, tend to behave that way.

Ivan Agenda

This cartoon by Andrzej Kranze, first appeared in the New Statesman *on 8 April 2002*

Ivan Agenda is a reporter who has come on this journey with us and is prepared to look at the values and practices of his profession from the outside. There are many who, like him, have developed a critical self-awareness. He is also Otto's sworn enemy. Otto is apt to emerge periodically from his hole in the ground, to splutter: 'The entire approach of Peace Journalism is... a contradiction in terms – it's agenda journalism.'[32]

Is there such a thing as 'non-agenda journalism'? That's how Objectivity presents itself – but we have shown how an agenda is, in reality, deeply embedded within it. To adapt a famous aphorism:

> 'Hostility to "agendas" really means an opposition to other people's agendas and an oblivion of one's own.'[33]

Journalism has been described as:

> 'Arguably the most important form of public knowledge in contemporary society. The mass media – of which journalism is one key, news-spreading part – have

become the leading institutions of the public sphere.'[34]

The governing assumption of this form of knowledge – 'we just report the facts' – presupposes a relationship between the facts and the report, the outside world and the way it is represented, which is natural, obvious and transparent. Hence the 'just'.

It is worth spending a little time here to emphasise how very odd this is. Journalism is a subject now taught in many universities. In any other university subject concerned with discourse and representation – including all the humanities and social sciences, and even (according to Thomas Kuhn) the sciences – this relationship is seen as problematic, meriting close scrutiny.

The governing assumption of all these other subjects is that all forms of discourse and representation have a built-in agenda. Among the key questions, therefore, are:

- What is the dominant agenda?
- Whose agenda is it?
- How is it derived and sustained?
- Is it revealed? How, and to what extent?
- What are its consequences?
- How are those whose agenda this is to be held accountable, and by whom?
- What are the alternative, or competing, agendas and how are they brought to bear on the dominant agenda?

We are going to take a short detour into some of the important theoretical insights which helped to bring them into focus.

In doing so, we are aware that the accounts we give are partial and simplified; our interpretations, contestable. The remainder of this chapter is intended to bring to bear, on issues in reporting conflicts, a shape and a way of thinking generally unfamiliar to journalism and journalists. We hope the usefulness of this exercise will become apparent; if only as a 'waymarker' to tempt you further along this journey for yourself.

Structuralism and the Linguistic Turn

Spring 2004, and an exhibition at the Tate Britain gallery, in London, of work by the Pre-Raphaelite Brotherhood of English painters. Their speciality, well displayed here: the painstaking capture, in oils, of Nature in all her glory. So painstaking, indeed, as to defeat the naked eye. The museum hired out magnifying glasses so patrons could appreciate the fine brush strokes used to convey details of flora and fauna.

The influential critic and cultural commentator, John Ruskin, a champion of these painters, once pronounced himself 'aghast' at the sheer amount of hard work their style entailed. They made a point of painting only on location, with their subject in front of them. Sketches, taken back to the studio for later elaboration, amounted to an unacceptable short cut. Never was there a more conscientious attempt to seek and reproduce 'meaningful facts'.

Across *la Manche*, at about the same time, the French were having none of this. They would bowl out into the countryside with a picnic and some pretty girls, dab a few blobs of colour on the canvas, then leave the painting to dry in the sun while they enjoyed a glass or three of wine…

This was Impressionism, and whatever it failed to exact from the artist in terms of time-consuming brushwork, it more than made up for in brainpower. The French had realised that it was not so much what was *there* – in nature or elsewhere – that was interesting, as *the way people saw it*.

These were the first stirrings of *painting about painting* – a project taken further by Post-Impressionism, Cubism and others, and a distinctive practice of Modernism, along with plays about the theatre and writing about writing.

Why writing about writing? Consider, once again, the claim: 'we just report the facts'. It contains an undeclared theory about language itself – as something we use to *express* experiences, or *reflect* a reality, that happened before we started writing. Hence, readers can recover that experience, and that reality, as they were, *through* our words.

This was what people generally thought, if they thought about it at all, before what is known, in retrospect, as the Linguistic Turn – chiefly attributable to the linguistic theory of Ferdinand de Saussure, and the intellectual movement, known as Structuralism, which drew heavily on his work.

DISCUSSION: The Cat sat on the Mat. It conjures up a familiar picture. But how? How do we know it means what it does?

Saussure's model of language was as a *structure*, or a 'closed system of signs'. In the words of one particularly lucid popularising account:

'Each sign was to be seen as being made up of a signifier (a sound-image, or its graphic equivalent), and a "signified" (the concept or meaning). The three black marks c-a-t are a signifier which evoke the signified "cat" in an English mind. The relation between signifier and signified is an arbitrary one: there is no inherent reason why these three marks should mean "cat", other than cultural and historical convention...

The relation between the whole sign and what it refers to (what Saussure calls the "referent", the real furry four-legged creature) is therefore also arbitrary. Each sign in the system has meaning only by virtue of its difference from the others.'[35]

This represents a crucial inversion – the 'structuralist emphasis on the constructedness of human meaning' – dependent, as it was, on a set of rules and relations established *before* the reality or the experience under discussion actually occurred.

'Meaning was not "natural", a question of just looking and seeing, or something

eternally settled... It was impossible to see reality as something simply "out there", a fixed order of things which language merely reflected. On that assumption, there was a natural bond between word and thing, a given set of correspondences between the two realms [but] if, as Saussure argued, the relation between sign and referent was an arbitrary one, how could any "correspondence" theory of knowledge stand? Reality was not reflected by language but *produced* by it.'[36]

As with the Impressionists, painting ways of seeing, suddenly our interest switches to the different ways of producing, or *constructing* this reality, and their consequences. Who said it should be that way, we start to wonder? How is *power* being exercised over it, by whom and for what end? If we wanted to, how could we construct it differently?

It brings us to another problem with Objectivity. As a way of reporting the news, it passes itself off as 'neutral', but even that may work on behalf of the kind of 'privileged groups' Chomsky and Herman refer to. Those who already enjoy power and advantage, in the order of things as presently constructed, have no interest in opening a conversation about how that order could be re-constructed.

This has a direct relevance in conflict – remember, in Chapter 2, we considered J K Galbraith's concept, the Culture of Contentment. The affluent may be sufficiently comfortable, in economic terms, to feel they do not have to worry about those who cannot gain access to many of the material benefits they themselves enjoy; consequently, underlying conflict issues cannot force themselves far enough up the political agenda to be properly addressed.

Another classic claim of Objectivity, never far from the back of Otto's mind, is the one Walter Cronkite, veteran presenter of *CBS Evening News*, used to sign off every night: '...and that's the way it is' (a catchphrase unashamedly nabbed, after Cronkite's retirement, by Brian Henderson of Australia's *National Nine News*).

If that is allowed to obscure, or stand in for, any examination of how and why it came to be that way, then its effect may be to *naturalise* the present arrangements, rendering them less open to challenge. And, as we have seen, it is when journalists seek to open up questions of how and why something has happened – like a bomb going off – that life, under the Objectivity conventions, gets difficult.

The CNN effect

The undeclared theory in the statement 'we just report the facts' is, in these terms, a 'correspondence theory' of the relations between language, meaning and reality. There is a reflex defensiveness in the word 'just'. Don't blame us for the way things are, it seems to say – we only reflect the world as it is. That world took shape independently of our involvement – only then did we come along to report it.

After the Linguistic Turn, however, we are on the alert for clues as to the *constructedness* of reality, and how language – and organised uses of language, or 'discursive practices', like news – is constructing it.

Perhaps the best-known theory about this is the 'CNN effect'. Derided, at its birth, as the Chicken Noodle Network, the channel came of age during the 1991 Gulf War – and was dubbed, in a comment attributed to then UN Secretary-General Boutros Boutros-Ghali, 'the sixteenth member of the Security Council'.

The proposition is that today's global media have grown so mighty as to be able to raise issues to the political agenda by their own efforts – issues which would otherwise hold little or no interest for the powers-that-be. TV crews may bring into our living-rooms evidence, for instance, of iniquities being visited on people far away, and generate in the process sufficient emotive power among audiences to force the authorities into a substantive policy response.

A new reality has been constructed according to this theory, not, strictly speaking, by the events themselves but by their representation in the media.

> DISCUSSION: Do the media work by raising issues of concern to the political agenda, off their own bat, and do they 'force' policy-makers to respond? If so, to what extent?

Of all the evidence for this view, two 'exhibits' in particular are put forward in its favour:

- Operation Restore Hope – the US intervention in Somalia, in 1992-3
- Operation Provide Comfort – protecting Iraqi Kurds fleeing the vengeance of a defeated Saddam Hussein in the winter of 1991

Examine these closely, however, and the relations of cause and effect become more blurred.

In Somalia, well before images of starving children started appearing on television, there were already moves afoot in Washington to build a case for military deployment. Ultimately the decision was 'based more on diplomatic and bureaucratic operations than press coverage'.[37]

Concerns raised independently by the media may sometimes be met with palliatives, but seldom, if ever, with a major policy shift. During the Rwandan genocide, the Pentagon was asked to use its military systems to jam hate radio broadcasts. Its response was to recommend sending food aid to succour those who, as refugees, managed to escape the bloodbath.[38]

How, then, to explain Operation Provide Comfort and the establishment of 'no-fly zones' in the north and south of Iraq, policed by the US, British and (initially) French air forces, ostensibly to protect the Kurds from aerial attack by Saddam Hussein?

This has been called 'TV news' finest hour'[39], based on the view that nightly coverage of Kurdish refugees, fleeing Iraqi helicopter gunships over the mountains into southern Turkey, prompted governments to decisive action they would never otherwise have considered.

However, this too gives way under closer scrutiny. Another account quotes Andrew Natsios, then director of the US Office of Foreign Disaster Assistance, which is part of the US government's Agency for International Development:

'Major geopolitical considerations drove policy at the time... The first was concern for Turkey, one of Washington's closest Muslim allies... Turkey, with its own Kurdish 'problem', had no desire to take in hundreds of thousands of destitute Kurdish refugees... Even if the cameras had not been there, the Bush administration would have made the same decision.'[40]

A more realistic model

The search for a more realistic model for the way news coverage influences the actions and calculations of parties to conflict takes us on a brief tour of Systems Theory. Consider:

'For every complex problem there is always a simple solution. And it is wrong.'

H L Mencken's aphorism raises a smile – but it is a smile of recognition. We are now familiar with the unpredictable consequences of applying what previous generations saw as simple solutions.

The roads are choked with traffic? OK, build more! The world's poor are starving? Send them food! Crime is rising? Lock up more criminals!

The fall-out from military interventions in Kosovo, Afghanistan and Iraq, as explored in Chapter 3, reminds us of a similar observation, one we have met before – Gandhi's equally famous dictum:

'I object to violence because when it appears to do good, the good is only temporary. The harm it does is permanent.'

> DISCUSSION: Why is it that an apparently simple solution to a complex problem such as the conflict over Kosovo – blame the Serbs, bomb them out – does not work, at least not in the long run?

Operation Allied Force freed the Kosovo Albanians from the straitjacket of direct rule by Belgrade. And it did, indeed, end with the pull-out of Yugoslavian forces. But this is to describe the consequences for just two individual parts of a system of relations.

Analysing conflicts as we have done, applying the insights of Peace Research, leads us to look at *the relations themselves*. Hence the call in the War Journalism/Peace Journalism table, for Peace Journalists to focus on the hidden costs of violence – the damage to psychology, structure and culture.

In conflict, as John Paul Lederach has observed, 'we are ill advised to focus our attention on the parts of a system. Rather, we must look at the system as a whole and to the relationships of its parts if we are to understand its dynamic and structure'.[41]

Systems Theory draws on paradigm shifts in science, in particular Quantum Physics. For the purposes of this book, we propose to leave Quantum Physics as a 'black box'. We don't have to know how it works; just appreciate what it does:

'The essential new quality implied by the quantum theory is... that a system cannot be analysed into parts. This leads to the radically new notion of unbroken wholeness of the entire universe. You cannot take it apart. For if you do, what you end up with is not contained within the original whole. It is created by the act of analysis.'[42]

This superseded the earlier, linear, Newtonian model of every action having 'an equal and opposite reaction' – implying that, once the action and reaction had taken place, equilibrium was restored. We went back to the *status quo ante*. Systems Theory suggests that the overall picture, the system, is augmented, and therefore altered, by every intervention in it; it can never revert to exactly the same state as before, and the change can manifest itself at any time, in any part of the system.

Actors across the system recalibrate their expectations, and adjust their behaviour, in response to every intervention. Build more roads and people are inclined to use them more, till those fill up too; imprison more wrong-doers and you initiate more people into a life of crime; send food to poor countries and you may undercut and bankrupt their farmers, weakening their ability to feed themselves.

NATO's war on Yugoslavia was followed by the mutation of the Kosovo Liberation Army (KLA) into the National Liberation Army, or NLA, and their campaign of destabilisation in the Former Yugoslav Republic of Macedonia – trying to repeat the trick of bringing armed intervention to their side. Neither did the system of international relations simply revert to its previous state. The US and UK governments drew on widespread media acceptance of key propaganda claims from 1999, examined in Chapter 4, as political collateral for invading Iraq four years later.

The Feedback Loop

In an important way, journalistic Objectivity is the equivalent of Newtonian physics:

'Conflict resolution is something on which I report, not something in which I engage. A side-effect of my reporting may be that it makes conflict resolution harder or easier, but that's a judgement that is made after our reporting.'[43]

This is a *linear* way of thinking. A source says or does something; what the source says or does is 'the facts'. A reporter comes along to report the facts, putting them into the media. Readers and audiences then receive their reports. There has been an action, a reaction and a return to equilibrium.

Any consequences can be safely ignored as *externalities*, a term from classical economics. (That's how economists came to leave out, say, the cost of decommissioning spent nuclear power stations from calculations about the cost of electricity they were to generate – 'too cheap to meter', in a vogue phrase of the 1950s.)

We have seen how linear ways of conceptualising relations of cause and effect can give us an equally partial and misleading picture of conflict. To grasp the dynamics of conflict as a system, we need an extra-linear view – hence the cycle of violence and the twin triangles of conflict and violence (see Chapters 2 and 3).

Their counterpart, in this discussion of news and why it is the way it is, is the Feedback Loop – a concept from Systems Theory, which gives an extra-linear account of cause and effect, refreshing the parts the 'CNN effect' cannot reach. What does it mean and how does it work?

We live in a media-savvy world in which any audience member could, at any time, be swept up in a 'human interest story' or chosen to appear on a reality TV show, and enjoy 15 minutes of fame. Actually it is possible, with a little guile, to spin this into rather more than 15 minutes.

Abi Titmuss attained minor celebrity status in the UK after entering the public eye as the girlfriend of a television presenter, John Leslie, who was accused, then cleared, of rape. Within months, she had posed nude on the front of the men's magazine *FHM*, been signed up by a porn TV channel as a presenter, told 'my hell' stories to popular newspapers about her experiences at drug parties, and been a contestant on a reality show for celebrity chefs. Interviewed about her meteoric rise, she commented:

'I have absolutely no idea why me. I have nothing that's different. Even I wonder sometimes what I might think of this Abi Titmuss character.'[44]

Just as the rape allegations against John Leslie were surfacing in 2002, at the other end of the news agenda another illuminating media event was taking place. The British government published its 'intelligence dossier' about 'weapons of mass destruction' in the possession of Saddam Hussein (pre-empted by the Simpson/Rangwala report but, as we have seen, virtually no one took any notice of that).

After the invasion, reports emerged about misgivings by some in the intelligence community that their 'product' had been misused in the compilation of the dossier, to exaggerate the threat. This was the basis for Andrew Gilligan's dramatic contribution to the BBC's *Today* programme (see Chapter 4).

The source for Gilligan's story was later unmasked as a government scientist, David Kelly, who was eventually found killed, apparently by his own hand, in an Oxfordshire wood. The Hutton Inquiry into the circumstances surrounding Kelly's death called, as evidence, confidential memos from within Downing Street, concerning the compilation of this dossier. The benchmark adopted by its authors, these memos revealed, was to ask themselves: 'What do we want to be the headline in the London *Evening Standard* on the day of publication?'

Like the invented character of 'Abi Titmuss' – scarcely recognisable, by her own account, to the previous Abi Titmuss – the dossier was a fact created, at least partly, *in order to be reported.*

The only way the sources in such cases can possibly know which facts to create, to be reported in a way they imagine will bring them fame, fortune or political advantage, is by observing previous reporting.

If, then, audience members can, in certain circumstances, become sources, so the sources

for stories also draw on their knowledge and experience as audience members. (Or they consult experts with a fund of knowledge and experience for hire – ace publicist James Herring in Abi Titmuss's case, and a veteran media team led by then communications director Alastair Campbell, in Downing Street.)

The two ends of the linear model of news have come together, forming a Feedback Loop of cause and effect.

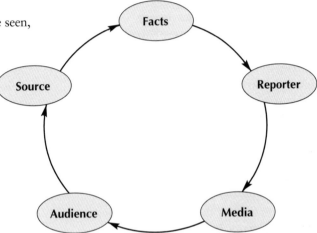

The Feedback Loop

In structuralist terms, the script for these stories – the roles to be played by the actors; the rules about what they should say – had already been written before the event. As the profile of Abi Titmuss put it:

> 'Take one demure, publicity-shy nurse, a minor TV presenter and a scandalous court case. Add the tabloid press, a porn channel and a liberal sprinkling of ambition. Stir in a new TV cookery show, and leave to rise…'

Equally, the British government's 'politics by dossier' had already begun over a year earlier, with the publication of intelligence material on the Taliban and al-Qaeda and their culpability in the attacks of September 11th. A government briefing paper – *Responsibility for the Terrorist Atrocities in the United States* – was eagerly reported:

PM NAILS BIN LADEN OVER SUICIDE ATTACKS

TONY Blair yesterday published 21 PAGES of proof linking Osama bin Laden and his terror network to the US attacks.

The PM braced Britain for imminent military strikes against bin Laden and the Taliban as he produced the damning dossier of evidence.

The document DETAILED how bin Laden and al-Qaeda henchmen meticulously planned the world's worst terrorist outrage.

It PROVED they worked hand-in-hand with Afghanistan's ruling Taliban regime.[45]

A pattern of reporting that passed an incentive around the Feedback Loop to the same source to provide another helping of facts, to the same recipe as before.

And the narrative of Iraq as a 'threat' had a much longer history, of course, stretching back through various claims from intelligence sources about 'drone aircraft', as discussed in Chapter 4.

The success of these claims as propaganda, however preposterous they may seem in retrospect, meant that journalists were, when it came to the Iraq dossier, 'asking for it'. The facts of tomorrow bear a discernible residue, or imprint, of the reporting of today.

The Feedback Loop effect depends, not on the reception of key messages by readers and audiences as such, but on assumptions, by the sources for those messages, about how they are *likely* to be received, if reported in such a way as to pass on a preferred or dominant reading.

Its influence on the actions and motivations of parties to conflict can be predicted, at least in outline, knowing what we do about conflict and the way it works. Report incidents of political violence without context, for example, and you are likely to incentivise a 'crackdown', because someone, somewhere, will assume the public have received, from such reports, an idea that this will form a fitting and effective response.

This knowledge cannot be unlearned. The linear reporting model underpins what is sometimes called a 'deontological' form of journalistic ethics, after the Greek, *deon*, meaning 'duty'. It's based on the universalising principle of Immanuel Kant:

> 'I ought never to act, except in such a way that I would will that my maxim [in so acting] could become a universal law'.[46]

For journalists, it means you do what you see as your duty in carrying out that part of the process up to and including publication or broadcast, without heed to the consequences. But the combined insights of Conflict Analysis and Systems Theory bring the consequences into much clearer focus, pointing us towards a 'teleological' form, after the Greek, *telos*, meaning 'goal' or 'outcome'.

That particular patterns of conflict reporting tend towards particular outcomes, or alterations to the overall system of conflict, is not in serious dispute. It brings a responsibility, at least, to identify those outcomes and to consider them before and during the reporting process as well. Max Weber proposed an 'ethic of responsibility' as the appropriate governing principle for public affairs. One should take into account the *foreseeable* consequences of one's actions, he argued, and adjust one's behaviour accordingly – it is foreseeability that confers responsibility. A deontological journalistic ethics is, in this sense, merely a teleological one 'in-waiting' – waiting for a convincing explanation of the relations of cause and effect.

> DISCUSSION: If you got the chance to interview Tony Blair, and he told you that we must 'deal with' the menace of Saddam Hussein, lest it 'engulf us', not next week or next month but at some unspecified time in the future, what would you do?

In a sit-down interview, this way of describing the 'threat' posed by Iraq would have invited demands for clarification:

- 'What do you mean by that, Prime Minister?'
- 'How would Iraq's weapons "engulf us", exactly?'
- 'Are you suggesting that Saddam Hussein would actually try to fire chemical or biological missiles at Britain?'
- 'Would overthrowing Saddam Hussein by force make it less likely – or more likely – that any such weapons he does possess would fall into the hands of "terrorists"?'

With every question, the claim would have looked more contingent, more hedged with 'ifs' and 'buts' – more threadbare. But there were no sit-down interviews with Blair at this point. Instead, the phrase was tailored to fit into a previously observed pattern, whereby Objective news reports – as distinct from persistent interviewers – would convey the Prime Minister's words into the public sphere, without picking holes in them.

Deconstruction

In Saussurean linguistics, meaning is generated by difference. But this is not limited to the difference between signs. Deconstruction concentrates on the problematical relationship between signifier and signified, to suggest that it is much more difficult to 'close our fist' over meaning than it might at first appear. After all, when you look up the meaning of a word – a signifier – in a dictionary, what do you get? More signifiers.

A signifier only signifies anything by virtue of its difference from other signifiers. But that is to say that, when we read it, we are also reading the difference – not only from other, similar signifiers but from all other signifiers. They are all *there*, each playing its own small part in defining the signifier, in creating its meaning. In the words of Jacques Derrida, who launched the seismic concept of

deconstruction on an unsuspecting world, in the 1960s:

> 'A text* is henceforth no longer a finished corpus of writing, some content enclosed in a book or its margins, but a differential network, a fabric of traces referring endlessly to something other than itself, to other differential traces. Thus the text overruns all the limits assigned to it so far (not submerging or drowning them in an undifferentiated homogeneity, but rather making them more complex, dividing and multiplying strokes and lines).'[47]

Precisely what is signified by a given signifier is forever altering. We may interpret someone's words today, and feel confident of their meaning; only to realise later, after hearing or reading something else, that they may have meant something entirely different. The possibility, that the meaning of any signifier may be altered by any subsequent one, hovers, ghost-like, around the edges of even the simplest sentence. Meaning is *deferred*, perhaps infinitely so:

> 'Each so-called "present" element, each element appearing on the scene of presence, is related to something other than itself, thereby keeping within itself the mark of a past element, and already letting itself be vitiated by the mark of its relation to a future element, this trace being related no less to what is called the future than to what is called the past, and constituting what is called the present by means of this very relation to what it is not.'[48]

As a method of reporting

Structuralism is a way of reading our experiences as structured before we have them – including the experiences of reporters,

---

*A 'text', to structuralist or post-structuralist writers, does not have to mean words. Any set of signs can be a text – a painting, television programme or even an all-in wrestling match.

reporting the facts. 'The facts' may be assembled according to familiar recipes, or narratives. They are 'always already' – to borrow Derrida's formulation – textual. His observations about texts and about writing, quoted here, may therefore also apply to 'the facts'.

As before, there is nothing pejorative in this. It doesn't mean the facts are any less real or authentic. It does mean the methods of deconstruction, commonly used to analyse literary or philosophical works, can be adapted to the job of reporting the facts. That is why Derrida is relevant in a book about journalism.

Deconstruction tends to seize on evidence that texts cannot help but overrun their limits. A text may have a 'governing system of logic' – assigning meanings and drawing distinctions – but its very textuality condemns the meanings to be divided and deferred; the distinctions transgressed.

We suggested earlier that War Journalism is the dominant discourse because it answers the needs, and fits the conventions, of Objectivity. One of them is to construct conflicts as a tug of war between two parties – a decision we scarcely notice because of its homology with the way so many other parts of life are constructed, and which can therefore pass as 'common sense'.

Indeed, one variant of structuralism – associated with the anthropologist Claude Levi-Strauss – proposes that experience is structured by deep-lying binary oppositions such as culture/nature, justice/mercy, civilised/savage and so on.

The last thing we need, in this discussion, is something else to authenticate the bipolar model of conflict. But Levi-Strauss was one of Derrida's early targets. Deconstruction is useful because it shows how *these binary oppositions, on a close reading, tend to evaporate*:

'The central move of a deconstructive analysis is to look at binary oppositions within a text... and to show how, instead of describing a rigid set of categories, the two opposing terms are actually fluid and impossible to fully separate. The conclusion from this, generally, is that the categories do not actually exist in any rigid or absolute sense.'[49]

In the story about asylum seekers in Chapter 5, the second version can be seen as deconstructing the first, with its binary opposition of 'us and them'. The second version, remember:

- transgresses the boundary, finding the 'other' in the 'self' and vice versa
- exposes the constructedness of this opposition in the first place – 'the beggars demonised in recent press coverage'
- highlights the possibility that the proposed 'remedy' will likely make the 'problem' worse, thus unravelling the relations of cause and effect implicit in the original

Another characteristic feature of deconstruction is to take a detail, banished to the margin of a text, and use that as a prism through which to view the whole. The detail often turns out to be anomalous, and therefore highly inconvenient to the ruling system of logic; the act of banishment, most revealing about its weaknesses. The very nature of writing makes this unavoidable, so any text, including whatever journalists think of as 'the facts', is automatically susceptible to such a process.

These insights are clearly potentially useful to Peace Journalism. It is, after all, an approach to reporting conflicts which:

- sets out to restore parts of the picture commonly omitted or marginalised
- excavates any evidence that parties to conflict may conceal, beneath stated positions, internal divisions or compatible needs and interests
- opens up war propaganda to negotiated or oppositional readings, by seeking and highlighting anomalies and contradictions

Can Peace Journalism survive contact with deconstruction?

Deconstruction explores the implications of the Linguistic Turn for our profoundest and apparently most settled ideas about our own identity. Not just our speech and writing, but all our thoughts and perceptions, consist of language. We use signs to look into our minds and search our souls, no less than when we interact with others. We have no identity, it proposes, that is not textual:

> 'Since language is something I am made out of, rather than merely a convenient tool I use, the whole idea that I am a stable, unified entity must also be a fiction.'[50]

> 'There is no experience consisting of pure presence but only of chains of differential marks.'[51]

DISCUSSION (a potentially fatal question): How, then, are we to make sense of our experience? Can there be any reliable set of first principles by which to interpret the reality around us?

Surely any attempt we might make to – for example – derive and set down a basis for making Gatekeeping decisions, to find anchorage, or cut 'the facts' down to size, would also prove susceptible to deconstruction? Indeed, according to Derrida, it would be fated to deconstruct itself: 'There is always already deconstruction, at work in works.'[52]

Why wouldn't Peace Journalism, too, fall foul of this? The very name 'Peace Journalism' automatically disperses one's meaning down chains of signifiers, betraying its apparent promise to act as a reliable organising principle in representing conflicts. The more so because peace is such a hotly contested term. In Chapter 2, we gave a number of definitions for peace. Perhaps the most resonant is Gandhi's: 'Justice lived by unarmed nations in the face of odds.'

But this, too, consists of other signifiers. 'Justice', 'nations' and 'odds' are every bit as contestable, in certain conflict situations, as 'peace' itself. What, then, *can* we identify as firm ground beneath our feet, when we put forward Peace Journalism as a vantage point from which to observe and report on conflict?

An African story

Consider this story, told to the South African Truth and Reconciliation Commission:

> 'Peter and John are friends. It happened that Peter stole a bicycle from John, and then after three weeks Peter came to John saying, "John, let's talk about reconciliation". And then John said, "I don't think we need talk about reconciliation at the present moment until you bring back my bicycle. Where is my bicycle?" And Peter said, "No, let us forget about the bicycle, let us talk about reconciliation". And then John said, "We cannot talk about reconciliation until my bicycle is back."'[53]

The bicycle is a signifier. For John, it may represent important 'signifieds' – what he thinks of as respect and restitution – but he may also feel the lack of *referents*: not only the machine itself but also perhaps the food that he cannot now fetch for his family. Here is a connection that is not arbitrary, but born of necessity.

What about justice? Stick with Peter and John, and ask it another way – is hunger a form of injustice? Sometimes – Gandhi's campaign for self-rule in India drew strength from the terrible famines of colonial times, as fields previously earmarked for growing food were given over, instead, to the production of cash crops, such as indigo, for the British. People were capable of feeding themselves, but not within the system devised under the Raj – a form of structural violence, denying their potential.

Today, the world's six billion inhabitants

could all have access to enough food, to clean drinking water and to basic medicine. There is plenty of each to go round; it's just that we choose to order things in such a way as to deny them to large numbers of our fellow human beings. That makes hunger and disease into forms of injustice.

> The essentials for life itself cannot be deferred, or deconstructed any further, and the Gandhian idea of justice – which is one of the underpinnings for the concept of peace in Peace Journalism – takes, as its first priority, the provision of these essentials for all.

Logocentrism and the 'transcendental signifier'

Deconstruction is sometimes criticised as a suggestion that we cannot, finally, 'know' anything – removing any basis to differentiate reliably between fact and fiction. Not really. Derrida identified, named, and thereby enabled us to inspect from the outside something called *logocentrism*. He noticed that many western ways of thinking, including those apparently antagonistic – liberalism and Marxism, for instance – shared one key characteristic: each was centred on its own single concept or *logos*, left sacrosanct as the underpinning for entire systems of signification and all the meanings – and binary oppositions – therein.

But various candidates for this role – God, Reason, Progress, Class, Nature – can also be shown to be under deconstruction; deferred, divided and decentred. They are, after all, signifiers – albeit 'transcendental signifiers'. Naming logocentrism helps us to think our way on to the outside of propositions such as:

- 'war is inevitable – it's human nature'
- 'shame these people must lose their way of life – but that's progress'

and even:

- 'media reflect the interests of the class who own them'

– with obvious advantages to our arguments here. But Derrida himself admitted it is very difficult, if not impossible, to 'opt out' of logocentrism: 'The notion of a structure lacking any centre represents the unthinkable itself.'[54]

In a later work, Derrida eventually nominated his own candidate for a 'transcendental signifier', something we need not attempt to deconstruct, or try to prove it is deconstructing itself:

> 'What remains irreducible to any deconstruction, what remains as undeconstructible as the possibility itself of deconstruction is, perhaps, a certain experience of the emancipatory promise.'[55]

This, too, we can read in light of the huge step forward for global justice, in the middle decades of the last century, brought about by the overthrow of colonial regimes – a collective experience of emancipatory promise. Promise, notice – not necessarily fulfilment. In the words of Bob Marley, a voice of post-colonial Jamaica, it was still necessary to:

> 'Emancipate yourselves from mental slavery
> None but ourselves can free our minds.'[56]

These elements – justice and emancipation, along with the principles of non-violence and creativity, introduced in Chapter 3 – give us a firm basis for *identifying* peace; establishing it as a vantage point from which to observe and report. We can be confident in the distinction we set out with, between War Journalism and Peace Journalism, even when theoretical perspectives, such as those of structuralism and deconstruction, have caused us to look again at so many distinctions in so many fields.

The majority world

Given the provenance of our idea of peace, it's perhaps not surprising that journalists in post-colonial societies are most ready to adopt it as an organising principle; their own teleological journalistsic ethic.

In many cases, it has chimed with ideals long cherished, that the fortunate should do their bit to improve the outlook for their society and the prospects for their fellow citizens. In Indonesia, where Peace Journalism, or *Jurnalisme Damai*, has made more headway than in most places, journalists can look to the example of Minke, a writer and newspaper editor who is the hero of a classic series of novels about the awakening of the Indonesian nation:

> '"Just think about it – who will urge Natives to speak out if their own writers, such as yourself, won't do it?" he is asked. Minke is told he should expect his people to look to him for help in articulating their aspirations: "He who emerges at the top of his society will always face demands from that society – it is his society that has allowed him to rise."'[57]

After the fall of the Suharto regime in 1998, and the subsequent set of sectarian conflicts in different parts of the country, this imperative took the form of promoting justice and non-violence to go with Indonesia's emancipation from both colonial rule and dictatorship. *Jurnalisme Damai* offered a practical way forward:

> 'Peace Journalism, as a development intervention in Indonesia, came in response to a clearly articulated demand from within. It blended readily with some of the constitutive assumptions about the profession of journalism... There was, before the advent of *Jurnalisme Damai* as such, a *Jurnalisme Damai*-shaped hole in Indonesian journalists' professional repertoire.'[58]

The minority world

Otto's view of these issues, when he pops his head out of the ground, is characteristic of what has been called 'the minority world' – a global elite of perhaps a billion or so of the richest people in the richest countries.

We have suggested that the patterns of newsgathering called Objectivity attained the status of industry conventions in response to commercial and political pressures in countries such as the US and UK with emerging consumer societies and liberal political institutions – among them, public service broadcasting.

Actually the governing concept, in many regimes of public service broadcasting, is slightly different – 'due impartiality'.

Consider this from the BBC *Producer Guidelines*: viewers and listeners should receive 'an intelligent and informed account of issues that enables them to form their own views'.

What does that remind you of? As a societal purpose for news, it's like the principle behind the liberal theory of press freedom. For John Stuart Mill, remember, the free flow of information was supposed to help us distinguish 'truth' from 'error'; the means, Madison said, whereby we might govern ourselves.

Consider how BBC journalists are supposed to see to it that audiences are equipped to form their own views. They must, according to the *Producer Guidelines*: 'Ensure that a full range of significant views and perspectives are heard', especially in dealing with 'major matters of controversy'. For news to fulfil the societal purpose envisioned in the liberal model may require it to project, into the public sphere, a diversity of perspectives – bringing them, to use Mill's word, into *collision* – perhaps weighing and testing them against each other, without necessarily *adjudicating* between them.

The conventions of journalistic Objectivity interfere with this. The dominant patterns of editing and reporting decisions amount to War Journalism, leading us – or leaving us – to overvalue violence, or apparently simple solutions to complex problems.

The case for Peace Journalism in the minority world, then, is *remedial* – a deliberate, creative strategy to seek out and bring to our attention those portions of 'the facts' routinely under-represented; the significant views and perspectives habitually unheard.

To get to this point, however, it is necessary to break the mould and embrace a critical self-awareness – examining systematically the assumptions and conventions inscribed in the dominant discourse of reporting and recognising the resulting patterns of omission and marginalisation. Purists may wince at our notion of 'using' deconstruction – but we have seen how a dose of Derrida can help.

When the philosopher died in October 2004, his obituaries listed the many disciplines influenced by his work. Journalism, the most important form of public knowledge, was notably absent – a curiosity we have set out to begin to change.

As one newspaper was moved to remark:

> 'What was important was that deconstruction held that no text was above analysis or closed to alternative interpretation... As a result, Derrida became popular among those willing to question the sterile idea of a 'western canon' who wanted to expand literary discourse so that writers such as Mary Elizabeth Braddon could sit alongside the Brontës. Thanks to Derrida, many new voices were heard.'[59]

For the 'western canon' you could substitute 'official sources' and the sterile discourse of War Journalism. Those new voices are equally urgently needed in news about conflict. In the words of Johan Galtung: 'Peace Journalism makes audible and visible the subjugated aspects of reality.'[60]

Conclusion

What is useful, albeit unusual, about the Peace Journalism model is that it leads us to take insights from theorising on the one hand, and from practical experience on the other,

and to feed each one through the other, relentlessly, back and forth. To review the fruits of this exercise so far:

- *Conflict theory:* We have a number of tried and tested propositions about conflict and violence, against which competing claims can be weighed and assessed.

- *Resisting propaganda:* We have a workable and comprehensive model of propaganda, what distinguishes it and the way it operates, as well as a set of tactics to resist it.

- *Objectivity's hidden biases*: We have subjected to close scrutiny the unexamined assumptions behind news that presents itself as Objective, or 'just reporting the facts'.

- *Bias towards War Journalism*: We have identified its consequences for the representation of conflicts, as predisposing news towards War Journalism.

- *The Feedback Loop*: A workable model for predicting the influence of journalistic responses on the actions and motivations of parties to conflict.

- *All news has an agenda*: We have established that the only choices are about which agenda and how to pursue it – something we have put into practice in several important stories.

- *Powerful analytical tools*: We have powerful analytical tools at our disposal, to challenge binary oppositions and excavate hidden details, as the basis for transcending the characteristic framings of War Journalism.

- *Peace*: We have a firm basis for claiming that peace is a valid organising principle for journalism about conflicts.

Endnotes for Chapter 7

1. Keith Spicer, director, Institute for Media, Peace and Security, – open letter, sent via email to the authors and others, 19 May 2004.
2. Roger Mosey, 'The Buerk vs Snow Show', London *Guardian* 'Review', 30 October 2004.
3. *Naked City*, ABC Television (US), 1958-63.
4. Lecture by Associate Professor Chris Nash, Centre for Independent Journalism at the University of Technology, Sydney.
5. Edward S Herman and Noam Chomsky, *Manufacturing Consent*, Pantheon Books, New York, 2002, p 298.
6. Noam Chomsky, *Necessary Illusions*, 1989, *ZMag* online version, Chapter One, 'Democracy and the Media', Segment 3/6.
7. Roy Greenslade, Damien Walsh Memorial Lecture, 4 August 1998.
8. Lali Javakhia, 'Tamaz Nadareishvili: "I Assess September 27 As the Day of Great Humiliation and Insult"', *Georgian Times*, 29 September 2003.
9. Pearson annual report 2003, operating performance, *Financial Times*, at http://www.pearson.com/investor/ar2003/ performance_ft.htm.
10. Speech to National Press Club, Washington DC, 8 October 2003.
11. Peter Gotting, 'Adland Bunkers Down for War', Melbourne *Age*, 10 March 2003.
12. Roy Greenslade, 'Don't Mention the War', London *Media Guardian*, 14 April 2003.
13. Mary B Anderson, *Do No Harm – How Aid Can Support Peace – or War*, Lynne Rienner publishers, Boulder and London, 1999, p 13.
14. Quoted in Johan Galtung, 'September 11, 2001 – Diagnosis, Prognosis, Therapy', in Johan Galtung, Carl G Jacobsen and Kai Frithjof Brand-Jacobsen, *Searching for Peace – The Road to TRANSCEND*, Pluto Press, London, 2002, p 95.
15. Howard Friel and Richard Falk, *The Record of the Paper – How the* New York Times *Misreports US Foreign Policy*, Verso, London and New York, 2004, p 2.
16. John Stuart Mill, *On Liberty*, on-line edition, Bartleby.com, 1995.
17. From a letter to W T Barry, 14 August 1822.
18. Robert A Hackett and Yuezhi Zhao, *Sustaining Democracy? Journalism and the Politics of Objectivity*, Garamond Press, Toronto, 1998, p 16.
19. Ben Bagdikian, *The Media Monopoly*, 6th ed, Beacon Press, Boston, Mass, p 176.
20. Robert A Hackett and Yuezhi Zhao, op cit, p 18.
21. Professor Jay Rosen, New York University, quoted in William Glaberson, 'Fairness, Bias and Judgement', *New York Times*, 12 December 1994.
22. Michael Kinsley, 'Osama Done Told Me – How Come Media Objectivity Is Suddenly Such a Bad Thing?', *Slate* magazine, 8 November 2001.
23. Mark Pedelty, *War Stories – the culture of foreign correspondents*, Routledge, New York and London, 1995, p 7.
24. Robert A Hackett and Yuezhi Zhao, op cit, 1998, p 78.
25. Ben Bagdikian, op cit, 2000.
26. Simon O'Hagan, 'When Kimberly Met Dominic', London *Independent on Sunday* 'Business' section, 5 December 2004.
27. Daniel C Hallin, *The Uncensored War – The Media and Vietnam*, Oxford University Press, Oxford, 1986, p 117.
28. Jake Lynch, 'Reporting Iraq – What Went Right? What Went Wrong?', in Anita Biressi and Heather Nunn (eds), *Mediawar, Mediactive* No 3, Barefoot Publications, an imprint of Lawrence & Wishart, London, 2004, pp 109-10.
29. Dilnaz Boga, unpublished MA paper, *Peacebuilding Media, Theory and Practice*, University of Sydney, February 2004.
30. Max Weber, *Essays in Sociology*, Oxford University Press, Oxford, 1946, p 78.
31. John Kampfner, 'Risk Averse and Running Scared', London *Guardian*, 26 September 2003.

32. Keith Spicer, email letter, op cit, 2004.
33. Terry Eagleton, *Literary Theory – An Introduction*, 2nd ed, Blackwell, Oxford, 1996, p x.
34. Robert A Hackett and Yuezhi Zhao, op cit, p 1.
35. Terry Eagleton, op cit, 1996, p 84
36. Ibid, pp 93-4.
37. Steven Livingston and Todd Eachus, 'Humanitarian Crises and US Foreign Policy: Somalia and the CNN Effect Reconsidered', *Political Communication*, Vol 12, October-December 1995, pp 413-29.
38. Alison Des Forges, 'Silencing the Voices of Hate in Rwanda', in Monroe E Price and Mark Thompson (eds), *Forging Peace*, Edinburgh University Press, 2002, p 249.
39. Martin Shaw, 'The Kurds Five Years On: TV News' Finest Hour', *New Statesman*, 5 April 1996.
40. Piers Robinson, *The Myth of the CNN Effect*, Routledge, London, 2002, quoted in Eric Herring, 'The No Fly Zones in Iraq: The Myth of a Humanitarian Intervention', *Cambridge Review of International Affairs* website, 2002, at http://www.aprl52.dsl.pipex.com/eric/EHNFZ2.htm.
41. John Paul Lederach, *Building Peace: Sustainable Reconciliation in Divided Societies*, United States Institute of Peace Press, Washington DC, 1997, p 26.
42. David Bohm, *Wholeness and the Implicate Order*, quoted in *Ecology as a Systems Theory* by David Rhoads and Andrea Orcutt at http://www.webofcreation.org/advocacy/stheory/basic.html.
43. Bob Jobbins, then news editor, BBC World Service, quoted in Jake Lynch, *Reporting the World*, Conflict and Peace Forums, Taplow, 2002, p 24.
44. Laura Barton, 'Abi's Road', London *Guardian*, 21 March 2004.
45. George Pascoe-Watson, 'Fight for Freedom – 21 Pages of Proof', London *Sun*, 5 October 2001.
46. Patrick Butler et al, *Journalism Ethics – The Global Debate*, International Center for Journalists, Washington DC, 2003, p 8.
47. Jacques Derrida, 'Living On', trans James Hulbert, in Harold Bloom et al, *Deconstruction and Criticism*, Seabury Press, New York, 1979, p 84.
48. Jacques Derrida, *Speech and Phenomena*, trans David Allison, Northwestern University Press, Evanston, Illinois, 1973, pp 142-3.
49. Wikipedia definition at http://en.wikipedia.org/wiki/Deconstruction.
50. Terry Eagleton, op cit, 1996, p 112.
51. Jacques Derrida, 'Signature Event Context', trans Samuel Weber and Jeffrey Mehlman, in *Limited Inc*, Northwestern University Press, Evanston, Illinois, 1988, p 10.
52. Jacques Derrida, *Mémoires – For Paul de Man*, trans Cecile Lindsay, Jonathan Culler and Eduardo Cadava, Columbia University Press, New York, 1986, p123.
53. Reverend Mpbambami, quoted by Bishop Carlos Belo, *Action for World Development NSW Newsletter*, AWD Australia, Spring 1999.
54. Jacques Derrida, 'Structure, Sign and Play in the Discourse of the Human Sciences', in *Writing and Difference*, trans Alan Bass, Routledge, London, 1978, p 279.
55. Jacques Derrida, *Spectres of Marx*, trans Peggy Kamuf, Routledge, London, 1994, p 59.
56. Bob Marley, *Redemption Song*, Island Records, 1980.
57. Pramoedya Ananta Toer, *A Child of All Nations*, quoted in Jake Lynch and Annabel McGoldrick, 'Reporting Conflict – An Introduction to Peace Journalism', in Thomas Hanitzsch, Martin Loffelholz and Ronny Mustamu (eds), *Agents of Peace*, Friedrich Ebert Stiftung, Jakarta, 2004, p 119.
58. Ibid, pp 142-3.
59. Editorial, 'Deconstruction: Our Debt to Derrida', London *Guardian*, 11 October 2004.
60. Personal conversation with the authors, on TRANSCEND training course, Manassas, Virginia, 21 March 2003.

Epilogue – Struggles and Opportunities

The philosopher Arthur Schopenhauer observed that a new idea tends to meet three phased responses in becoming established – first ridicule, then violent opposition, before finally being accepted as self-evident.

Experience of introducing Peace Journalism, to journalists and others, has familiarised us with all three, along with a number of recognisable interim stages:

- 'You're asking the impossible'
- 'We already do this'
- 'I'm an exception'

The crunch often comes when they are presented with incontrovertible evidence of *patterns* of omission and marginalisation, which keep important parts of important stories outside the frame.

The sheer mismatch in size between short news reports on the one hand and the practically infinite category, 'the facts', on the other does not lead to some bits being left out at random. Instead, they are usually the same bits. In reports of conflict, there is a discernible dominant discourse of War Journalism.

News, as we have seen, is not as simple as 'reflecting' or 'expressing' something that happened outside and before itself; something which is *there*, waiting, as it were, to be uncovered and reported. To realise this is to begin to focus on what journalism is doing *to* the facts as it represents them to readers and audiences.

Consider, once again, the famous Gestalt diagram of the old – or is it a young – woman in black (Chapter 2). Both are present. But if we have been brought up looking only at pictures of young women, then that is all we are likely to see. This concept is, to the journalistic Objectivity paradigm, as Kryptonite is to Superman:

> 'All observation is theory-laden in the sense that what we see is mediated by our existing theories, and to that extent knowledge is inherently problematic.'[1]

Peace Journalism *announces* itself as a theory. But the alternative is not to do without theory; it is to apply different theories, whether acknowledged or not. 'When we open our mouths to describe what we see, we in effect describe ourselves, our perceptions, our paradigms.'[2]

Journalism education

By the time journalists begin describing what they see, many will have switched paradigms already. Most, today, are graduates, and these insights about knowledge, theory and observation are founding principles for any serious inquiry in the subjects they study at university, including virtually any branch of the humanities and social sciences.

Admission to professional ranks often requires them to be checked in at the door, however. So the place where the two paradigms meet – university journalism education – is one where anomalies come readily to the fore. It is, therefore, a site of struggle, where the ideas put forward in this book are gaining a foothold in the teeth of sporadic opposition of the kind Schopenhauer would have recognised.

A couple of years ago, at the most prestigious journalism school of them all, Columbia University in New York, President Lee Bollinger had been expecting to toast the appointment of a new Dean, but the selection process revealed such varying views as to what students should actually learn that he launched a root-and-branch review, with the words:

> 'To teach the craft is a worthy goal, but clearly insufficient in this new world and within the setting of a great university.'[3]

Contemporary contributions to this debate recount a sense of 'identity crisis'[4] among J-schools, and of journalism itself as an anomaly in higher education, in never having undergone 'conceptual reform'.[5] Indeed, according to one commentator, President Bollinger should restore some fizz by encouraging the further integration of theory and practice:

> 'The success of the project of enrichment will only be partial if teachers of the craft stand aloof from the formalization of knowledge, just as success will be limited if scholars stand aloof from journalistic experience. Journalism educators must take a step back into thought and combine the urge to cover the news with a scholarly urge to formalize an understanding of how journalism texts are made.'[6]

What is more usual is to 'add bits on', like one department that offers a foundation year taking in 'readings... from the *Epic of Gilgamesh* to Foucault in seven months – without any mention of their application to journalism'.[7]

It's no use encouraging journalism students to 'collect' interesting theories as if they were geological or biological specimens, by way of a hobby. The responsibility is to give them tools to apply a critical self-awareness to *their own journalism.*

Many journalism departments do attempt

this, of course, or at least some individuals within them take this responsibility seriously. Latterly, the Toda Institute for Peace and Policy Research has sponsored an international collaboration among scholars and professionals to develop Peace Journalism itself as a full-length university course, a project based explicitly on 'mating' the two paradigms, the journalistic and the academic:

> 'The application of "constitutive rhetoric" to the construction of a media peace discourse is based on the premise that the *assignment of meaning* is a central feature in the symbolic role of the media [emphasis added].'[8]

Journalist training

Journalist training has become a big business, especially in the years since the fall of the Iron Curtain. What place is there in this for Peace Journalism? Initially, the rationale was that new democracies needed a free press to help them work properly, and that journalists with no experience of working in such conditions therefore needed a crash course in western-style 'Objective' reporting methods.

Then came the Rwandan genocide. The media's influence – creating conditions in which violence became more likely, then aiding and abetting it – focused international attention on the role of journalism in conflict, not only as a potential threat but also as a resource for interventions to reduce violence and the likelihood of violence. It triggered a 'second wave' of journalist training initiatives, as 'peace' was added to 'democracy' in the list of desiderata to be realised with the help of the media:

> 'The influence of the media has caught the eye of international agencies and NGOs closely involved in peace-building during the last decade. Over ten years an estimated one billion dollars has been invested in interventions relating to the media in conflict-ridden societies. There is an emerging belief that the media may well

be the most effective means of conflict resolution and preventing new wars.'[9]

Can training in 'Objective' reporting achieve these aims? We have suggested that the set of conventions most western journalists think of as 'Objectivity' includes a dualistic model of conflict – two parties in a tug of war. So it would not necessarily have offered any antidote to the polarising and provocative effect of Rwandan media, at least in the phase when the basis for the later 'hate speech' was being established.

In October 1990, an attack was staged on the Rwandan capital, Kigali. 'Staged' is the word – the shots were actually fired by the FAR, the Rwandan army, as citizens cowered in their homes – but the official version, of 'marauding Tutsis at our doors', was faithfully reported by the media, led by the government-controlled Radio Rwanda. The authorities cited this incident as 'proof' that the country was 'under threat' and used it to justify a security clampdown – the arrest of thousands of Rwandan Tutsis and opponents of the MRND party of President Habyarimana.

Again, there is nothing in the Objectivity conventions necessarily to interrupt such a sequence of cause and effect. Unlike Radio Rwanda, media in the UK in 2002-3 were not directly under the control of the government. And yet, in previous chapters, their response to another series of events staged in order to be reported, the publication of the British government's dossiers on Iraq's supposed 'weapons of mass destruction', has been weighed and found wanting.

The Kigali incident was crude, the British dossiers more sophisticated, but the political aim in each case was the same – to convince people that they faced a 'threat'; and to use that as legitimation for a policy of violence.

Both worked, thanks partly to misleading news reports – misleading, not because they breached the conventions of Objectivity, but because they conformed to them. As we saw with the extended study of Globelink News in Chapter 6, the convention is for information from official sources on one's own side to be

treated as facts waiting to be discovered, not as part of the conflict itself.

No one would argue that many media in poor countries could not benefit from help in improving basic professional skills – note-taking, accuracy, sorting and assembling story components – or that western trainers have nothing to offer them.

Cris Maslog, a Filipino journalist-turned-professor, gave this assessment:

'No longer the good old who, what, where, when and how, but more important now, answering the why. Explaining why is the most difficult and this needs training and logistics, even scholarship, with which most Third World journalists are not equipped.'[10]

To help with this, western-style professional methods need to be combined with Peace Journalism if training is to be effective in creating space and opportunities for developing and transitional societies to consider and to value non-violent responses to conflict.

Public service and media campaigning

Both the 'frontlines' we have visited so far are, ultimately, located in the individual journalist. Journalism education and journalist training represent important new mediating structures. The struggles being waged within them may alter the overall balance by *supplementing* the influence of existing structural factors on the journalism produced by individuals who pass through them. However, no serious endeavour to bring about Peace Journalism can afford to ignore those larger structural factors themselves.

This is the thinking behind a development proposal by Toda Institute Director Majid Tehranian:

'Structural pluralism may be considered a *sine qua non* of content pluralism...

For Peace Journalism to take on a sustained life, the voiceless in global communication must be empowered. To do so, it takes more than pious ethical codes or perfunctory international declarations. Major resources must be allocated to the development of the global information infrastructure.'

This, or something similar, has been suggested before; indeed, at one point, none other than the World Economic Forum seriously considered a proposal to fund it.[11] Tehranian's suggestion is for a World Media Development Bank as a UN specialised agency, financed out of taxes imposed on the two communication global commons – the geo-stationary orbit and the electromagnetic spectrum – and 'providing low interest loans to media organisations:

- committed to a Peace Journalism code of ethics
- aimed at audiences with low or no access to the media
- supporting independent media and interactive communication'[12]

Another task worthy of the Bank's support could be efforts to make the structual pluralism we already have work properly. Built into broadcasting systems the world over is the concept of public service, as a *quid pro quo* for the use television and radio companies make of global commons.

This concept is, in turn, written into codes and guidelines for journalists. The BBC policy of ensuring that a 'full range of significant views and perspectives' are heard – quoted in Chapter 7 – is amplified still further in its *Producer Guidelines*:

'There are usually more than two sides to any issue.'

From the Ofcom *Programme Code* for commercial UK broadcasters, including news providers ITN and Sky:

'In dealing with major matters of controversy, licensees must ensure that justice is done to a full range of significant views and perspectives.'

From the Canadian Broadcasting Corporation code, *Journalistic Standards & Practices*:

'• to achieve balance and fairness, the widest possible range of views should be expressed
- there must also be depth, the capturing of dimensions and nuances. Without these elements, the programming becomes too simplistic to permit adequate comprehension'

From the Australian Broadcasting Corporation's *Editorial Policies*:

'• "balance" should be achieved by presenting "a wide range of perspectives"
- in serving the public's right to know, editorial staff will be enterprising in perceiving, pursuing and presenting issues which affect society and the individual
- pursuing impartiality should not mean endorsing the status quo. The Corporation is also required to be innovative... The ABC seeks to be a pace-setter in community discussion'

Television in America is less overtly regulated, but the First Amendment to the US Constitution protects freedom of expression. In a famous ruling in 1969, the Supreme Court said that should mean 'an uninhibited marketplace of ideas... It is the right of the public to receive suitable access to social, political, and other ideas which is crucial.'

A Peace Journalism analysis shows how conflict reporting produced within the structures we already have fails to fulfil the public service requirements on which they are based. It is also inaccurate, being at odds with what is known and has been observed about conflict. This is essential content for debates about those structures, the need to make them work better, and whether we need new ones to go with them.

Media monitoring

The Oxford philosopher Onora O'Neill lamented the fact that journalism was short on 'assessability' and therefore accountability.[13] To assess journalism, many groups around the world carry out media monitoring for sundry purposes, using different sets of criteria.

Once you can assess Peace Journalism, you can compare the extent of it in different media – an opportunity to 'raise through praise'. It's given rise to media peace awards such as:

- The Media Peace Award run by Australia's United Nations Association, now over 20 years old
- An award scheme run by Media Watch in Surabaya, Indonesia, and devised by its Director, Sirikit Syah, based explicitly on Peace Journalism

The four-point ethical checklist set out below was devised as a set of monitoring criteria for UK media, specifically to measure War Journalism and Peace Journalism:[14]

How is violence explained?

- How does the explanation arise from the way violence is reported?
- Does it offer a classic 'blow-by-blow' account?
- Or does it cover the workings of structural and cultural violence on the lives of people involved?
- Does it illuminate the intelligible, if dysfunctional, processes which may be reproducing the violence?
- What are we led or left to infer about what should, or is likely, to happen next?

What is the shape of the conflict?

- Is the conflict framed as 'tug of war' – a zero-sum game of two parties contesting a single goal?
- Or as 'cat's-cradle' – a pattern of many interdependent parties, with needs and interests which may overlap, or provide scope for integrated solutions?

Is there any news of any efforts or ideas to resolve the conflict?

- Is there anything in the report about peace plans, or any image of a solution?
- Must these aspects of a story wait until leaders cut a 'deal'?
- Do the reports of any 'deal' equip us to assess whether it is likely to tackle the causes of violence?
- Do we see any news of anyone else working to resolve or transform the conflict?

What is the role of Britain; 'the West'; the 'international community' in this story?

- Are 'our' stated goals of intervention the same as our real goals? Do we get any exploration of what the unstated goals might be?
- Is there anything about interventions already under way, albeit perhaps undeclared?
- Is there any examination of the influence of previous or prospective interventions on people's behaviour?
- Does it equip us to assess whether more, or less, intervention might represent a solution, or to discriminate between different kinds?

These are some of the underpinnings for media campaigning to bring about more Peace Journalism. Media representations of conflict are a key site for the exercise of power, and therefore a field of interest in their own right for anyone engaged in struggles for democracy, peace and justice – including, in their different ways, journalists, students and concerned citizens of the world. The arguments, examples, and conceptual and practical tools in this book are intended to help them.

Endnotes for Epilogue

1. Alexander Wendt, *Constructing International Politics* v 20 International Security 71, p 75.
2. Stephen R Covey, *The 7 Habits of Highly Effective People*, Simon & Schuster, London, 2004 edn, p 28.
3. Quoted in Emanuella Grinberg, 'Columbia President Challenges King's', *King's Journalism Review*, Vol 6, October 2002.
4. Grinberg, op cit.
5. Michael Janeway, 'Rethinking the Lessons of Journalism School', *New York Times*, 19 August, 2002.
6. G Stuart Adam, (Academic Vice-President, Carleton University, Canada), 'The Education of Journalists', in *Journalism*, Sage Publications, London, 2001.
7. University of King's College, Halifax, Nova Scotia, Canada – the quote is from Grinberg, op cit.
8. Dov Shinar, 'Media Peace Discourse: Constraints, Concepts and Building Blocks', paper circulated to Toda Group, 2004, p 7.
9. Ross Howard, 'The Media's Role in War and Peacebuilding', in Marina Caparini (ed), *Media in Security and Governance*, Geneva Centre for the Democratic Control of Armed Forces, Baden-Baden, 2004, pp 147-8.
10. In response to the Reporting the World Global Survey, 2003.
11. Worldwide Media Network, devised and developed by Hannes Siebert, 1999.
12. Majid Tehranian, 'Peace Journalism: Negotiating Global Media Ethics', *The Harvard International Journal of Press/Politics* 7, 2002, pp 58-83.
13. BBC Reith Lecture, 2002.
14. Adapted from Jake Lynch, *Reporting the World – a practical checklist for the ethical reporting of conflicts in the 21st Century*, Conflict and Peace Forums, Taplow, UK, 2002.

List of Exercises

Here is a list of exercises that appear throughout the book.

For lecturers and facilitators, they are designed as longer pieces of work that can be set between seminars or training sessions, or for break-out groups to study together. Some provide sufficient material for written assignments.

For students and general readers, they represent punctuation points, places to pause and reflect on what you have read and are about to read.

Generally, our suggestions on the answers follow the exercises in the text, in some cases highlighted as a commentary.

Chapter 1 The Peace Journalism Model

Exercise One – Identifying War Journalism and Peace Journalism p 20

Read the following scripts from two television news reports on a suicide bombing in Jerusalem. In the first, can you identify at least two characteristics of War Journalism? In the second, can you identify at least two characteristics of Peace Journalism?

Questions
- How is the violence explained?
- Who or what is to blame for the violence?
- What might we therefore expect the solution to be?

Exercise Two – Creating a PJ/WJ Table p 27

Compile a War Journalism/Peace Journalism table on a conflict of your choice.

How is the reporting of this conflict, in general:
- War/violence-orientated?
- Propaganda-orientated?
- Elite-orientated?
- Victory-orientated?

In what ways could it be reported in order to be:
- Peace/conflict-orientated?
- Truth-orientated?
- People-orientated?
- Solution-orientated?

Chapter 2 Conflict Analysis – Anchorage for Journalists

Exercise One – The Conflict Orange p 40

Two neighbours are in dispute over an orange.
- What happens next? How do the parties behave? How might their Attitudes to each other influence their Behaviour? List as many different outcomes to this conflict as you can.
- Can you give a 'score' for each of these outcomes? (Example: where the two neighbours fight, and A overpowers B and picks the orange for himself, A wins 1-0.)
- Of particular interest is the fact that many who do this exercise suggest cutting the orange in two, as a compromise solution. What score does this give? 1-1? Are you sure? What does it tell us about the problems of compromising?
- What might be better than compromise? What does it take to create something better than compromise?

Exercise Two – Reporting the Orange Conflict p 41

Now imagine you are a journalist, sent to cover this dispute:

- How could you help the neighbours, and their village, region or even their country, to think about this conflict in such a way as to make a non-violent outcome more likely?
- Who would you interview, what would you ask them, and why?
- You can invent as many complications as you like to make it more interesting. For example – what if A is a member of ethnic group C, and B is a member of ethnic group D?
- What if group C is in a majority locally, but the next-door province or republic has a majority of group D?

Exercise Three – Partisan Perceptions p 47

Choose a conflict situation of which you have some detailed knowledge, perhaps involving groups A and B.

Draw up a table and ask:

- What are the important 'facts' as seen by group A?
- What does group B think of these 'facts'?
- What are the important 'facts' for group B?
- What does group A think of these 'facts'?

Think about how the answers would help a Peace Journalist in knowing what to look for, and what to ask about, in any development in the conflict?

Devise plans for news stories which convey each side's perceptions of each issue.

Exercise Four – Using Conflict Analysis in Reporting p 48

Read the following two articles about the bombings in the Moroccan city of Casablanca in May 2003.

What understanding of key concepts from Conflict Analysis does each contain?

The first article is adapted from material filed from the scene for London-based broadsheet newspapers at the time, the second is from the London *Guardian*.

Chapter 3 Reporting and Understanding Violence

Exercise One – Thinking about Violence p 60

Take a conflict you know:

- List five examples of structural violence.
- List five examples of cultural violence.

Exercise Two – Explaining or excusing violence? p 69

Read the script for a television news report conceived as one of a series of follow-ups to the issues raised by the bombing in Jerusalem covered in Chapter 1. It's based on the story of a suicide bomber's brother. Read it and answer the following questions.

- How does it explain violence?
- Does it excuse violence?
- If not, how does it avoid doing so?
- Does it demonise the perpetrators of violence?
- If not, how does it avoid doing so?

Chapter 4 War Propaganda

Exercise One – Test the Propaganda p 98

In NATO's war on Yugoslavia, in 1999, how effective was the propaganda?

Can you remember, at this distance:

- Why NATO went to war?
- Why diplomacy failed?
- Whether NATO won?
- Whether its initial aims were achieved in the final agreement?
- How NATO won and how the bombing achieved its effect?

Exercise Two – Decoding Propaganda p 113

- Come up with your own list of propaganda terms, from a conflict you are familiar with.
- How are they misleading?
- What other words would you use in their place?
- How would you explain the facts so as to avoid misleading readers and audiences?

Chapter 5 Scenarios and Dilemmas

Any of the scenarios in this chapter can be put to groups as the basis for an exercise. In addition, two are marked up as exercises in their own right:

Exercise One – The British Media's Coverage of Asylum Seekers p 131

Read the scripts for two television reports about asylum seekers in Britain and ask, in each case:

- How are the asylum seekers described?
- Who are 'they' and who are 'we'?
- What are we told about the asylum seekers' reasons for coming to Britain?
- What is diagnosed as the 'problem' here?
- What are we led – or left – to infer is the 'solution'?

Exercise Two – How was the Rwandan genocide characterised in news reports? p 144

Use an Internet search engine of English language media for the period between 7 April and 30 April 1994. Enter the following pairs of search terms and see how many times they occur together (answers for UK newspapers given at the end of the chapter):

- Rwanda AND anarchy.
- Rwanda AND chaos.
- Rwanda AND tribal.
- Rwanda AND savage OR savagery.
- Rwanda AND genocide.

Chapter 6 Doing Peace Journalism

Exercise One – Writing Peace Journalism p 161

- Read the following news story from the *Jakarta Post* about a violent incident.
- Imagine you are the *Post*'s Palu correspondent.
- Rewrite the article as an on-the-day story, transforming it into Peace Journalism.
- Word limit – 800 words.
- Read the steps that follow the article before you begin the task.

For more information for your story, interview the characters in a role-play for two people p 164.

Instructions:

- Begin with person A playing the role of one of these characters.
- Person B is the interviewing journalist.
- Conduct the interview to reveal the character's part in breaking or diverting the cycle of violence (see Chapter 3).
- Then person B assumes the role of the other character, and person A that of the interviewing journalist.
- Each journalist must then write the story of the Palu bombs, drawing on the notes about their own character and their interview with the other character.

Exercise Two – Israel's Military Refuseniks p 173

Read the script for a TV report about Israel's military refuseniks and explain what it contributes to Peace Journalism:

- How does it affect the model and shape of the conflict?
- How does it add to the explanation for violence?
- Who or what is to blame for the violence?

Exercise Three – Reporting on Iraq's 'dossier' submitted to the UN on its 'weapons of mass destruction' (referring to the scripts for an episode of a leading international TV news bulletin) p 182

1. List the sources used for these reports, including those speaking:
   – on the record
   – off the record
2. What do they have in common?
3. Do these sources disagree on anything? If so, what? How would you describe the degree of disagreement between them? What views or perspectives do they all have in common?
4. What perspectives are left out of these reports?
5. Look again at how the sources are used by the reporters, especially those quoted anonymously, ie speaking off the record. What do the reporters use them to do?
6. What assumptions have the reporters made about what their sources are saying, and why?

7. Do you agree with their assumptions? What other possibilities are there?
8. What *effect* might the sources be trying to bring about:
   – on debate about the war?
   – on public opinion?

Exercise Four – What would you do? p 185

What would you do, in order to weigh and test, if you were one of the reporters on this bulletin:

- Dolly Dipcorr?
- Dick Defcorr?
- Wally Washcorr?
- Percy Polcorr?
- Their editor?
- The presenter/news anchor?

What alternative sources would you use? And what would they add?

Use the material from their existing packages and devise ways to 'turn the corner' into any of your alternative sources.

Exercise Five – Working with the Sliding Scale p 187

- Spot the connections between elements from either end of the WJ/PJ sliding scale in two stories from the Philippines.
- Write the top line and opening paragraph(s) for each story.
- With further research on the background to the bombings in Manila and two southern cities – and the conflict in Mindanao – write an 800-word Peace Journalism article on each story.
- Online resources could include mindanews.com, reuters.com, pcij.org (Philippine Centre for Investigative Journalism), (*Philippines Daily Inquirer*) inq7.net.

Chapter 7 Why is News the way it is?

Exercise One – Testing the Big 'O' p 206

Read two newspaper reports from September 2002, highlighting competing claims about Iraq's 'weapons of mass destruction', and say:

- Which one is Objective?
- If both are, which is more Objective?
- If neither is, which is less Objective?
- What makes them Objective – or not Objective?

Appendix B – Physical and Psychological Security for Journalists Covering Violent Conflict

Exercise One – The Emergency Bag p 249

Imagine you are alone in a hostile environment, perhaps a conflict-affected area. Your guide has left. What do you need to come through safely? Think of the items you would like to have with you in your bag.

Exercise Two – Exploring Trauma p 250

- Think about a traumatic incident that has happened to you that you can talk about with another person – an incident that is meaningful but 'medium-range'.
- Write it down in notes.
- Distinguish the three stages of before, during and after.
- Note separately the facts, the feelings, and the future – ie what you were thinking would happen next.
- Discuss the incident with another person.
- Notice what they say that puts you at ease and helps you to talk.
- Take a guess at how much stress your colleague absorbed.

Exercise Three – Trauma Jargon p 250

- Write the following four terms on four separate large pieces of paper:
  – Trauma
  – Stress
  – PTSD
  – Counselling and psychotherapy
- Give one sheet to each group.
- Ask each group to write out everything they may have heard or know about each term.

List of Discussion Points

Here is a list of discussion points that appear throughout the book. For lecturers and facilitators, they are designed to stimulate group discussions.

For students and general readers, they represent punctuation points, places to pause and reflect on what you have read and are about to read.

Chapter 1 The Peace Journalism Model

- What connects a decision to frame a conflict as a battle between two parties with the question in the middle – who will win? p 7
- What was the cause of the Iraq conflict, and what should be the outcome, the 'exit'? To find the answers, where should we begin looking? p 8
- Does Peace Journalism mean journalists 'resolving conflicts'; or becoming advocates for particular solutions or initiatives? p 18
- Looking back at the Galtung table, come up with a checklist of simple recommendations to avoid slipping into War Journalism. p 28

Chapter 2 Conflict Analysis – Anchorage for Journalists

- Read the following two quotes from newspaper articles. Consider the difference between the definition of conflict from Peace Research, and the notion of conflict written into two typical pieces of news reporting. p 34

- What happened on each of the dates listed? How might they be relevant to the conflict of today? p 35
- Go back to the definition of conflict given here and ask yourself – how many conflicts are you involved in?
    - In your family?
    - Your workplace?
    - Your community?
  How do you respond to them? p 38
- What will happen if only one part of a conflict is dealt with? p 38
- What inluences the way people are likely to respond to conflict? In what circumstances do conflicts arise and what factors make parties more – or less – likely to respond violently? Or non-violently? p 39
- What do you think is useful in needs and fears mapping, for journalism about conflict? p 44
- What does each formula for peace mean, how would it work and what would each look like in practice? What is likely to happen next, after each different kind of peace? p 47
- Go back to the theories about what causes conflict, given in the earlier part of this chapter.
    - What theories can you find in each of these articles?
    - What do they suggest is 'the problem' here?
    - What do they lead you – or leave you – to infer would be an appropriate remedy? p 52
- What is Osama bin Laden's view of the issues underlying al-Qaeda's conflict with

the US in particular, and the West in general? p 53

Chapter 3 Reporting and Understanding Violence

- What do we mean by violence? p 59
- During the Rwandan genocide:
  - What was the direct violence?
  - What was the structural violence?
  - What was the cultural violence? p 61
- Where does evil 'come from'? Are some people born evil or are they 'made that way' by the conditions in which they find themselves? p 64
- Who are the heroes of non-violent struggle? How many can you name? p 78
- Why do we need an intervention in the Cycle of Violence at the point of anger? p 86
- Can you think of any similar projects, particularly grassroots initiatives, that have made a tangible difference in a conflict zone? p 87

Chapter 4 War Propaganda

- How can journalists continue to offer a reliable account of what is really going on, in the face of sophisticated and determined war propaganda? p 106
- Come up with a 'neutral' dictionary-style definition of 'terrorism'. Could you apply it neutrally, so that all situations meriting this description could be reported as 'terrorism'? p 114
- If you see a piece of propaganda which you believe is misleading, should you call it a 'lie'? What would you expect to happen if you did? p 114
- Look at the picture of Fikret Alic, a Bosnian refugee standing on the other side of a barbed wire fence. What does it remind you of? p 116

Chapter 5 Scenarios and Dilemmas

Work through the following nine dilemmas and decide how you, as a journalist, would tackle them.

1. Tension is rising – before direct violence p 126
   Do you:
   a) Talk it down – ignore the story?
   b) Talk it up – sensationalise the story?
   c) Devise a Peace Journalism approach?
- What are the important distinctions between these two articles? p 130
2. The beginnings of violence p 140
   Do you:
   a) Say the situation is getting worse and call for international intervention to stop it? Or
   b) Devise a Peace Journalism approach?
- What would you have done, as an editor or reporter, to try to alert the outside world to the dangers in Rwanda between 1990 and March 1994? p 141
3. What is your responsibility as a journalist if parties to a conflict are not communicating? p 146
4. What if you can only report on one party? p 148
   Do you:
   a) Accept and reproduce claims that the violence is all in the pursuit of a greater good?
   b) Ridicule and scorn claims that the violence is all in the pursuit of a greater good?
   c) Devise a Peace Journalism approach?
5. Reports filter through of a 'massacre' p 151
   Do you:
   a) Splash it as an atrocity, demanding urgent action, likely to change the course of war?
   b) Ignore or downplay it?
   c) Devise a Peace Journalism approach?
6. Reporting on refugees p 153
   Do you:
   a) Seek out the most extreme horror stories?
   b) Play it down?
   c) Devise a Peace Journalism approach?
7. Stalemate. How do you get it on the news? p 154
   Do you?
   a) Ignore it?

b) Sensationalise it and say the situation is about to explode into all-out war?

c) Devise a Peace Journalism approach?

8. Peace proposals p 156

Do you:

a) Report this as an important offer?

b) Describe it as 'Peace in our Time!'?

c) Devise a Peace Journalism approach?

9. A facility with the men of violence – do you accept or decline? p 158

Chapter 6 Doing Peace Journalism

- Go back and read the two reports of the suicide bombing in Jerusalem from Chapter 1 p 168
  – What is missing?
  – What do you want to hear more about?
  – Has it aroused your interest to find out?
- How do these 'missing elements' change the framing and supplement official narratives? p 173

Chapter 7 Why is News the Way it is?

- Consider – 'The purpose of journalism is [nothing] more than to seek meaningful facts'. Can that be right? Can it be the full story? If not, what is missing? p 195
- Does War Journalism predominate because it is in the interests of those who own the media and their clients? p 197

- When the hard commercial interests of media owners and clients are against war, or against violence, why do we not see a sudden outbreak of Peace Journalism? p 200
- What does Objectivity mean and where does the idea come from? p 203
- The Cat sat on the Mat. It conjures up a familiar picture. But how? How do we know it means what it does? p 213
- The CNN effect – Do the media work by raising issues of concern to the political agenda, off their own bat, and do they 'force' policy-makers to respond? If so, to what extent? p 214
- Why is it that an apparently simple solution to a complex problem such as the conflict over Kosovo – blame the Serbs, bomb them out – does not work, at least not in the long run? p 215
- If you got the chance to interview Tony Blair, and he told you that we must 'deal with' the menace of Saddam Hussein, lest it 'engulf us', not next week or next month but at some unspecified time in the future, what would you do? p 218
- Deconstruction – How are we to make sense of our experience? Can there be any reliable set of first principles by which to interpret the reality around us? p 221

Appendix A – *Dialogue with the Devil's Advocate*

'Reading maketh a full man, conference a ready man, and writing an exact man' – so said Sir Francis Bacon, English philosopher at the court of Queen Elizabeth I.

Having read, thus far, so much about writing and the different ways it can be done, what about 'conference'? Here we deal with some common objections to Peace Journalism, matching them with some ready answers, in a Dialogue with the Devil's Advocate.

Devil's Advocate: Peace Journalism? Isn't that a bit of a dodgy label – sounds a bit hippie-ish?

Peace Journalism Book: It has been given plenty of alternative names:

Post-Realist Journalism
Solutions Journalism
Empowerment Journalism
Conflict Analysis Journalism
Change Journalism
Holistic Journalism
Big Picture Journalism
Open Society Journalism
Analytical Journalism
Reflective Journalism
Constructive Journalism
Process Journalism

'If a fish were an anthropologist, the last thing it would discover would be water' – Margaret Mead.

To put it another way, 'if you inhabit an orthodoxy you do not name it'[1] – you only need to call it something when you inspect it from the outside. If you think of conflict coverage as 'just reporting the facts', you have no need to call it War Journalism; and no need to define Peace Journalism against it.

There may be many circumstances, therefore, where announcing the ideas in this book as Peace Journalism would be poor tactics – likely to close ears, not open them, to what you have to say.

You could think of the methods in this book as giving a new set of terms for the everyday work of a journalist:[2]

From old role	**To new**
Watchdog	Enabler
Commentator	Communicator
Independent of issues covered	Independent yet interdependent
Spectator/observer	'In the boat'
Style/Stories	
Debate	Dialogue
Difference	Common ground and difference
Polemic	Discussion
Approach to journalism	
Seeks simplicity	Explores complexity
Reactive to violent events	Strategy to understand/uncover the conflict
Event-based reporting	Process-based reporting
'I am objective'	'I am fair'
Balance = cover both sides equally (quantity)	Balance = represent all sides' stories and perceptions (quality)
Approach to audiences	
Bodily damage/gore increases circulation	Public participation in problem-solving builds audiences/readership
Newsroom sets agenda	Public has role in setting agenda
Leaders/experts know best	Ordinary people need to be consulted
Right to know	Right to participate in democratic processes
'This is the way journalism is done'	Exploratory and flexible; rooted in values

Devil's Advocate: Sounds like you are telling us not to report violence?

Peace Journalism Book: No, there is no point in concealing violence. Show it, but show also images and statements which provide an explanation for it other than the violence itself, probably by focusing on how the conflict is affecting people in everyday life – between episodes of direct violence.

Devil's Advocate: But gore and sensation sell papers and get viewers tuning in.

Peace Journalism Book: Do they? Dramatic eyewitness reports of battles, in the invasion of Iraq, for instance, did not all increase circulation or audience figures. And there are many ways to sell a story – human interest, something counter-intuitive, some startling exposition or juxtaposition. There are many ways to cause a sensation.

Devil's Advocate: Doesn't it mean just reporting 'good news'?

Peace Journalism Book: No, like all journalism, PJ seeks to report on something new. It just recognises that 'something new' in a conflict may be brought about by, for instance, people working to promote understanding at the grassroots as well as by men firing guns or leaders negotiating. It is about seeking out the sources of change, unburdened by the assumption that official sources always know best.

Devil's Advocate: You talk about Peace Journalism, but isn't Peace a loaded word? Peace for whom, anyway?

Peace Journalism Book: If peace is *for* someone in the sense of being *against* someone else, it is not peace. Yes, sometimes a party to conflict will put forward an idea and call it a 'peace plan' when in fact it is just another version of that party's demands.

The whole essence of PJ is based on understanding what is needed to create a *lasting* peace, addressing the genuine needs and interests of all sides. This book is intended to equip you with the tools to assess those plans for yourself.

Devil's Advocate: At least what you call War Journalism holds leaders to account. It sounds like you are just currying favour with the authorities.

Peace Journalism Book: There is a difference between PJ and what is sometimes called 'Critical Journalism'. PJ says: 'I do not necessarily accept your claims, but for the purposes of this exercise let us take them on their merits.'

It then examines the demands and position of the speaking authorities to see whether, equipped with a sophisticated understanding of what is required to make peace, they appear to be the best way of achieving the stated aims.

Devil's Advocate: To do what you call for would mean every story being half an hour or several thousand words in length!

Peace Journalism Book: Of course, not every piece can give a full explanation of a conflict. What is at stake is the *shape* of the explanation, either given or *implied*. After reading a short news report, what do I expect as the next logical step? What do I seek to hear more about? Will it be an understanding of how common ground can be built upon through sustainable development – or another escalation of violence? A short segment of a straight line is still straight; a short segment of a circle has a noticeable curve.

Devil's Advocate: All this talk of the 'grass roots' suggests to me that you are in danger of missing the story, which is where the leaders are.

Peace Journalism Book: It is not 'either/or' but 'both, and'. We have to treat as important the experiences, hopes, fears and grievances of the reading, listening and viewing public. If we don't, who will?

And after all, signed agreements cannot by themselves make people live together in peace. As part of society, we are as responsible for 'social negotiation' as anyone else, even if it takes a long time.

Devil's Advocate: Excuse me, but Peace is not in my job description. I just report the facts.

Peace Journalism Book: Every time you report something, you add another layer to the cumulative understanding among sources, and potential sources, of how you are likely to respond in future to facts presented, packaged or even created for you to report.

All those future facts will therefore contain a residue of decisions you have already made.

The Feedback Loop means there is no 'just the facts' – PJ is about taking responsibility for the impact and consequences of our reporting.

Devil's Advocate: What you are calling for is just Good Journalism, really.

Peace Journalism Book: There is plenty of good War Journalism and good Critical Journalism. We need both. But they offer a distorted picture by routinely missing out certain factors which the insights of Conflict Analysis tell us are essential to a proper understanding.

It is this pattern of omission which is dangerous unless counterbalanced by Peace Journalism. In particular, making peace and non-violent initiatives visible, a focus on prevention and the need for therapy to overcome trauma, and making the conflict transparent – something we can understand by comparing our own lives with those of people affected by it.

Devil's Advocate: I think journalists do a pretty good job already in very difficult circumstances. Why give them something else to worry about?'

Peace Journalism Book: PJ is a set of tools, not a list of extra tasks. Firstly, in a time of rapidly proliferating media, PJ's ability to deliver unusual, different angles is all the more valuable.

Also, think of just a couple of the benefits by the criteria journalists already use to measure their work – independence and being proof against manipulation.

The history of conflict coverage is replete with examples of journalists being manipulated because they believed they were 'just reporting the facts'. PJ, by setting down this burden, leads us to apply an equal scrutiny to all sides: 'Who wants me to believe this and why?'

Devil's Advocate: That sounds a bit cynical.

Peace Journalism Book: No, there is nothing pejorative in the observation that sources in the news devise and calibrate their behaviour in order to get the coverage they believe will advance their interests.

Would we think better of a government which, for instance, neglected one of the most important and powerful tools for winning arguments – for creating the political space and endorsement it needed to carry out important policies?

Better to accept that all the sources journalists use have their own agenda, and that their words and deeds, the messages they send to journalists, are part of that agenda. What's important is to ensure that, as the BBC *Producer Guidelines* put it, 'no significant perspective remains unreported or under-represented'.

Devil's Advocate: So, you're one of these post-modern johnnies who say there's no such thing as the truth, so why bother trying to report it?

Peace Journalism Book: No, the basic duty of a Peace Journalist is the same as a War Journalist – you report honestly the facts in front of you, as you see them.

But 'The Truth' is bigger than any newspaper or programme – we can only report some bits of it. The question is, which bits?

Do you, as a reporter, tend to find certain kinds of facts habitually cropping up in front of you, while others remain out of the picture? Is there a cumulative – perhaps systematic – pattern of omission? What might be the consequences of this?

Does it tend to give readers and audiences a distorted view? PJ is a remedy to patterns of omission and distortion, easily discernible in the reporting of conflicts.

The Senegalese singer and UN youth ambassador Baaba Maal says: '... no one has the definition of truth. It can only come out of people who talk.'[3] Journalists are, of course, people who talk, so they can, by all means, report the truth, as long as they accept that no one (emphasising one) can define it, but that it is multi-faceted.

Devil's Advocate: What about Fox News? You've had plenty to say about Objectivity, but aren't you aiming at the wrong target? Doesn't Fox prove the real menace is partisan news?

Peace Journalism Book: Sure, Fox is partisan, and more clearly tied to a political party than most TV news. But it still tries to conceal its agenda. Hence its presenters challenge interviewees, on terms suggested by the Bush White House, with the words 'some people say', camouflaging a perspective as a fact. That's also why it went to court to stop the humorist, Al Franken, using its slogan 'fair and balanced' to tease it – looking ridiculous was a price Fox was prepared to pay to safeguard its vicarious claim to the credibility television news has built up over the years.

Its existence certainly does not alter the analysis we present here, that news overall shows a dominant discourse of War Journalism, or that the remedy is more Peace Journalism.

Devil's Advocate: What about Indymedia? It's not worth trying to reform corporate media, is it? They just serve their own interests – the solution for the problems you describe is to follow Jello Biafra's advice and *be* the media.

Peace Journalism Book: In the first place, the interests of corporate media may not be that easy to pin down when it comes to reporting conflicts (see Chapter 7). Also, 'corporate media' represent a colossal concentration of wealth and power, crying out for some form, or forms, of social discipline – a goal that should not be relinquished or ignored.

The first step to that is greater media literacy, realising what we're getting – War Journalism – and more to the point, what we're missing. And remember, corporations have already been brought, by public awareness and pressure, to improve their environmental and ethical behaviour.

All forms of professional journalism are distinguished by two common factors – trained observers and edited copy. The latter is particularly important as it means that someone other than the writer takes or at least shares responsibility for the content. If you report something, you have to satisfy that person that what you've said is fair, truthful and accurate, before it can reach readers or audience. 'Indymedia' lacks that safeguard.

The fact that anyone today can produce something that looks like journalism is a challenge to professional journalists, who would be wise to begin thinking of themselves as being in an implicit dialogue with their audience:

'Big media... treated the news as a lecture. We told you what the news was. You bought it, or you didn't...

Tomorrow's news reporting and production will be more of a conversation or a seminar. The lines will blur between producers and consumers, changing the role of both in ways we're only beginning to grasp. The communication network itself will be a medium for everyone's voice, not just the few who can afford to buy multimillion-dollar printing presses, launch satellites, or win the government's permission to squat on the public airways.'[4]

Endnotes for Appendix A

1. From Jake Lynch, *Iraq, peace journalism and the construction of truth*, Media Development, World Association for Christian Communication, December 2001, available online at http://www.wacc.org.uk/modules.php?name=News&file=print&sid=732.

2. Table by Lesley Fordred, University of Cape Town, quoted in Jake Lynch, *Reporting the World*, Conflict and Peace Forums, Taplow, UK, 2002, p 36.

3. Quoted in Chris Thompson and Dominic Elliott, 'Move Over Bob Geldof', *New Statesman*, 14 March 2005, p 24.

4. Dan Gillmoor, in 'We the Media – Grassroots Journalism By the People, For the People', O'Reilly, 2004.

Appendix B – *Physical and Psychological*
Security for Journalists Covering Violent Conflict

The concept of Peace Journalism is based on examining the way journalists – their agendas, concepts and conventions – affect the stories on which they work. This appendix deals with the obverse – how the stories affect the journalists, their physical and emotional security. It's a subject deserving of consideration here because it exerts a powerful and, it could be argued, growing influence on the circumstances of news production.

The methods we advocate in this book may themselves bring journalists into greater danger. To report on conflict by making contact with grassroots activists rather than sticking by the military; and taking issue, at times, with the way the situation is presented by officialdom, can increase the potential risks. All the more important, then, to consider ways to safeguard reporters and editors who wish to decide for themselves how important stories should be covered. These notes are intended as a starting-point for that process.

Safety – a brief introduction

Richard Sambrook, director of Global News at the BBC, was, at the time of writing, chairing an international committee set up by the International News Safety Institute (INSI) to investigate the dangers facing journalists around the world and to recommend ways of protecting them. Announcing the details, he said:

'Journalists are now at risk to a greater extent than they have ever been before. Where once their neutrality was widely recognised and respected, today they are targeted and sought out [by aggressors], seen as high-profile representatives of their countries or cultures.

Increased partisanship in our media may have played a part in that; there may be other factors, too. But with 85 journalists and support staff killed in the last year, we, as an industry, cannot carry on and do nothing. It is now one of the biggest inhibitions on freedom of reporting.'[1]

How does this predicament manifest itself in practice? What are the global trends making the 'newsface' more inherently risky? And what can be done? Take, for instance, the growing toll among editors and reporters in the Philippines – the second most dangerous place to be a journalist, according to international organisations, after Iraq.

One of them – the latest at the time of writing, in March 2005 – was Marlene Esperat, a veteran campaigner against corruption, gunned down in her home, in front of her children, on the southern island of Mindanao. Why is the death toll growing among Philippines journalists, and what if any connections are there with broader global developments?

Impunity and indivisibility

The first issue is that of impunity. Shortly after Marlene Esperat's death, army and police chiefs posed for local media issuing solemn orders to one another to find her killers, and shaking hands with members of her family. The outcry occasioned by the slaying sent a useful incentive around a Feedback Loop of cause and effect, promising a good news story to the authorities if they were seen to be taking decisive action.

However, as many as 14 journalists were killed in 2004, with Esperat the fourth to be killed in 2005 and, at the time of writing, none of the killers have been brought to justice. A special police unit, Taskforce Newsmen 7, was set up to investigate, but journalist trade unionists complain that it is engaged as much in smearing some of the victims as in hunting their murderers, thereby lessening the political pressure for a solution.[2]

The second issue is the indivisibility of human rights. In an earlier incident, MindaNews, a news agency in Mindanao that offers Peace Journalism to its clients and readers, saw one of its photographers, Gene Boyd Lumawag, shot dead.

In the words of a local peace activist, Bishop Felixberto Calang:

'We believe there is a direct correlation between escalating violence against mediapersons and growing summary executions in Mindanao. When the press is attacked with impunity, it is reflective of the general breakdown of respect for the human rights of ordinary citizens especially those who are poor and underprivileged. And under such a condition, it is the State that should take full accountability because it has failed to perform its supposedly inherent duty to protect and uphold human rights.'[3]

Concerns over journalists' own safety were mounting by this stage, late 2004, and not only in the Philippines. In Iraq, the system of 'embedding' journalists with US and UK forces, during the invasion and after, attracted controversy over allegations that reports reaching the public were skewed to a military point of view. At the same time, reporters intent on providing, for the sake of balance, some other perspective on the war were encountering great dangers.

Veteran British Independent Television News (ITN) correspondent Terry Lloyd was the first of a number of journalists killed by the US-led forces themselves. The International Federation of Journalists (IFJ) has complained of a 'culture of secrecy and deceit' among military authorities over Lloyd's death. According to some reports, he might have survived if he had not been shot for a second time in the head, by a US helicopter gunship, while being transported to safety.

Hamid Aglan, the businessman in whose minibus Lloyd was being driven, said:

'The helicopter killed him. It should not have happened. The journalist would have lived if I had got him to hospital. I was told he would have died instantly. There was nothing anyone could have done for him after he was hit.'[4]

Then there was the attack on the hotel used by media companies in Baghdad as US-led troops entered the city. In the words of IFJ Secretary-General Aidan White:

'If one incident sums up the frustration, anger and head-shaking bewilderment of journalists over their treatment during the Iraq war, it is the attack on the Palestine Hotel on April 8, 2003, when scores of reporters covering the battle of Baghdad came under deadly fire from US forces.'[5]

Two journalists died in the attack and many more were injured. The IFJ dismissed the Pentagon's report on the incident as a 'cynical whitewash' and called for a formal public inquiry, under independent jurisdiction, to determine the truth.

The IFJ have also expressed concerns over the apparent repeated targeting of Al Jazeera, which reaches up to 300 million Arabs living in 22 countries around the world. Given that US forces have bombed Al Jazeera offices three times, first in Kabul in November 2001, then Basra on 2 April 2003, and then a third time in Baghdad on 8 April 2003, 'it is impossible not to detect a sinister pattern of targeting,' White says.

After the end of what President Bush called 'major combat operations', journalists also faced the danger of kidnap and attack by various elements opposed to the US-led troop presence in Iraq. According to the veteran London *Guardian* reporter Jonathan Steele:

'It has become virtually impossible for journalists to function... Our translators are getting death threats. Reporters who used to rent houses have received anonymous notes warning them to get out... these are the worst working conditions I have had to face. Only Chechnya comes anywhere close.'[6]

The sequence of events in Iraq reminds us, once again, of the indivisibility of human rights. Many noticed that kidnappings of foreigners started only after the world saw pictures of US troops abusing inmates in Abu Ghraib prison in early 2004. Some hostages pictured in videos released by their captors were rather pointedly dressed in orange uniforms, shackled and caged in the manner of the detainees at Guantanamo Bay.

These detainees were, of course, stripped of the rights they would have enjoyed as prisoners of war when the Pentagon decreed that, as 'enemy combatants', they were not covered by the Geneva Convention; or by US terrestrial law, since they were being held in Cuba, which is not part of US sovereign territory.

The Philippines – returned to its alliance with the US under President Gloria Macapagal Arroyo and a key participant in the 'war on terrorism' – could usually expect to face censure from Washington for abrogations of human rights. A State Department report named the country among

98 with the most abuses including 'arbitrary, unlawful and, in some cases, extrajudicial killings; disappearances; torture and arbitrary arrest and detention'.[7]

Such assessments have traditionally offered firm backing and a larger context for activists concerned about particular issues. The killing of Gene Boyd Lumawag, for instance, was met with protests from US-based campaign groups, including the Media Breakfast Club of Los Angeles.

However, critics charge that America is now running a 'gulag of prisons and planes' to keep detainees in 'judicial oubliettes' like Guantanamo and Bagram air base in Afghanistan, or to transfer them in secret to friendly countries where torture is practised.[8] They accuse the Bush administration of squandering US moral authority to criticise others, thereby undermining respect for human rights by governments around the world.

Kenneth Roth, executive director of Human Rights Watch:

'Since September 11th... the military has systematically used third-degree techniques around the world on detainees... We're giving the world a ready-made excuse to ignore the Geneva Conventions. [secretary of defense, Donald] Rumsfeld has lowered the bar.'[9]

Self-help

Journalists, then, may find themselves alongside many others on the receiving end of violence and human rights violations – sometimes officially sponsored or inspired and covered by deceit, secrecy and impunity. Their experience may reflect a rising global trend.

There is, clearly, an important job to do in making sure, via one's own journalism, that these issues remain 'on the map' and in keeping a record – as many Philippines media do, by reporting them as front-page news – rather than, in Martha Gellhorn's words, 'just letting things drift away'.

In the meantime, what can editors and reporters do to protect themselves? The first priority has been to raise the profile of safety issues and overcome residual industry machismo which has marked them with a certain stigma. In the words of psychiatrist Raj Persaud:

> 'It seems that ambition, coupled with a belief that war reporting enhances a career by giving a high media profile, leaves journalists reluctant to speak out about their fears and insecurities.'[10]

Part of the answer is institutional. The International Code of Practice for the Safe Conduct of Journalism represents a comprehensive list of what is required of responsible news organisations. They are to provide journalists with:

- equipment for the job
- risk awareness training
- social protection including life insurance
- free medical treatment

Moreover, similar provision is to be made for freelances; and news organisations are called upon to avoid taking risks for competitive advantage.

INSI's own International Safety Code says: '… assignments to war and other danger zones must be voluntary. No career should suffer as a result of refusing a dangerous assignment.'[11]

In major news organisations in rich countries, the lesson is sinking in. Leaders in the location safety field include Reuters, CNN and the BBC. But institutional support is being made gradually more widely available through development aid to media in developing and transitional countries, by Reporters sans Frontières, the IFJ and many others.

Safety training

A key part of these efforts is safety training for journalists. INSI's code says media workers 'must not contribute to the uncertainty and insecurity of their conditions through ignorance or reckless behaviour'.

This means, among other things, avoiding 'hunting alone'. To let someone know where you are going, and when to expect to hear from you, is standard practice. You are also safer, in most situations, working in pairs or in groups. The possible survival of witnesses is a deterrent to attack – the rationale for volunteer monitors from Peace Brigades International as they accompany humanitarian workers in conflict zones.

Being prepared for danger

A list of questions you need to ask

- *Who* – who is asking/telling you to go? Is it work pressure? Do you have a genuine free choice or will you be regarded as weak or unreliable if you choose not to go?
- *Who* – who is helping you? Do you have contacts who will also protect you? Are they an armed group?
- *Who* – who knows you are going and will monitor your progress while you are in the danger zone, raising the alarm if you are not back on time?
- *Who* – who will accompany you or are you going alone? Is there a benefit in working together with other journalists – a safety in numbers? Or if you work for a local news organisation, could you travel with an international reporter whose safety may carry a higher political premium than yours?
- *Why* – if you are pressurising yourself, why? For career accolades, the buzz of danger, or because you have a genuinely excellent lead on a story with lots of people to help you?
- *What* – what will be gained from the story? Will it show one particular party in great light? Is it for the promotion of your news organisation? Are you illuminating hidden aspects of Peace Journalism?

- *When* – look at your timing: might a different, safer, phase of the conflict be more conducive to doing Peace Journalism? Are there other, safer, ways of achieving the same objectives? After the siege of Fallujah in April 2004, several journalists, desperate to investigate what could be 'the greatest US blunder of this war', were seized by gunmen. London *Guardian* correspondents Jonathan Steele and Rory McCarthy decided it was not worth the danger of entering the city, and instead found Fallujah families who escaped to Baghdad, using their testimony as the basis for some vivid reporting.

Equipment you might need

Some basics
- Accreditation – do you need government passes to work as a journalist? For example, in Indonesia it is illegal to work as a journalist without government permission, and in Israel and the West Bank you would hardly get through a checkpoint without official Israeli government passes for journalists.
- First aid kit
- Flak jacket
- Helmet
- Travel documents, visa, passports etc
- Water bottles and sterilising tablets

**Exercise One
The Emergency Bag**

Imagine you are alone in a hostile environment, perhaps a conflict-affected area. Your guide has left. What do you need to come through safely? Think of the items you would like to have with you in your bag.

This is what the UK security firm Centurion recommends if 'the deterioration of local circumstances, a local guide's withdrawal of services, or the forced seizure of transport may necessitate isolated travel on foot within a hostile environment':

- Rucksack (25-30 litres) with waterproof liner
- Spare clothes (suitable for season/environment)
- Wind-proof jacket and over-trousers
- Gloves
- Woollen hat/sun hat
- Metal water bottle and water sterilising tablets
- Day food and emergency food
- Map of area and compass
- Watch
- Whistle
- Penknife
- Candle
- Waterproof matches/lighter
- Radio (short wave)
- Notebook and pencil
- Torch, spare bulb and batteries
- 20m length of strong cord (many uses)
- Toothbrush and toothpaste
- Sanitary towels/tampons
- Sun barrier cream
- Comb/brush
- Insect repellent
- First aid kit (sterilised + contents)
- Personal medication
- GPS (if owned)
- FFD (first field dressing)
- Money (US dollars)
- Photocopy of passport/visa (in separate waterproof bag)[12]

Trauma – a brief introduction

Why does trauma matter?
'I've had about ten friends killed this past decade. I've been wounded myself. I've been taken prisoner, beaten, kidnapped, shelled, mortared, shot at, knocked down by the blast of an explosion.'[13]

The voice of an anonymous war correspondent displays an extreme of human endurance and begs the immediate question – what was the effect on those involved and on their capacity to do the job, to write an accurate story?

Journalism in many places has a tradition of stoicism, a macho culture in which to acknowledge any sort of personal distress may invite discrimination and threaten one's career prospects.

The anonymous journalist went on to say: 'When you've seen things and experienced things that you'll never forget no matter how much you want to, it's important if the situation is bothering you that you should seek some kind of help.'

This person took part in the first study of its kind, by Canadian psychiatrist Dr Anthony Feinstein, who discovered that nearly three in 10 frontline journalists develop post-traumatic stress disorder during their career – about the same as frontline soldiers.

The study also highlighted increased use of alcohol: '... the females (in the war group) are drinking five times as much (as those in the control group), the males about twice as much'. And 21 per cent of the war group were suffering from major depression, well over twice the rate of depression amongst Canadians as a whole.

The DART Center for Journalism & Trauma, based at Washington State University, Seattle, has taken a lead in promoting what is now a growing awareness of a need for 'emotional literacy' among journalists covering conflict. According to the director of DART Centre Europe, Mark Brayne (a former BBC foreign correspondent and editor who is also a trained psychotherapist):

'A better awareness of trauma and how it affects people – both in the story and those telling it – can make for better journalism. It can also protect journalists from being drawn too deep into situations where, beyond telling the story, they cannot help.'[14]

Here are some basics of a training programme designed to open up issues of trauma and develop this awareness.

Exercise Two
Exploring Trauma[15]

- Think about a traumatic incident that has happened to you that you can talk about with another person – an incident that is meaningful but 'medium-range'.
- Write it down in notes.
- Distinguish the three stages of before, during and after.
- Note separately the facts, the feelings, and the future – ie what you were thinking would happen next.
- Discuss the incident with another person.
- Notice what they say that puts you at ease and helps you to talk.
- Take a guess at how much stress your colleague absorbed.

Exercise Three
Trauma Jargon

- Write the following four terms on four separate large pieces of paper:
  – Trauma
  – Stress
  – PTSD
  – Counselling and psychotherapy
- Give one sheet to each group.
- Ask each group to write out everything they may have heard or know about each term.

What do we mean by trauma?

'Trauma' comes from the Greek word for 'wound', a piercing of the skin, and symptoms are the body's and psyche's response to being wounded.

A *natural response* to reporting on events ranging from the September 11th attacks to the opening of mass graves in Bosnia can include:

- Sleeping difficulties/nightmares
- Exhaustion
- Flashbacks/nightmares
- Aggressive behaviour/resentment, anger
- Startled response/hypervigilance
- Inability to maintain relationships
- Social withdrawal (avoiding people, places)
- Anxiety/fear/depression
- Feeling of numbness
- Substance abuse (drink, drugs etc)
- Grief
- Cynicism
- Shame/loss of self-respect
- Loss of sense of meaning and hope
- Fear
- Physical symptoms, body pain, headaches
- Anxiety/panic/irrational fears
- Self-harming, a shadow of former self
- Tearfulness
- Feeling 'scattered'[16]

Gabrielle Rifkind, Institute of Group Analysis:

'If the trauma does not find a language the symptom will mumble on, and the conflict that has not been expressed is at risk of being re-enacted. Every enactment becomes an attempt to resolve the conflict but if the process is unconscious it is more likely to be an enactment or acting-out rather than finding a way to resolve it. We are therefore caught in a trauma, unable to find a way to speak about the loss.'[17]

Stress

'Stress is the natural, healthy response to any kind of pressure we are under, when adrenaline gets pumped round the body. But when stress is overwhelming, the heavy, persistent and unprocessed flows of adrenaline and other stress hormones can do deeper damage to how we function.'[18]

Post-Traumatic Stress Disorder

PTSD is a medically recognised illness, showing three main clusters of symptoms, and the significant fact is that these symptoms must last for more than a month:

- *Re-experiencing:* nightmares, flashbacks as if the event was happening again
- *Avoidance/numbing:* avoiding any situation or reminder of the past trauma
- *Hyperarousal:* persistent symptoms of being on permanent alert and in an agitated state – as if the threat could return at any moment

This is how it affected one journalist at the BBC:

'Chris for example did a reporting spell in Iraq after the 2003 war. He saw many bombings and death, and was in a Humvee with the Americans when it came under fire. Chris had been terrified, and on his return to London, walking quietly home from the Saturday supermarket run, suddenly found himself under a table with his shopping scattered across the pavement. A car had backfired in the street, and before Chris knew what was happening, his body – mistaking the backfire for gunfire and a threat to his life – had thrown him to the floor.'[19]

Who is at risk?
- Those with previous exposure (not just at work) to trauma/violence
- The experienced who take the attitude, 'It won't happen to me'

- The inexperienced – who want to get a career boost from doing something dangerous and daring
- Those with poor social support (family, friends, colleagues)
- Those whose stress levels are already high
- People who find it difficult to talk about emotions
- Anyone with a history of past emotional/psychological problems
- Those who are inclined to feel responsibility, and feel in some way responsible for what they have witnessed
- Those who use drugs and/or alcohol to deal with stress

How to take care of yourself

Take a break, but keep to your usual routine – this is not always the best time to take a holiday. Britain's Royal Marines, pioneers of training to deal with trauma and stress, believe someone who has witnessed a traumatic event needs three meals and a sleep, rather than being withdrawn altogether. Their other top tips include:

- Physical self-care at this time is important, so don't miss meals; and remember your adrenaline rates are high, so avoid tea and coffee where possible and get plenty of sleep.
- The basic message is do not bottle up your feelings, talk to someone you feel comfortable with, whether it is a member of your family, someone in your team, a close friend or a professional counsellor or therapist.
- Accept it may take some time for the memories to go away – healing can be painful and take some time. The less judgemental you can be with yourself, the better.
- Take time to review the experience yourself, whether during walks in the countryside or through writing a personal journal. But at the same time do not become isolated, spend time with your family and children – often a good antidote at such times.

- Take more care – accidents can happen when you are preoccupied emotionally, as your concentration may be affected; driving may require more care and attention than usual.

The BBC's Trauma booklet advises:

'• Trauma can be deeply distressing – and it can change us as people. But if we can come to recognise and accept what's happened, we can integrate that experience – and without having to push them away, put the distress associated with traumatic memories safely in the past.
- It's not about forgetting, but it is about moving on.
- Trauma is also an opportunity to grow and learn from what we've witnessed and been through.
- When recounting or mulling over things you may have been through, it's helpful to concentrate on the positive aspects of what you experienced. This does take some effort, but like physical exercise it gets easier with practice.'[20]

Victims and survivors of trauma

One reason for journalists' reticence in addressing their own trauma is that many have interviewed people with much worse experiences. There can be a feeling that it might be 'self-indulgent' to complain on one's own behalf after talking to people who have lost loved ones, say, or undergone torture.

Caring about others and about oneself need not be alternatives, of course. The DART Center also produces tips, informed by an awareness of trauma and its effects, for interviewing victims and survivors:

'1. Always treat victims with dignity and respect – the way you want to be treated in a similar situation. Journalists will always seek to approach survivors, but reporters should do it with sensitivity, including knowing when and how to back off.

2. Clearly identify yourself: "I am Fred Smith from (your news organisation), and I am doing a story on Joan's life." Don't be surprised if you receive a harsh reaction at first, especially from parents of child victims. However, do not respond by reacting harshly.

3. You can say you're sorry for the person's loss, but never say "I understand" or "I know how you feel". Don't be surprised, too, especially when covering acts of political violence, if a subject responds to your apology by saying, "Sorry isn't good enough". Remain respectful.

4. Don't overwhelm with the hardest questions first. Begin with questions such as, "Can you tell me about Carol's life?" Or, "What did Antonio like to do? What were his favourite hobbies?" Then listen! The worst mistake a reporter can do is to talk too much.

5. Be especially careful when interviewing survivors of anyone who is missing, and try to clarify that you seek to profile their lives before they disappeared and not to write their obituaries. If you're unable to contact the victim or other survivor, try calling a relative or the funeral home to request an interview or obtain comments. If you receive a harsh reaction, leave a phone number or your card and explain that the survivor can call if she or he wants to talk later. This often leads to the best stories.'

6. 'Try to avoid asking the clichéd question, "how do you feel?" Be more creative with your questions, try asking "what is running through your mind right now? What would you like others to know about what is happening to you, your family, your community?"[22]

7. Be alert for any hint that they may be prepared to appeal for restraint in the response to their loss or for dialogue with the perpetrators. Can you draw this out? Such individuals often make powerful advocates for peace. The story can prove to be more interesting because it is not what people are expecting.

✳

Endnotes for Appendix B

1. From a lecture by Richard Sambrook at Columbia University, New York, 28 October 2004.

2. Personal testimony from members of the National Union of Journalists in the Philippines, during Peace Journalism training workshop led by the authors, March 2005.

3. Quoted in Cheryll Fiel, 'Government Scored in Mindanao Press Protests', in *Bulatlat*, Vol 4, No 42, 21-27 November 2004.

4. Tom Newton Dunn, 'ITN Demand Pentagon Answers', *Daily Mirror*, 11 September 2003.

5. Aiden White, *Justice Denied on the Road to Baghdad*, International Federation of Journalists, p 25.

6. Jonathan Steele, 'How Do You Cover Events Like This?', London *Guardian*, 26 April 2004.

7. 'Supporting Human Rights and Democracy – The US Record, 2004-5', State Department, 28 March 2005.

8. Stephen Grey, 'America's Gulag', *New Statesman*, 17 May 2004.

9. Quoted in Seymour Hersh, 'The Gray Zone', *New Yorker*, 25 May 2004.

10. Dr Raj Persaud, 'The Battle We Don't Report', London *Guardian*, 28 April 2003.

11. International News Safety Institute, 'The International Safety Code, published in *Justice Denied on the Road to Baghdad*, International Federation of Journalists, p 46 Appendix 4.

12. 'Hostile Environments and Emergency First Aid Aide-memoire', *Centurion*, October 2002, p 17.

13. Quote read by John Owen speaking at 'Risking More Than Their Lives – The Effects of Post-Traumatic Stress Disorder', the Freedom Forum, European Centre, London, 12 April 2001. The journalist quoted is interviewed Dr Anthony Feinstein, University of Toronto, in his study of war correspondents and

Post-Traumatic Stress Disorder (PTSD) in journalists.

14. Mark Brayne, *Traumatic Stress – A Training and Support Handbook*, BBC, May 2004.
15. An exercise given by Surgeon Lieutenant Commander, Royal Navy, Neil Greenberg, during a training course at Bush House, London, run by the BBC and Dart Centre Europe for Journalism and Trauma, 6-8 February 2003.
16. Mark Brayne, Journalism and Traumatic Stress, BBC and Dart Centre Europe for Journalism and Trauma, January 2002, p 10.
17. Gabrielle Rifkind speaking at 'Emotions, Trauma and Good Journalism', a Dart Centre Europe conference held at the Center for Counselling and Psychotherapy Education, 15 January 2002.
18. Mark Brayne, Journalism and Traumatic Stress, BBC and Dart Centre Europe for Journalism and Trauma, January 2002.
19. Quoted in Mark Brayne, *Traumatic Stress – A Training and Support Handbook*, BBC, May 2004.
20. Mark Brayne, *Traumatic Stress – A Training and Support Handbook*, BBC, May 2004.
21. Joe Hight and Frank Smith, 'Tragedies and Journalists – For More Effective Coverage', Dart Centre for Journalism and Trauma, www.dartcenter.org.
22. William Cote and Roger Simpson, *Covering Violence – A Guide to Ethical Reporting about Victims and Trauma*, Columbia University Press, 2000.

Appendix C – Resources

An eclectic, though far from comprehensive, list of organisations involved in Peace Journalism or complementary activities around the world. All web addresses correct at time of going to press.

Arab Media Watch – London, UK
www.arabmediawatch.com
A British media monitoring and campaign group, focusing on representations of the Arab world, in particular the conflict between Israel and the Palestinians. Gives content analysis, as well as contacts and tips for letter-writing to news organisations.

Australian Centre for Peace and Conflict Studies – Brisbane, Australia
www.polsis.uq.edu.au/acpacs/
Academic teaching and research department specialising in Peace and Conflict Studies at the University of Queensland. MA module in Peace and Conflict Media from January 2005, offered in conjunction with the School of Journalism.

Australian Centre for Independent Journalism – Sydney, Australia
www.acij.uts.edu.au
An independent not-for-profit foundation associated with the Journalism School of the University of Technology, Sydney, Australia. The school also accredits students who take an option in Conflict-resolving Media at neighbouring Sydney University (see CPACS, below).

Australian Conflict Resolution Network – Sydney, Australia
www.crnhq.org
Australia's first peace and conflict organisation. The CRN has a broad focus of teaching, researching and developing conflict resolution ideas, locally, nationally and internationally. Launched the Media Peace Award over 20 years ago, which is now run by the UN Association Australia.

BASIC – British American Security Information Council – Washington DC, USA and London, UK
www.basicint.org
Useful source of information for a Peace Journalist, especially on security threats; helpful in countering propaganda such as that in the run-up to the invasion of Iraq in 2003. Researches a variety of global security issues, including nuclear policies, military strategies, armaments and disarmament.

Centre for Peace and Conflict Studies (CPACS) – Sydney, Australia
www.arts.usyd.edu.au/centres/cpacs
The first university department in the world to launch, in October 2000, an MA module in Peacebuilding Media, Theory and Practice, taught by the authors (now known as Conflict Resolving Media). CPACS offers Masters and PhD qualifications through the University of Sydney.

Conciliation Resources – London, UK
www.c-r.org
A small group working to support grassroots peace initiatives, they also produce the

substantial and detailed *Accord* publications – an international review of peace initiatives. CR runs a Media & Conflict in Africa programme, providing training opportunities for journalists – particularly in West and East Africa. Like Peace Journalism, their training workshops teach conflict resolution theory and highlight the responsibilities of journalists in reporting conflicts and peace processes.

Center for War Peace and the News Media (CWPNM) – New York, USA
www.nyu.edu/cwpnm
New York University's CWPNM supports journalists and news organisations worldwide with a variety of projects include media and conflict, a global reporting network – featuring the weekly resources: Global Beat and Global Beat Syndicate – and the Mid-East/American Media Project.

Committee to Protect Journalists
www.cpj.org
A US-based non-profit organisation founded in 1981. Promotes press freedom worldwide by defending the right of journalists to report the news without fear of reprisal, by publicly revealing abuses against the press and by acting on behalf of imprisoned and threatened journalists.

DART Center for Journalism and Trauma – Seattle, USA and London, UK
www.dartcenter.org
A US-based charity, also with a centre in London, offering support and information for journalists who cover trauma and violence. Works to raise these issues within major news organisations, to change the macho culture about emotions and highlight the prevalence of post-traumatic stress disorder among frontline correspondents.

Fahamu (learning for change) – Oxford, UK
www.fahamu.org
Specialises in training by supported distance learning, including a programme in Peace Journalism to be offered from 2005. An innovative education organisation utilising information technologies to help civil society organisations to bring about social change and promote and protect human rights. The word *Fahamu* means 'understanding' or 'consciousness' in Kiswahili.

FAIR (Fairness and Accuracy in Reporting) – New York, USA
www.fair.org
US-based media monitoring and activism group. An archive on their site of all media criticism articles on the Web means you can find almost anything. They also give tips on organising your own media activism, along with contact details of all major US news organisations.

Glasgow University Media Unit – UK
www.gla.ac.uk/departments/sociology/units/media.htm
A communications research and teaching department within Glasgow University with a special interest in war and peace reporting.

In 2004, the group launched a major study on the reporting of Israel and the Palestinians, *Bad News from Israel* (Pluto Press), adduced several times in this book.

International Federation of Journalists – Brussels, Belgium
www.ifj.org
The world's largest organisation of journalists, representing around 500,000 members in more than 100 countries. Acts as a lobby group for issues of safety, justice and free speech. Active in training journalists in issues like human rights and safety, particularly in Eastern Europe and Africa.

International News Safety Institute (INSI) – Brussels, Belgium
www.newssafety.com
Set up in 2003 by news organisations and journalism support groups to provide information and resources for journalists in hostile environments. The group lobbies for risk reduction, and encourages employers to implement safety procedures. Updated briefings on its website.

Institute for Media, Peace and Civil Society (IMPACS) – Vancouver, Canada

www.impacs.org

IMPACS runs a Media and Peacebuilding Programme, which includes research and training. Research is focused on developing policy options for a variety of media interventions, from TV soap operas to news. One early report mapped the whole field of media interventions as a continuum from mainstream news to intended-outcome media.

Institute for War and Peace Reporting (IWPR) – London, UK

www.iwpr.net

The Institute for War and Peace Reporting is both a useful source of information and a training institute. Local journalists attend IWPR training sessions in their home city, after which they become accredited correspondents, writing for regional reporting services, posted on the IWPR website both in English and in their own languages.

It's a way for them to air, sometimes under pseudonyms, stories that are too risky for the local press; a notable contribution to media freedom. Payment is channelled to journalists themselves, so any risk of corruption is cut out. The IWPR training programme includes Peace Journalism.

Internews Network – centres around the world

www.internews.org

Internews Network is an international non-profit media organisation with the brief of using media to reduce conflict within and between countries. In Indonesia they ran Reporting for Peace training workshops with the South African trainer Fiona Lloyd. Their website keeps track of stories around the globe on media and conflict, in a special section called *Media, War and Peace.*

International Media Support (IMS) – Copenhagen, Denmark

www.i-m-s.dk

A media support group focused on promoting peace, stability and democracy through media training and other interventions.

Their handbook on *Conflict Sensitive Journalism* was based closely on our Peace Journalism material, and talks about the need for journalists to understand the dynamics of conflict and violence to play a positive role.

Media Channel – New York, USA

www.mediachannel.org

A useful resource bringing together more than a thousand affiliates engaged in democratising the media. From here you can connect with just about every organisation engaged in investigative reporting, monitoring, supporting, training or challenging the media around the world.

Includes the *News Dissector's Blog*, by veteran journalist, author and media analyst Danny Schechter. There is a specific focus on conflict reporting issues with the *War and Peace Monitor*. Schechter has been a supporter of Peace Journalism since the early events at Taplow Court from 1997.

Media Diversity Institute – London, UK

www.media-diversity.org

Grew out of the Center for War Peace and the News Media in NY. MDI focuses on using the media to lessen inter-group conflict, advance minority and human rights, and support deeper public understanding of all types of social diversity. Based in London, it has offices in Armenia, Azerbaijan and Georgia.

Media Foundation of West Africa – Accra, Ghana

www.mfwaonline.org

A regional independent, non-profit, non-governmental organisation established in 1997 to defend and promote the rights and freedoms of the media in West Africa, and generally to help expand the boundaries of freedom of speech and expression there 'around the issues of human rights, democracy, peace, security and development'.

MediaWise – Bristol, UK

www.mediawise.org.uk

A media charity providing advice, information, research and training on media ethics. The brief: 'providing a new understanding between journalists and the citizens they serve'. Their website also provides a useful set of links to most of the world's journalism codes of ethics and conduct.

Medios Para La Paz – Colombia

Website (in English)

http://www.mediosparalapaz.org/index.php?id categoria=1285

A non-profit organisation created by a group of 80 Colombian journalists aimed at 'fostering responsible journalism to cover war and negotiation efforts for a political way out'. It takes, as its remit, 'the disarmament of speech'.

Among its activities are awards for good reporting, as well as training and education programmes.

Mindanews – Mindanao, Philippines

www.mindanews.com

Website is a project of the Mindanao News and Information Cooperative Center, 'the leading provider of accurate, timely and comprehensive news and information on Mindanao'.

The group has a long-standing interest in Peace Journalism.

Oxford Research Group – Oxford, UK

www.oxfordresearchgroup.org.uk

Global security research group. Regular briefing documents including original analysis and creative ideas for solutions, notably by Professor Paul Rogers, concentrating on the security situation in Iraq and Afghanistan.

OneWorld Online – London, UK

www.oneworld.net

OneWorld is a major human rights and sustainable development Internet gateway focusing on giving a voice to those typically overlooked by mainstream media and policy-makers. A useful source of information and contacts, including country guides edited by local volunteers offering a broad introduction to the sustainable development and human rights issues in each location.

Pambazuka News – Durban, South Africa and Oxford, UK

www.pambazuka.org

Pambazuka means 'arise' or 'awaken' in Kiswahili. It is a weekly electronic newsletter covering news, commentary and analysis, and a range of other resources on human rights and development in Africa, reaching more than 60,000 people. There is a weekly section on 'Media and Free Expression'. Editorials recently collected into a book.[1]

PATRIR – Cluj, Romania

www.patrir.ro/

The Peace Action, Training and Research Institute of Romania (PATRIR) is an institute, organisation, training centre and network, linking together scholars, practitioners and grassroots activists throughout Romania.

As a major centre for TRANSCEND's work, the Institute holds a number of Peace Journalism related activities, including onsite courses and online courses.

Peace Direct – London, UK

www.peacedirect.org

Grew out of the Oxford Research Group (see above) as a way of supporting people on the front line prepared to take non-violent action.

They also establish partnerships linking those on the front line with groups/individuals in the UK to give direct support – financial and as moral encouragement – to grassroots activists working to promote alternatives to violence or to ameliorate its effects.

Responding to Conflict (RTC) – Birmingham, UK

www.respond.org

RTC provides advice, training and longer-term support to people working for peace. Highly regarded ten-week residential course, 'Working with Conflict', offered every year to participants from some of the world's most intractable conflicts. Includes a module on Peace Journalism.

Saferworld – London, UK

www.saferworld.org.uk

Human security think-tank with particular emphasis on the trade in small arms. They work with governments and civil society internationally to research, promote and implement new strategies to increase human security and prevent armed violence.

Saferworld have been supportive in the work of Peace Journalism and helped organise joint discussions as part of their 'Iraq Conflict' project.

Search for Common Ground – Washington DC, USA

www.sfcg.org

A conflict resolution group using media as one of its primary tools, making TV productions and radio soap operas with a peace-building message.

They use an approach similar to Peace Journalism called 'Common Ground Journalism'. This includes journalist training in Africa, the Middle East, and the Aegean region 'to diminish inflammatory reporting and promote mutual understanding'.

Transnational Foundation for Peace and Future Research (TFF) – Lund, Sweden

www.transnational.org

Specialises in peace research, conflict-mitigation and education. Its fieldwork has focused on the Balkans, Iraq, Burundi. TFF's homepage offers analyses, commentaries, ideas and debates, usefully distilled into regular PressInfos.

Toda Peace Institute – Tokyo, Japan and Hawaii

www.toda.org

A peace research institute backed by the Soka Gakkai International (SGI), a Japanese-based lay Buddhist organisation.

Due for publication in 2005: the Institute's book, *Democratising Global Media: One World, Many Struggles*, under the Rowman and Littlefield imprint; includes a chapter by the present authors, 'Peace Journalism – a global dialogue for democracy and democratic media'.

The Toda Institute is presently embarking on a major research programme, to develop courses in Peace Journalism.

TRANSCEND Peace and Development Network

www.transcend.org

A network of practitioners working for conflict transformation by peaceful means. Founded by Professor Johan Galtung, who first defined Peace Journalism. The website has a list of all the members, their contact details, various lectures and articles, and information on how to apply for online Transcend Peace University courses, including one on Peace Journalism.

World Association for Christian Communication (WACC)

www.wacc.org.uk

WACC is funded by Protestant churches of Europe and North America. Has published several articles on Peace Journalism in its globally distributed magazine, *Media Development*.

US Institute for Peace (USIP) – Washington DC, USA

www.usip.org

Although the board of directors is appointed by the US President and confirmed by the US Senate, the Institute claims to be independent and non-partisan. 'Provides for innovative approaches to human capacity building for peace and working with public and private partners to manage and resolve international conflicts.'

USIP currently have a research programme on 'Media-Based Conflict Interventions': a long-term study of how the media can perform conflict-transforming tasks foreseen by conflict resolution theory while at the same time preserving the professional norms of journalism.

Endnote for Appendix C

1.   African Voices on Development and Social Justice, eds Firoze Manji and Patrick Burnett, Mkuki na Nyota, Dar es Salaam, 2005

Select Bibliography

Dispatches from the front – insights into the politics of the news agenda

Hammond, Philip and Herman, Edward S, (eds), *Degraded Capability*, Pluto, London, 2000.

Kampfner, John, *Blair's Wars*, Freedom Press, London, 2003.

Knightley, Phillip, *The First Casualty*, Prion, London, 2000.

Pedelty, Mark, *War Stories*, Routledge, New York, 1995.

Overviews

Carruthers, Susan, *The Media at War*, Palgrave, Basingstoke, 2000.

Greenslade, Roy, *Press Gang – how newspapers make profits from propaganda*, Pan, London, 2004.

Hackett, Robert A and Zhao, Yuezhi, *Sustaining Democracy? The Politics of Objectivity*, Garamond Press, Toronto, 2000.

Hargreaves, Ian, *Journalism – Truth or Dare*, Oxford University Press, Oxford, 2003.

Herman, Edward S and Chomsky, Noam, *Manufacturing consent – the political economy of the mass media*, Pantheon, New York, 1988.

Schechter, Danny, *The More You Watch, the Less You Know*, Seven Stories Press, New York, 1997.

Conflict and Peace

Ackerman, Peter and Duvall, Jack, *A Force More Powerful*, Palgrave, New York, 2000.

Galtung, Johan, *Peace by peaceful means*, Sage, London, 1996.

Galtung, Johan et al, *Searching for Peace – the road to TRANSCEND*, Pluto, London, 2002.

Lederach, John Paul, *Building Peace – sustainable reconciliation in divided societies*, United States Institute of Peace Press, Washington DC, 1997.

Fisher, Simon et al, *Working with conflict, Responding to Conflict*, Zed Books, London, 2000.

Rees, Stuart, *Passion for Peace – exercising power creatively*, University of New South Wales Press, Sydney, 2003.

Rogers, Paul, *Losing Control – global security in the 21st Century*, Pluto, London, 2002.

Critical theory

Eagleton, Terry, *Literary theory – an introduction*, Blackwell, Oxford, 1983.

Royle, Nicholas, *Jacques Derrida*, Routledge Critical Thinkers series, Routledge, London, 2003.

Index

Abu Graib jail 65, 66, 247
Abu Sayyaf Group (ASG) 188, 190, 192
Adnan, Indra 48
Afghanistan 80, 81
African National Congress (ANC) 152
'agenda journalism' 211–212
Ahtisaari, Mahti 104
aid resources diverted 103
Al Jazeera 111, 246, 247
'al-Hayat' 67
al-Qaeda 49, 53, 75, 115, 116, 188, 217
Albania, National Liberation Army (NLA) 129
Alexander River Project 170
Ali Ahmeti 129
Amanpour, Christiane 99
Americans Talk Issues Foundation 97
Amnesty International, Kosovo 79
anchorage 57, 120, 141, 204
Arab grievances/hopes 53, 75, 76
Arab-Iraeli conflict 21–27, 70–73, 158, 168, 170–173
Arafat, Yasser 157, 158
Arguillas, Carolyn 190
Arusha Accord, Rwanda 143
Ash, Timothy Garton 106
Ashdown, Paddy 116
Ashrawi, Hanan 150
asylum seekers 127, 128, 131–139
Aung San Sun Kyi 79
Avnery, Uri 106

Bacon, Kenneth 105, 114
Bagdikian, Ben 202, 204
Bagram Air Base 247
Bali Bombing 75, 76–77
Barak, Ehud 157
BBC 1, 109, 248
    Guidelines 9, 184, 223, 242
    Iraq 110, 111, 112
    World Service 113

Black, Ian 101
Blackman, Oonagh 208
Blair, Tony
    Iraq 2, 7, 11, 141, 205
    Kosovo 98, 100, 103, 104, 49–150
    WMD 14, 179, 181, 184, 206, 207, 209, 217
Blix, Hans 181
Blunkett, David 35
Bosnia, media bias 99
Boutros-Ghali, Boutros 214
Boyce, Admiral Sir Michael 180
Brandeis, Amos 170
Brayne, Mark 250
Bremer, Paul 82
Bretton Woods Agreement 39, 144
British Ministry of Defence 106
broadcasters' Codes of Conduct 230
Brown, Gordon 199
Browne, Lord 13, 199
Brzezinski, Zbigniew 12, 145
Bulger murder 68–69, 74
Bush, President George W.
    election 10, 12, 80
    Iraq 2, 7, 11, 109, 116, 206, 247
Butler Report 115

Camp Bondsteel 146
Camp David talks 157
Campbell, Alastair 104, 109, 114, 186, 217
Center for Strategic and International Studies 186
Centre for Oil Depletion Analysis 13
Channel 4 News 172, 186
Cheney, Dick 10, 116, 199
Chernomyrdin, Viktor 104
Chomsky, Noam 197, 200, 201, 204, 205, 211, 213
Clark, General Wesley 105, 106
Clinton, Bill 99, 104

CNN 156, 248
'CNN effect' 214
Cohen, William 103
Columbia University, School of Journalism 228
conflict 34, 36, 38, 39
    ABC triangle 38, 39–40, 119, 120
    diagnosis & remedy 37–38
    explanations 36
    mapping 42–44
    outcomes 39, 40–42, 45
    overcoming 37
    partisan perceptions 46–47, 51
    responses 36–37, 39
    study of 33
    transcendence 42, 45
Conflict & Peace Forums 48
Conflict Analysis 13, 33, 34, 36, 48, 53, 57, 120, 141, 143, 144, 211, 218, 234, 240, 242
    news reporting 53–54, 143, 242
Convention on Refugees (1951) 134
Cook, Robin 109, 114
    resignation 114
Cordesman, Anthony 109
'corner turns' 185, 186, 187
Cosic, Dobrica 121
creativity/non violence 84, 85, 149
critical journalism 241, 242
Croat nationalism 121
Cronkite, Walter, catchphrase 213
Crooke, Alastair 76
Cycle of Violence 57, 74, 173
    interrupting 86–89, 91, 171, 209
        Liberia 89–90
        Mozambique 89

Daily Mail 134, 135
Daily Mirror 150, 206, 207

Dallaire, General Romeo 144
Damazer, Mark 111
DART Centre for Europe 250, 252
DART Center for Journalism & Trauma 250
Deconstruction (Derrida) 219–222
Dejevsky, Mary 17
demonisation 69
    Sadam 16, 69
    Serbs 118–120, 121, 122
    Taliban 81
Derrida, Jacques 219, 220, 221, 222
Detroit Project 13, 186

Economist 1
Einstein, Albert 48
Elworthy, Scilla 86
embedded journalism 17, 110, 111
encoding-decoding meaning 96, 197
European Broadcasting Union 110
Evening Standard 134, 135, 217
evil, concept of 64, 65
Express 206

Faleh Abdel Jabar 83
Falk, Richard 201
Fareed Zakaria 66
'Feedback Loop' 135, 149, 216, 217, 218, 242, 246
Fikret Alic 116, 117, 118, 120
Financial Times 1, 82, 199, 206
'First Casualty, The' 106
Fisk, Robert 145, 148, 185, 205
Fleurot, Olivier 199
Foley, James B. 101
Fox News 109, 243
Franks, General Tommy 112
Friel, Howard 201

Galtung, Johan 6, 47, 224
Galtung table 6, 7, 8, 16, 17, 27, 47
Gandhi, Mahatma 48, 78, 79, 84, 215, 221
Gapon, Georgii 78
Gellhorn, Martha 247
Geneva Accord 171
genocide, UN definition 143, *see also* Rwanda
Georgia conflict 198–199
Gilligan, Andrew 114, 217
Global War on Terrorism 189, 190, 247

Goldenburg, Suzanne 17
Good Friday Agreement 45, 46, 198
Gowing, Nick 98, 108
'Grand Chessboard, The' 12
Greenslade, Roy 200
Guantanamo Bay 247
Guardian 17, 101, 200, 206, 247
Gulf War 115, 206
Gush Shalom 77, 106, 158

Hall Stuart 96, 197
Hallin, Daniel 205
Hamid Karsai 80
Hazem Saghiyeh 66, 67, 68
Herman, Edward 197, 201, 204, 211
Herring, James 217
Hilsum, Lindsay 17, 107
Himal Association 112
Holbrooke, Richard 80
Hoon, Geoff 180
Howarth, Gerald 180
'Human Development Report on the Arab World' (2002) 53
Human Rights Watch 76, 247
Hume, Mick 117
Hutton Enquiry 217

Ignatief, Michael 121
IMF 82, 143
Independent Television News (ITN)
    Bosnia 116, 117, 118, 120
Independent, The 145, 171
    asylum, the facts 139
    Peace Journalism 205
India, guide to reporting violence 54
Indonesia
    Bali bomb 76–77
    creative initiatives 164–166
    Palu bomb 161, 162–168
    Peace Journalismm 88, 89, 91, 223
    reporting unrest 127, 128
Inkatha Freedom Party (IFP) 152
'Inside Indonesia' 127
International Code of Practice for the Safe Conduct of Journalism 248
International Development Select Committee report (migration & development) 134, 135
International Federation of Journalists (IFJ) 246–247, 248
International Herald Tribune 19

International News Safety Institute (INSI) 245, 248
International Solidarity Movement, Palestine 171
Intifada 171
Iraq, ' Peace' 81–83
    United Iraqi Alliance (UIA) 82
Iraq Body Count project 112
Iraq War 1, 2–4, 81–83
    arguments for war 9
    'Dishonest Case for War on Iraq, The' 207
    BBC coverage 4, 182, 183
    causes 35, 36
    civilian deaths 113
    Coalition War plan 108
    coverage analysed 7–11
    manipulation of media 108, 184
    media coverage 2–4, 178–181, 204, 207
    oil theory 9–13
    parties to conflict 13, 14
    price paid by business 199
    propaganda 107, 108, 109, 110, 112
    restricted sources 182–183
    sources – own agenda 183, 184
    study of coverage(Maryland University)3–4 5, 9, 35
    UK Govt. briefing 217, 218
    'victory' 102
    warnings unheeded 83
    WMD – evidence 14, 15, 16, 178, 182, 207–208
Israel Palestine Centre for Research & Information (IPCRI) 171, 172
Israel security wall 186, 187
Israeli Committee Against House Demolitions 171
Israeli peace initiatives 174–177, *see also* Arab-Israeli conflict
ITN 116, 117, 118, 120, 246

Jakarta Post 164, 151, 238
Jane's Dictionary of Unmanned Aircraft 107
Jemaah Islamiya (JI) 76, 77
Johnson, Hiram, 95
journalism
    choosing words 112–114
    Codes of Conduct 230
    creating realities 200
    deconstructing the facts 220
    'dualism' bias 210
    education 227–228
    'ethic of responsibility' 218

the future 229, 230
influence of advertising 202
intermediary rôle 146–147
'just facts' 196, 214
linguistic theory 213, 214
official source bias 203–204
press freedom 210–212
principles questioned
    195–196
reflexivity 18, 83, 196, 211
report underlying reasons
    210, *see also* violence,
    reporting
sliding scale 187
societal purpose 197, 201
working with trauma victims
    252–253
Journalist
    Security 245
        Codes of Practice 248
        high risks 245
        Iraq 246
        Philippines 245–246
        Post-Traumatic Stress
            Disorder 251
        safety training 248–249
        self-help 248, 252
        trauma 249–252
    training 228–230
'Justice & Charity' 51, 73

Kagame, Paul 63
Kagan, Donald, 10
Kagan, Robert 85
'Kangura' 62
Kant, Immanuel 218
Karadzic, Radovan 118
Karen National Liberation Army
    (KNLA) Burma 155
Kay, Alan 97, 102
Kelly, Dr David 217
Kerry, Senator John 80
King, Martin Luther 78, 84
King, Martin Luther Jnr. 48
Knightley, Phillip 106, 110
Kosovo 79–80, 98, 120, 144
    bombing 114
    Liberation Army (KLA) 100,
        101, 104
        CIA involvement 100
    media reports 101, 110
    peace options suppressed 100,
        144, 145
    war propaganda 100, 102,
        103, 115
Kosovo Verification Mission
    (KVM) 102
Kuhn, Thomas 205, 212
Kurds 82, 136–139

Laity, Mark 148, 149
Lancet, The 113
language/Saussure's model 213,
    219
Large, Judith 48
Lawson, Dominic 204, 205
Ledeen, Michael 12
Lederach, John Paul 18, 215
Leipzig demonstrators 79
Leonard, Mark 85
Levi-Strauss, Claude 220
'Linguistic Turn' 213, 221
Little, Alan 108
Little, Alistair 150–151
Lloyd, Terry 246
'LM', libel case 116, 117, 118,
    120
Loyn, David 77, 80, 81, 183
Lynch, Jake 117, 136–138, 149

McCarthy, Rory 249
Macedonia 58, 59, 102, 129, 130
McGoldrick, Annabel 25, 155,
    156, 173
McVicar, Sheila 100
Madison, James 201, 202, 223
'Madres de La Plaza Mayo' 78
Mainali, Mohan 112
Mandela, Nelson 78
Marshall, Penny 117, 118
Mason, Paul 11
massacres, reporting 151–152
Médecins sans Frontières 80
media
    24 hour news 108, 109
    corporate power 243
    force for moderation 163
    influence questioned
        214–216
    manipulated by sources 184,
        185
    monitoring 21
    new thinking needed 106,
        107–108
Melvern, Linda 143
Middle East Policy Initiatives
    Forum 172
Mill, John Stuart 201, 202, 223
Miller, James 172
Milosevic, Slobodan 98, 100,
    101, 102, 106, 120, 200
Mkhize, Khaba 152
Mohammed, The Prophet 84, 85
Moro Islamic Liberation Front
    (MILF) 188, 190
Morocco, bombing 49–53, 75,
    210
Murdoch, Rupert 67, 135
Museveni, Yoweri 62

Muson, Ken 107
Mussomeli, Joseph 189, 191

'9/11' 53, 66, 67, 75
Naif Naik 81
Natal Witness 152
National Asylum Support Service
    (NASS) 134
NATO
    bombing of Yugoslavia 79,
        105–106, 144, 148, 149,
        206, 216
    Kosovo crisis 79, 80, 102,
        103, 104, 145
    propaganda 98–106
    Rules of Engagement 106
    'US in Europe' 145
Nepal Centre for Investigative
    Journalism (NCIJ) 112
Nepal, journalists 113, 114
Neve Shalom/Wahat al-Salam 172
New York Magazine 66
New York Post 66
*New York Time*s 105, 145, 185,
    201
news
    'gatekeeper theory' 196, 203
    propaganda 197
    'values' 196–197
newsmedia *see* media
Newsweek 66, 67
Non Governmental
    Organisations (NGOs) 89,
    153, 154
non violent action 18, 19–20,
    77–79, 84, 86–90
Northern Ireland 44–46, 198

Oberg, Jan 19
'objectivity' 203–204, 211
    ignores consequences 216
    not neutral 213–214
    War Journalism 209, 210,
        223, 229
official sources not neutral 18
oil interests 81, 199, *see also*
    Iraq War, oil theory
O'Neill, Onora 231
OPEC 10, 11, 12
Organisation for Security & Co-
    operation in Europe (OSCE)
    98, 100
'Orientalism' 51–52, 63
Osama bin Laden 12, 53, 67, 69,
    75

Palestine *see* Arab-Israeli conflict
Parents Circle 171
peace 47–48, 221, 241

Peace Brigades International 89, 248
'peace building',four pillars 87
Peace Journalism 5–7, 120, 161, 195, 211
   17 point plan 28–31
   in action 17, 150, 163–168
   alternative sources 18–19, 91, 164–168
   anchorage 57, 120
   challenging power 145
   conflict reporting 33–34, 91, 128–130, 141
   Deconstruction 220–222, 224
   early warnings 141, 142
   ethical checklist 231
   extra-linear thinking 74
   follow-ups 168–173
   hidden costs of violence 215
   Indonesia 88, 89, 91, 151, 223
   Kosovo 144–145
   non-violent responses 18
   peace initiatives 141, 144
   peace proposals 156, 157
   sliding scale War/Peace 187, 192
   strategy for change 21, 106
   The Independent newspaper 205
   University studies 195, 227, 228
'Peace Journalism', Indonesia 88, 91
'Peace Journalism Option, The' 48
'Peace Journalism in Poso' 168
Peace Research 6, 13, 18, 59
   anchorage 120
   Conflict Theory 33, 36, 57
   new discipline 34
Peace Studies 6, 33, 75
Perle, Richard 66, 67
Pew Research Center 11, 104
Philippines, conflict 188–189
   human rights 247
   journalists at risk 245, 246
   New People's Army (NPA) 189, 190, 192
Pilger, John 101
Pilkington, Ed 3
Powell, Colin 115
   WMD 178, 179, 181, 182
Project for a New American Century (PNAC) 10
propaganda 95, 97, 98
   advertising techniques 109
   Bosnia 116–118

dealing with 108, 109
decoding 113, 114
dehumanisation 16
entertainment industry 96
graphics stacks 109
Gulf War 115
Iraq War 16, 107ff
Kosovo 100, 102, 103, 104, 105
Manichean analysis 99
media manipulation 108, 109
military 108, 109
misleading images 116
NATO/Yugoslavia 98–105
partial accounts 115
psychology of 121
US 96, 97
words used 112, 113, 114
Putin, President Vladimir 14

'Radio Television Libre des Mille Collines' 62
Rambouillet Accord 100, 101, 102, 105, 144
Rangwala, Glen 186, 207, 208
Ranson, Jenny 99, 200
'realism' 85
Rees, Stuart 78
Refugee Council (GB) 128, 133, 135
   exploding media myths 133, 134
refugees 134, 153–154
Reporters sans Frontières 248
restrictions on newsgathering
   Iraq 10, 111
   Nepal 111, 112
Reuters 1, 113, 248
Rice, Condoleezza 27, 186, 187
Ridder, Tony (Knight Ridder) 199
Road Map to Peace 186, 187
'road to Basra' 150
Robertson, George, Lord 104, 115
Roche, Barbara 132
Rogers, Paul 75
Rose, General Sir Michael 99
Roth, Kenneth 247
Rubin, James 68
Rugman, Jonathan 186
Rugova, Ibrahim 100
Rumsfeld, Donald 10, 247
Rusbridger, Alan 17
Rwanda, genocide 17, 61–63
   analysis 62, 63, 143, 144
   failure of reporting 143
   international community 210
   local media 141, 228–229

Patriotic Front 62, 63, 142
   warnings 141, 142

Saddam Hussein
   al-Qaeda 116
   demonised 16, 69, 95
   obstinacy 181, 184
   oil 10, 11
   overthrown 102, 205
   regime change 2, 3, 97, 141, 149, 185, 204
   WMD 8, 14, 95, 178, 182
Said, Edward 51, 52
St Petersburg Times/Florida 115
Sambrook, Richard 245
Saud, House of 75
Saussure, Ferdinand de 213, 219
Saxton, Jim 104
SBS Television, Australia 189
Schmidt, Rosemarie 53, 54
Schopenhauer, Arthur 227, 228
Schwarzkopf, General Norman 115
Science 66
Security for Journalists *see* Journalist, Security
'sequencing' political tactic 184
Serbs
   demonised 118–120, 121, 122
   national identity 101, 102
Shea, Jamie 110
Short, General Michael 105, 114
Simons, Tom 81
Simpson, Alan 186, 207, 208
Sinn Fein 146
Sintuwo Maroso Youth Covoy 165
Sky News 109, 156
'sliding scale' Peace/War 187
Smith, Dan 87
Snow, Jon 186
Soyuz Karta 115
stalemate, reporting 154–156
Stanford Prison Research Experiment 65, 120
Steele, Jonathan 247, 249
Stock, Jean ref 110
Straw, Jack 132
   WMD 178, 179, 181, 184
Structuralism 213, 219, 220
   Levi-Strauss 220
'Structure of Scientific Revolutions, The' 205
Suara Bangsamoro Partylist 188
Sun 135
Sunday Telegraph 204, 206
Sunday Times 103, 107

Sykes-Picot agreement 53
Systems Theory 215, 218

Taliban 80, 81, 217
Tehranian, Majid 229, 230
Telegraph 103, 211
Tenet, George 116
tension , reporting 125–128
terrorism 75–77, 113–114
Time 66, 67
Times 15, 68, 102
Times of India 208
Titmuss, Abi 216, 217
Toda Institute for Peace and
    Policy Research 228, 229
TRANSCEND 172
Transnational Futures
    Foundation (TFF) 19
Tudjman, Franjo 119

UN High Commission for
    Refugees (UNHCR) 103
UN Security Council 105
United Nations (UN)
    membership 128
    Rwanda 142, 143
United States (US)
    National Security Strategy 12
    occupation of Iraq 82, 83,
        see also Iraq War
    oil/war 9–13
    propaganda 96, 97
    Yugoslavia 103, 104, *see also*
        NATO
Urban, Mark 105, 129

van Klinken, Gerry 127, 128
Vietnam war, news coverage 205
violence 57, 59–61
    context 63, 66, 67, 68,
        198–199
    cultural 59, 60, 61, 172, 173
    direct (visible) 59, 60, 61
    early warnings 140
    explaining/not excusing 69,
        73
    hard cases 74
    hidden costs 84, 215
    invisible legacy 83, 103
    legacy of
    Afghanistan 80, 81
    Iraq 82–83
    Kosovo 79–80, 103
    murder 68–69
    reporting 53–54, 57–59,
        70–73, 83–84
    structural 59, 60, 61, 62, 63,
        168
    typology 60–63
    see also Cycle of Violence
Von Sponek, Hans 19, 186

War Journalism 5, 6, 20, 197
    acceptance of violence 83
    Arab-Israeli confict 21–23,
        27, 28
    bad for business 199, 200
    bipolarity 7, 8
    elite orientation 17, 18
    ethical checklist 231
    Iraq coverage 199
    linear explanations 74

links with Peace Journalism
    192
news biased 106
Northern Ireland coverage
    198
'objectivity' 140, 209, 210,
    220
official sources 18, 140
pattern of omission 18, 200
propaganda 99, 201
Republic of Georgia 198
sliding scale Peace/War 187
violence compounded 200,
    201
Washington Post 202
Weber, Max 209, 218
Welesa, Lech 78
White, David Manning 196
Willetts, David 133
Williams, Ian 118
Wolf, John 27
Wolff, Michael 3, 66
Wolfowitz, Paul 8, 10, 49, 51
World Wars/peace arrangements
    38, 39
Wynne-Jones, Ros 150

Younge, Patrick 127
Yugoslav Army (VJ) 100, 105
Yugoslavia 121, 144, *see also*
    NATO, bombing of Y.

'zero sum game' 7, 43
    Iraq War 8, 14, 16
Zimbardo, Philip 65

Ordering books

If you have difficulties ordering Hawthorn Press books from a bookshop, you can order direct from:

Booksource
32 Finlas Street, Glasgow G22 5DU
Tel: (08702) 402182
Fax: (0141) 557 0189
E-mail: orders@booksource.net

or you can order online at
www.hawthornpress.com

For further information or a book catalogue, please contact:

Hawthorn Press
1 Lansdown Lane, Stroud
Gloucestershire GL5 1BJ
Tel: (01453) 757040
Fax: (01453) 751138
E-mail: info@hawthornpress.com
Website: www.hawthornpress.com

Also from Hawthorn Press

News from the Holy Land
Theory and Practice of Reporting Conflict
A Peace Journalism Video
Jake Lynch and Annabel McGoldrick

Journalists Jake Lynch and Annabel McGoldrick made this film in 2004 to help viewers analyse how conflict is reported. News from the Holy Land examines the way the Israeli-Palestine conflict is presented by the media, and shows different ways of reporting that help resolve, rather than escalate conflict. The Video and Teaching Notes offer an invaluable resource for NGOs, peace groups, and school and university courses in journalism, media studies, politics and history. The authors run Peace Journalism seminars internationally.

48pp; 198 x 114mm; 1 903458 54 4 (PAL – UK); 1 903458 55 2 (NTSC – US); pb

Confronting Conflict
A first-aid kit for handling conflict
Friedrich Glasl

Conflict costs! When tensions and differences are ignored they grow into conflicts, injuring relationships, groups and organisations. So, how can we tackle conflict successfully?

Dr Friedrich Glasl has worked with conflict resolution in companies, schools and communities for over 30 years, earning him and his techniques enormous respect.

Confronting Conflict will be useful for managers, facilitators, management lecturers and professionals such as teachers and community workers, mediators and workers in dispute resolution.

192pp; 216 x 138mm; 1 869 890 71 X; pb

Ken Sprague – People's Artist
John Green

This lively portrait shows how everyone can be a special kind of artist - how art can transform lives, deepen social engagement and build bridges. Ken Sprague's goal as a people's artist was, 'to build a pathway to the Golden City, and to help people dream again.' Here, for the first time is a selection of Ken's pictures, including his Guernica cartoon as a boy, poster for Martin Luther King, the labour movement, the Anti Apartheid Campaign and war pictures from Iraq and Kosovo.

Ken Sprague was a print-maker, posterman, painter, cartoonist, muralist, banner maker, psychodrama tutor and art teacher. He was a legendary storyteller, with moving and amusing stories to enliven his pictures. John Green is a journalist, film maker, artist and trade union official, with a life-long interest in art.

160pp; 275 x 215mm; 1 903458 34 X; pb